YUKON

The Last Frontier

YUKON
The Last Frontier

Melody Webb

University of Nebraska Press
Lincoln and London

First Bison Book printing: 1993
Most recent printing indicated by the last digit below:
10   9   8   7   6   5   4   3   2   1

Library of Congress Cataloging-in-Publication Data
Webb, Melody, 1946–
[Last frontier]
Yukon: the last frontier / Melody Webb.
p.   cm.
Originally published: The last frontier. 1st ed. Albuquerque: University of New
Mexico Press, 1985. With new introd.
Includes bibliographical references and index.
ISBN 0-8032-9745-9 (pbk.)
1. Frontier and pioneer life—Yukon River Valley (Yukon and Alaska)   2.
Yukon River Valley (Yukon and Alaska)—History.   I. Title.
F912.Y9W43   1993
979.8'6—dc20
93-12536   CIP

Reprinted by arrangement with Melody Webb
Originally published under the title *The Last Frontier: A History of the Yukon
Basin of Canada and Alaska*

Published in Canada by the University of British Columbia Press, Vancouver

∞

For my husband, Robert M. Utley

Contents

List of Maps		viii
Preface to the Bison Book Edition		ix
Introduction		xiii
I	The Yukon: A Setting for Successive Frontiers	1
II	The Russian and English Frontiers	21
III	The Trader's Frontier	51
IV	The Early Miner's Frontier: Fortymile and Circle	77
V	The Explorer's Frontier	99
VI	The Klondike Frontier and Its Backwash	123
VII	The Soldier's Frontier	143
VIII	The Missionary's and Settler's Frontier	171
IX	The Transportation Frontier: Riverways	205
X	The Transportation Frontier: Trails and Roads	225
XI	The Transportation Frontier: Railways, Highways, Airways	247

XII   The Twentieth-Century Miner's Frontier   269

XIII   The Enduring Frontier   291
       Notes   313
       Bibliography   359
       Index   395

List of Maps

1   Alaska Superimposed on Continental US   9
2   The Native World following page   11
3   The Russian and English Frontiers   23
4   Frontiers of the Middle Yukon   49
5   Missionaries, Explorers, Soldiers   101
6   Goldfield Approaches: Klondike and After   126
7   Yukon Goldfields: Dawson to Fort Yukon   135
8   Yukon Goldfields: Fort Yukon to Tanana   139
9   Transportation   231

Preface

Since 1985 and the first edition of this book, a group of scholars have banded together, calling themselves "the New Western Historians." They assail Frederick Jackson Turner and his frontier thesis. Instead, seeking a new synthesis, they focus on the West and its victims—Indians, Hispanics, women, blacks, even the environment. While Turner heralded triumphs and progress, the New Western Historians dwell on failures and injustices. Where Turner saw the frontier molding new institutions and shaping the unique American character, these historians see continuity in capitalistic and exploitive practices.

At the risk of being characterized a "historical artifact," I still believe that Turner's thesis of successive frontiers helps explain the westward movement to the north country. Few historians accept Turner's thesis at face value, but even the New Western Historians concede its interpretive and metaphorical power to withstand a century of attack. No other interpretation organizes the movement of people in terms non-historians can understand and accept. My goal was to help all readers comprehend the history of the Yukon, not as a unique land with its own distinctive past and problems, but as part of a shared experience.

True, Turner neglected minorities, especially Native Americans. I tried to remedy that failing by folding their story in with the gradual development of the river basin. No culture, however, remains stagnant. Alaska Natives changed as they encountered each new frontier. Ironically, next to the Klondike Gold Rush, the single greatest impact on Natives was the passage of the Alaska Native Claims Settlement Act of 1971. Drawing lessons from mistakes made with Native Americans in the American West, Congress tried to meld the traditional Native culture with twentieth-century capitalism. The law offered (1) enough land to sustain a subsistence economy for those Natives who chose to retain their traditional lifeways—forty-four million acres, (2) a just monetary settlement for extinguishment of Indian title to remaining land—nearly a billion dollars, and (3) Native control over the money and land they received through the establishment of thirteen Native corporations. By 1992, like the American economy in general, some of the Native corporations were profitable, others millions of dollars in debt. Although the New Western Historians may perceive this law as another example of white dominance and exploitive capitalism, alcohol—a substance most Native Americans cannot metabolize properly—has caused more cultural dysfunction than any other factor.

Turner also ignored women. While few of my peers would accuse me of being insensitive to women's history, I did not focus on their contributions in *Yukon: The Last Frontier*. Instead, I tried to select characteristic people to represent each frontier. The one frontier most often perceived as masculine—trapping—I illustrated with a woman. Women also played large roles on other frontiers, most notably the "Soldier's Frontier" and the "Missionary's and Settler's Frontier." Other minorities, however, were not recognized. Their story remains to be told. I might also add that if I were writing the book in 1992, I would use a more gender-free prose.

Although I personally concur with the New Historian's belief that white culture has "messed up" the environment, the application of that generalization to Alaska is difficult. Despite the deforestation caused by the mining and steamboat frontiers, the Yukon looks much as it did prior to 1890. What saved the Yukon from a fate similar to that of the American West was the scarcity of people. It has had time to recover. It may not be immune to development, but its climate and environment may limit its attraction to permanent migration and settlement.

Thus, I still accept Turner's thesis as an organizational device. I also accept his emphasis on environmental history over other analytical theories. And I still applaud his belief in narrative and anecdotal history. The issue of whether westering humans were conquerors or heroes, however, is not one to be resolved through study of the history of the Yukon Basin.

Readers of my original "Introduction" often ask me what became of Dave Evans. He left the Yukon in the early 1980s. Despite his animosity to the National Park Service in 1976, he found that his skill in building and maintaining log cabins was an asset the National Park Service needed. In 1992, after nearly ten years of seasonal labor in Denali National Park, he became a permanent employee, working in Anchorage, Alaska.

I left the Yukon and Alaska in 1979 to pursue my doctorate, but with concrete plans to return. Instead, I spent nine years in Santa Fe, New Mexico, as the National Park Service's regional historian of the Southwest Region. Then in 1989 I moved out of history and into management as the superintendent of Lyndon B. Johnson National Historical Park. Recognizing that my new career path required broader experience, I transferred in 1992 to the assistant superintendent position in Grand Teton National Park. Here, my Alaska seasoning gave me credibility and respect.

So after seven years, I am delighted to find that the University of Nebraska believes this book worthy of its prestigious Bison series. I hope that it continues to inform both scholars and the public on "the last frontier."

Introduction

A rifle cracked in the distance. I shivered as water dripped off a spruce tree and trickled down my neck. I moved closer to the campfire sputtering uncertainly in the rain. Fervently I hoped Dave's aim had been true this time. Two hours earlier he had missed and ever since had been patiently awaiting another chance. Meanwhile, I was cold, wet, hungry, and apprehensive about our prospective dinner—beaver.

Next morning we made our way back to the Yukon along an old trapping trail. As we hiked, we became aware that we were probably the first humans to use the trail in perhaps half a century. The blazes on the trees had scarred over, the path often faded and even vanished in the muskeg, and several antique steel traps lay sprung but near their trapping sets. Obviously some spring, years ago, a trapper who planned to return in the fall trusted his neighbors enough to leave his traps here. What changed his mind? What kind of man was he? Did he build the fallen cabins we found at the mouth of the creek? Was this trail a short-cut between the Kandik and Yukon rivers as Dave surmised? Did Canadian Chris Peterson and American Larry Dennis cut the trail as they trapped the upper Kandik—one on each side of the border? Or did Pete Summerville cut it before a cow moose trampled him to death? Or was it some trapper whose name never found its way into written records and now was lost even from oral traditions?

Many such experiences filled my three months on the Yukon River in the summer of 1976. Almost as much as the long hours in libraries and archives, this "outdoor research" helped me to deal authoritatively with Yukon frontiers. To David Evans, Yukon trapper, I am indebted for introducing me to a river life-style in many ways unchanged from a century—even two centuries—ago.

Three months before my first taste of beaver tail, Dave had strolled into my office at the University of Alaska in Fairbanks. Shaggy, bearded, broad-shouldered, he sported a picturesque felt hat and, with weathered good looks, resembled the Hollywood stereotype of the mountain man of the frontier past. Because he had studied history in college, he had grown curious about the history of "his land." He had come down to the university to learn more about it.

Coincidentally, the National Park Service had recently assigned me to study the history and historic sites of "his land"—two million acres near the Canadian border proposed for addition to the National Park System as Yukon-Charley National River. I had completed my documentary research. Now I was insecure about embarking on a survey of historic places in this roadless wilderness.

Fortune had it that Dave Evans agreed to serve as my guide for the coming summer—but only if I did it his way. He scorned freeze-dried foods and gave me a list of groceries that included flour, baking powder, tea, beans, peas, rice, and potatoes. He would carry a gun, he said, and if opportunity arose would kill fresh meat. I was not to bring my national park ethic or Sierra Club values into his world. I agreed.

By living a modern trapper's life-style, I hoped to gain insights into the life and times of an earlier Yukon. Coming to terms each day with swarming mosquitoes and biting gnats, burning sun and pouring rain, low water and protruding trees, monotonous camp chores and time-consuming meals, long hikes over punishing terrain and gentle floating trips on a placid river, might give me a feeling and perspective for my subject that the documentary evidence failed to impart.

Thus I benefited from skills and insights that few historians enjoy. I learned not only to eat beaver and bear, but to like them. Specialized techniques in trapping and mining took on real relevance through exposure to prospectors, miners, and the river people, not all of whom were comfortable with a woman as historian rather than kitchen drudge. I even practiced panning for gold and crafting simple trapping sets. Most important, I accommodated to the Yukon environment and accepted it without insulating layers of "civilization." I am, therefore, deeply grateful to Dave for his patience and insights, which contributed to an immensely valuable personal perspective of Yukon history.

The study completed for the National Park Service in 1977 provided the foundation for my doctoral dissertation and subsequently this book. I expanded the scope of the initial study to cover the entire Yukon Basin and corrected several premature interpretations suggested in the earlier version. I have sought in particular to perceive the history of the Yukon as an extension of the westward movement. Therefore, this is not a history of Alaska, but the history of a region that extends through Canada's Yukon Territory and into British Columbia as well. To achieve this goal, I used Frederick Jackson Turner's thesis of successive frontiers as a means of understanding and interpreting the history of a largely unknown geographical area—the Yukon Basin.

While no one theory can explain or define human behavior, Turner's metaphorical concept of successive frontiers provides a highly effective scheme for organizing complex and contradictory information into a meaningful synthesis. Thus the westward movement can be perceived through successive waves of distinct occupational or cultural groups that confronted and modified a new land. Although these groups overlapped and competed with one other, examination of each group or frontier facilitates understanding of the whole.

Just as Turner used this thesis to focus attention on a little-known West, so I have applied it to a little-known Yukon. Since his successive frontiers did not readily fit the coastal history of the continental United States, he ignored it. Likewise, the Alaskan and Canadian coasts developed their own social and economic institutions that did not influence or extend to the vast interior and, thus, cannot be studied through this interpretive lens.

At the same time, while Turner ended his frontier with the development of towns or with the arrival of "civilization," he essentially terminated his theory with the beginning of the twentieth century—his present day. Contrary to the opinions of some historians, Turner's thesis may be extended through the twentieth century to help Americans understand today's social order. Thus instead of physical frontiers, the twentieth-century frontiers become technological frontiers, which modify the American character and culture as much as or more than the environmental frontiers of the previous century.

To study multiple frontiers, by necessity Turner emphasized an interdisciplinary approach. In his landmark thesis, he used theories from such diverse fields as geography, political science, economics, and demography. To study Yukon frontiers, I have used the disciplines of anthropology, archaeology, geology, mining and civil engineering, geography, theology, and economics.

In addition, to have validity for a nation, regional or frontier history should be a part of national history. It should not be studied in isolation or as a unique entity. Therefore, for the north country's history to become meaningful, I have presented it as part of the westward movement and intimately tied it to unfolding themes of American history.

Finally, particular people associated with certain frontier themes provide a focus for human interest while also offering a personal perspective of a major event or cultural experience. Individual lives illustrate and illuminate broader forces of human history. I have tried in these pages to look at some of the important aspects of the Yukon's past through the eyes and experiences of such people, both significant and merely typical. In some instances, I have also carried their lives further beyond the Yukon than some readers might believe warranted. I have done this deliberately, because it has seemed to me that an unusual number of people—Henry Allen, Roald Amundsen, and Billy Mitchell are examples—went on to national or international distinction. For many, their Yukon experiences have been largely forgotten, and I think it worth pondering to what extent their youthful Yukon seasoning equipped them to conquer adversity and achieve great purposes.

While the field survey was the most exciting and dramatic part of my study, most of my time was spent paying appropriate homage to libraries and archives. I visited the Library of Congress, the National Archives, the National Archives and Record Center at Seattle, the universities of Oregon and Washington, the Oregon Province Archives of the Society of Jesus at Gonzaga University, the Huntington Library in San Marino, California, the Alaska State Historical Library at Juneau, the Alaska Resources Library in Anchorage, and the indispensable Elmer E. Rasmuson Library at the University of Alaska, Fairbanks. I wish to thank collectively all librarians who helped me in my search. Specifically, however, I want to mention Martin F. Schmitt at the University of Oregon, Reverend Clifford Carrol, S. J., at Oregon Province Archives of the Society of Jesus, Renee Blahuta of the University of Alaska Archives, and the several competent and supportive librarians at the Alaska Resources Library who took an active interest in my project.

Several persons dug into their photograph collections to find appropriate illustrations—my deep appreciation goes especially to Virginia S. Burlingame, Eileen Edmunds of the Yukon Archives, Fr. Neil R. Meany, S.J., and Jerome A. Greene. Superintendent David A. Mihalic of Yukon-Charley Rivers National Preserve sent me more than thirty of the park's original and best slides for previewing. Such trust and genuine interest merit special commendation.

There are numerous people who also deserve thanks. First and foremost, my husband, Robert M. Utley, freely gave his time, knowledge, and editing skills to improve my style and interpretation. He also took time away from his own writing projects to draft the essential and complicated maps. More important, he lent support and encouragement as my writing and revision absorbed evenings and weekends for more than two years. My dissertation committee—Richard N. Ellis, Donald C. Cutter, W. James Judge, Ferenc M. Szasz, and Richard W. Etulain—read my work closely and critically and offered insights and improvements. My editor, Dana Asbury, ensured editorial consistency throughout the work.

Several persons in the National Park Service merit recognition. William E. Brown arranged the funding for the initial project, and Zorro A. Bradley assumed many of my administrative responsibilities and allowed me time for fieldwork, research trips, and writing. Robert L. Spude extended to me the riches of his own research excursions to the Bancroft, the Public Archives of Canada, and the Alaska Steamship Records in San Francisco. My supervisors and colleagues both at the Services's Alaska office in Anchorage and the Southwest Regional Office in Santa Fe have followed my academic endeavors with interest and enthusiasm.

R. N. DeArmond of Juneau, whose knowledge of Alaskan history is only exceeded by his generosity in sharing it, not only read my manuscript for historical accuracy, but pointed me toward a number of obscure sources and even lent me his indices of the *Alaska Weekly* and other Alaskan newspapers. Elizabeth Andrews and Orlando W. Miller of Fairbanks read portions of the work and made valuable suggestions. Linda Finn Yarborough graciously translated the important François Mercier manuscript. Most especially, my gratitude extends to my dear friend, David S. Grauman, who actively shared in the evolution of the project. His excitement, enthusiasm, and intense interest spurred me on when my own spirits flagged.

Finally, I owe a debt of appreciation to the local people of Alaska and the Yukon Basin. I wish to thank all those who offered me hospitality and others who gave me their time and shared with me their memories. Most particularly I want to thank George Beck and Charlie Biederman, whose knowledge of the twentieth-century Yukon far surpasses the synthesis of this study.

CHAPTER 1

The Yukon: A Setting for Successive Frontiers

"Stand at Cumberland Gap," historian Frederick Jackson Turner declared in 1893, "and watch the procession of civilization, marching single file—the buffalo following the trail to the salt springs, the Indian, the fur-trader and hunter, the cattle-raiser, the pioneer farmer—and the frontier has passed by. Stand at South Pass in the Rockies a century later and see the same procession with wider intervals between."[1]

Stand beside the Yukon River near the Alaskan-Canadian border fifty years after South Pass and watch Turner's frontiers, modified by the north country's unique environment, flow past in similar succession: Indian, trader, explorer, missionary, miner, soldier, riverboat man, dog-team driver, woodchopper, and finally townsman.

Although Cumberland Gap and South Pass never witnessed so orderly a procession as Turner pictured, his idea that moving and changing frontiers shaped the peoples and institutions of the United States has retained substantial validity, even though parts have fallen before the attacks of revisionists.[2] By 1893 Turner had rejected contemporary historical concepts that ignored the westward movement and environmental factors. Instead, he thought that the distinctive environment of the United States, coupled with the presence of free land on the western edge of advancing settlements, explained basic American character and institutions. Attracted by dreams of economic improvement or adventure, people took into the wilderness established political, economic, and social practices. Against the hostility of a new environment, these sophisticated practices gave way to new or adapted ways of life. Slowly the frontier grew more and more complex as various groups with different skills and abilities passed through, and finally a fully developed society evolved. This society, however, differed from those farther east by its separate evolution and its unique social environment. Although with essential differences because of time, place, and individuals, this same process repeated itself for three and a half centuries.

Although Turner did not mention Alaska in his classic paper of 1893, he was probably not wholly ignorant of the unknown giant. Indeed, during the next thirty years he read articles on Alaska, studied maps of Alaska, collected data on Alaskan economics, and compared the natural resources of Alaska with those of Scandinavian countries.[3] In 1926, near the end of his career, he recognized Alaska as the last frontier. "The opening of the Alaskan wilds," he wrote, "furnished a new frontier and frontier spirit to the Pacific Northwest as well as to the nation."[4] Thus, within the broad conceptual framework he had created, Turner visualized the frontiers as extending to Alaska. More explicitly, he perceived that "civilization . . . followed the arteries made by geology."[5]

The mightiest of these arteries in the north country is the Yukon River. The Yukon and its tributaries create the heartland of Alaska and Canada's Yukon Territory. It is a geographical curiosity that this great river extends almost from sea to sea: rising less than twenty miles from tidewater, it reaches the ocean through 1,900 miles of channel, draining 325,000 square miles of British Columbia, Yukon Territory, and Alaska.[6] It is bounded on the north by the Brooks Range in Alaska and the Mackenzie Mountains in Canada, extensions of the Rocky Mountain System, and on the south by the Coast and Alaska ranges, extensions of the Pacific Mountain System. The Yukon Basin includes tributary basins vast in themselves—the Tanana, Koyukuk, Porcupine, White, and Pelly.

Although one of North America's greatest natural arteries, the Yukon was the continent's last major river system to be discovered, explored, and settled. In contrast to the Appalachian barrier to frontiersmen of the Old West, more than mere mountains impeded the opening of the Yukon. Physical detachment from the continental United States and remoteness from the centers of Canadian development discouraged and slowed the Yukon frontiers. Where isolation failed to halt growth of temperate California, hostile climates and formidable terrain combined to create a unique and forbidding environment throughout the Yukon Basin.

This environment evolved through millions of years of uplift, ero-

The Yukon River. Nearly two thousand miles long, the Yukon is one of North America's largest rivers. Although among the last of the great rivers to be explored and settled by whites, it served throughout human history as the major means of travel. *J. Wise, National Park Service.*

sion, and deposition. Throughout geologic time, the earth's crust buckled, fractured, pulsated, and produced uplift and troughs as ancient seas and later glaciers emerged and submerged the land.[7]

More than thirty thousand years ago, as the climate slowly cooled, waters evaporated from the oceans of the world and fell on the high mountains as snow. As a result, giant glaciers formed in the mountains. Although waxing and waning, they generally left the Yukon Valley free of ice. The forces causing glaciation culminated in lowered oceans and enlarged land masses. Most particularly, a wide land bridge between Alaska and Siberia took shape. Early man and other mammals may have crossed this bridge and migrated along the ice-free Yukon corridor toward the United States and Mexico.

Following the last glacial period, abrupt environmental changes caused the extinction of many of early man's food sources, such as the mastodon and musk oxen. Nevertheless, early man continued to adapt and change along with his environment.[8] Meanwhile, the Yukon, whose waters and tributaries had carried away the melting glacier water, dwindled in size.

The Ice Age left behind a momentous legacy. With enough moisture, coupled with a mean annual temperature below freezing, permafrost formed. Thick moss insulated the ground and guarded the permafrost against thawing temperatures. Once established, permafrost prevented the infiltration of ground water, melt, and rain. The mosses also impeded surface drainage, and thus, despite meager precipitation, swamps, marshes, and tundra developed.[9]

As geologic time approached historic time, the environment known to the early Indian grew similar to that known to the twentieth-century Yukon trapper. The glacier-scraped highlands, descending from the two mountain systems, dominate a horizon that gently slopes down to the rounded hills, even-topped ridges, and open valleys of the Yukon. The Yukon cuts through complex geologic structures as it flows toward the Bering Sea, leaving behind benches and terraces as testimony to its previous course and might. Willow, alder, and black "scrub" spruce cover its banks. As the elevation increases, the black spruce gives way to groves of white spruce, birch, and aspen. Berries of all kinds, rosebushes, and spongy muskeg form the undergrowth. As the Yukon nears the sea, the terrain flattens, and an open, treeless tundra supports little diversity in vegetation.

A string of lakes in British Columbia gives rise to the Yukon. Once free of the lakes and confined to time-hardened rock, it forms a single dominant channel. Flowing to the northwest, it picks up two of its largest Canadian tributaries, the Pelly and White rivers. From the White River, the Yukon acquires its muddy color and load of silt. Two hundred miles after crossing the international border into Alaska, it breaks free on flat plains and meanders in a bewildering maze of channels. Known as the Yukon Flats, the area comprises a great swampy, lake-pocked lowland two hundred miles long and forty to ninety miles wide. Here the Yukon absorbs the flow of the Porcupine River, which drains the barren slopes of the Brooks Range.

Below the Yukon Flats, a steep-sided valley once again confines the river to a single channel. Called the Ramparts, this stretch of valley is less than three miles wide and 120 miles long. As it approaches the mouth of the Tanana River, the gorge opens abruptly to a broad lowland twenty miles wide. Receiving its largest tributary, the 400-mile-long Tanana, the Yukon divides into several channels, broken by numerous islands and sand bars, as it makes its way to the delta.

At the delta the Yukon separates into a number of divergent chan-

The Yukon Basin. The muddy river flows swiftly through metaphoric rock, divides into multiple channels through lowlands, and grows sluggish and meandering as it nears the sea. *Robert Belous, National Park Service.*

nels, which flow northward to the Bering Sea. More than seventy-five miles separate the northernmost channel from the southernmost. Between them lies an intricate maze of waterways that shift constantly with the ebb and flow of the tides, the current, and scouring ice. Here too Alaska's second largest river, the Kuskokwim, reaches the sea. With the deposition of soil from the two rivers, the delta stretches for more than two hundred miles along the coast. Like all deltas, the land is flat and only a few feet above tidewater. Drained by sluggish, meandering rivers and dotted with a myriad of lakes, this vast, treeless tundra harbors thousands of nesting waterfowl and mosquitoes unto infinity.

The influence that most severely distinguishes the Yukon frontier from the Cumberland Gap and South Pass of Turner is climate. Temperatures range from seventy degrees below zero in the winter to more than ninety above in the summer. Sheltered by the Brooks Range to the north and the Alaska and Coast ranges to the south, the Yukon Valley annually averages only ten to twelve inches of precipitation—comparable to the deserts of the Southwest. Snow cover lasts at least seven months a year, while daylight wanes to less than three hours.

Throughout human history, climate coupled with geography made travel extraordinarily difficult. During the summer months, swampy, moss-covered, mosquito-infested terrain discouraged movement by land and forced travelers to Turner's time-honored "arteries of civilization," the rivers. But in the winter the rivers froze, and travelers evolved new methods to confront snow, ice, and extreme cold in order not to be immobilized altogether.

Newcomers to the Yukon Valley found that they had to learn to cope in extremely personal terms with an environment brutal in its consequences for the uninitiated. Two seasons prevail, summer and winter, fleetingly separated by breakup and freeze-up. Breakup, the worse time of year, occurs when the sun begins to provide enough heat to melt the winter's snow but not enough to warm the ground. As a result, the ground remains frozen, and the melted snow has no place to go. The top few inches of soil become water-logged, a soggy, muddy morass that bars all travel. Freeze-up, in contrast, signals the beginning of cold weather, which brings easier travel and more effective means of preserving the meat from fall hunts. Spring and fall pass in less than three weeks and leave little but pleasant memory.

Initially all "cheechakos," or greenhorns, eagerly greet the summer, with its long hours of daylight. But summer has its drawbacks. For one thing, the extended days seduce people into maximizing the daylight hours and, leaving only four or five hours for sleep, gradually wear themselves out. For another, insect life is everywhere a persistent scourge. Historically, smudge fires kept the ever-present swarms of mosquitoes at bay, as insect repellent does today, but the incessant humming still dominates all other sounds and hounds people and animals alike to seek quiet refuge. A diverse assortment of other hostile insects such as gnats, yellow-jackets, and "no-see-ums" make up in tenacity and ferocity what they lack in numbers.

While summer travel along riverways is relatively simple, movement across country becomes nearly impossible, even with modern technology. The terrain does not lend itself to natural trails, and game paths seldom lead in directions that humans want to go. Moreover, the permafrost, sustaining swamps and muskeg, makes movement slow, tedious, and exhausting. Every step on muskeg sinks the feet two to three inches, and walking is thus far more laborious than on sand. In contrast, the traveler in the swamps confronts stagnant water and, worse, tussocks. Tussocks are clumps of grass resembling miniature palm trees that protrude above the swamp floor about eight inches apart. The hiker has the choice of slogging through knee-deep swamp water or wobbling precariously from tussock to tussock, struggling constantly to maintain balance and direction. Even in timber, thick underbrush retards progress. Wild rosebushes claw the unwary while impenetrable thickets of alder and willow force interminable detours. Rain, sleet, hail, and even summer snow showers add unexpected bursts of discomfort, surprise, and dismay.

Winter, however, provides the dimension of greatest contrast and requires the most adaptability. The long, cold, dark winter nights bring on depression, hallucinations, bad tempers, and culminate in a mental disorder known as cabin fever. While newcomers find winter the most difficult season to cope with, sourdoughs welcome it as a quiet, calm, and restful time that encourages visiting with friends and the development of support networks. Sharing the environment's adversities fosters camaraderie and community spirit, as essential today as in Turner's time. When temperatures drop to fifty below zero for weeks at a time, the day-to-day chores of survival, mutually shared, create bonds of friendship that cross all walks of life.

Winter's extreme cold changes the properties of the commonest materials of everyday life. Even the thickest metal grows brittle and breaks easily. Bare flesh that touches cold metal burns, and the slightest dampness from perspiration glues it securely to the metal. Rubber also cracks readily, and vehicular tires flatten into lopsided squares. Wind does not usually blow during cold snaps, but temperatures drop low enough to freeze mercury thermometers. Cold this severe will transform a cup of hot coffee thrown into the air into a cloud of black steam, with nary a drop falling to the ground.

Unlike summer, winter carries inherent lethal dangers. Frostbite occurs when ice crystals form in the body fluids and underlying soft tissues of the skin. It resembles and acts like burns. In some cases the frost destroys the tissue, and extremities—the most vulnerable to frostbite—may require amputation. Improperly dressed travelers face exposure or hypothermia, an abnormal lowering of the body's temperature. Unless diagnosed at once and the victim thoroughly warmed, death follows quickly. Ironically, overdressing often leads to greater dangers than underdressing. If perspiration forms, it freezes on the garment closest to the skin and negates the value of additional layers of protection. Even breathing the super-cooled air requires caution to prevent frostbite to the throat and lungs. While travel becomes easier across snow-covered swamps, muskeg, and rivers, broken equipment may leave the wayfarer subject to winter's deadly perils.

In addition to the three factors of climate, ground cover, and terrain, size and distance set Alaska and western Canada apart from more southerly frontiers. Alaska alone is one-fifth the size of the continental United States and contains 586,400 square miles or 365 million acres. Superimposed on a map of the forty-eight contiguous states (see illustration), Alaska stretches from the Atlantic Ocean to the Pacific and from the Canadian border to the state of Arkansas. It once embraced four separate time zones, now merged to two. Fairbanks, in the heart of the Yukon Basin, lies nearly five hundred miles from the Bering Sea on the west and another five hundred from the eastern border of Canada's Yukon Territory. Such immense distances, crowded by all manner of hostile terrain and gripped by extremes of climate, form one of the world's most formidable and unique environments.

Thus the environment of the Yukon demanded greatly modified behavior patterns, radically new perceptions, and skills and abilities without precedent in America's frontier experience. As individuals adjusted and adapted, some innovative social and economic institutions evolved as well. The first adaptations and evolutions began with the

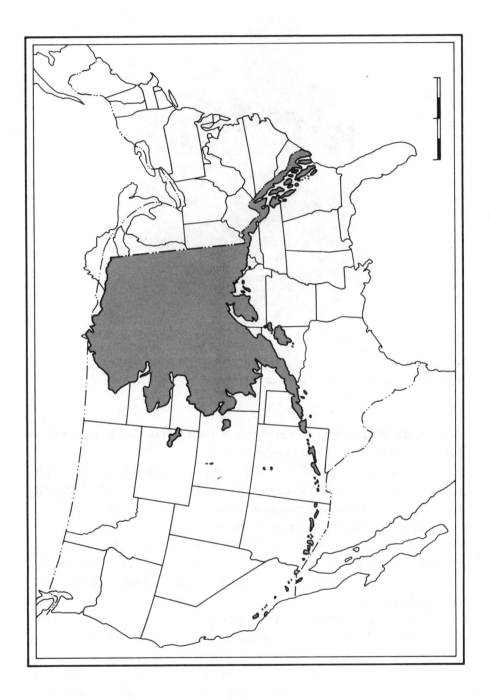

9

Coastal Eskimo. Yukon Eskimos took advantage of the rich environment of the delta to exploit the resources of both land and sea. While the fur of land animals gave warmth, skins of sea mammals provided waterproof shells. From Frederick Whymper, *Travel and Adventure in the Territory of Alaska.*

Native American, whose experiences formed a foundation on which successive generations of white pioneers built.

Long before whites "discovered" the Yukon River, however, a rich mosaic of cultural groups exploited the land's resources and adapted to its harsh and demanding environment. Of all peoples confronting a land, the Natives of North America epitomized Turner's environmentally determined man. Nonetheless, with his Anglo-Saxon bias Turner largely ignored the Indian and his relationship to the land.[10] But as elsewhere on the continent, the Yukon Native met the land on its terms and adjusted accordingly.[11]

Two different cultures evolved, each in its way exploiting its diverse and cyclic world. The coastal Eskimos at the mouth of the Yukon focused on the sea's largess. The Athapaskan Indians of the interior accommodated to the mountains, rivers, lowlands, and ridges and their varied bounty. The Eskimos developed independently and uniquely from other American cultural groups. The Athapaskans, on the other hand, re-

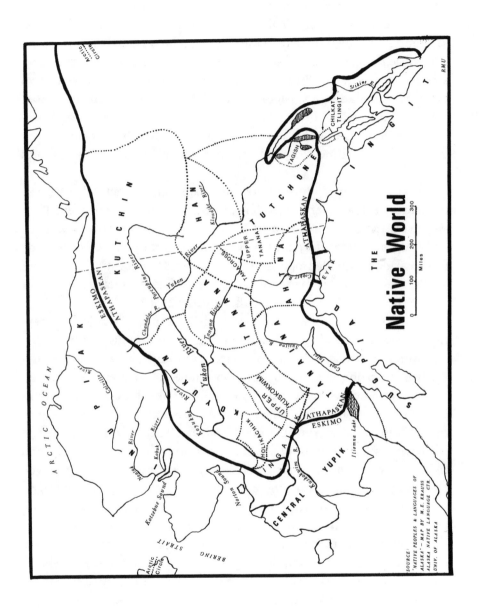

THE

Native World

SOURCE:
"NATIVE PEOPLES & LANGUAGES OF
ALASKA" - MAP BY M.E KRAUSS
ALASKA NATIVE LANGUAGE CTR
UNIV. OF ALASKA

0   100   200   300
     Miles

ARCTIC OCEAN

ARCTIC   OCEAN

ESKIMO

INUPIAK

ATHAPASKAN

KUTCHIN

HAN

KOYUKON

Yukon River

Koyukuk River

Yukon River

Chandalar R.

Porcupine River

Klondike River

Tanana River

TANANA

UPPER
TANANA

TANACROSS

TUTCHONE

ATHAPASKAN

ATHABASKAN

AHTNA

Copper R.

EYAK

Susitna R.

Cook Inlet

UPPER
KUSKOKWIM

KUSKOKWIM

HOLIKACHUK

INGALIK

ATHAPASKAN

ESKIMO

Iliamna Lake

TANAINA

SUGPIAQ

CHILKAT
TLINGIT

TAGISH

Stikine R.

T L I N G I T

RMU

Arctic
Circle

Kobuk River

Noatak River

Selawik River

Kotzebue Sound

Norton Sound

Kuskokwim R.

Nushagak R.

CENTRAL

YUPIK

BERING STRAIT

Arctic
Circle

11

presented the most widespread linguistic group in aboriginal North America. They spread across the bulk of Alaska and Canada, along the Pacific Northwest coast, and into the southwestern deserts.

The Eskimos of the Yukon Delta exploited one the richest environments of the northland. Unlike their relatives farther north, who confronted long months of sea ice, darkness, and sparse but diverse resources, those of the Yukon enjoyed the abundant spawnings of two large river estuaries, a warmer and more productive ocean, and a flat, treeless, lake-pocked lowland congenial to migratory waterfowl. Possibly because the resources were ample and diverse, the Eskimos of the delta had more time to spend on ceremonies, story-telling, art, and crafted tools.

Like all Eskimos, those of the delta displayed distinctively Mongoloid features. They were short, lean, muscular, and broadheaded. They wore straight black hair and had little facial hair. Weakly developed browridges shielded deep brown eyes. To cover the body, clothes made from caribou provided optimum warmth and durability. Waterproof shells, made from sea mammal skins or bladders, protected the wearer during inclement weather and while hunting at sea.[12]

The Eskimos of the delta located their permanent villages where they found an abundance of game or fish, a continuous water supply, and ample firewood. In adjusting to the environment two families generally lived in one rectangular, semisubterranean house, entered through an underground passageway designed to limit heat loss. Permanent villages fostered group unity, encouraged ceremonies and festivals, and promoted communal sharing. During the fall and winter months, they were the base of seasonal subsistence activities—hunting seal or caribou and fishing through the river ice. Each spring Eskimos temporarily moved to sealing or fishing camps where they hunted spring seals, snared migratory waterfowl, or fished for salmon, herring, and smelt. As fall approached the people returned to their permanent villages.

Just as subsistence needs determined village location, they were also reflected in Eskimo religion. The land-and-sea dichotomy of Eskimo subsistence, moreover, became magnified in Eskimo religion. For example, the spirits of the land and sea opposed and repelled each other. Thus one could not mix the hunting or eating of land and sea animals. In addition, the complexity of the spirit world required intermediaries, or shamans, who understood the spirits and, with gifts or rituals, compensated or propitiated the spirits for human failings. Thus, shamans

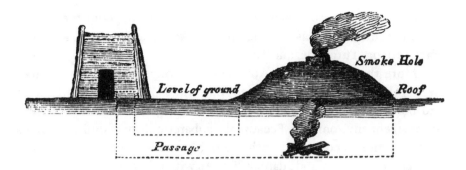

Semisubterranean house. Often two families shared these houses. Entrance through an underground passageway limited heat loss. From Frederick Whymper, *Travel and Adventure in the Territory of Alaska.*

became important authorities with real political power that derived from spiritual power. Nevertheless, other leaders, lacking such formal power, were still able to influence the community through widely acknowledged wisdom and skills in subsistence activities.

Knowledge of the land and its resources created a sophisticated technology and stimulated complicated adaptive strategies for exploiting them. Oriented to the sea, Eskimos of the delta emphasized open-sea hunting from skin-covered boats. They used harpoon darts, throwing boards, and bladder floats rather than weapons designed for land or ice. A multitude of diverse hooks, seines, nets, floats, and traps testified to the importance of fish to the economy.

Because of the bountiful coastal environment and its unique adaptive techniques, few Eskimos exploited the interior forests. This vast but difficult land was left to another people and other cultures. The primary characteristics of these people, who became known as Athapaskans, were mobility and flexibility. Lacking the rich resource base of the coast, they followed their prey. Thus they kept their material culture simple and easily replaced.

Whatever the common origin of the Athapaskans, their language changed enough to set off some Athapaskans from others. Unlike other American Indian groups, no formal tribal organization evolved. Instead, only kinship-related groups, sharing a common language and a particular territory, joined as regional bands. As time passed and Athapaskans moved into diverse environments, they borrowed some cultural traits from neighboring groups and created others. As a result, cultural diversity developed. Those Athapaskans that spread throughout the Yukon Basin became known as the Ingalik, Holikachuk, Koyukon, Kutchin, Han, Tanana, Tutchone, and Tagish.[13]

More than twenty-five Athapaskans groups, totaling more than twenty thousand persons, occupied Alaska and Canada.[14] Through time and borrowing, they acquired adaptive strategies for mastering their intransigent environment. Because the subarctic climate limited sources of sustenance as compared with the richly endowed coast, they developed great flexibility and adaptability. As with other Native Americans, nearly every aspect of their culture reflected a fusion with the land. Subsistence activity, settlement patterns, religious beliefs, social organization, as well as dress, tools, and travel, betokened dependence on the land.

Differences in quantity, quality, and stability of food resources of particular interior environments produced slight differences in individual Athapaskan groups.[15] Additional differences came from trading and intermarrying with neighboring cultures.

Despite differences in environment, subsistence activities, and borrowed characteristics, the Athapaskan groups had much in common.[16] Illustrative of the Athapaskans were the Kutchin and their close relatives, the Han. These two groups resembled each other in language and culture and occupied the middle Yukon. The Kutchin, one of the largest and most widespread of the Athapaskans, extended from the ramparts of the Yukon along the Porcupine River, one of its major tributaries, to the Mackenzie River in northern Canada. The Han, smaller and more compact, straddled what later became the international boundary. Because they required game as well as salmon, they ranged over a large territory. As a consequence, their population before the white advent was small—less than one thousand for the Han and approximately twelve hundred for all the Kutchins.[17]

In contrast to the squat coastal Eskimos, the Han and Kutchin looked like other North American Indians. They were tall, generally slender, with high cheekbones and black hair and eyes. Apparel and ornamentation reflected the distinctive features of their environment as well as their trading relationships. Men and women wore caribou shirts decorated with porcupine quills or shell beads. Both wore trousers with footwear attached. During the winter they added a rabbit-skin shirt, moose-skin mittens, marten- or rabbit-skin caps, and caribou-skin pants tanned with the hair on and worn next to the skin.

Athapaskan Indian. More than twenty-five Athapaskan groups inhabited Alaska and Canada. This Kutchin, drawn by Alexander Murray, illustrates dress, trade goods, and facial ornamentation. *Public Archives of Canada.*

For personal decoration and individual distinction, the Han and Kutchin coated the skin with grease followed by red ochre on the face. The women tattooed patterns of vertical lines on the chin and horizontal lines from the corners of their eyes toward their ears. Both sexes wore earrings and necklaces of dentalia shell or colored porcupine quills. For dress they inserted a straight bone or beaded ornament horizontally through the septum of the nose. Their hairdress, probably the most obvious cultural mark, was worn long and tied in the back of the head with liberal applications of grease, red earth, goose or duck down, and shells. As the years went by the hair became so heavily loaded with beads, shells, and accumulated dirt that the neck bent forward, giving a stooped appearance.

In adapting to climatic extremes, the Han and Kutchin developed different types of shelters. During the coldest months, two families built and shared a twenty-five-foot-square pole house covered with moss and soil. For winter hunting, they used a semispherical skin-covered shelter, which could be easily carried. During the summer they moved out of their moss house and into a light-weight skin-covered shelter, similar to that used for winter hunting. These skinned shelters allowed flexibility and mobility in traveling for subsistence and trade.

During the summer, the Han and Kutchin traveled on their diverse navigable rivers in several kinds of boats. Most characteristic of all Athapaskan groups was the birchbark canoe. On a spruce frame the craftsmen sewed the birchbark sheets together with spruce-root line. Then with the bare hand they applied melted pitch over the seams and cracks. Travel in winter required novel innovation—the Athapaskan snowshoe with upturned toes and a lacing or webbing of caribou skin. In addition, a ten-foot birch sled carried the family's belongings and occasionally a freshly killed animal.

Most Athapaskans traveled extensively for subsistence purposes. During the summer those along the Yukon partook of nature's predictable run of salmon, generally smoking, drying, and caching them for winter's food. In the fall, many Athapaskan groups dispersed and hunted caribou, which moved in large herds conducive to corraling and butchering. In late winter, after the depletion of cached stores, individual hunters sought moose, rabbits, and grouse. With spring thaw, the Indians snared or shot migrating waterfowl, completing the seasonal subsistence cycle.

Athapaskan institutions arose almost entirely from this day-to-day

Athapaskan winter shelter. Drawn by Alexander Murray in the late 1840s, this lithograph depicts life when temperatures drop to sixty degrees below zero. The skin shelter allowed greater ease and mobility in following winter game. *Public Archives of Canada.*

struggle to subsist in an exacting environment.[18] Moreover, the changing seasonal economic relationship of the Athapaskans to their environment ordered their social organization. Although basically tied to the village, they broke up several times a year to exploit the resources more efficiently. During the early fall they cooperated in communal caribou drives, but in the late winter they hunted moose and other animals individually. In the spring they joined with a partner to hunt waterfowl. By summer they had separated into individual fish camps but still maintained close contact with the nearby village. Family ties, friendship, and a sense of community sharing bound them to their village.

Within the village the family embodied the basic unit of social organization. During the periods of comparative isolation and seminomadism of the arctic winters, the family depended on the contributions of each individual. Since survival required the man as hunter to cover a large territory in search of game, he traveled lightly, with little besides his weapons. The woman, on the other hand, bore the packs and trudged slowly but directly to a new camp. When the man returned exhausted and hungry from hunting expeditions, the woman willingly fed him first. The man regarded the outside world as his, whereas the woman exercised her authority over the home. The division of labor worked comfortably and harmoniously with nature.[19]

Less stable were the bands of separate families that grouped together during the winter hunting period and the larger tribelike groups that formed villages during the fishing season. Economic pressures generated by insufficient food resources often caused these larger groups to disintegrate. Thus, while the family remained cohesive, circumstances dictated a flexible band and group structure.

Athapaskan religion, as with other North American Indians, was highly individualistic. Just as subsistence depended on independent and individual skills, religion, too, emphasized individual rituals rather than community rites. Within the general framework of Athapaskan beliefs, each person developed specific attitudes and ideas about the supernatural. Certain individuals established a recognized relationship with the spirit world and functioned as shamans. Through dreams, medicinal potions, and magical songs and dances, shamans prevented or cured disease. Each shaman sought help from his guardian animal spirit and used it to banish evil spirits. He also predicted weather, game, and the future. Religion thus proved highly functional and personal.

Although the culture stressed self-reliance and individualism, a flexibility existed that encouraged cooperation when necessary. Accordingly, Athapaskan social organization and religion responded to the task at hand and the demands of the environment at different times of the year. Mythology and religion went hand-in-hand with the importance of the movements of game. The more a man knew about his environment and the multitude of exploitative techniques that were part of his cultural heritage, the better equipped he was to deal effectively with the environment. Though each person acquired his own skills and abilities, he did so through the culture's socializing process. Thus the rigors of the environment tempered both social and individual impulses and fused them into a unifying culture.

Besides the two major cultural groups of Eskimos and Athapaskans, one other group used the Yukon Basin. The Chilkat Tlingit Indians, residing around the Lynn Canal in the southeastern panhandle, fully exploited the resources of sea and forest. Located among abundant and stable resources, the Chilkats became the wealthiest and most powerful of Native groups. Most important, they controlled the two major passes to the interior—the Chilkat and Chilkoot. As a result, they dominated the trade with the interior Indians. Secure with ample subsistence, the Chilkat dwelled in permanent, year-round villages. These communities, in turn, developed strong community loyalty and territorial consciousness. With power and wealth went an aggression and belligerency that set the Chilkats apart from the more peaceable Athapaskans and Eskimos.[20]

Of the three major Native groups of the Yukon, the Athapaskans adapted to the river environment and played a central role in its evolving history. Because their forest resources differed substantially from the wealth that the sea provided, their culture strongly contrasted with those of the Chilkats and Eskimos. Lacking the abundant resources of their seafaring neighbors, the Athapaskans did not develop permanent villages. As a result, they were more mobile, individualistic, and flexible. Loyalty to the village, band, or territory was less important than loyalty to the family. Even warfare most often occurred to avenge the death of a kinsman. On the other hand, they freely adopted aspects of other cultures that made their life easier or more enjoyable. Thus, at the advent of white contact, the Athapaskans displayed a willingness to adjust and adapt to changing conditions.

The impact of the environment on the evolution of the Yukon Native culture provided a northern dimension to the hypothesis that Turner applied to the continental frontiers of the United States. Moreover, the Native symbolized many of Turner's character traits of the unique American—individualistic, self-reliant, innovative, adaptive, and yet socially dependent.[21] In contrast to the frontiersmen that followed, however, the Natives of the Yukon Valley pursued a harmonious relationship with their natural environment. With the arrival of the white man and his goods, skills, and institutions, this relationship changed.

CHAPTER 2

The Russian
and English Frontiers

The Native world of the Yukon could not remain forever undisturbed. From east and west, Europeans closed in. During the seventeenth century, England and France ventured into the northeastern quarter of North America while Spain pushed north from New Spain. Russia, the sleeping giant, yawned and stretched eastward to Asia. For the next two centuries rivalries for the power and leadership of the continent exploded in full-scale wars that rocked Europe and the New World. Determined to win military glory and political prestige, each country expanded its imperial boundaries. As land came to connote power, colonial possessions took on major significance. Trade with China for tea, silk, and drugs intensified competition in ocean commerce and stimulated the development of new industries. America yielded tobacco, sugar, and furs. Trade and commerce became synonymous with power.

Oblivious to impending invasion, Natives of the Yukon nevertheless felt ripples of the approaching tide long before they confronted white men in the flesh. In fact, a vast trading network connected Siberia through the Yukon to what later became Canada, and through this network moved Native goods and European manufactures. Through groups on both east and west serving as commercial intermediaries, the people of the Yukon Valley obtained tobacco, metal pots, knives, steel flints, and other useful products of Europe.[1] Concepts of land ownership and other strange customs of the whites, however, did not flow in this early network and remained alien and unknown.

Russia owed her American empire first to Peter the Great, then to Vitus Bering. As Russia expanded early in the eighteenth century, Peter the Great sought to westernize his vast realm, to expand trade, industry, and shipping, and to augment his territories even more. After gaining "windows" on the Baltic and Black seas, he looked east, to Siberia. From fur traders there he heard of new and unexplored lands still farther east, across the cold waters of the North Pacific. In 1725 he sent a Danish navigator in Russian service, Vitus Bering, to Siberia with orders to find and reconnoiter the coast of northwestern America. When Bering failed, Peter's successors sent him again, in 1733, this time to establish Russian sovereignty in the New World and exploit its fur and mineral resources.[2] In 1741 Bering succeeded at last. He touched on American shores and claimed them for Russia. Enroute home, however, winter storms of the North Pacific battered his little craft, eventually shipwrecking the crew on uncharted islands that were populated with scores of sea otters, walruses, and polar foxes. While awaiting rescue, the survivors of the ill-fated voyage gathered furs that later reaped high profits in China.

During the next sixty years more than ninety-two expeditions followed the course Bering charted from Siberia to the fur-rich islands and coast of Alaska, called Russian America.[3] Drawn by high profits, Siberian fur traders, legendary *promyshlenniks*, risked foul weather, unreliable vessels, hunger, scurvy, and eventually hostile Natives. As they pressed the Natives to hunt increasingly scarce furbearers, they also, incidentally, explored and charted the islands and coast of Russian America.

Russia's eastward surge challenged Spain and England, and they responded. Spain pushed New Spain's frontiers northward along the California coast, and her explorers charted the very waters Bering had sailed. In 1776 Great Britain sent her greatest navigator, Captain James Cook, to investigate the northern shores of Siberia and Russian America. Throughout the eighteenth century a steady stream of British ships penetrated Russian-claimed seas. In answer Russia planted settlements to ratify and protect her claim—first on the Aleutian Islands, then on the mainland. By 1788 between 450 and 500 promyshlenniks in the service of at least five trading companies inhabited Russian America.[4]

From Natives the men of each imperial power learned of the other and, secondarily, of the Yukon that lay between them. In 1789 Alexander Mackenzie, a trader with the Canadian North West Company, descended the mighty river that later acquired his name all the way to its mouth. Here Natives told him of another and even greater river on the other side of the mountains. White men lived there, the Indians said.

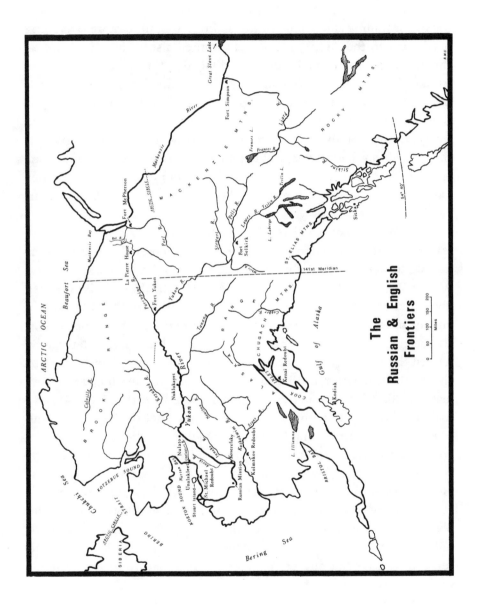

The
Russian & English
Frontiers

Aware that Russians had settled Cook Inlet, Mackenzie assumed that this great river flowed southward and emptied near the Russian redoubt of Kenai.[5] As the first to pioneer the Mackenzie River, later to become the major trading and supply route tapping a vast fur empire stretching northward to the Arctic, Mackenzie wanted also to find and explore this mysterious river of which he had heard, but he could find no one to guide him. Ironically, the journals of his remarkable trek, when translated into Russian in 1808, prompted Russian authorities to seek for themselves the elusive river of Mackenzie's informants. At the same time, promyshlenniks had heard from local Natives of a great river in the interior but had not been able to find it. Three of the world's greatest navigators had sailed past its mouth without discovering it—James Cook in 1778, Joseph Billings in 1790–93, and Otto von Kotzebue in 1815–18.

But the Russians persisted. During the early 1790s Aleksey Ivanov, leader of a group of traders of the Lebedev-Lastochkin Company, left in midwinter on skis from Iliamna Lake, the great body of water on the Alaska Peninsula that is Alaska's largest lake. Led by Natives whose obedience they ensured by holding their families as hostages, Ivanov and his promyshlenniks traveled north, recording an abundance of Native settlements and furbearers. They crossed a broad river—later to be named the Kuskokwim—through a summer portage and pushed on to the north, at length reaching the banks of still another broad river. At last—the date is no more exactly known than the early 1790s—Ivanov had found the river of which the Russians and English had heard vague reports for so many years. One day it would take the name Yukon, a corruption of its name in Native tongue. The Natives of this valley, Ivanov recorded, eagerly traded furs for beads, especially white ones. He also noted the presence of various metal articles, large knives with copper embossing, and blunt axes. As he skied along the coast, he observed that the Kuskokwim and the Yukon flowed into the sea with only "a day and a night's journey between them."[6] By Easter he had returned to Lake Iliamna, completing a circuit that would not be duplicated for forty years.

As the nineteenth century opened, the forces that governed the history of empires in the North Pacific began to shift. In 1799, while the promyshlenniks tentatively examined the fringes of Russia's colonial empire, politicians and businessmen in St. Petersburg consolidated all the rival fur companies of Russian America into the Russian-American

Company and set out to eliminate foreign competition. Twenty-two years later, in 1821, the British likewise ended ruinous competition with the merger of the Canadian North West Company into the British Hudson's Bay Company. During the years in between, while England confronted war and economic chaos in America, Russia emerged from the Napoleonic wars as the strongest nation in Europe and strove to keep Great Britain at bay. As part of that program the czar issued an imperial edict forbidding foreign ships to venture within one hundred miles of the coast of America north of fifty-one degrees north latitude. For four years the United States and Great Britain resented the proscription and sparred with Russia over disputed territory. Finally, in 1824, Russia and the United States recognized the Russian boundary at fifty-four degrees forty minutes north latitude. To secure American friendship, Russia allowed American ships to enter Russian-American ports to fish and trade with the Natives. A year later the British and Russians signed a similar treaty, defining the mainland boundary between the two colonial empires as the 141st meridian.

As Russian and British diplomats wrangled over the terms of the Treaty of 1825, both countries pursued exploration of the Pacific Northwest to buttress their claims. Although the main focus for the Russians remained the southeastern panhandle, they cautiously probed the vast interior drained by the Kuskokwim River. Hudson's Bay Company traders, on the other hand, aggressively moved into the lower Fraser River and attempted to build a trading post on the Stikine River. With high-quality goods and low prices, British traders hoped to steal the coastal fur trade from the Russians. In the process all moved ever closer to the remote country of the Yukon on which Aleksey Ivanov had gazed almost three decades earlier.

Pitted against each other in the early decades of the nineteenth century stood two giants of the north country—George Simpson and Baron Ferdinand Petrovich von Wrangell. Competent, energetic, and aggressive, the one governed the Hudson's Bay Company and the other the Russian-American Company. Hard-nosed but rigidly loyal to crown and company, George Simpson ruled the Hudson's Bay Company with an efficient iron hand. As an illegitimate child, he had learned cynicism and the value of discreetly placed gifts. Baron von Wrangell, on the other hand, came from noble German parents with uncompromising ethics but proved equally efficient and exacting in his leadership of the Russian-American Company.[7] Threatened by the Hudson's Bay Company's domineering and effective trading practices, Wrangell confronted Simpson's forces on the Stikine River and dispatched expeditions to explore and scientifically examine the southwestern coast. While Simpson governed for nearly forty years, Wrangell's rule lasted only five, from 1830 to 1835. Even after Wrangell returned to Russia, however, he continued as a director of the company. Throughout his life he remained a staunch supporter of the company and champion of the value of Russian America. In 1839, in the Germanic Confederation city of Hamburg, the two adversaries met face to face and resolved the two companies' difficulties. The English leased from Russia a strip of territory along the coast of the southeastern panhandle, and in exchange the British agreed to supply Russian posts with wheat, peas, meats, and butter at fixed prices.

Meanwhile Wrangell also looked to the interior. In 1833 he established a trading post on the Kuskokwim and sent veteran navigators Adolf Karlovich Etholen and Mikhail Dmit'rievich Teben'kov to chart Norton Bay. Although Etholen failed to find Ivanov's great river, he knew that it existed and believed it could best be exploited by planting a trading post or redoubt near Stuart Island. The following year Lieutenant Teben'kov sailed around Stuart Island, then chose another island for his redoubt, which he named for himself—Mikhailovskii or St. Michael Redoubt.[8] With the help of Natives and prefabricated structures, he completed the redoubt within ten days.[9] And so the Russians advanced a step closer to the land of the Yukon.

Almost immediately Wrangell insisted that communication routes be explored to facilitate the trade and scientific discoveries foreshadowed by the founding of St. Michael Redoubt. In Native skin boats from Pastol Bay First Mate Andrei Glazunov, a Russian Creole born and educated in Russian America but capable of speaking Kodiak Eskimo, reached the Yukon, which his Eskimo informants called the Kvikhpak.[10] Although he floated thirty miles down the Apoon, the northernmost stream of several that form the mouth of the Yukon, Glazunov failed to reach the sea or explore the other mouths. He did succeed, however, in visiting at least four Native villages and stimulating in their residents an interest in trading at St. Michael.[11]

In the winter of 1833–34 Glazunov with four Russian companions once again set forth to explore the Yukon to find a route to Cook Inlet and Kenai Redoubt.[12] Rather than negotiate the maze at the mouth of the river as well as confront potentially hostile Natives, Glazunov por-

St. Michael Redoubt. Russia's first Yukon trading post served as supply base for subsequent posts in the interior. Because of the maze of channels at the Yukon's mouth, travelers took a shortcut directly east from St. Michael to reach the river. From Frederick Whymper, *Travel and Adventure in the Territory of Alaska.*

taged from St. Michael Redoubt to the Anvik River and followed down it to the Yukon. Although he and his men tried to live off the land, they more often found themselves living off the generosity of the Natives. All the way down the Yukon they fought fierce head winds and bad weather. When they finally reached the Native village of Koserefsky, at the mouth of the Innoko River, the women and children fled to a nearby mountain. After Glazunov calmed their fears and explained his purpose, an old man said: "Now we shall no more believe what has been said to us of the Russians, that their nails and teeth are of iron; we see that the Russians are men like us and we are thankful to know the truth. We will come to visit your forts and are all disposed to trade with you."[13]

With guides from this village Glazunov crossed into the Kuskokwim drainage and met Creole Semen Lukin, who had explored the Kuskokwim and helped establish a trading post soon to be known as Kolmakov Redoubt. Despite Lukin's warnings, Glazunov forged forward up the Stony River, seeking a nonexistent portage to Cook Inlet. Almost immediately his guides abandoned him, his supplies diminished, and the weather grew increasingly cold. Recognizing that he could go no farther, he turned back, barely able to crawl feebly into a Native village. Here he recuperated until he could return to St. Michael Redoubt. Although he did not reach Cook Inlet in his 104-day ordeal, he succeeded in opening the Yukon to the fur trade. For his achievement Wrangell provided him with a monetary reward.

In February 1835 Glazunov returned to the Yukon and thoroughly explored the lower river. In 1836 he came back once again and established the first settlement on the river at the Native village of Ikogmiut, near the later Russian Mission.[14] The trading post had good access for supply and trading purposes to St. Michael Redoubt and also to Kolmakov Redoubt, on the Kuskokwim River. In 1838 a devastating smallpox epidemic wiped out more than half the aboriginal population and most of the local tribal leaders, or *toyons*. Believing that the Russians had deliberately introduced the disease, the Natives sought revenge. Later that year, a dozen Eskimos from the lower Kuskokwim Valley journeyed to Ikogmiut. Under the pretense of trading, they killed the arrogant manager and his men. Despite sporadic efforts by Glazunov and others to revive the trading post, in 1845 the Russian-American Company abandoned it.[15]

Next to push the Yukon frontier farther upriver was Petr Malakhov, son of Vasilii Malakhov and founder of what eventually became Kenai Redoubt on Cook Inlet. Petr was a Creole, but no ordinary Creole. With his father's connections to Governor Aleksandr Andreevich Baranov, he had attended the Kronshtadt Navigation College near St. Petersburg. Following graduation, he had accepted the task of surveying what was known to the Russians as the upper Yukon Basin. Using Glazunov's Native guide, he left St. Michael Redoubt on February 8, 1838, and eighteen days later reached the Yukon. In spite of Native stories of horrors awaiting him, Malakhov pushed upriver, collecting furs as he traveled. On March 10 he reached the mouth of the Nulato River, which he learned played host to a major trading fair each spring. Examining the area, he concluded that it would make an ideal trading post. Continuing up the Yukon, he entered the mouth of the Koyukuk River, where he stayed until spring. When the ice went out on May 3, Malakhov floated down the Yukon to St. Michael Redoubt—the first to do so.[16]

In November 1838 Malakhov set off to settle Nulato. During this voyage he learned from a young Native of an easy shortcut to Nulato

Nulato. Drawn here by American artist Frederick Whymper in 1866, Nulato became the farthest outpost of the Russian-American Company. Nearly wiped out twice, once by smallpox and once by Native attack, Nulato survives today. From Frederick Whymper, *Travel and Adventure in the Territory of Alaska.*

via the Unalakleet River. Heretofore shrewd Native traders, fearing that the advent of new Russian posts would cost them their middleman status, had guided the Russians on a tortuous trail to the interior; but now their secret was out. Trading as he traveled, Malakhov reached Nulato on March 28, 1839. Unfortunately, the smallpox epidemic was at its height and had decimated the population. With no Natives to hunt and fish, Malakhov and his men were starving by spring. Even so, he built a cabin half a mile upstream from the Native village, assigned an overseer to conduct such trade as proved available, and left Nulato on May 31.[17]

For the remaining years of the Russian presence, Nulato was their northernmost post. In 1841 a new manager arrived. An energetic Creole who had traveled with both Glazunov and Malakhov, Vasili Deriabin found the company's buildings burned and the village in ruins. With winter approaching, he moved the location to a patch of timber below the village and commenced rebuilding the post. Over the next two years the Natives slowly drifted back, and Nulato had a new beginning.

To the east, meanwhile, the British fielded a trader of energy and ability, Robert Campbell, who was twenty-six years old in 1834. The rugged Scottish hills of his father's sheep farm had strengthened his tall, broad-shouldered physique for the deprivation of the North American frontier. He chose the Hudson's Bay Company for the challenges of exploration and living in an unknown land. At the same time he turned a sensitivity, unusual in rough traders, on the Natives. A devout Presbyterian, he carried a Bible wherever he went and piously believed that the products of his civilization should be used to help lift the Natives from poverty and misery.[18]

After learning the fundamentals of the fur trade, Campbell took an active interest in expanding the trading boundaries of the Hudson's Bay Company. In 1840, with a companion and two Indians, he poled and tracked his boats up the Liard River and its tributary, the Frances River, crossed the continental divide, and looked down onto a westward-flowing river. Campbell called it the Pelly, in honor of a former governor of the Hudson's Bay Company, and in fact it flowed into the Yukon. Campbell thus became the first white man to cross from the Mackenzie into the Yukon drainage.

Sir George Simpson, governor of the Hudson's Bay Company, was certain that the Pelly eventually flowed into the Pacific and ordered Campbell to explore it further. Following Simpson's orders, in the spring of 1843 Campbell once again crossed the mountains and descended the Pelly in birchbark canoes. He and his eight men carried only three bags of pemmican, some powder and shot, and a few pounds of tobacco, beads, and other trade items. Campbell recorded abundant wildlife, especially at the junction with the Lewes, and also Indians who had never seen white men. These Indians were Athapaskans, presently known as Tutchone. "They were tall, stalwart, goodlooking men, clad from head to foot in dressed deer skins, ornamented with beads & porcupine quills of all colours," Campbell wrote. "They spoke in very loud tones, as do all Indians in their natural state, but seemed peaceable & kindly disposed towards us." The Indians discouraged further travel down the Pelly, however, warning of bad Indians who would kill and eat them. Campbell scoffed at such stories, but his men became frightened. Reluctantly, therefore, he agreed to turn back. On the return trip he confronted a large band of Indians who stood with "bows bent & arrows on the string." With a bold but conciliatory approach, Campbell succeeded in securing an amicable interview. The rest of the voyage proved uneventful, and the explorers arrived at Frances Lake in July.

When Sir George Simpson reviewed Campbell's report and maps, he concluded that the Pelly River was either "Turnagain [Cook Inlet] or Quikpok [Yukon]." Because of the richness in furbearers, he agreed that the forks of the Pelly and Lewes rivers would make a good site for a trading post and urged Campbell to start one. He also recognized Campbell's desire to proceed down to the sea, but cautioned that that "would be impolitic, as it would bring us into competition with our Russian neighbours, with whom we are desirous of maintaining a good understanding."[19] Simpson had no wish to jeopardize the fragile truce he had so recently worked out with Wrangell at Hamburg.

As Campbell worked his way toward the Pelly, another Hudson's Bay Company officer, John Bell, opened a second inland route to the Yukon. Like Campbell, Bell was Scottish, as was his assistant, Alexander Kennedy Isbister. In 1840 they explored the Peel and Rat rivers.[20] Following this trip in 1840, Bell received orders to establish a trading post on the Peel to be called Fort McPherson. In 1842, after Isbister returned to England for further schooling, Bell retraced his route up the Rat River. Then, after a rugged portage over the Richardson Mountains, he came to a river later named for him. From here he made his way to a larger river, the Porcupine. Then, concluding the overland route too difficult for communication and supply, he returned to Fort McPherson.[21]

Nonetheless, in 1844 Sir George Simpson ordered Bell to explore the Porcupine to its mouth. For the third time Bell crossed the Richardson Mountains by the five-day portage connecting the Rat and Bell rivers. After building canoes, he descended the Bell to the Porcupine and on to its confluence with a still larger river. For the first time an Englishman gazed on Mackenzie's mysterious river. He named it the Youcon—the Kutchin Indians' name for what turned out to be the fourth largest river in North America. These Indians assured Bell that no Russian traders inhabited the area. Six days later, on June 22, he left the marshy, lake-pocked land and returned to Fort McPherson.[22]

While Campbell and Bell fulfilled Simpson's orders to explore the upper Yukon, another able Russian took the field, one destined to leave a lasting imprint on Russia's map of her American empire. He was Lt. Lavrentiy Alekseyevich Zagoskin, and his interest in exploring interior Russian America happily coincided with the interest of Baron von Wrangell, now Director-in-Chief of the Russian-American Company, in having it explored. A graduate of the Kronshtadt Naval Cadet Corps, Zagoskin had served on the Caspian and Baltic seas. To relieve the boredom of official life, he read voraciously. Literary greats such as Pushkin and Gogol and world travelers like Krusenstern and Kotzebue stimulated the irrepressible youth to emulate them. His first essay, on his Caspian Sea experiences, verified his literary skills and his keen observations of common people. During the deterioration of the Russian Imperial Navy during the 1830s, Zagoskin like most idealistic young officers became demoralized and depressed. In 1838, therefore, he transferred his services to the Russian-American Company and traveled from Siberia to New Archangel—present Sitka. Later he commanded one of the last ships to service Fort Ross, the distant Russian outpost in present California. Here he met a young assistant from the Academy of Sciences who taught him the principles of science and the skills of collecting plants, animals, and ethnographic information. By 1840 an experienced explorer, the thirty-two-year-old Zagoskin wrote to Wrangell requesting the opportunity to document the interior valleys of Russian America for science and the company.[23]

Wrangell, still smarting from the aggressive tactics of the Hudson's Bay Company on the Stikine, required reliable data about the interior. He wanted to know communication routes between forts and the coast and where best to establish forts and trading posts. He feared that, if trade promised, either the British or the Siberians—competing Russian traders—would dominate it unless his company obtained a better understanding of the land and its people.

To Lieutenant Zagoskin, therefore, fell the task of exploring and mapping the interior. His orders required him to follow the Yukon and Kuskokwim to their sources, report on the abundance of furbearers, and ascertain the most practical portages between the two rivers. His orders also included exploration of Kotzebue Sound and determination of the ways in which trade then flowing to Siberia might be diverted to company posts. Since he had initiated the idea, Zagoskin happily accepted the assignment.

The young officer's enthusiasm dampened somewhat, when he arrived at St. Michael Redoubt and recognized the immensity of his task. By 1842 the Creoles and interpreters from earlier expeditions had grown accustomed to the comforts of the fort and refused to accompany him. He also learned that he had to outfit his command with winter clothing and food, oversee the construction of sleds, and purchase dogs and skin boats. Regretfully he had to admit that he could not explore Kotzebue Sound and still fulfill the other portions of his assignment.

Finally, on December 4, 1842, after four months of preparation, Zagoskin set forth for the Yukon. He had five men, five sleds, twenty-seven dogs, and sixteen hundred pounds of supplies. At Unalakleet he added another sled and eight hundred more pounds of food and equipment. Halfway to the Yukon, along the shortcut portage, he discovered that his guides had never been to the Yukon. Moreover, the weather turned bitterly cold—so cold the mercury in his thermometer froze. His men suffered from frostbite and lack of proper food. But at long last, on January 15, 1843, the expedition reached Nulato.

As soon as the explorers recovered from their ordeal, they assisted the post manager, Deriabin, in rebuilding the post. They also checked fish traps, hunted for grouse, and bartered for furs. Within a few weeks Zagoskin began to ready his expedition for a trip up the Koyukuk. Since he planned to go where no Russian had been, he carried trade goods and astronomical instruments.

On February 25 Zagoskin left Nulato and headed for the Koyukuk. Within a week he had traveled farther than had Malakhov before him. Because the smallpox epidemic had left its scars and fears, one Indian village insisted on purifying his expedition by setting fire along the trail. Other Natives, however, gratefully supplied shelter and food in exchange for trade goods. From these willing Natives, Zagoskin learned of their trade route to Kotzebue Sound. He also became convinced that the Yukon Natives communicated with Kotzebue Natives and indirectly with Siberian Natives. Nevertheless, when his food ran low, he returned to Nulato.

Zagoskin prided himself on his expedition's self-sufficiency. They hunted and fished rather than buying provisions from the Natives. The advantages were multiple: his expedition cost less than all others, his men subsisted in the wilds longer, they learned more about the country, and they remained independent of the Natives, whose respect was essential. With the arrival of spring the expedition spent days killing waterfowl for their rations. "I am a good enough shot, but missed many a duck or goose," he admitted, "as I watched with pleasure how it played in the bright waters of the Nulato, or came to rest on the shore after its exhausting journey."

Finally on May 5 the ice in the Yukon moved. "After the first crack," rhapsodized Zagoskin, "mountains of ice reared up on the sand bars; after a minute everything broke loose: the ice heaped up again, and again broke apart—death again was magnificently vanquished by

L. A. Zagoskin. At thirty-two years of age, Zagoskin launched the first Russian scientific exploration of the Yukon. Despite hardships, he explored more of the Yukon than any other Russian. An observant amateur naturalist and ethnologist, his writings and collections formed the basis for Russian knowledge of a remote empire. From Henry N. Michael (ed.), *Lieutenant Zagoskin's Travels in Russian America, 1842–1844.*

life." Such poetic musings set Zagoskin apart from his contemporaries. While the Yukon cleared itself of ice, he assiduously collected birds, insects, and plants—all the while bemoaning his ineptitude.

On June 4 Zagoskin and his men left Nulato in his skin boat to seek the source of the Yukon. He remained convinced that the "Great River" of Mackenzie's account was no other than the Yukon. He quickly learned that summer travel carried its own hardships. Mosquitoes drove them all to the brink of madness. "To say nothing about the midges and mosquitoes would be to remain silent about the most acute suffering we had to bear on this trip," he groaned, " a suffering to which one becomes accustomed, as to an inevitable evil from which there is no escape." Sandbars, logs, and sand spits required strenuous efforts to detour. Fast water necessitated crossing and recrossing the mile-wide river in search of slower and friendlier water. Headwinds, rain, and portages slowed progress even more.

Despite the adversities, the expedition journeyed upriver, seeking Natives with whom to trade. Different Native groups greeted the adventurers in different ways. Some had never seen white men, even though they possessed iron tools, beads, and wire rings. Most welcomed the Russians and exchanged information for trade goods. Others, however, trade middlemen to Indians farther up the Yukon, resented Russian intrusion into their territory and feared disruption of their economy. Strangely, Zagoskin observed greater friendliness when his Native guides did not accompany him.

When the party reached the Yukon's junction with the Nowitna River, a multitude of problems confounded them. First, the rainy season raised the water in the river, made poling impossible, also towlining from shore, and rotted the skin boat from the inside out. Moreover, Zagoskin learned the hard way that skin boats needed frequent waterproofing with sea mammal grease, which was not available on interior rivers. Next, they confronted shallows jammed with logs and boulders. Rather than waste time that could be used to complete his other commissions, Zagoskin turned back. His thorough surveying and mapping provided more information than all other expeditions put together, but for at least twenty years the Nowitna would mark the limit of Russian knowledge of the Yukon.

Within a week Zagoskin was back at Nulato. Convinced anew of the richness of the Yukon for fur trading, he also recognized the pervasive influence of Siberian trade in which the Siberian Natives traded goods acquired from Siberian merchants and thus undersold the Russian-American Company. Nonetheless, the Nulato traders, even as new and inexperienced as they were, still brought in more beaver pelts than any other. In his report Zagoskin recommended that more men be sent to the outposts to ensure safety and provide greater opportunity for hunting and fishing. Moreover, he noted, the Natives had begun to acquire an interest in European dress, and the trading goods should be changed accordingly. Competition between St. Michael Redoubt and the interior posts he found self-defeating and frustrating.

In August 1843, with considerable regret, Zagoskin left Nulato. "Here I had been more than a year in the company of common people and daily with those who are called savages," he observed; "the first are truly concerned with the welfare of their fatherland and talking with the second was far from boring but often very instructive. The natives stimulated my curiosity."[24] He and his expedition floated down to Russian Mission, which he made his headquarters. From there he explored the upper and lower portages to the Kuskokwim, investigated the Innoko River, and scouted what was called the upper Kuskokwim. As he completed his journeys, he compiled his ethnographic notes. Significantly, he recognized not only the basic difference between coastal Eskimos and interior Indians, but discerned differences of dialect and culture among the Indians.

Nearly two years after leaving St. Michael Redoubt, Zagoskin returned. Several months later he departed Russian America via Sitka and Siberia. In 1847 he published his report and displayed his collections. He had collected thirty-eight species of birds, seventy species of insects, fifty different rocks, and recorded statistical and ethnographic information about interior Natives with examples of their weapons, clothing, and cooking utensils. On the basis of his achievements, the Russian Geographical Society elected him a full member, and the Academy of Science awarded him its highest prize. In 1848 he left the naval service only to return as a commander of the local militia during the Crimean War. Following the war he retired to his estate in Russia to experiment with horticulture and write essays opposing serfdom and the sale of Russian America. He died in 1890 at the age of eighty-two.

While Zagoskin explored the Yukon and recorded his ethnographic observations, the Russian Orthodox Church sent a missionary to St. Michael Redoubt and neighboring villages to save Native souls. In 1845, following Zagoskin's two-year trip, the Bishop of Russian America sent a Creole priest, Iakov Netsvetov, to establish a mission in the interior. Although the company had recently abandoned Russian Mission as a trading post, he chose the village because of its proximity to Natives on the Kuskokwim and Yukon rivers. After a cold and hungry first winter, Netsvetov built a house, dried his winter's fish, and began to travel and convert Natives. Whenever he could win the trust and confidence of the people, he vaccinated them against smallpox. Others resisted, explaining: "We did not know God before and we don't want to know him now." Nonetheless, in 1851 he succeeded in building a church, and by 1853 he had 1,720 converted Natives as his congregation. Although the Russian-American Company retreated and retrenched, the Russian Orthodox Church continued to grow and attract converts.[25]

While the Russians worked their way toward the middle Yukon, Sir George Simpson audaciously ordered a new post on the Yukon, at the mouth of the Porcupine. Although he knew this to be in Russian territory, he recognized it as good fur country with a population of unexploited Indians. Ironically, he did not choose Bell or Campbell, veteran explorers, to establish the post. Instead he turned to a newcomer to the Hudson's Bay Company—Alexander Hunter Murray.

Another of the ubiquitous Scots who turned to fur trading in the New World, Alexander Murray was twenty-seven years old but a veteran of several years with the American Fur Company in the United States. On the company's boats as he traveled north in 1846 was the seventeen-year-old daughter of a colleague, Anne Campbell. As the artistic Murray taught the young woman to sketch, they fell in love. They married immediately, and Anne went with him to La Pierre House, a newly established post on Bell River near the head of the Porcupine on Bell River. Back and forth over the Rat River portage Murray trekked with supplies. When Anne became pregnant, Murray left her at La Pierre House as he plodded on to the Yukon.[26]

Murray knew full well that he and his company trespassed on Russian soil. Indians also seized every opportunity to remind him of his transgression. Even as he started down the Porcupine, a group of Kutchin hailed him and warned that Russian traders had traded at the mouth of the Porcupine the year before.[27] On June 25, 1847, Murray reached the Yukon. Here the Yukon Flats Kutchin described their trading contacts with the Russians on the lower Yukon. Their accounts detailed the vast supply and selection of trade goods, the Russian promise to explore the Yukon to its source in 1847, and well-armed men with pistols traveling in boats of sheet iron.[28] With the Russians in mind, Murray insisted on strong fortifications. "When all this is finished," he assured himself, "the Russians may advance when they d——d please."

The Yukon did not impress Murray. "As I sat smoking my pipe, and my face besmeared with tobacco juice to keep at bay the d——d mosquitoes still hovering in clouds around me, my first impressions of the Youcon were anything but favourable," he fumed. "I never saw an uglier river, everywhere low banks, apparently lately overflowed, with lakes and swamps behind, the trees too small for building, the water abominably dirty and the current furious."[29] Even so, on a rare piece of high ground, his post went up. He named it Fort Youcon.

Trading began immediately. Quickly Murray realized that his trading supplies were inadequate—a chronic complaint of such far-flung outposts. For lack of trade goods he reluctantly turned away prime furs. The cunning Kutchin tormented him with descriptions of the Russians' large stock of goods that were reportedly underselling his.[30] The Indians also reported that the Russians promised once again to meet them upriver with plenty of goods. According to the Indians, the Russians blamed the British for the epidemics and called them "bad people." In spite of all, the winter passed well enough, for plentiful game and fish kept Murray and his men well fed. With the arrival of spring he hurriedly poled his way back to La Pierre House, where his wife and new daughter awaited him.

The Murrays returned to Fort Yukon (new spelling) for three more years. Despite the rough surroundings, Anne took up housekeeping and bore three daughters. "We have a good house," she wrote her mother-in-law, but "we are far from old friends and have no society but ourselves."[31] Meanwhile Murray worked hard to establish good trading relations with the Kutchin and Han. Acute observations while traveling and trading led him to divide the Kutchin into eight tribes and calculate the population of the Yukon and its tributaries to include one thousand adult males—that is, men who could hunt.[32] His accurate sketches of Indian life and culture illustrated Sir John Richardson's *Arctic Searching Expedition*. In 1851, as his daughters approached school age and his own health declined, Murray requested and obtained a transfer. After numerous positions, he finally attained the coveted chief-tradership. In 1874, still in his fifties, he died. Anne outlived him by thirty-three years, dying in 1907.

In 1848, while Murray completed his first year at Fort Yukon, Robert Campbell set out to fulfill Sir George Simpson's orders of 1844 to establish a post at the forks of the Lewes and Pelly rivers. Like Murray, Campbell struggled with "a miserably insufficient outfit." On the other hand, he found the Indians at the forks surprisingly friendly and strictly honest. Campbell named his post Fort Selkirk. Later in the season he confronted the coastal Chilkats, who served as middlemen between the coastal and interior trade. With frustration Campbell watched as the Chilkats undersold him with a better supply of trade goods, obtained from American and British ships.

Not only were trade goods in short supply; bare essentials were too. After a near famine during his second winter, Campbell in desperation drew up a bold plan for evacuating his men westward, to the Russian outposts. Rather than risk another winter without supplies, he would drift downstream until he reached the "Russian trading posts along the river on the Pacific Coast."[33] Thereby he staked his life and those of his men on his belief that the British Yukon and the Russian Kvikhpak were the same river. Campbell even sent word of his plan with some Chilkats to the coast, where a company ship captain duly alerted the Russians. Fortunately, however, the winter supplies arrived, and Campbell did not have to resort to his plan. Nonetheless, trade goods remained in chronic short supply because of the hazards of transporting them over the treacherous route he had opened.

Meanwhile the debate over the identity of the Yukon continued. Governor Simpson insisted that the Russian Kvikhpak emptied into Cook Inlet, as Mackenzie had suggested. The Yukon, he believed, emptied into the Arctic Ocean, and its mouth carried the name Colville.[34] Alexander Murray, who had studied the Yukon Kutchin, believed like Campbell that the Pelly and Yukon were the same. Some of his Indians had visited Frances Lake and the forks of the Pelly and Lewes.[35] At last, in April 1851, Simpson judged relations with the Russians sufficiently cordial to grant Campbell permission to explore as much of the Pelly as he wished.

Eagerly Campbell left on June 4, 1851. Although rumors whispered that the Russians had traveled the middle Yukon, Campbell became the first recorded white man to make the trip. After two days and nights of travel, he met a group of Indians, later known as the Han, who delivered a letter of welcome from Alexander Murray written a year earlier, thus reinforcing his faith in his hypothesis about the nature of the Yukon. Campbell named the White and Stewart rivers for colleagues in the Hudson's Bay Company. On June 8, after only a four-day journey, he reached his goal—Fort Yukon. "I had thus the satisfaction of demonstrating that my conjectures from the first—in which hardly anyone concurred—were correct & that the Pelly & the Youcon were identical."[36]

When he landed at Fort Yukon, Campbell learned that Murray and his family were on their way up the Porcupine to a new assignment. The next morning Campbell rushed up the Porcupine and overtook Murray. Together they crossed the rugged Rat River portage and ascended the Mackenzie to Fort Simpson. Despite the longer voyage— along the Pelly-Yukon, then up the Porcupine, over the Rat River portage, and then up the Mackenzie—Campbell recognized that he had pioneered another supply route to Fort Selkirk. His earlier route, via Liard River and Frances Lake, was dangerous and had caused at least fourteen deaths.[37] With his winter supplies Campbell returned along this new route to Fort Selkirk.

The following summer brought a disaster that ended Campbell's enterprise. Once again he traveled down to Fort Yukon and obtained enough trade goods to test the potential of his fort. But he reckoned without his old adversaries, the Chilkats of the southeastern coast. Fort Selkirk challenged their monopoly of trade with the Indians of the upper Yukon, and that summer they showed up at the fort angry and hostile. Campbell failed to appease them, and indeed he was lucky to escape with his life as they burned his trading post. He sought permission to rebuild the fort but failed to convince the company managers of its importance. Discouraged and cynical, he left for Scotland. A year later, with bride in train, he returned as a Hudson's Bay Company administrator. Never again, however, did he cross the Rockies to the Yukon. After forty-one years, the company suddenly and unjustly fired him, and he finished his life cattle ranching in Manitoba.

While Murray completed his last winter at Fort Yukon and Campbell readied his men for his first trip down the Yukon, in the fall of 1850 a countryman of theirs arrived at Russian St. Michael Redoubt. He was Lt. John J. Barnard of HMS *Enterprise*, and he was looking for another Englishmen, Sir John Franklin. This pioneering Arctic explorer had failed to return from his third voyage, and a massive search was under way. Barnard was part of the effort. He had heard vague rumors that Indians of the Koyukuk River had seen strange white men in the valley. As he quizzed Russian authorities at St. Michael Redoubt, he

Robert Campbell. Into the Yukon Basin from the east came Scotsman Robert
Campbell of the British Hudson's Bay Company. He explored new trading
routes, established Fort Selkirk, and proved that the British "Yukon" and the
Russian "Kvikhpak" were the same river. *Hudson's Bay Company.*

met the Nulato manager, Vasili Deriabin, who planned to return to Nulato after obtaining his winter supplies. Barnard traveled with him to Nulato and remained to investigate the rumors.

Unwittingly Lieutenant Barnard struck the spark that set off a powder keg whose contents had been growing in volatility for a decade. The conservative leadership of the Russian-American Company had ignored Lieutenant Zagoskin's wise counsel contained in his final report of 1844. St. Michael Redoubt, Nulato, and other posts had not been strengthened, and competition among Russian posts for the interior trade continued. In addition, Russian trade goods from Siberian Natives still competed with Russian trade goods from Russian-American Company traders. Animosities within the Native world compounded the instabilities introduced from outside it. In 1846 Nulato raiders fell on a village of their kinsmen on the Koyukuk River, killed and pillaged, and thus in the inevitable Indian scheme of things created an obligation of revenge. More important, Russian traders, especially Vasili Deriabin, had bad reputations among the Natives. Vastly outnumbered, several traders resorted to intimidation and cruel tactics to subdue the Natives. Deriabin's brutality caused the Indians around Nulato to hate and fear him. In 1851, when Lieutenant Barnard reached Nulato, the fuse was stretched and needed only the smallest of sparks to explode into flames. He innocently requested that the Indians on the Koyukuk River come to Nulato and be questioned.[38]

That was too much for the Koyukons on the Koyukuk. First they killed Barnard's Russian emissaries. Then they came as ordered, but at night and stealthily. They crept into the village of their old foes at Nulato. Stumbling on their enemies' birchbark canoes, they chopped them up, set fire to them, and then pushed the blazing wood into the smoke holes of Nulato's subterranean houses. Taken by surprise, many of the Nulato Indians suffocated in the smoke, others burned, and still others, trying to escape, were shot down with arrows or spears. Because the attackers used no firearms, no sound traveled to the nearby Russian post. The avenging Indians now appeared at the post and seized one of their tribesman who served as an interpreter for the Russians. "If you do not kill the *bidarshik* [Deriabin]," they threatened, "we will kill you." The interpreter surprised Deriabin getting out of bed and stabbed him repeatedly in the back. Lieutenant Barnard, reading in bed, reached for his gun and fired two wild shots before receiving a mortal wound. Barnard's shots, though, warned the Russians in their barracks.

They quickly barricaded the door and opened fire. With the death of one Indian, the rest withdrew. They had avenged the old Nulato raid as well as Deriabin's brutality. Deriabin and Barnard were buried in the Nulato cemetery—victims of the closest thing to a "massacre" that history records on the Yukon River.[39]

As British and Russian traders competed for the Native trade, so missionaries competed for Native souls. More than twenty years after the Russian Orthodox Church sent missionaries to the Yukon, the Anglican Church in 1861 sent the Reverend William West Kirkby to the Yukon. Thirty-three years of age, Kirby had grown up in Uffington, England. For the previous ten years he had served as a missionary schoolmaster at Fort Simpson. The journey to La Pierre House fatigued him exceedingly mostly from the "badness of the walking, intense heat of the sun—and myriads of the most voracious mosquitoes."[40] From La Pierre House he continued down the Porcupine with trader Strachan Jones.

The fort and the Kutchin Indians greeted him so enthusiastically that he spiritedly wrote his church's missionary magazine: "Gladly would I, if it were not for my family, live permanently among them. They require a single man to be their Missionary."[41] Despite his welcome he stayed only a week. His second trip to the fort, in 1862, he stayed nine days. Oblate Father Jean Sequin of the Roman Catholic Church, who accompanied him on the trip, spent two years on the river and traveled as far as Nuklukayet. Although he worked hard and risked his life on a little-traveled river, he made no headway among Indians or Englishmen.[42] Kirkby's reports and letters, however, aroused interest in England, and in October 1862 he found his permanent missionary—Robert McDonald.

McDonald was well qualified for the new post.[43] He had grown up on the frontier, worked with the Indians of Manitoba for nine years, and had a gift for languages. As soon as he reached the Yukon, he began to learn the Kutchin language. Within two years he had translated hymns, prayers, and parts of the Bible into Kutchin and had instructed his converts in reading and memorizing these passages. He even married a Kutchin woman. At this time, however, devastating epidemics of influenza and scarlet fever wiped out large numbers of Indians and felled McDonald himself. Expecting death, he requested a replacement. William Carpenter Bompas arrived from London in the dead of winter. By this time, however, McDonald had recovered and could continue his duties. Rather than send the thirty-four-year-old Bompas back to

Fort Yukon. In 1847 Alexander Murray established Fort Yukon fully aware that it lay in Russian territory. Ironically, the Russians never challenged or contested the British post. Not until the Americans acquired Alaska were the British forced to leave. From Frederick Whymper, *Travel and Adventure in the Territory of Alaska*.

London, Kirkby made him priest-at-large. This assignment marked the beginning of extensive travels and expanding responsibilities destined to have great impact in the latter half of the century.

Despite contrary rumors, the English and Russian trading frontiers still had not met. In 1860 the Russians commissioned Ivan Lukin, the son of Semen Lukin, founder of Kolmakov Redoubt on the Kuskokwim River, to spy on the English at Fort Yukon. Lukin accompanied a group of Indians traveling to the trade fair at Nuklukayet, at the junction of the Tanana with the Yukon. From there, pretending to be a runaway from Russian service, he gained the assistance of the Kutchin. After scouting the strengths and weaknesses of the British, Lukin left by night and floated to Nulato. He was the first recorded white man to ascend the Yukon from the sea and establish definitively that the British Yukon was in fact the Russian Kvikhpak.[44] The Russians, however, made no use of this disclosure.

Following Lukin's exploratory visit to Nuklukayet and Fort Yukon, the Russians began to visit the trade fair at the mouth of the Tanana. At the same time, to keep competition keen, the British manager at Fort Yukon, Strachan Jones, sent several parties of Kutchin to the trade fair. In 1862 he descended the Yukon to the Tanana and participated in the trading. Then, further challenging Russian sovereignty, he floated to the Nowitna—the farthest point of Zagoskin's exploration and survey.[45] Because breakup occurs at the headwaters of a river before it makes its way downriver to the mouth, the British reached Nuklukayet first each year. Consequently they succeeded in taking the majority and the best quality of the Natives' furs. Each year they usually left the trade fair even before the Russians arrived.

As the Russian and British trading frontiers neared each other and finally touched on the Yukon, competition and friction proved not as intense as might have been expected. In truth, Russia had lost her taste for the American adventure. Throughout the 1850s and 1860s events elsewhere commanded national attention and energy. In 1853 the Crimean War broke out with Turkey and later Great Britain, and almost immediately British naval superiority threatened the isolated and indefensible American colonies. The Russian-American Company agent negotiated a fake sale of the colonies to a San Francisco company, but before he could complete the fraud, company officials in St. Petersburg obtained from the Hudson's Bay Company a mutual guarantee of their respective holdings in northwestern America. Although the Treaty of Paris of 1856 preserved Russian America, it opened the Black Sea to Russia's enemies, reduced Russian influence in Europe and the Balkans, and exposed Russia's social and financial weakness.

The war also left a huge budget deficit, and herein lay an enormous portent for Russian America. The czar's brother conceived the idea of solving the problem by selling the American colonies, and to whom more fittingly than the Americans themselves. Other motives reinforced the proposal. Russia wanted the United States as a counterweight to her continuing rival, Great Britain. Rumors of a Mormon migration to Russian America coupled with the troubles posed by growing numbers of smugglers and unauthorized whalers made the colony less attractive at the very time rising interest in China's Amur Valley absorbed the attention of St. Petersburg's imperialists. Predictably, the old American hand Baron von Wrangell, now chairman of the Russian-American Company's board of directors, objected vehemently. Among other things, he disliked Americans, whom he felt abused privileges and cheated Natives. But the proposal won out, and in 1857 Russia's envoy in Washington, Edouard de Stoeckl, cautiously broached the matter with United States diplomats.

The United States was definitely interested—especially in furs, whales, and trade. Also, Russian America would provide a strategic link with Asia and make possible a land route for an around-the-world telegraph line. But the United States in the 1850s grappled with the great struggle over slavery, and virtually every issue, however seemingly remote, became embroiled in it. Like the Mexican Cession of 1848, such a huge territorial acquisition would be sure to inflame the question of slavery in the territories.

The issue remained alive, but barely. The United States plunged into civil war. Russia's preoccupation focused on Europe and the Balkan question. At the same time, however, the ties to Russian America weakened even more. With the Treaty of Peking in 1860, giving Russia access to China, the Russian-American Company's commercial link to Asia lost importance. Also, investigations of the Russian American Company turned up poor management, insensitivity to Natives, fur pelt depletion, rampant smuggling, and no diversified colonial economy. Increasingly the colonies came to be viewed as a luxury Russia could not afford.

Then the American Civil War ended. While England had sided with the Confederacy, the czar had conspicuously supported Lincoln and the Union. Northerners were grateful. Once more diplomats took up the question of the sale of Russian America. At four o'clock on the morning of March 30, 1867, representatives of the two nations signed the historic accord ceding Russian America to the United States for the sum of $7.2 million.[46] "Seward's Folly" or "Seward's Icebox" critics of the United States Secretary of State called it. But American forces moved in, hoisted the national flag, and took possession of what they renamed Alaska—believed to be an Aleut word meaning "great land."[47]

Meanwhile on July 1, 1867, three eastern political units—Nova Scotia, New Brunswick, and the province of Canada—formed one "dominion" under the name of Canada and began to build a continental nation. Although the Hudson's Bay Company exercised proprietary rights over much of the West, known as Rupert's Land, negotiations commenced immediately to purchase the company's holdings. In 1868, the government of Canada agreed to pay the Hudson's Bay Company 300,000 pounds, and in 1870 a settlement was secured with boundaries for provinces and territories. Thus by 1870 both British and Russian authority had vanished from the Yukon Basin.

However lightly the Russian frontier had directly touched the Yukon and its tributaries, it had left a legacy not without consequence for the future. Its most significant impact was on the Natives, especially those of the lower Yukon, and was most noticeable in a European material culture that the Natives had eagerly adapted to their own. The first Russian trade goods had come from Siberia, through Siberian Natives, and these had prepared the way for direct trading relationships when the Russians appeared on the Yukon. Then, more often than not, these Russian newcomers were Creoles—offspring of Russian unions with Native women. They readily took to Native ways—wore Native dress, ate Native foods, fished using Native techniques—and thus, seemingly less dangerous and alien, were more warmly welcomed than pure-blood Europeans. Many took Native wives and thereby cemented ties of kinship that further facilitated commerce. As a result the Yukon Natives rapidly incorporated European manufactures into their material culture and cultivated a dependence on trade that did not vanish with the Russians.

In ways other than material, the Russians left their mark. They appointed *toyons* or chiefs, for example. This practice tended to undermine the Native political system and give the Russians a measure of dominance. Natives who received Russian favors grew wealthier and more influential, but also more dependent. The Russian withdrawal left consequent political instabilities. And ranking near the top of any list of Russian influences must be disease, which killed more than one-half of the Native population.

The changes hardly added up to a revolutionary cultural transformation. Partly because the new diseases seemed a betrayal of trust to the Natives, the Russians failed to integrate Natives into the fur trade. Moreover, the scarcity of trade goods, the decline in beaver and its marketability, and the reluctance to trade firearms further limited the Russian potential to alter the economic lives of the Yukon Natives. Subsistence patterns remained intact, Native dress and shelter continued, and the Russian Orthodox Church, blamed for the smallpox epidemic, made little headway. Even so, as the Natives embraced facets of Western culture, they forfeited some measure of self-reliance and independence. They grew dependent upon the trader, his trading post, and his demand for fur. Any change in any of these three variables brought a corresponding change in the Native life-style. Thus the Russians introduced a new variant to the environment of the Natives. The British and Americans perpetuated this variant.[48]

Besides the Natives, the Russians also influenced the British. Bering's thrust eastward had spurred them northward and westward. Through greater resources, aggression, and commitment, by 1867 the Hudson's Bay Company had firmly entrenched itself along Alaska's southeastern panhandle and throughout the Mackenzie drainage, and its agents had even trespassed successfully on Russian soil.

For the Americans, therefore, the Russians left behind Native customers, British customers, and a residue of tangible assets. In San Francisco, soon after the Alaska purchase, seven men from various parts of the country formed Hutchinson, Kohl & Company. Purchasing the assets of the Russian-American Company, this firm then took in two other groups and formed the Alaska Commercial Company. Swiftly it came to dominate the fur trade of Alaska.[49] The Hudson's Bay Company found these newcomers not as appeasing, passive, or accommodating as their Russian predecessors. Instead the Americans, conditioned by two hundred years of frontier adaptations, exhibited aggression, innovation, and impatience.

Americans wasted no time moving to the Yukon. In 1868 a company of traders wintered at the mouth of the Tanana and participated in the trade fair held there each spring. British traders showed up as usual, to be greeted with anger and thinly veiled threats of force.[50] These foreigners trespassed on United States soil, the Americans charged, and they complained to Maj. Gen. Henry W. Halleck, commander of the United States Army's Military Division of the Pacific. British diplomats denied any intent to trespass and promised to withdraw if United States authorities determined through astronomical observation that the Hudson's Bay Company's Fort Yukon in fact lay within American territory. General Halleck therefore directed Capt. Charles W. Raymond of the Corps of Engineers to determine the latitude and longitude of Fort Yukon and to report on the activities of the Hudson's Bay Company in Alaska.

Enroute to this assignment, Captain Raymond witnessed a historic first on the Yukon. He reached St. Michael on the Alaska Commercial Company's ship *Commodore*. Lashed to the *Commodore*'s deck was a fifty-foot sternwheel steamer whose prow exhibited its name in black letters—the *Yukon*. On July 4, 1869, the *Yukon* entered the Yukon's mouth—the first of hundreds of steamboats to navigate the river whose name it bore. It caused great excitement and consternation among the

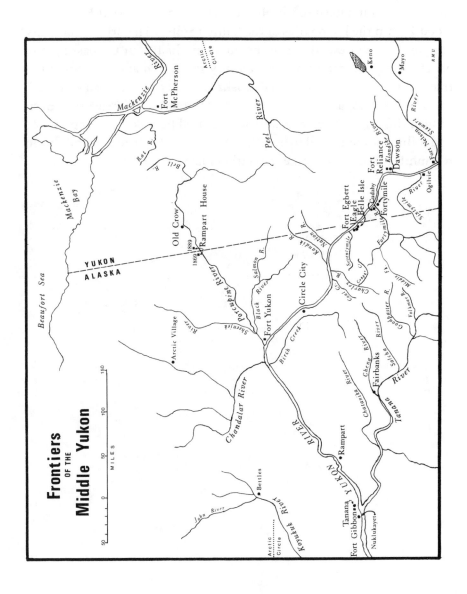

Frontiers
OF THE
Middle Yukon

MILES

0   50   100   150

Beaufort Sea

Mackenzie Bay

Mackenzie River

Fort McPherson

Arctic Circle

Rat R.

Bell R.

Peel River

Keno

Mayo

R M U

Fort Nelson

Stewart

Klondike River

Dawson

Fort Reliance

Ogilvie

Sixtymile R.

Fort Egbert
Eagle
Belle Isle
Ludahy
Fortymile
Seventymile R.
Fortymile R.

Rampart House

Old Crow

1889
1869

YUKON
ALASKA

Porcupine River

Sheenjek

Salmon R.

Black River

Kandik R.

Nation R.

Charley R.

Coal C.

Seventymile R.

Goodpaster River

Volkmar R.

Middle R.

Circle City

Fort Yukon

Birch Creek

Chena River

Fairbanks

Salcha R.

Tanana River

Arctic Village

River

Chandalar River

Chatanika River

Rampart

YUKON RIVER

Koyukuk River

Bettles

John River

Arctic Circle

Tanana
Fort Gibbon
Nuklukayet

49

Natives as it "appeared to them as a huge monster, breathing fire and smoke."[51]

Raymond debarked at Fort Yukon. After making celestial observations, he announced to the Hudson's Bay Company that Fort Yukon stood within the boundaries of the United States. The British company obligingly withdrew. Because the company had been trespassing and poaching, the Secretary of the Treasury refused to allow it to sell the trading post to the newly formed Alaska Commercial Company. Instead, in 1871, the company rented it from the United States Treasury.[52] Even though the British had physically left the middle Yukon, their presence and influence continued to be felt.[53] An artificial political boundary did not inhibit the free movement of either Natives or traders.

CHAPTER 3

The Trader's Frontier

The fur-trapping and trading frontier of the American West repeated itself in Alaska a generation later. The breed of men, the fierce competition, the transportation of supplies by steamboats, the development of strategically located trading posts—all marked the continental frontier of 1807-40 and the Yukon frontier of 1867-85. Even the consequences recurred: traditional Native culture changed to accommodate that of the white invaders, new routes of travel were found in a hostile land, and enticing tales held promise of economic opportunity to newcomers.[1] One major difference, however, separated the two frontier experiences. Shortly after the Alaska purchase, Congress turned control of the fur-bearing animals over to the Secretary of the Treasury, and he issued regulations prohibiting anyone but Natives from taking such animals. In Alaska, therefore, Natives trapped. Whites traded.

But fur traders were not the first Americans to Alaska. As early as 1860 a young American scientist found his way to Fort Yukon. Robert Kennicott, born in New Orleans but reared in Illinois, battled ill health despite the efforts of his physician father. Believing his health too poor for a classical education, he invested his energy in becoming a naturalist, winning the favor of the renown scientist, Spencer Fullerton Baird, who served as Assistant Secretary and later Secretary of the Smithsonian Institution. By the age of twenty-one Kennicott had a number of scientific publications to his credit. Within a year he acquired the title of curator of the Northwestern University Museum of Natural History and traveled to Canada's Red River for collections.

With further support from the Smithsonian Institution and the Audubon Club of Chicago, and the promised hospitality of the Hudson's

Bay Company posts, Kennicott launched a three-and-a-half-year collection trip into British and Russian America. In April 1859 he left Chicago for British America. A year later he descended the Mackenzie to the Peel and then over the mountains to La Pierre House. From there he floated the Porcupine to arrive at Fort Yukon in September 1860. Here he spent the winter and the following summer in the company of Hudson's Bay Company traders. As Indians throughout the Yukon Basin came to Fort Yukon to trade, Kennicott observed and even participated in the trading rituals. As a result, he collected valuable ethnographic information and museum specimens of their material culture. Occasionally the Indians called on him to perform medical feats. Delightedly, he obliged them. When he left Fort Yukon in August 1861, he stayed at La Pierre House until the following January, when he began his long journey to Chicago, arriving on October 17, 1862.

The joyous, high-spirited enthusiasm of the young naturalist left its mark on remote British posts. With good cheer, Kennicott threw himself into the traders' activities. He not only hunted, fished, and trapped but also chopped wood, carried water, and did his share of the onerous chores. As a result, the traders liked him. Most important, he inspired them to gather specimens. For the next ten years Hudson's Bay Company traders sent collections to the Smithsonian Institution. Kennicott's own collection numbered forty boxes and more than three thousand pounds of skins of mammals and birds, eggs, nests, skeletons, fish, insects, fossils, plants, Indian skulls, dresses, weapons, and utensils. Swiftly, he gained recognition as the only American expert on Russian and British America.[2]

Between 1865 and 1867 more Americans appeared on the Yukon with an expedition fielded by the Western Union Telegraph Company. When attempts to lay an Atlantic cable failed five times, businessman Perry McDonough Collins convinced Secretary of State William H. Seward, the United States Congress, and the Western Union Telegraph Company of the feasibility of building a telegraph line from British Columbia through Russian America and then across Siberia to Europe.[3] In 1865, with charters and approvals from Russia and Great Britain, the project got under way. Overall responsibility lay with Col. Charles Bulkley and Capt. Charles M. Scammon, while the Scientific Corps, charged with exploring and collecting data and specimens, was led by the only American with knowledge of Alaska—Robert Kennicott.

Personality conflicts, logistical problems, and unsuitable tempera-

Robert Kennicott. In 1860, under the auspices of the Smithsonian Institution, Kennicott spent three years in British and Russian America. As America's only expert on the region, he was selected to head the Scientific Corps of the Western Union Telegraph Expedition. While on the Yukon in 1866, his heart failed, and the post fell to William H. Dall. *Bancroft Library.*

ment made Kennicott a nervous wreck even before reaching St. Michael. Always in poor health, he performed best when alone. His temperament did not allow for human frailties nor inspire men to follow him. Moreover, he was sensitive and easily provoked. He had little patience to cope with the countless frustrations of a project the size of the Russian-American Telegraph Exploring Expedition.

Arrival in Russian America only increased Kennicott's irritability. The river steamer failed to function, local interpreters, guides, and helpers demanded inflated wages, and sled dogs were scarce. Slowly, from Kennicott's base at Nulato, exploration began. During the first year the Americans only retraced Russian paths. Kennicott had planned a winter trip to Fort Yukon but had to postpone it. Then in May 1866 his heart gave out. Two of his men found him on the river bank, dead at the age of thirty.[4]

William H. Dall succeeded Kennicott as chief of the Scientific Corps, while Frank Ketchum and William H. Ennis continued his telegraph responsibilities. Dall, like Kennicott, had trained as a naturalist under the world-famous geologist Louis Agassiz. He was only nineteen years of age when he joined the Telegraph Expedition. Exploration of the Yukon, however, was left to Ketchum. In late May he and another expedition member, Michael Lebarge, guided by Creole Ivan Lukin, set out in a skin boat for a quick round trip to Fort Yukon—the first since Lukin's journey in 1860 to link the Russian and British frontiers. Then that winter, while Dall collected and prepared specimens and English artist Frederick Whymper sketched and painted from their base at Nulato, Ketchum and Lebarge departed overland for the upper Yukon. In June 1867 they reached Robert Campbell's Fort Selkirk at the mouth of the Pelly, which marked the limit of their exploration and the farthest distance up the Yukon that white explorers had traveled. Dall and Whymper met them at Fort Yukon, and together the telegraph team floated back to Nulato. There they learned that the Atlantic cable had been successfully laid. Instantly, the Russian-American Telegraph Expedition became defunct. The expedition returned to San Francisco that summer, although Dall obtained permission to stay for another year to continue his collecting.

The Western Union Telegraph Expedition left a modest though not insignificant legacy. It broke no new ground, explored no new territory, developed no new resources. But it did yield the first systematic scientific investigation of interior Alaska, and it provided Americans for the

The Western Union Telegraph Expedition. With the approval of the British and Russians, the Western Union Telegraph Company sought to stretch a telegraph line from British Columbia through Russian American and then across Siberia to Europe. The expedition's Scientific Corps led American exploration of the Yukon; some members even reached as far upriver as Fort Selkirk. From Frederick Whymper, *Travel and Adventure in the Territory of Alaska.*

first time with explicit knowledge of their immense new possession. Several members of the expedition wrote books and articles about their experiences that enticed adventurers northward. Four—Frank Ketchum, James M. Bean, Ferdinand Westdahl, and Michael Lebarge—returned to seek their fortunes and play a part in opening the country. Dall's extra year accumulated a wealth of information on geography, history, climate, fisheries, fur trade, and mineral resources.[5]

Americans lost no time in laying the foundations of a trading empire to supplant those of the Russians and British. William Dall saw it begin to take shape as early as June 1865. Learning from Russian friends of the United States purchase of Alaska, he had floated from Nulato down to St. Michael as soon as spring breakup opened the river. There he found an old friend from the telegraph expedition, Mike Lebarge, back in Alaska as a trader for Hutchison, Kohl & Company. Almost at once, however, Lebarge decided to strike out on his own, and he teamed up with other former telegraph employees, some disenchanted Hudson's Bay Company traders, a few French Canadians, and even several Rus-

Americans recently arrived on the Yukon had to learn new methods of travel. Sleds pulled by dogs offered rigorous experiences for the Western Union Telegraph Expedition and the for American traders who followed. From Frederick Whymper, *Travel and Adventure in the Territory of Alaska.*

sians who chose to remain with their Native families in Alaska rather than return to a Russia that was less home than foreign country. Together these men organized a loose trading association they called the Pioneer Company. At the junction of the Yukon and Tanana rivers, they established Nuklukayet, the first American post in Alaska. They also explored the Yukon and gained valuable experience with furs and Natives. The Pioneer Company lasted only a year, but the knowledge Lebarge and his associates acquired contributed greatly to the eventual success of the firm that absorbed it late in 1869—the Alaska Commercial Company.[6]

Among the Pioneer adventurers who joined the Alaska Commercial Company was François Mercier, who was destined to dominate the Yukon trading frontier for the next seventeen years. Of striking height, broad shoulders, and flowing hair, Mercier served as the Alaska Commercial Company's general agent for the Yukon, Tanana, and Kuskokwim rivers. He and his brother Moise descended from a long line of rugged French-Canadians—*coureurs de bois*—who had extensively explored from the upper Mississippi to western Canada. They seemed to thrive on hardship, deprivation, and adventure. Both men received their training and experience from the Hudson's Bay Company. In 1869, when François took charge of the Alaska Commercial Company's opera-

François Mercier. Among the first to fill the vacuum left by the Russian-American Company were former Hudson's Bay Company traders. Mercier established several new trading posts, encouraged the visits of Catholic missionaries, and used steamboats to supply the Alaska Commercial Company's far-flung posts. *Public Archives of Canada.*

tion based in St. Michael, Moise acquired the most remote yet most profitable post, Fort Yukon.[7]

From St.Michael, François Mercier established trading posts, with only one small steamboat, the *Yukon*, provided them annual provisions and merchandise, won the loyalty of the unruly independent traders now in company employ, competed with rival companies, and developed friendly relations with the Natives. He also initiated the practice of supplying his posts from the mouth of the Yukon rather than over the difficult Mackenzie-Porcupine route, and, disdaining the international boundary, he boldly made a company highway of nearly the whole navigable length of the Yukon.

By 1871 Mercier had the organization of the river trade well under way, but a serious problem loomed as the restless Americans confronted the leisurely ways of the Alaskan Natives. Following the trading rituals the Russians and British had evolved, the Natives enjoyed spending several days drinking tea, smoking, and feasting at the traders' expense before settling down to barter their furs.[8] The Americans, however, wanted to get down to business at once. Moreover, when the Hudson's Bay traders left Fort Yukon in 1869, they merely moved up the Porcupine beyond where they guessed the boundary lay and established Rampart House. There the Kutchin Indians continued to trade for familiar and preferred goods and delighted in playing the British and Americans against each other. Friction quickly developed between the American and Native temperaments.

Mercier left on the first steamboat to San Francisco in 1872 to discuss the potential Native problem with company managers. He believed that if the Natives got out of hand, the lives of his traders would be in jeopardy. The company president, sympathetic and concerned, suggested a force of two hundred armed men to protect the traders, possibly with government aid. Wisely, Mercier counseled less provocative measures. Roman Catholic missionaries, he suggested, might be more effective. After Mercier talked with his parish priest in Montreal, Oblate Father Isidore Clut, who had spent a number of years in the Canadian Athapaskan and Mackenzie regions, appeared the ideal choice.[9]

Within weeks after receiving a request for help, Father Clut, accompanied by Father August Lecorre and a servant, left Great Slave Lake via the Mackenzie and the Porcupine. For more than three months they journeyed, sleeping without shelter in rain and snow and breaking the ice as they advanced on slightly frozen rivers. Finally they reached Fort Yukon and such comforts as Moise Mercier could provide. The following May 1873, they continued down the Yukon to Nuklukayet, where they met François Mercier. Throughout the summer, as Mercier stopped to trade at each village, Monseigneur Clut taught Catholicism to the

Natives and baptized their children. In turn the Natives named Mercier as godfather. With the end of summer approaching, Mercier released Father Clut to return to Fort Simpson via Fort Yukon, the Porcupine, and the Mackenzie. Father Lecorre, however, stayed at St. Michael for the winter and visited communities along the lower Yukon. In the summer of 1874, he learned that Alaska had become the jurisdiction of Bishop Charles J. Seghers of Vancouver Island. Thus, at the first opportunity, he sailed for San Francisco. Despite Mercier's hopes, the Catholic missionaries failed to produce miracles. The trader and the Native would have to learn to adjust to the other.[10]

While Mercier struggled to establish a Yukon River fur-trading empire, a group of Yukon-bound prospectors wintered in Canada near the junction of the Liard and Nelson rivers. Among the group, three men stood out, three who would leave an indelible stamp on Yukon history. They were Leroy Napoleon McQuesten, Arthur Harper, and Alfred Mayo.[11]

Tall and muscular, "Jack" McQuesten grew up on a farm in New England, but the California gold rush lured him west. A series of gold strikes on the Fraser and Finlay rivers drew him into Canada. With a restlessness common to fur traders, he longed to join the Hudson's Bay Company and share in the *voyageurs'* adventurous discovery of new lands. When he observed the hundred-pound loads these men carried over portages, he knew that he must train and discipline himself to absorb the punishment voyageurs stoically, even joyfully, endured. After a rigorous training course, the Hudson's Bay Company reluctantly accepted the young man. On the first portage of the first trip northward, however, he staggered under nearly two hundred pounds of load and then fell his full length over the first log he attempted to cross. He knew without a doubt that he was not physically cut out to be a voyageur and returned to the factor in charge of the expedition to design himself another job. For several years he traveled, traded, and learned skills that he would use for the rest of his life. A full-flowing mustache and good-hearted spirit characterized the man later called "The Father of the Yukon."

Like McQuesten, Harper came north looking for gold. He was born in Antrim, Ireland, in 1832 but emigrated to New York at age eighteen. For twenty years he followed the stampedes, prospecting and dreaming of a bonanza. As he studied Arrowsmith's *Atlas of North America*, he pondered the discoveries of gold throughout the Rocky Mountains, from

Leroy Napoleon 'Jack' McQuesten (left) and Arthur Harper (right) arrived on the Yukon together and stayed until after the Klondike stampede. First Indians and then miners came to depend on their trading posts for food staples, grubstakes, and companionship. *University of Alaska Archives.*

Mexico to northern British Columbia, and wondered if it might also occur at the northern extremities of the range. Piercing eyes and full, untrimmed beard betrayed an intense and driving temperament.

In contrast, Kentuckian Alfred Mayo, a former circus acrobat, exuded good humor and a dry wit and loved practical jokes. He was smaller than either McQuesten or Harper, but driven by the same restlessness and search for excitement that led them to prospecting. Like them, when gold could not be found, he turned to trading.

Hearing tales from a former Fort Yukon trader of potential gold and easily caught marten and fox in Alaska, the three men and their companions decided to try the new American territory. Because McQuesten and Mayo had business near Great Slave Lake, Harper and his friends went ahead. McQuesten, Mayo, and company floated the Bell River on a raft, then built a boat and continued down the Porcupine to the Yukon.

Here, on August 15, 1873, they met Moise Mercier. He treated them like kings. "Some of us had not had such good living in ten years," relished McQuesten.[12] Harper had already left Mercier's post and had pushed on up the Yukon to the White River to spend the winter prospecting. McQuesten and Mayo took life more leisurely and wintered downriver near the ramparts of the Yukon. They built a cabin, killed three moose, one large bear, numerous geese and ducks, and caught some of the largest and fattest whitefish that they had ever seen. Lacking window glass, they cut a two-foot square of ice every week or so from a nearby lake and installed it on the cabin. Although they had planned to do some trading, they saw not a single Indian all winter. When spring arrived, they returned to Fort Yukon and then traveled back down to Nuklukayet, now renamed Tanana Station by the Alaska Commercial Company. Here they reunited with Harper and his party.

Since all of the prospectors lacked provisions, they decided to continue to St. Michael. Here François Mercier offered them employment with the Alaska Commercial Company. McQuesten and Mayo accepted, but Harper declined, preferring instead to prospect for gold near Tanana Station. Mayo was assigned to the company post there, but McQuesten drew an assignment far upriver. Mercier reckoned to tap the Han Indian country, unexploited since the destruction of Campbell's Fort Selkirk in 1852. Father Clut had known McQuesten well on the Mackenzie River and had recommended him as an honest man and a good trader. Mercier decided to establish a new post there with McQuesten in charge.

Aboard the *Yukon*, the company's little steamboat, Mercier and McQuesten left St. Michael in July 1874 with three barges in tow containing supplies and merchandise for the forts on the Yukon. The crew spent six hours a day chopping wood to burn in the craft's boiler. Above Fort Yukon, the steamer entered an unfamiliar part of the river. The pilot had difficulty finding the channel and frequently went aground. Eventually Mercier chose a site for the new trading post on Canadian soil across from the Han village of Nuklako, six miles below the mouth of the Klondike River. He named it Fort Reliance. Mercier established the post to accommodate the Han Indians, who previously had to travel hundreds of miles to trade their furs at other posts. "It was, then, to shorten at least a little this long and painful journey," explained Mercier, that he established Fort Reliance.[13]

After spending two days to help clear a site for the new post, Mercier left McQuesten and an Englishman named Frank Bonfield to construct the fort and initiate trade while he returned to St. Michael. McQuesten hired Han Indians to carry logs and others to hunt and dry meat for winter. Next, he and Bonfield built a house, measuring thirty feet long and twenty-five feet wide, of large logs, squared on one side, with a roof of small birch logs covered with pieces of birch bark about six or seven inches in size. Then came the store and storage buildings of similar construction. When winter arrived, McQuesten and Bonfield had warm dwellings and plenty of dried meat. Before winter ended they had exchanged all their trade goods for furs. Fort Reliance had proved its value. Later it became the major landmark in the area. Fortymile River was estimated to be that distance downriver from Fort Reliance and Sixtymile River a similar distance upriver.

In striking contrast to the hundreds of adventurers who scoured the American West for beaver and Indian trade, during the trading season of 1874 only thirty-two white men lived on Alaska's three major rivers—the Yukon, Kuskokwim, and Tanana.[14] In Alaska marten, not beaver, brought the greatest value in quantity and quality, followed by land otter, black bear, and finally beaver. Beaver had once been the great staple fur of the Alaskan interior just has it had throughout the American West during the early 1800s. Whereas overtrapping in the American West nearly decimated the population, in Alaska two bitterly cold successive winters froze the beavers in their lodges or blocked their entrances with ice until they starved. Thus, the severe environment, not the trappers, nearly wiped out the whole Alaskan beaver population.[15]

More similarities than differences, however, marked the two trading frontiers. Isolation in both cases forced a self-reliance and self-assurance typical of the frontier. The traders, recognizing that the Indian culture had already adapted successfully to the environment, embraced much of their life-style. The Indians, in like manner, acquired from the traders those aspects of Western culture that made life easier if less secure and independent. Often the traders, like their earlier counterparts, completed the union between the two cultures by marrying Native women. McQuesten, Harper, and Mayo were not exceptions.

One such union produced a family that played a major role in developing the Yukon Basin during the trading and early mining frontiers. In 1867, while in the employ of the Russian-American Company, Ivan Pavaloff, half Russian and half Koyukon Indian, hosted the Western Union Telegraph Expedition at his post at Nulato. Later he guided William Dall and Frederick Whymper of the Western Union Telegraph

In 1884 a self-taught artist, Pinyit Everett, captured the setting of Fort Reliance (above) and Nuklukayet (below). Fort Reliance came to demark distance on the upper river—Fortymile and Seventymile rivers were respectively those distances from Fort Reliance. Nuklukayet, at the junction of the Tanana and Yukon, capitalized on the annual spring trading fairs of the Indians. *University of Alaska Archives.*

Expedition from Nulato to Nuklukayet. Dall characterized him as short, thick-set, swarthy, and low-browed. He appeared good humored, willing to assist in data gathering, generous, hospitable, and honest. Nonetheless, he was an insatiable drinker and unmanageable when drunk. He legally married a Nulato Koyukon Indian woman named Malanka or Marina and had nine children, whom he treated well. Three of the children came to prominence in the years ahead: Ivan (better known as John Minook or Manook), Peter (called Pitka), and Erinia, who married a Nulato Creole, Sergi Gologoff Cherosky, when she was just sixteen years old. From Nulato the family observed and participated in the changes in trading practices from Russian to American. After the purchase of Alaska, Pavaloff stayed on at Nulato to serve as interpreter for Mike Lebarge and later for Ivan Korgenikoff.

Like the Russians and British before them, American traders devoted most of their time and effort to staying alive in a hard land. Since they carried only the staples of flour, tea, and sugar, much time had to be allocated for hunting moose, bear, and caribou, and for drying and storing meat. Dogs, essential to winter travel, had to be fed. Thus salmon, the main dog food, had to be caught and dried or bought from the Indians. Cords of firewood had to be chopped and stacked in anticipation of seventy-below-zero temperatures. If any of these resources were in short supply, the winter would be even harder.

When McQuesten, Mayo, and Harper met at St. Michael in the spring of 1875, they discovered that the Alaska Commercial Company had been reorganized. Trading posts were now leased to independent traders working on commission. The Mercier brothers left the company at this time either in disagreement with the new policy or as a result of the reorganization. Moise had even left Alaska, never to return. Since Harper had not found enough gold to live on and most of his companions had returned to San Francisco, he joined with Mayo to trade at Fort Reliance for the next three years, prospecting the surrounding country each fall. Meanwhile McQuesten went to Fort Yukon.[16]

In 1877 unusually fierce competition excited the Natives of the Yukon and led to serious trouble. Another San Francisco firm, the Western Fur and Trading Company, appeared on the river. So strenuously did the two companies compete that they drove the price of fur higher than the market value in San Francisco. The Natives capitalized on the rivalry—as they had between the Russians and British—and played one company against the other. The traders soon began to have trouble with the Natives. At Fort Reliance Harper and Mayo caught some of them stealing goods. Disgusted and discouraged, they abandoned the post. Meanwhile François Mercier reappeared in the employ of the new firm. He opened a post near the mouth of the Tanana River and created such severe competition that the Natives quickly gained the upper hand.

The competitive environment provoked the first hostilities between American fur traders and Indians on the Yukon River. In May 1878 one of the early adventurers of the Pioneer Company, James M. Bean, wearied of the stiff competition and decided to strike out on his own. He loaded his American wife, his two-and-a-half-year-old son—the first American born on the Yukon—a twelve-year-old Russian Creole girl, his baggage, and some trading goods into a large skin boat. With the help of five Indians, he launched his boat from the Alaska Commercial Company post at Nulato. He initially planned to establish a trading post at the mouth of the Tanana, but upon arriving on June 7 he learned that McQuesten held one post and Mercier another, both within seven miles of each other. Instead Bean chose to move up the Tanana River and establish trading in an unexploited area. McQuesten had spent a month the previous winter with the Indians there, the first white man to trade and visit with them, and he had found them "a kind of wild set and not to be depended upon."[17] He therefore advised Bean to leave his family behind. A belligerent and headstrong old man, Bean ignored the advice. He traveled thirty miles up the Tanana, built a trading post, and commenced trading.

Because he pioneered new trading territory and hoped to make enough money to leave the country, Bean charged more for his goods than the two companies. At the same time his brusque manner and greedy trading style alienated the Indians. Toward the end of September 1878 two young Indians came to trade. After completing the transaction, they followed custom and asked to spend the night and eat dinner with the Beans. Rudely Bean refused. Angry and humiliated, the Indians waited until the Beans sat down to eat. While one distracted Bean, the other crept up behind him, shoved a gun under his colleague's arm, and shot Mrs. Bean in the back. As she fell to the floor, Bean sprang up and ran for his gun. The second Indian's gun misfired and both fled to the woods. Panicked by fear, the old man threw his son and the young girl into the Indians' birchbark canoe and attempted to maneuver it into the fast current. Almost instantly his abrupt moves capsized the boat, fortunately in shallow water. Coincidentally an old Indian woman arrived in a large birch canoe to trade dried salmon. Bean forced her to take him and his surviving family to Mercier's post at the mouth of the Tanana.

When the frightened party arrived at the Western Fur and Trading Company post, Mercier immediately sent for Harper and Mayo to help him deal with the problem. Harper, with a group of Indians, returned to Bean's post to recover the body of Mrs. Bean. Later at Tanana Station two old Indian women washed and dressed the body while Mercier made a coffin. Meanwhile, Bean expressed no sorrow nor even any thanks for the services. Instead he took the coffin, his son, and the Creole girl and cast off for St. Michael. An early winter, however, forced him to inter his wife's body at Nulato, next to those of Lieutenant Barnard and Vasili Deriabin—the first white woman buried on the Yukon and one of only two violent deaths recorded on the Yukon during the period of the traders' frontier.

The second violent death involved Indian revenge. In the fall of 1879 an old Russian Creole, known as Ivan Korgenikoff, served as trader for the Alaska Commercial Company at Nulato. When his son Elia killed an unarmed Nulato Indian boy seemingly without provocation, Korgenikoff sent him to Tanana to keep him out of harm. Meanwhile, the Indian's family approached Korgenikoff demanding a settlement. Korgenikoff had recently arrived from the lower river, where the Russians had made the Indians subservient. Behaving as arrogantly as he had on the lower river, he offered the boy's relatives forty dollars, "as that was enough for a dog," and warned them that if they did any harm to his son he would kill them.[18] Since he had in fact killed four or five Indians on the lower river, the family did not want to raise his wrath and appeared to accept the offer. They all trekked over to the Western Fur and Trading Company post to have a neutral party witness the settlement.

Before Korgenikoff left, his interpreter, Ivan Pavaloff, warned him to be careful. Pavaloff was half Koyukon himself and had married into the Native group. He did not believe that the Koyukon Indians would be satisfied with such a paltry sum. His premonition proved correct. On the return trip the brother of the slain Indian pulled a pistol and killed Korgenikoff. The remaining traders accepted the revenge murder because the Indians had "settled it according to their laws and customs."[19]

A third incident with potential for violence found a peaceful resolution because of the good sense of the Han Indians. When Harper and Mayo abandoned Fort Reliance in 1877, they left some arsenic mixed with grease to kill off the mouse population. In 1879, moved by the severity of competition downriver, McQuesten decided to reopen Fort Reliance. Enroute, at Charley's Village at the mouth of the Kandik, he learned that two old women and a blind girl had eaten the arsenic and had died. Fearing for McQuesten's safety, Chief Charley tried to convince him to remain at his village and trade, but McQuesten did not want to incur the expense and labor necessary for a new post. Consequently, when he arrived at Fort Reliance and the Natives greeted him with joy, he was immensely relieved. They paid for the goods their people had stolen from Mayo, and McQuesten gave a dog in exchange for the young girl's death. Both parties acknowledged that the old women should have known better and were no loss to the village. A still closer bond was created when McQuesten fell and broke a rib while prospecting. Every day a messenger came from one of the three bands of Indians inquiring of his recovery and stating that their shamans were making magic for him.

Despite the competition of the two trading firms, the traders depended on one another to survive in the harsh environment. For example, in 1880 François Mercier took the Western Fur and Trading Company's new steamer *St. Michael* up the Yukon at the same time the traders of the Alaska Commercial Company went up in the *Yukon*. Since the *Yukon* was "liable to break down any time," Mercier offered to carry the Alaska Commercial Company traders to Fort Reliance on the *St. Michael*. Gratefully McQuesten and his crew accepted the offer and laid up the steamer in a protected slough. Not surprisingly, the following spring McQuesten found that during breakup ice had smashed the *Yukon*. The company, however, had anticipated its eventual demise, and at St. Michael a new seventy-five-foot boat, also named the *Yukon*, was launched.

Although most of the trading took place on the Yukon, St. Michael remained the headquarters for the Alaska Commercial Company and the Western Fur and Trading Company. The village had changed little since Russian occupancy. The fort was still an enclosure of dwellings and warehouses joined together with a high wooden fence, designed to protect inhabitants not from hostile Natives but from the incessant wind. Many of the buildings dated to the Russian period and were constructed of driftwood logs, roughly tongue and grooved into each other, and caulked on the inside and out. Loose dirt piled up around the outside of each building kept the wind from entering beneath the flooring.

Outside the enclosure were the Russian Orthodox Church and the gardens of the two companies.

Russian traders still played a major role in both companies. For example, Moise Lorenz, a Russian Jew from Odessa, served as commissary agent for the Alaska Commercial Company. His life-style, however, contrasted greatly with that of the typical Russian trader, who married a local Native woman and adopted her culture. In 1880 Lorenz married a beautiful and refined American woman from Maine, who brought with her the trappings of her culture—wallpaper, carpet, canary birds in gilded cages, flowering plants, and a library.[20] Mercier, on the other hand, spent most of his time on the river.

To compete with the Alaska Commercial Company's post at Fort Reliance, Mercier decided in 1880 to establish a post for the Western Fur and Trading Company in Han territory at David's Village (near present Eagle), the largest Han village on the Yukon. After dropping off McQuesten and his crew at Fort Reliance, Mercier returned to David's Village and built a trading post three-quarters of a mile from the village. He left his steamer captain in charge and boated back to St. Michael for the winter.[21] By spring the trader at David's Village had grown disgusted with the poor trading season and abandoned the post, taking with him the windows and stove.

During the summer of 1881, Harper, a man known only as Bates, and two Indians left David's Village to hike over the highlands into the Tanana drainage to prospect new country. As they crossed the North Fork of the Fortymile River, the current swept Bates off his feet and nearly drowned him. While he dried his clothes, Harper prospected and collected a sample of sand. Bates carefully stored it away, and they continued to the Tanana River. At the Tanana, the two Indians made their traditional moosehide boat. Fighting snags, sweepers, and rapid water, the party descended five hundred miles to the Yukon. This trip documented for the first time an area that later played a major role in the development of interior Alaska and recorded the first trip down Alaska's third largest river. Bates left the Yukon and returned to San Francisco, where he took Harper's sand from the Fortymile to an assayer. To his surprise it assayed at $20,000 worth of gold to the ton. The following winter, when Harper learned of the sand's value, he returned to the Fortymile but could not find the locale where it was collected.

Although McQuesten, Harper, and Mayo spent time each summer and fall prospecting for gold, they found no claims worth staking. Nevertheless, they explored various tributaries of the Yukon—the Tanana, the Fortymile, the Sixtymile, the White, the Stewart—and in the process acquired a general familiarity with broad relief features, drainages, and gold-bearing gravel. Through letters to friends in the placer camps of British Columbia, they publicized the mineral potential of the Yukon. Furthermore, their trading posts offered prospective gold-seekers an assured source of provisions.

Reports of gold were nothing new. Rumor had prospectors reaching the Yukon overland from the coast for a decade or more.[22] George Holt was the first who can be documented, in either 1874 or 1875.[23] Somehow he circumvented the belligerent, territorial Chilkats and, crossing either Chilkoot Pass or White Pass, traveled as far as Marsh Lake, the headwaters of the Yukon River. His reported discovery of coarse gold excited his friends in Sitka, but the Chilkats cowed even the most courageous.

In 1879 Captain L. A. Beardslee of the United States Navy, an able and responsible officer commanding the USS *Jamestown*, used an imaginative stratagem to try to open up the Chilkat territory. When word reached Beardslee of an intra-Chilkat war, fueled by the illegal distillation of hooch—a potent mixture of hops, molasses, and assorted other ingredients—he recruited a number of Sitka Chilkat to visit their kinsmen and emphasize the "value of white friendship and the danger of the opposite." Moreover, his emissaries were to request the opportunity for white traders and miners to explore the interior for precious minerals, which "if found, would enrich the Indians also." By February 1880 the Sitka Chilkats had returned with an invitation to white miners to enter the hitherto forbidden land. Eighteen men chose Edmund Bean (no relation to James Bean of the Tanana disaster) as their leader. Beardslee sent the *Jamestown's* launch, three naval officers, thirteen men, two interpreters, and a pilot to accompany them. The military precautions proved unnecessary. The Chilkats not only permitted the pioneer crossing of Chilkoot Pass, but also packed the miners' gear to the headwaters of the Yukon—the beginning of what became a profitable occupation for the Chilkats. Later that year the James "Slim Jim" Winn party followed. Before the summer passed, all miners returned, but with only a few traces of gold. Nonetheless, these prospectors opened a major route to the Yukon that later became highly significant.[24]

Meanwhile in 1882 François Mercier returned to the Alaska Commercial Company and built a post at David's Village near the Western Fur and Trading Company's post, which had been abandoned for a year. He named it Fort Bell, for a company backer in San Francisco who was also his friend. Later the fort became known as Belle Isle. Erinia Pavaloff Cherosky, daughter of Creole Ivan Pavaloff of Nulato, and her Creole husband, Sergi Gologoff Cherosky, served as Mercier's interpreters. The Western Fur and Trading Company also decided to return to its post at David's Village that year, and competition between the two exceeded previous limits. "The Indians had a picnic that winter," quipped McQuesten, "as they both had quite a supply of flour and they were both out in the Spring."[25]

The year 1882 was also notable for the appearance on the Yukon of two parties of prospectors destined to leave their mark on early Alaskan mining history. They came from opposite directions—the one up the Yukon, the other down. Edward Schieffelin headed the first. He had already made a name and a fortune for himself by discovering the rich silver mines of Tombstone, Arizona. In 1881 he had sold his Tombstone claims and with his brother Eff set forth for the Alaska Yukon. In March 1882 the brothers mistakenly landed in the new boomtown of Juneau, in southeastern Alaska. When they learned of the high coastal mountains they would have to cross to reach the Yukon, they decided to return to San Francisco, build a steamer, and ascend the Yukon from its mouth. They also made a quick trip to Arizona to recruit Charles Farcoit to serve as the steamer's engineer and to pick up two more prospectors. They left San Francisco in a chartered ocean schooner with three years of supplies stored in the hold and a fifteen-ton steamer, *New Racket*, lashed to the deck.

The expedition disembarked at St. Michael to learn that they had to shift for themselves. They could hire a pilot to guide them through the maze of islands and channels at the Yukon's mouth, but once on the river Schieffelin became steersman, captain, and pilot. Without serious mishap, they reached Tanana in August. Using the steamboat to tow logs, some of the "boys" began building winter quarters several miles up the Tanana River. Ed and Eff, meanwhile, took a skin boat and started prospecting. They found a fair prospect near the ramparts of the Yukon, but winter came on suddenly and the river began to freeze. Begrudgingly they floated with the ice back to their winter quarters. Although Schieffelin took a dog team to St. Michael with plans to prospect the Kuskokwim and the highlands between it and the Tanana, a bad winter storm changed his mind. He returned to Tanana in April 1883. He and his party spent the summer digging the gulch they had prospected the previous fall and prospecting for other signs, but they failed to find the bonanza they sought. Finally, they decided, there must be mines in countries where the climate was not "so terribly rigorous," and in August they voted to abandon Alaska. Schieffelin sold the *New Racket* to the newly organized firm of McQuesten, Harper & Mayo, and Charley Farcoit agreed to remain behind as engineer. The Schieffelin venture, though small, represented the first significant capital invested in Yukon mining.[26]

The second set of prospectors that reached the Yukon in 1882 came through Chilkoot Pass, through the coastal mountains above Juneau that had intimidated Schieffelin. Unlike their predecessors, the Bean and Winn parties, this group decided to winter on the Yukon rather than return to Juneau. Among these men were the French Canadian Joseph Ladue, Howard Franklin, and Harry Madison—all destined to play major roles in the development of the Yukon. The men wintered next to McQuesten at Fort Reliance. Impatient to find gold, some of them began to thaw the frozen ground with fires. After spending three days to sink one hole ten feet deep, which water promptly filled, they quit to wait for spring. For the first time McQuesten had people to talk with during a winter. Each evening they met at his store to play cards and tell stories. During this winter they decided they needed an orderly process to follow in the event gold should be struck, and they drew up "laws" governing the size of placer claims, the right to water, and recording practices. Appropriately they elected McQuesten recorder.

When spring arrived, McQuesten launched the *Yukon* downriver to pick up the traders and their furs at the various Alaska Commercial Company posts. Mercier came aboard at Belle Isle. Here, too, the Western Fur and Trading Company's trader joined them in the *St. Michael*. On the first day out the *St. Michael* ran aground. When they failed to dislodge it, McQuesten and Mercier left and continued to St. Michael. After waiting twenty days for the water to rise and float his grounded boat, the trader was forced by lack of provisions to abandon it. Meanwhile, at St. Michael, McQuesten and Mercier learned that the Alaska Commercial Company had bought out the Western Fur and Trading Company. The severe competition had ended. Now came the delicate task of raising the price of trade goods and lowering the value of furs without angering the Natives.

A series of misfortunes during the fall of 1883 relieved the problem. Since the *St. Michael* had gone aground and could not be refloated before fall, supplies for the winter depended on the ability of the Alaska Commercial Company—or more accurately, McQuesten, Harper & Mayo— to provide for the upper river. After the partners purchased the *New Racket*, they loaded it with winter supplies and headed for Fort Reliance. Reaching the *St. Michael*, they succeeded in refloating it and tied it up for the winter. Then, within only ten miles of Belle Isle, the *New Racket* broke a crank pin. McQuesten had no choice but to leave a few supplies with the Indians to help them hunt through the winter while he and his party returned to winter at Tanana. The prospectors of the upper Yukon, who had hoped to find provisions at Fort Reliance, were forced to journey all the way to Tanana or St. Michael. But the hardship caused the Indians by these accidents heightened their appreciation for even the higher-priced goods when they finally arrived the following spring.

The Alaska Commercial Company found it had to abandon, for a while, its posts upriver from Tanana and operate the upper river from the steamboat. The rapid rise in prices and the demand for immediate payment of credit so bewildered and angered the Indians that the traders did not want to risk wintering alone among them. Even what had been the most profitable post, Fort Yukon, fell into disrepair, and its stockade gradually disappeared into the steamer's firebox.[27]

While the fur traders fought ruinous competition and prospectors struggled to find a profitable stream, Catholic and Anglican missionaries competed for Native souls. Despite the American purchase of Alaska and an international boundary, the Anglican Church Missionary Society of London continued to fund Robert McDonald's work on the Yukon. Meanwhile in 1877 two Roman Catholic priests, Charles John Seghers and Joseph Mandart, reached St. Michael from Vancouver Island.

No ordinary priest, Charles Seghers came from Flemish stock and graduated one of the "brightest, most pious, and zealous seminarians of Ghent."[28] Although a young man of thirty-eight, he had a family history of tuberculosis, and his own body was consumed with the disease. Nonetheless, he devoted his life to American missions and in 1873 became the bishop of the Diocese of Vancouver Island, which included Alaska. Although he had planned a permanent mission for Alaska's interior to counter the Russian Orthodox and Anglican advances, Father August Lecorre refused to return to Alaska. Instead, Seghers sought time from his hospital and teaching responsibilities to travel to St. Michael. Father Mandart accompanied him.

Arriving in July 1877, Seghers decided that the whalers and their intoxicating drink had "spoiled" the Eskimos of the coast, and he decided to move into the interior. After quizzing the fur traders, Bishop Seghers chose Nulato for his base. On the long overland walk from Unalakleet to Nulato, he and his companions fought the marshy lowlands and their scourge, the mosquito. "They [mosquitoes] unceremoniously drop into your cup of tea," Seghers complained, "they are uncooth [sic] enough to fill your spoon before you take it to your lips, you open your mouth either to speak or breathe and half a dozen of mosquitoes sail into your throat and give you a fit of coughing." The missionaries also ran low on food and energy before they finally reached Nulato. Seghers's initial experiences with the logistics of traveling and getting provisions to Alaska's interior gave him second thoughts about establishing a resident missionary. "I cannot yet assume such a grave responsibility," he reported.

Using Nulato as a base, manned by Father Mandart, Seghers radiated in all directions throughout the fall and winter. He reached Natives along the river by birchbark canoe. With snowfall he learned to use dog sleds. Traveling with fur traders stationed at Nulato, he attempted to convert Koyukon Indians along the Koyukuk River. Once he even confronted a shaman who challenged him to test each other's respective powers; he refused. Later, during the coldest months of winter, he journeyed along the river to Russian Mission. Because of the presence of a Russian Orthodox priest, Seghers refrained from instructing in Catholicism but expressed contempt for the priest's missionary activities.

At the invitation of François Mercier, Mandart and Seghers tried evangelizing at the spring trade fair at Nuklukayet. Assured by Mercier that Indians from throughout the interior traded there, they succeeded only in baptizing seven children and conducting the first Catholic funeral in Alaska. Somewhat discouraged, Seghers found that the Anglicans on the upper river had been too successful and had prejudiced the Fort Yukon Indians against Catholic missionaries. To other Indians, however, he taught "the truths of religion" in their own language. Linguistically inclined, he had learned not only Russian during his fourteen-month stay but several Athapaskan languages as well. Despite the frustrations and the distractions of the fair, Seghers felt that the trading station would make a splendid mission. In June, the missionaries departed with Mercier for St. Michael and later for Vancouver Island. Seghers had traveled more than 2,500 miles preaching "Christ's Gospel" and had provided a firm basis for a permanent mission at Nulato and possibly at Nuklukayet. As he left Alaska, he planned to return immediately but subsequently and disappointedly learned of his appointment as coadjutor (successor) to the Archbishop of Oregon City. Thus he placed his dreams on hold.

When word of Catholic missionaries reached the Anglican Reverend McDonald, he stepped up his activities and campaigned vigorously for an assistant. He continued to instruct Kutchin lay readers, whom he called "Christian Leaders," and encouraged them to travel and preach the Protestant gospel to their kinsmen. Like the traders and prospectors, McDonald did not think that international boundaries should inhibit the Lord's work. In 1878, to counter the influence of Father Seghers, McDonald and his Kutchin wife traveled to Fort Yukon and Tanana. Here he learned that the traders, believing that he brought a beneficial influence to the Indians, wanted to fund a mission for Fort Yukon.[29] Finally, in 1881, the long-awaited assistant joined McDonald.

A dedicated, hard-working, selfless churchman, Rev. Vincent C. Sims immediately took over McDonald's Yukon responsibilities. With the help of the Kutchin Indians, he built a small church at La Pierre House. Later, in 1882, he visited the Hudson's Bay Company's post at Rampart House, where he met Han and Yukon Flats Kutchin who had come to hear his services. With the help of the local Kutchin, Sims constructed a mission to better serve the whole district. The following year he journeyed to the Yukon. "There are perhaps few places in the world," Sims wrote a fellow minister euphorically, "where the natives are so clamorous for Christian teaching."[30] He found Fort Yukon deserted so continued upriver to Han country. At David's Village he discovered that the dialect of the Han was different from the Kutchin and difficult to understand. When McQuesten's steamboat, *New Racket*, broke down, Sims canceled his plans to go farther up the Yukon, went back to the Porcupine with McQuesten, and from there returned to Rampart House.

Sims's main worry concerned Tanana. He feared that the Roman Catholics would get established there first. Moreover, he had heard that the traders near Tanana would help to found a mission. The following year, therefore, he hastened to Tanana and observed the Han and the Kutchin and the books that had been introduced among them. Indian lay readers or McDonald's "Christian Leaders" at David's Village had taught them reasonably well. Next Sims went two hundred miles up the Tanana River to preach. Then he floated back to the Yukon and down to Nulato, where he caught a steamboat for Fort Reliance. From there he traveled back to Fort Yukon and up to Rampart House.

Such an exhausting schedule had its consequences. In 1885 Sims suffered a nervous breakdown and contracted pneumonia. "Tell the Committee to send out a man in my place and another for the Yukon," his last letter read. "It is too much for one man."[31] The religious fervor that drove Sims to his death, however, died with him on May 11, 1885.

The year 1885 marked a major turning point on the Yukon River. As more and more prospectors arrived, McQuesten recognized that the Alaska Commercial Company, which financed his firm, focused on fur trading and thus neglected the growing needs of the mining community. While Mayo went to Fort Reliance and Harper, accompanied by Mercier's interpreters, the Cheroskys, wintered at Belle Isle, McQuesten headed for San Francisco to urge a change of policy on the company's directors and also, he hoped, to order mining supplies. In the summer of 1885 he returned with fifty tons of mining supplies. Coincidentally, prospectors on the Stewart River had struck pay dirt that very spring. It was a small strike, but it launched the Yukon mining frontier. At the same time, McQuesten's shift from the Indian trade to the mining trade signaled the passing of the trading frontier. Appropriately, François Mercier, the king of the traders, chose this time to go home to Montreal, never to return to Alaska.

CHAPTER 4

The Early Miner's Frontier: Fortymile and Circle

The new frontier opened by the discovery of a few thousand dollars worth of gold on the Stewart River in 1885 followed patterns established on older western mining frontiers. The great California gold rush had graduated many experienced miners and prospectors who roamed the West seeking new bonanzas.[1] Those who found their way to the Yukon represented the same type of miner-prospector who followed the stampedes from California to Colorado, Nevada, Idaho, Montana, and British Columbia. Restless, impatient, individualistic, they had no time or money to develop lode deposits. Rather they looked for placer gold—"poor man's gold"—that nature had already partially mined.

Most of these men understood the basic geologic process that formed placers. After the injection of gold-bearing quartz veins into the Yukon strata, 60 to 130 million years ago, the land folded, faulted, and eroded in processes that loosened the gold particles from the host rock. Rainwater and melting snow picked them up and carried them into ancient rivers. As the rivers slowed, the heavy gold particles dropped first, followed by sand and gravel. Later, glacial rivers again swept up the gold and gravel, carried them still farther and, as the torrent slackened, dumped and buried them once more. To these ancient stream beds men from other mining frontiers brought their training, experience, and social institutions.

The minor gold strike on the Stewart River in 1885 and McQuesten's return to the Yukon with mining supplies marked a change in policy of the Alaska Commercial Company, the firm that stood behind McQuesten, Harper & Mayo and would eventually absorb them. No longer were Indians and their furs the main source of trade, which now catered to miners. Consequently, in the summer of 1886 Harper and McQuesten abandoned Fort Reliance, in the Indian country, and moved to accommodate the miners at Stewart River. They named their new trading post Fort Nelson, for Edward William Nelson, who had been stationed at St. Michael with the United States Army Signal Corps from 1877 to 1881 and who later became known for his extensive biological and ethnographic collections.[2] During that winter nearly seventy-five men wintered at the new post. Meanwhile word passed out of Alaska with departing miners that gold had been discovered on the Yukon. More than a hundred miners arrived in the spring of 1887 to try their hand in the arctic gold fields.

Typical of the early Yukon prospectors was Walter H. Pierce. Learning skills and techniques in the Colorado and Idaho gold fields, Pierce moved north through the Cassiar District of British Columbia and the new boomtown of Juneau to cross the Chilkoot Pass in 1884. As he and his partners floated the Yukon, they tested the mouths of tributaries for gold and then worked up the Stewart. As the river bars became dry, they built rockers and rocked for gold, earning an encouraging twenty-five dollars a day. Further mining, however, recovered only fine and limited gold. Discouraged with the summer's output, the party returned to Juneau. Recognizing that the Yukon summers allowed little time to prospect and return, Pierce decided to take supplies for eighteen months. Once again, in 1885, he and a group of prospectors worked their way down the Yukon, testing "favorable looking streams, sometimes staying a week in one place."[3] During each stay he and a partner would take a trip upstream forty or fifty miles. Depending largely on game for food, they traveled light, with only a pick, pan, shovel, Winchester rifle, Colt revolver, one-half a blanket, and a little flour, bacon, sugar, and coffee. Usually they found signs of gold, but not much in any one place. They even prospected up the Fortymile River, constructing canoes or rafts when required. During the winter some of Pierce's companions developed scurvy, and eventually two of them died. With spring breakup of 1886, Pierce and six others decided to float down to St. Michael, prospecting as they went. There they boarded a government revenue cutter for Sitka. By fall 1886 Pierce was back in Juneau embroiled in a dance-hall murder trial. Acquitted of the murder, he confronted an even greater ordeal—tuberculosis. By 1890, not yet forty years old, he was dead.

Although the Stewart strike proved disappointing to Pierce and others like him, from it men fanned out in greater numbers to search other streams and rivers. Harry Madison and Howard Franklin, two miners who had arrived with Joe Ladue in 1882, traveled from Fort Reliance forty miles downstream to the Fortymile River. Arthur Harper had searched the Fortymile years earlier, and later so had Ladue. But this time Madison and Franklin tracked their boat twenty-three miles upriver, into American territory. Here, in 1886, they struck coarse gold—the first rich placer on the Yukon.[4]

Once again the firm of McQuesten, Harper & Mayo planned to move its post, Fort Nelson, from the Stewart to the mouth of the Fortymile. At this time McQuesten was in San Francisco buying supplies. Harper recognized the value of Franklin's gold discovery and knew that hundreds of prospectors would arrive in the spring. He feared that starvation might ensue if McQuesten did not bring in more stock than had been planned. Even though winter had set in, a young steamboat pilot and an Indian boy volunteered to carry a letter across Chilkoot Pass. The pilot died, but the message got through to McQuesten.[5] Harper's premonition held true. Several hundred gold-seekers arrived in the spring of 1887, even ahead of McQuesten.

The unexpected change in trading policy caught the Indians by surprise and left them confused and frustrated. Suddenly they found their furs second to the miners' gold. But more important, by 1887 they saw the abandonment of both Fort Reliance and Belle Isle. Unfortunately for the Indians, they had grown dependent on these posts: their diet had broadened to include flour, lard, sugar, and tea; their clothing now incorporated items of cotton, flannel, and wool; their weapons included the all-important firearms; matches replaced flint; metal pots supplanted woven basketry; and alcohol had been introduced. Although Indians complained of the long and often dangerous journey to the new Fortymile trading post, they went. For the company, economics, not sentiment, dictated policy.

By 1887 many prospector-miners had entered Alaska and would stay through the Klondike rush. George Matlock appeared on the Fortymile as well as Frank Buteau, Henry Davis, Gordon Bettles, Michael O'Brien, and Jack Wade. They knew and depended on one another as each in turn depended on the reliable firm of McQuesten, Harper & Mayo. Generally the early miners cooperated with one another. In fact, a group known for their tall tales as the Sixteen Liars decided to locate claims of three hundred feet each instead of the fifteen hundred feet allowed, thereby generously leaving room for others. A few undesirables, however, also showed up. One man known only as Leslie tried to poison his partners with strychnine. He was fortunate that no one died and that the miners took no more drastic action than to order him out of the country. To explain his departure from the Yukon in the middle of winter, Leslie spread stories of hostile Indians.[6]

The only two recorded Indian problems of the early mining frontier occurred in 1888. The first involved John Bremner, who had come to Alaska in a party that included Lt. Henry T. Allen of the United States Army. The group pioneered a new route to the Yukon, starting at Valdez and ascending the Copper River to a portage across Mentasta Pass to the Tanana, but the expedition had nearly starved to death. Afterwards Bremner had joined with others to investigate the Koyukuk River. He separated from them to explore a tributary now known as the John River. After he left the John River and floated down the Koyukuk, he stopped one day for lunch. His fire and coffee attracted two Koyukon Indians—a twenty-year-old youth and an aged shaman. Satisfying custom, Bremner shared his meal with them. Then, as he packed his boat, the old man ordered the boy to seize Bremner's gun and shoot him. In fear of the medicine man's magic, the boy did as he was told. Together they weighted the body, sank it, and took the tools, supplies, and boat. When Bremner did not return, his friends began to search. Through John Manook, son of Ivan and Malanka Pavaloff and thus three-quarters Koyukon Indian, the murder was uncovered. He and the rest of the party hurried to Tanana to report the deed.[7]

At Tanana a posse of prospectors collected to enforce the miners' law and teach the Indians not to kill whites. At the mouth of the Koyukuk they commandeered a small riverboat, the *Explorer*, and steamed upriver. The two Pavaloffs, John Manook and Pitka Pavaloff, regarded themselves as friends of Bremner and volunteered as interpreters. The group found a cache of drying whitefish containing tools clearly marked with Bremner's name. A short distance farther upriver they came to an Indian camp. When the steamer landed, two Indians ran into the woods but were quickly apprehended. They were the culprits, and the youth at once admitted his deed. The vigilantes took the two back to the Yukon and, after dinner, put them on trial. When asked why he had killed Bremner, the youth replied that he wanted the victim's gun, blanket, and tobacco. When told that he would die for killing a white man, he replied that he wished he could kill more whites as they were no good anyway. Fearing the shaman's power worse than death, he claimed full responsibility for the murder. Lacking evidence to hold the shaman, the posse released him. Without further delay but with great ceremony, the miners hanged the boy and left him hanging as an example to others. In good spirits and feeling well satisfied, they started back to Tanana. Not far from the Koyukuk they met another group of Indians. When told of the deed and warned against killing white men, the chief replied, "We won't kill any prospectors but we are not afraid of you white men, if you start anything."[8]

The second episode resulted from a cultural misunderstanding. An Indian witness to a murder, taken to Sitka to testify for the prosecution, returned to St. Michael to report to his people that the murderer now lived in a "big house," kept there in peace and plenty by the government. Such, the Indians concluded, was the reward for killing a white man.

In the summer of 1888, as miners stampeded down the Yukon to the Fortymile, Red Tom O'Brien and his partner, known only as Frenchy, suffered the consequences of this misunderstanding. At the mouth of the Charley River a young Han Indian killed Frenchy. When other stampeders found the body, they approached the Han fish camp. The young Indian met the miners and asked in broken English what they wanted. They replied that they wanted to know who had killed the white man. To their surprise the Indian announced that he had. The older Indians explained that he had promised to kill the first white man he met on the river so that he could go to San Francisco, live in a "skookum" house, get good clothes, and have a fine life. To ensure that there would be no further misunderstandings about the murdering of whites, the informal posse hanged the youth from a tree and riddled his body with bullets. The hanging discouraged others from following his example.[9]

Unlike Indian-white relations of the American West, the years between 1867 and 1896 on the Yukon were remarkably peaceful. Indians killed only four persons, and two of these gave ample provocation. Bean and Korgenikoff violated traditional customs of the Natives. Bremner and Frenchy, on the other hand, were innocent victims of greed—an excess not peculiar to any one culture.

Scholars have not satisfactorily probed why Native-white relations on the Yukon were so much less violent than in the American West. For one thing, the Natives had to devote almost all their time and energy to the quest for food. For another, they welcomed the techniques and tools the whites brought. White traders and prospecters, moreover, seem to have approached the Natives less belligerently; a hard and demanding land encouraged mutual respect and dependence. And alcohol, though it found its way to the Yukon, flowed less copiously. However valid these speculations, ethnohistorians have yet to gather the data from which clear conclusions may be drawn.

In addition to a different native people, miners confronted a different environment, one for which their experience elsewhere had not prepared them. Permafrost especially confounded them. Below a depth of only a few inches the ground was permanently frozen. Although the Fortymile bedrock on which the gold lay was shallow, the miners grew impatient waiting for the spring sun to thaw the soil enough to dig. On Franklin Gulch during the winter of 1887 Fred Hutchinson built a fire to start the thaw—and discovered that permafrost could be a boon as well as bane. Beginning to dig, he found that the permafrost made supporting timbers unnecessary. Not only could the industrious miner now, by artifical thawing, mine year-round, but he did not have to timber his mining shaft.[10] At the end of winter a large mound of gold-bearing gravel lay piled high near his diggings awaiting the spring thaw. Once the snow and ice melted and flowed into rushing creeks, the miner could wash his winter dump. Despite year-round operation, however, the early Fortymile miners averaged only $800 a year.[11]

Even though the California and subsequent gold rushes had developed sophisticated equipment for the mining of placer deposits, each gold rush had to evolve through the placer-mining cycle of gold pan, rocker, and sluice box. The gold pan was shaped like a very large pie tin. The miner filled it with gold-bearing gravel, added water, and swished it around to carry off the dirt. Eventually, after repeated washings, only gold was left. The rocker was a box on rockers with a perforated metal top and a sloping blanket inside. The miner dumped in water and gravel together and vigorously rocked the mixture. The gold fell through the perforations and lodged on the blanket. The more complicated sluice box depended on a constant flow of water. The box could be any length, generally between three and fifteen feet, with open ends. Riffles were fastened to the floor. As the gravel and water flowed freely through the box, the riffles caught the gold.

Finally, in 1890, the California technique of hydraulic mining reached the Fortymile. Frank Buteau, George Matlock, and their partners built a flume from Franklin Gulch to their claim to create twenty-four feet of pressure, an amount sufficient for hydraulic mining. The water was then channeled into metal pipes and nozzles that directed

Panning for gold (above) and drift mining with a rocker sluice (below) demonstrate the basic techniques of placer mining. Boiler-heated steam points driven into frozen ground thawed gold-bearing gravel. A windlass brought the gravel to the surface where gold pans, rockers, or sluice boxes separated gold from gravel. *University of Alaska Archives.*

highly pressurized jets onto river banks and hills. The force crumbled the banks and washed the gravel into waiting sluice boxes.

Although traders now could furnish supplies sufficient to last the miners through the winter, they continued to be unreliable. The miners, however, discovered that they need not be wholly dependent on the trading posts. This became evident in 1889 after the Alaska Commercial Company's new steamer, the *Arctic*, struck a rock and could not continue upriver with the winter provisions for the Fortymile. Notice went out of the disaster with a suggestion to come down the Yukon and winter at St. Michael. Instead, George Matlock, Frank Buteau, and two others decided to stay in the Fortymile area and work on their flume. They killed forty caribou and supplemented their meat diet with three sacks of moldy flour and a few beans. When the newly repaired *Arctic* arrived in the spring, the partners, recalled one, were "all well and happy." Reluctant again to trust the company so completely, the following autumn they constructed a fish trap, patterned after those used by the Natives, and caught a ton and a half of grayling to help them through the winter. Meanwhile the ubiquitous Arthur Harper moved to the mouth of the Pelly and near the site of Robert Campbell's old Hudson's Bay Company post established a new trading post, which he appropriately called Fort Selkirk.

The shift from bar diggings (the Stewart strike) to gulch diggings (the Fortymile find) not only demanded new techniques, but also fostered long-term communities. Bars, found along bends in rivers, were often flooded or washed away, and thus the diggings were risky and brief. Gulches, on the other hand, contained a small amount of water that could easily be diverted. They could be worked as long as the gold held, even, using drift mining techniques, throughout the winter.

Because of the extreme isolation and the commitment of time and labor, Fortymile miners required supplies, equipment, and general companionship. To meet these needs, a number of cabins sprouted haphazardly around McQuesten's store at the mouth of the Fortymile. They included a blacksmith shop, a sawmill, and at least ten saloons. On an island opposite the town stood the Anglican mission, school, and associated Indian settlement. The place took the name Fortymile and, although servicing claims mostly in Alaska, the community lay on the Canadian side of the boundary.[12]

Initially the miners of the Fortymile made the most of what little they had. They lacked stoves, stovepipes, and windows. Typical fron-

Fortymile. As the Yukon's first mining town, Fortymile became a prototype of others that followed. Although the town lay on the Canadian side of the boundary, the flag flying in the photograph is American. *University of Alaska Archives.*

tiersmen, they improvised. They made stoves and chimneys out of rocks and mud, using flat rocks for the tops of the stoves. For windows they cut clear pieces of Yukon River ice slightly larger than the window openings and fastened them in place with wooden buttons. Additional supplies and a few amenities came more frequently when the larger and faster *Arctic* was launched. The new boat could make several round trips from St. Michael each season.

One of the first to observe the life-style of the earlier miners was Josiah Edward Spurr of the United States Geological Survey. He found the miners hospitable, eager for news from the outside world, keenly interested in political developments, and generally more intelligent and better informed than other isolated miners of his experience. Their taste for Shakespeare, philosophy, and science surprised him.[13] A few women had followed their husbands to the Yukon and made rough-hewn cabins into comfortable homes. Missionaries and schoolteachers also became a part of the growing community.

Conflicts occasionally shook the camp. One night several men were gathered in a cabin when a man named Washburn became angry at George Matlock and stabbed him in the back. Bent on revenge, Matlock

Early prospector's cabin. The early miners depended for warmth on the ubiquitous Yukon stove. Refinements to cabins included squared-off logs to resemble houses left behind. *University of Oregon Special Collections.*

returned with his gun, aimed for a flesh wound, and shot through the window at Washburn. The bullet struck Washburn in the thigh. They were "even up" and later even shook hands and became friends.

Some in Fortymile did not enjoy free-spirited and raucous activities Chief among these, an unsociable man of sour disposition, was John J. Healy. Healy knew the goldfields of Montana and Idaho as a miner, trader, and sheriff. He arrived in Alaska in 1886 to develop a trading post at the trailhead to Chilkoot Pass that later became the town of Dyea. Observing the traffic over the pass, he believed that he could compete successfully with the entrenched Alaska Commercial Company. In 1892 he convinced Chicago millionaires Jack and Michael Cudahy

John J. Healy. Healy was the motivating force behind the establishment of
the North American Transportation and Trading Company—the primary
rival to the Alaska Commercial Company. In contrast to Jack McQuesten's
generosity, Healy offered no credit but did maintain lower prices. His
complaints about the American miners' lack of order and respect brought the
North-West Mounted Police to Fortymile. *Virginia S. Burlingame.*

of meat-packing fame and P. B. Weare of the Chicago Board of Trade to
form the North American Transportation and Trading Company. By fall,
at St. Michael, Healy had assembled the *Portus B. Weare*, a steamer
about the size of the *Arctic*, and before winter set in he steamed upriver
as far as Nulato.

Shortly after breakup in 1893 Healy arrived at Fortymile. Separating himself from McQuesten and the Alaska Commercial Company,
he constructed his house, store, and warehouse a mile downstream and
across the Fortymile River at a site he called Cudahy. In contrast to
McQuesten, Healy refused to offer credit, but he did have lower prices.
His personality also contrasted with McQuesten's. Healy was cranky,

stingy, even vindictive. Thus, when a serving girl brought minor charges against him, the miners' court joyfully assessed him a considerable amount of money.

Furious with Fortymile's supposed lack of justice and order, Healy complained to his good friend Superintendent Samuel B. Steele of the North-West Mounted Police. At the same time Canadian surveyor William Ogilvie expressed concern that the number of American miners collecting in Canada threatened an American takeover unless Canada exercised its sovereignty on the Yukon.[14]

In response to these two initiatives, Inspector Charles Constantine of the North-West Mounted Police arrived in Fortymile in August 1894 to assess the situation. He found the community quiet and orderly with law enforced through a committee of miners. Nonetheless, he made a number of recommendations. The international boundary, he said, should be surveyed so that miners would know in which country their claims lay. If the Yukon were to develop, schools and mail delivery would have to be improved. Thousands of dollars were going uncollected in customs because there was no collector. Finally, something had to be done to control the liquor traffic. In 1894 he estimated that more than three thousand gallons would find their way to miners and Indians alike. Many of these recommendations, he concluded, could be carried out by a force of thirty-five to forty Mounted Police.[15]

In 1895 Constantine returned to Fortymile with twenty red-coated constables—the first tangible evidence of Canadian sovereignty in the Yukon Basin. In addition to his police responsibilities, Constantine's duties included those of magistrate, gold commissioner, land agent, and collector of customs. Through the labor of his men, he erected Fort Constantine near Cudahy. Police work proved unexacting with no serious crimes for the Mounties to handle.

Meanwhile, because the Fortymile yielded no bonanza, prospectors toiled up and down the tributaries of the upper Yukon in search of other deposits. McQuesten extended liberal credit and grubstaked miners to explore further.[16] During the winter of 1890 Barney Hill and Capt. Billie Moore hauled a year's supply of goods by sled from Fortymile to a point forty miles up the Seventymile River (seventy miles from Fort Reliance, thus thirty miles from Fortymile). They built a ditch, a flume, and several whip-sawed sluice boxes. Six to eight other miners worked the river at the same time, all with poor results.[17] In 1894, as mining interest increased, Harper once again moved his trading post to meet

Charles Constantine and original Yukon contingent of North-West
Mounted Police. Fearful that the dominance of American miners in the
Canadian mining district of Fortymile might cause a rebellion, the
Canadian government sent Inspector Constantine (seated in center to right
of boy) of the North-West Mounted Police to assess the situation and
then, a year later, to provide Canadian law and order. *Yukon Archives.*

demand. He left Fort Selkirk and joined Joe Ladue at Sixtymile to establish Ogilvie. Like McQuesten, they extended grubstakes or a season's
food and supplies to miners for a percentage of a claim should gold be
found. Among those grubstaked was Robert Henderson, who searched
the drainages of the Klondike River. Miners routinely traveled the length
of the Yukon, tracked or poled their way up tributary streams, and subsisted on bare essentials in order to try their hand at a good prospect.

Two men found promise on Birch Creek. In the summer of 1892
Sergi Gologoff Cherosky, Mercier's and Harper's Creole interpreter at
Belle Isle, and his brother-in-law, Pitka Pavaloff, hunted moose up Birch
Creek and did panning on the side. On one bar of the creek they saw
color in their pans. After staking a claim and naming it Pitka's Bar, they
killed a moose and with the skin made a canoe to float down to Tanana
Station.[18] Here they picked up their families, boarded the steamer, and
went upriver to Fortymile. Cherosky and Pitka approached McQuesten
for a grubstake or a year's outfit on the Birch Creek prospect. McQuesten
agreed: he wanted information from an unprospected area and also hoped
to cash in on a new strike.

By autumn the families were back downriver at a place approximately thirty miles above what later became Circle City. They had begun building cabins when other miners, drawn by word of gold on Pitka's Bar, showed up. More than a hundred men wintered at the place, which became known as Old Portage. To accommodate that many people, Manny Hill built a store. At the first sign of spring 1893, Pitka and Cherosky, followed by other hopeful miners, crossed to Birch Creek. Still others headed for creeks that turned out to be less rich. Although Pitka and Cherosky had staked claims, they made no fortunes. As Erinia Cherosky explained it: "Not knowing anything about mining and how to stake claims, they lost all their claims to the white men."[19]

These mines lay sixty to eighty miles from the Yukon. Eventually a connecting trail wound across swampy muskeg and around a multitude of small ponds guarded by clouds of persistent mosquitoes. Roadhouses sprang up approximately every twelve miles and furnished weary travelers a meal and a floor to sleep on. For the roadhouse proprietors and for the miners, the greatest problem was obtaining supplies from the Yukon. During the winter dog sleds freighted mining equipment and food at seven cents a pound, but in the summer freighting costs jumped to forty cents a pound.[20]

By the first winter, 1893–94, mines on Mastodon, Deadwood, and Mammoth creeks had yielded $9,000, and by the end of 1895 the output from all the streams in the Birch Creek district was $150,000.[21] Since these mines were even more shallow than those at Fortymile, the miners resorted to open-cut methods. This method required that the ground be stripped clear of the vegetation and worked from the surface down to bedrock. There the gold pan, rocker, or sluice box came into play to separate gold from gravel. Since open-cut mining could only be employed during the summer, the miners spent the winter in town.

"Town" was "Fish Camp," downriver from Old Portage. Manny Hill had moved his store there to be closer to the creeks. McQuesten joined him later that fall of 1893 when reports of the discoveries filtered up to Fortymile. During the spring breakup of 1894 a number of cabins at Fish Camp washed away, so McQuesten moved still farther downriver. Here Barney Hill, from Seventymile, and Robert English staked out a townsite. Since the miners thought the town was north of the Arctic Circle, they called it Circle City.[22]

Leaving the Fortymile post to Mayo, McQuesten encouraged the development of the Birch Creek diggings. He offered any Fortymile miner outfits on credit, and eighty men accepted his offer. By November 1893 the two major creeks, Mastodon and Deadwood, had been entirely staked. Deadwood Creek, in fact, was known as "Hog-um" Creek because some people hogged it all when they staked the creek. This selfishness contrasted with the altruism so prominent at Fortymile. Geologist Spurr commented on the "remarkable difference" between the attitudes at Birch Creek and those at Fortymile. At Birch Creek few showed hospitality or friendliness, and all seemed to lead cheerless lives.[23]

Circle City rambled along the left bank of the Yukon at the edge of the Yukon Flats. Dog freighter Arthur Walden described it:

> A person approaching the town by water for the first time
> saw a steep bank with small boats of all descriptions
> moored along the edge. On top of the bank were piles of logs
> to be whip-sawed, and crude scaffoldings for this purpose,
> with their accompanying machinery of a man above and a
> man below. Then came a stretch of fifty feet or more which
> was the street, and on the other side were rows of log
> cabins, with a few larger buildings also of logs. These cabins
> were moss-chinked and dirt-covered, with the exceptions of
> the warehouses, which were built of corrugated iron. In the
> mosquito season every cabin had its little smudge in front.[24]

In winter it was a "City of Silence," he added, muffled by snow and cold. More critically, Englishman Henry De Windt saw that "four hundred log buildings line the wide straggling thoroughfares . . . [in a] motley collection of sodden dwellings and dripping roofs."[25] He scoffed at Circle City's claim to be "the Paris of Alaska." By 1896 the town had a population of seven hundred and was the largest settlement on the Yukon and said to be the largest log-cabin city in the world.[26]

Like Fortymile, Circle City attracted a settlement of Indians. Some built log cabins on the edges of town and mixed freely with the miners and townspeople. Others, more traditional or less acculturated, lived in tents and semisubterranean houses on an island two miles down the Yukon.

The leading citizen of Circle City was Jack McQuesten. Now fully in the employ of the Alaska Commercial Company, which had purchased his firm, he built a two-story log building for a store and a fireproof, corrugated-iron warehouse. He was also postmaster and banker.

Circle. "The Paris of Alaska" was Circle's boast. A more accurate boast was "the largest log-cabin city in the world," which included McQuesten's two-story store. *University of Alaska Archives.*

In this latter role he not only continued to extend credit but also boasted the only safe in town.

McQuesten did not bask in unchallenged monopoly for long. From Fortymile in 1894 came his arch-rival, John J. Healy. Healy and the North American Transportation and Trading Company were no more popular in Circle City than in Fortymile. McQuesten, on the other hand, remained generous and likable. In 1894 he extended more than $100,000 in credit and had collected nearly all of it by the following autumn. Nevertheless, what some regarded as the high prices, poor quality and quantity of goods, and "greedy" profits of both commercial companies antagonized some of the townspeople.[27]

Aside from McQuesten's store, Circle's eight to ten dance halls and saloons offered warm, comfortable places to meet and enjoy the lights and music. Gambling went on all the time. A few professional gamblers arrived from Juneau when they heard of the rush. The gamblers, saloonkeepers, and dance-hall girls lived well, dressed well, took life easy, and in a sense were the aristocrats of the camp. Since the few respectable women kept to themselves, the dance-hall girls furnished nearly all the miners' feminine society. Although of easy virtue, they were treated with respect and social equality. Theater came to Circle City with George Snow, a New York actor who arrived on the Yukon via California, Juneau, and the Stewart River. He presented theatrical performances in Harry Ash's "Opera House," which was actually nothing more than a dance hall.

Visitors reported in garish detail Circle's famed "balls." Sometimes they were merely extensions of the "dollar-a-dance" balls nightly staged by the dance halls. Other times they were held for special occasions such as to raise money for a school, hospital, or library. Of all the visitors, Spurr best captured the spirit of these dances:

> The couples gyrated in eccentric curves around in obedience to the [director's] cries; and a row of miners too bashful to dance, or who could find no partners, sat on boxes close to the wall, hunched up their legs and spit tobacco juice until the middle of the floor was a sort of an island. In short it was the most brilliant affair Circle City had ever witnessed.[28]

Illustrative of the morality of pre-Klondike society, doors lacked locks, and even gold dust was left in unlocked cabins. Caches of food and supplies along the trail and at the mines remained undisturbed. Claims were bought and sold orally. Robbery was a rarity, murder even more so. There was little open quarreling, but the long winter nights and close contacts developed intense hatreds that were usually settled by not speaking or by dividing all jointly owned possessions and moving elsewhere.

As on other mining frontiers, miners' associations arose out of the feeling of brotherhood and loyalty demanded by close living in a hostile environment. These fraternal organizations provided relief to members in sickness or distress as well as social companionship. The first was the Yukon Order of Pioneers (Y.O.O.P), organized in Fortymile in 1893 with McQuesten as president, then reorganized in Circle in 1895. The Miners Association was formed by men who did not care for the liquor element in the Y.O.O.P.[29] Both associations required an initiation fee, password, and good moral conduct. Most miners belonged to both. The Miners Association added to the library McQuesten had brought down from Fortymile. Eventually it numbered two thousand

Yukon Order of Pioneers. As on other mining frontiers, fraternal associations sprang up in Fortymile and Circle. The Y.O.O.P. included such old-timers as Frank Buteau, George Matlock, Al Mayo (standing third–fifth from left), and Jack McQuesten (seated fourth from left). *University of Alaska Archives.*

volumes. Among them were the Bible, the *Encyclopedia Britannica,* and such authors as Darwin, Hume, Huxley, and Macaulay. For a substantial fee, these books were lent to the miners at the diggings to help relieve the tedium.

As in earlier mining camps elsewhere, the Yukon prospectors improvised institutions of law and order. They took as their model California practice as modified by the Oregon Code. At Circle the "miners' meetings" of the California gold rush, which tended to be vigilante in character, were refined into instruments of fairly judicial respectability.[30] If no official judicial office existed, the miners could elect a judge, officers of the court, and a jury, and the finding would be as binding as if reached by a regularly constituted court. The procedures were simple. A man with a grievance, either civil or criminal, posted notice and called a meeting. The miners assembled and elected a chairman. The prosecutor presented his case and the defendant his. Cross-examination and summation in favor of each side followed. The chairman then called for a vote and the matter was settled. The usual punishment was banishment from the community regardless of weather or other adverse conditions.

Generally the meetings ruled in favor of women complaining of breach of promise. In winter thieves were fortunate to escape with a handsled instead of a hanging. For shootings, although uncommon, the miners used self-defense as a rule of thumb and usually favored the nonaggressive party. Yet judicial decorum did not always prevail, as disclosed by the demand of one meeting that a prostitute pay court costs, including two gallons of liquor drunk by the jury. Although the miners planned to return the money in trade, wiser heads prevailed before the prank could be consummated.

By 1897 this institution had outlived its usefulness. One complaint was that, despite good intentions, the miners could not decide cases impartially.[31] Another was that the disreputable class drawn to every mining frontier to prey on the miners settled in the towns. Gamblers, con artists, and owners of saloons and dance halls came to dominate the miners' meetings. In Circle the proliferation of such parasites made the productive miners reluctant to settle in town the disputes that occurred on the creeks; they claimed that justice could no longer be obtained there.

The Klondike gold rush of 1898 opened a new era, one that was decidedly less orderly. Then, as Arthur Walden cynically reported, "civilization, with its religion, laws, disorder, stealing, education, murder, social life, commercial vice, comforts, and broken pledges crept in; justice cost money and disease raged."[32]

Other social institutions sprang up in Circle. As more women came and families burgeoned, the townspeople built a school and sent for a teacher. The United States Bureau of Education assigned Anna Fulcomer, a graduate of the University of Chicago, to serve as schoolteacher. Although the schoolhouse had not been completed, school opened in 1896 with thirty students: four white, twenty Native, and six half-Native. A few adults even received reading lessons in her spare time. Without heat, teacher and students spent the first few months bundled in furs. Since there was a shortage of books, Miss Fulcomer resorted to frequent use of the blackboard. The rush to the Klondike shortened her term to only one year.[33] At the same time the Episcopal church built a mission administered by Rev. Jules L. Prevost and his wife. Eventually government officials also reached the Yukon: United States Commissioner, inspector of customs, United States Marshal, collector of Internal Revenue, and postmaster.

Circle boasted citizens who lent flavor and spirit to the town. The famous Tex Rickard, founder of New York's Madison Square Garden, owned a gambling house briefly in Circle. Swiftwater Bill was a dishwasher in a Circle roadhouse before he became the millionaire Don Juan of the Klondike. The Reverend Jules Prevost moved the *Yukon Press* from Tanana Station and continued its claim as the first newspaper on the Yukon. The first dentist in the interior, Benton S. Woods, arrived in 1895 and crafted his own dentist's chair of twisted saplings. He doubled as Circle's mining recorder. A remarkable Mrs. Willis, forty-five years old but stout and rugged, pulled her own sled weighing 250 pounds into Circle and started a laundry and bake shop. Men such as George Matlock, Tom King, and Casper Ellingen appeared briefly as horse freighter, miner, and saloon owner respectively.

One who left a record of Circle in this period was William Douglas Johns. He had grown up in Chicago, studied law, raised cattle and wheat in North Dakota, and run a newspaper. The depression of the 1890s led him to look for a life independent of business vagaries. He arrived in Circle in 1896, staked a claim on Birch Creek, then wintered in Circle City. He rented a twelve-by-fourteen-foot cabin. Heavy moss between the logs and on the roof insulated it, but still during the cold months he could scrape ice from the logs behind his bunk. His bunk consisted of spruce boughs for a mattress covered with blankets and robes. He recorded prices similar to those in Fortymile: flour, $37 per hundred pounds; whiskey, $50 a gallon; dogs, $150 each; and firewood, $16 per cord.

One of the first things Johns learned—though he faltered in expressing it—was that "nothing will test out men as to their real character, resourcefulness, courage, endurance of difficulties, kindliness, willingness, and readiness to do their part and not shirk their duties as Life on the Trail in that hard frontier country would do." He saw numerous partners break under the stress of simply trying to survive. The usual food was sourdough, beans (known as Yukon strawberries), and coffee. Saloons provided warmth and companionship even for those who did not have money. Women of all classes won respect as "one phase of the free and easy democracy of the remote frontier." Indians, too, drew his compassion as he observed what "trading companies had 'done' to them." Although the Alaskan vote did not count, on election day in 1896 Circle City voted anyway and went solidly for William Jennings Bryan. Evening featured a torchlight procession led by an illuminated banner bearing Bryan's likeness. Miners' meetings, even to one with a background in law, gained Johns's approval. Like his fellow townspeople, he was governed by the unwritten but no less binding customs of the Yukon. They contributed to his philosophy—not unlike that of Frederick Jackson Turner—that "the frontier life developed a man's self-respect, a regard for the rights of others, and a mutual helpfulness."[34]

Fortymile and Circle City reflected the pattern made typical by the mining camps that predated them in California and elsewhere. Men outnumbered women, and respectable women were rare. Communities were cosmopolitan: college graduates dug next to illiterates while various nationalities mixed with sourdough Alaskans. The promise of easy gold eventually attracted lawless outcasts, gamblers, and harpies. In these early Alaskan camps they had to solve problems stemming from their unique environment by developing democratic institutions and administering their own brand of justice.

In the autumn of 1896 the structure and character of Fortymile and Circle changed drastically. The cry, "Gold on the Klondike," emptied the mining camps almost overnight. It marked the end of a frontier and the beginning of a new phase in Yukon mining. For once, McQuesten, Harper, and Mayo failed to capitalize on the rush. Although Harper and Joe Ladue moved their sawmill from Sixtymile and staked out the Dawson townsite, McQuesten and Mayo met severe competition in the commercial business and decided they were getting too old for that kind of life. In 1897 Harper left Alaska, ill and on the charity of the Alaska Commercial Company. He died the following year of tuberculosis in Arizona. Tuberculosis also killed his colleague, Joe Ladue, not long after the Klondike find. McQuesten, the "Father of the Yukon," also abandoned Alaska for California in 1898. Because of a lucky investment in a Klondike mining share, he left relatively wealthy. Only Al Mayo remained in Alaska to survive a succession of subsequent gold rushes. Outliving his two partners by twenty years, he died in Rampart, Alaska, in 1923.[35]

The year 1898 proved a major watershed in Yukon history. The simple and trusting life-style dependent on fur or minor gold discoveries changed with the development of new frontiers of multiple occupations and diverse values. Knowledge of the Yukon's environment increased, and methods evolved that allowed fuller utilization of the river's resources. At the same time, technology diminished time, distance, and the severity of the environment. As a result, changes came in successive waves or "frontiers."

CHAPTER 5

The Explorer's Frontier

Long before the discovery of gold on the Klondike in 1896 made the Yukon a common household word, scientists and explorers had revealed some of its mysteries. Although these one-time visitors played little role in the unfolding frontiers, their maps, scientific observations, and narrative descriptions exposed a receptive audience—popular as well as scientific and military—to the rigors of arctic life. More importantly, their work laid the basis for formal knowledge of an unknown land. Just as in the American West, government scientists led organized exploration and mapping expeditions to the Yukon.[1]

The Russian-American Telegraph Expedition of 1865 gave rise to three books. First to appear, in 1868, was a travelogue by the expedition's artist, Frederick Whymper, appropriately titled to stimulate the armchair adventurer *Travel and Adventure in the Territory of Alaska*. In 1869 the Chicago Academy of Sciences published posthumously Robert Kennicott's journal of his trip to the Yukon in 1860. Unfortunately, the Chicago fire of 1871 destroyed the original manuscript and most of the printed copies, thereby preventing widespread acknowledgment of his achievement. Finally in 1870 the best source of all, William H. Dall's *Alaska and Its Resources*, was published. The volume not only included a narrative of the expedition's adventures and discoveries, but also provided the only synthesis to date of the area's history, geography, geology, and potential resources. Dall subsequently published a number of articles in scholarly journals.[2]

Although Dall continued his Alaskan research on the coast, scientific observations of the Yukon fell to yet another of Spencer Baird's protégés, Edward William Nelson of the United States Army Signal

Corps. He arrived at St. Michael in 1877 to record weather observations and collect data on geography, ethnology, and zoology. Between 1877 and 1881 Nelson explored the Yukon Delta—the swampy marshland between Alaska's two largest rivers—as far inland as the Innoko River. Although his official report contained no new geographic revelations, his ethnographic descriptions proved exceedingly rich and detailed. Nelson eventually became chief of the United States Biological Survey and instituted major conservation methods to protect Alaskan wildlife.[3] Following his tenure, the Signal Corps made little further contribution to scientific or popular knowledge of the Yukon Basin.

The next observer on the Yukon was the enigmatic Ivan Petrov. Despite a checkered career, he matched William Dall in the great body of information on nineteenth-century Alaska he laid before the American public. In 1874 Petrov went to work for Hubert Howe Bancroft as a researcher for Bancroft's *History of Alaska.* That work, which Petrov himself largely wrote, contains many inaccuracies. Not surprisingly, so does the biographical sketch of himself that he wrote for Bancroft, which is riddled with fanciful fabrications and omits such details as two desertions from the U.S. Army.[4] Even so, it is a mistake to discount, as some have done, Petrov's contribution to knowledge of Alaska.

While researching for Bancroft in official archives in Washington, D. C., Petrov won a commission from the Superintendent of the Census to collect population and natural resources data on Alaska for the census of 1880. His itinerary remains vague, but it is known that McQuesten gave him a ride as far as Nulato on his steamer and that from there he went by skin boat to the Nowitna River.

Petrov compiled a straightforward and balanced census report. Not content with his own observations, he synthesized data from Raymond, Nelson, Dall, and the Russian-American Company. In fact, he obtained, even paraphrased, most of his ethnography from Dall. Petrov dealt authoritatively with economics. Agriculture, he wrote, would never be profitable because of swampy soil, short growing season, poor transportation, and small market potential. Although the rivers and streams showed "colors," mining would be difficult because of the obstacles to travel and transportation. Rather he predicted, the fur trade would dominate Alaska's economy; the Yukon fur trade alone he calculated at $75,000 per year.[5]

Petrov's population figures, obtained largely from missionaries and traders on the river, have been questioned, but they now furnish the

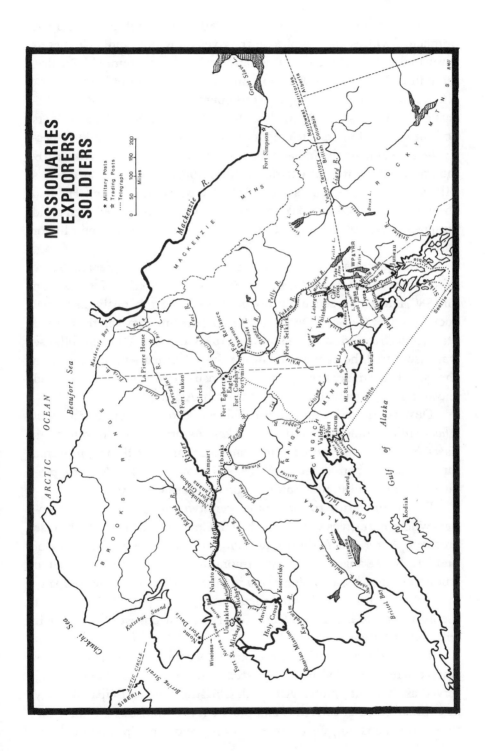

MISSIONARIES
EXPLORERS
SOLDIERS

★ Military Posts
☆ Trading Posts
···· Telegraph

0 50 100 150 200
Miles

only enumeration for the period.[6] In 1880 St. Michael had the largest number of whites and Creoles on the river—4 whites and 5 Creoles as compared to 100 Eskimos. At Russian Mission Petrov counted 5 Creoles, including the Russian Orthodox missionaries, and 143 Eskimos. At Nulato he recorded the largest settlement on the Yukon—163 Athapaskans, 2 whites, and 3 Creoles. On the Koyukuk and Tanana rivers he lumped the Indian settlements together with 150 and 700 respectively. At Rampart the Indian village contained 110, at Fort Yukon 109 Indians and 2 whites, at Charley's Village only 48 Indians, at David's Village 106 Indians, and at Fort Reliance 82 with 1 white.[7] He also observed the toll disease took upon the Natives and predicted their rapid disappearance, but he provided little other information on their life or culture.

Although the superintendent of the eleventh census selected Petrov to collect census data for Alaska in 1890, his contribution was less than for 1880. During his census duties, he forged and erroneously translated documents for the State Department in the dispute between the United States and Great Britain over sealing in the Bering Sea. When his offense was discovered, he confessed, but the State Department did not press charges. The Superintendent of the Census fired him, however, and another man prepared the report of 1890 for Alaska.

Despite Petrov's improprieties, his work for Bancroft's *History of Alaska* left an indelible mark on Alaskan historiography. In spite of its flaws and sometimes pure fabrications, the work is still a major source for the Russian period. His tenth census, along with Dall's work, provides the most substantial information for Alaska prior to 1880.

Following Petrov to the Yukon were two groups of foreign scientists whose narratives were published in German. The first, the Krause brothers, Aurel and Arthur, represented the Geographical Society of Bremen. No strangers to Arctic exploration, they had just completed studies on the Chukotsk Peninsula in Siberia when a trading company in southeastern Alaska invited them to stay at its post at Chilkoot, at the north end of Lynn Canal, and observe the strongest of the Tlingit tribes, the Chilkats.

The brothers arrived at Chilkoot in December 1881. The trader's Native wife, who had been educated in an English mission school, served as their interpreter. Although Christian, she participated freely in Chilkat cultural activities and provided the Krauses with information about behavior, customs, traditions, and kinship relationships.

After a long, severe winter, Aurel left to compare the Chilkats with Tlingits in Sitka and farther south, while Arthur stayed to make natural history collections and carry out geographical research. Guided by Chilkats, Arthur crossed the coastal mountains via the Chilkoot Pass to Lake Lindeman and became the first scientific explorer to map the area. The Chilkoot route later played an important role in the history of the upper Yukon. At summer's end, in 1882, Arthur left Alaska and eventually joined his brother in Bremen. In addition to Arthur's scientific description and mapping of the headwaters of the Yukon, Aurel's ethnography of the Tlingits became the standard text on the tribe.[8]

The second foreign scientific expedition was that of Norwegian Johan Adrian Jacobsen, who represented the Berlin Museum. Not professionally schooled in either natural history or science of any kind, Jacobsen nonetheless learned the prerequisite skills through experience and natural aptitude. He grew up a fisherman who graduated to piloting ships. Seeking adventure more than knowledge, he volunteered to collect Eskimo ethnographic materials from Greenland and promised to return with an Eskimo family to tour Europe. Despite the hard work, Jacobsen learned to enjoy his trips. Later he went to Lapland and then back to Greenland for more collecting.

In 1881 the Berlin Museum commissioned Jacobsen to make collections along the northwest coast of America and Alaska. While in San Francisco he made the acquaintance of the Krause brothers, who had spent the winter in Alaska. At the same time he joined forces with the prospecting party led by Ed Schieffelin. Upon reaching St. Michael, Schieffelin in his steamer the *New Racket* generously towed Jacobsen's skin boat. As the party moved upstream, Jacobsen helped Schieffelin's crew keep the steamer supplied with wood.

From the first evening, Jacobsen experienced what he called "the plague"—mosquitoes. "It is no wonder," he expounded,

> that all travelers in the tropics or up in the north
> immediately mention the nuisance inflicted by these
> bloodthirsty insects. One can overcome dangers, and against
> ambushes one can protect oneself with vigilance; accidents
> can often be prevented or lessened by energy and quick
> action; one can overcome all kinds of situations, but against
> the relentless pursuit during waking and sleeping carried on
> by mosquitoes, which are constantly replaced by millions of
> new ones, there is no defense.[9]

At the mouth of the Tanana Jacobsen turned back. As he floated downriver, he stopped at as many villages as he could to collect ethnographic material but complained bitterly of high prices. After reaching St. Michael he spent time in other parts of Alaska before returning to Berlin.

In 1883, shortly after his return, Jacobsen published a book that summarized his ethnological expedition. The following year a ghost writer took his journals, notes, and lectures and published still another book. Through his collection of more than seven thousand specimens, his lectures, slide shows, and semiscientific articles, Jacobsen acquainted a European audience with the wonders of Alaska.

At the same time, the United States Army moved to make its presence felt on the Yukon. Even though the army had been withdrawn from Alaska in 1877, Gen. Nelson A. Miles, commander of the Department of the Columbia, believed that Alaska fell under his military jurisdiction. Because of his experience in the American West, he strongly pressed for authority and funding to explore the unknown land and to gather information on its Indians. Congress preferred to let the matter drift, so Miles, characteristically, found his own authority and squeezed his budget to send a small party to explore Alaska's interior. In 1882 he seized upon the rumor of Indian discontent that followed the price war between trading companies as the pretext for exploration.[10]

Miles chose 1st Lt. Frederick Schwatka to head the expedition. Schwatka was not a typical soldier. Born in Galena, Illinois, he moved to Salem, Oregon, where in 1867 he received an appointment to the United States Military Academy at West Point. Following graduation and assignment to the Third Cavalry, he continued studies in law and medicine. In 1875 the Nebraska Bar Association admitted him, and the following year he received a medical degree from Bellevue Hospital Medical College in New York. In 1879 he took a leave of absence and outfitted an expedition under the auspices of the American Geographical Society to search for Sir John Franklin, missing in the Arctic since 1847. Following rumors from Eskimos on King William Island, Schwatka spent two years in the quest. During this time he explored new country, found graves and records of the Franklin Expedition, and completed the longest sledge journey in history. Returning to his regiment in 1880, he welcomed Miles's Alaskan assignment.

Ordered to determine the number, character, and disposition of all Natives, their relations with one other, and their attitude toward the

Frederick Schwatka. In addition to his army commission, Schwatka had degrees in law and medicine. Because of his Arctic experience, in 1883 General Miles sent him to explore and map the Yukon. *Harper's Weekly,* 1878, courtesy of *Jerome A. Greene.*

encroachment of whites, Schwatka left Portland on May 22, 1883—or as he later described it, "stole away like a thief in the night."[11] A surgeon, topographer, and three enlisted men accompanied him.

Schwatka chose to enter the interior through Canada, and it turned out that his greatest contribution lay in mapping the Canadian segment of the Yukon between Lake Lindeman and Fort Selkirk. Canadian officials and the American Congress reproached Miles for Schwatka's impolitic judgment, but Miles, though also dismayed, defended his subordinate.

Schwatka climbed Chilkoot Pass—already fully mapped by Arthur Krause—built a raft at Lake Lindeman, and began to float the Yukon.

With arrogant disdain for Canadian sensibilities, he renamed each river and geographic feature he passed, including Lake Bennett, Marsh Lake, and Miles Rapids and Canyon. Surviving the run through Miles Rapids, he moved on to Fort Selkirk, where he found only the chimneys remaining of Campbell's old fort. Here at the junction of the Lewes and the Pelly, he made another significant and enduring decision. After measuring current rate, width, and depth, he decided that, contrary to tradition, the Lewes, not the Pelly, was the true mother of the Yukon. As a result, all subsequent maps had the Yukon forming from Lake Marsh.

As Schwatka floated downriver, he continued his mapping and observation of Natives. The river below Fort Selkirk, however, was well known, especially that portion Lieutenant Raymond had mapped in 1869. His assessment of the interior Indians provided no new information beyond that given by Dall and Petrov. Schwatka, however, did form a high opinion of the traders, whom he called "men of good judgment" whose behavior would make "collisions [with Indians] less probable than would generally be supposed."[12] Moreover, he found that the traders conciliated the Indians, and when hostilities threatened, the traders avoided the Indians altogether. The Indian threat, the excuse for his expedition, had resulted in no more than the traders changing their trading style and temporarily abandoning their upriver trading posts.

At the mouth of the Tanana the expedition abandoned its battered raft for a small decked vessel, that McQuesten lent them. He called it a "barka" and it had only one small sail, a jib. They drifted down the river to Anvik where the *Yukon* overtook them and towed them to St. Michael. They were in luck: ten days later the schooner *Leo*, returning from Point Barrow with another army party, picked them up and took them to San Francisco.

When Schwatka reached the States, he immediately published an account of his Yukon adventures in newspapers and magazines, even before his official report was printed. Two years later he wrote an entertaining book, *Along Alaska's Great River*, which brought great publicity to Alaska and its resources. In 1885 he resigned his army commission and engaged in several private exploration ventures, including an unsuccessful attempt to climb Mount Saint Elias and an exploration of the headwaters of the White River.

The success of Schwatka's expedition inspired General Miles to plan an even more ambitious reconnaissance of Alaska's interior. For this assignment he chose his aide-de-camp, Lt. Henry Tureman Allen.

Born in Sharpsburg, Kentucky, in 1859, Allen attended Peekskill Military Academy and then West Point. Tall, good-looking, well bred, he radiated a southern charm and grace that made him popular with women. Although vain, he carried himself with confidence and poise. In 1882, following his commissioning, he reported to Fort Keogh, Montana Territory, where he helped guard the construction of the Northern Pacific Railroad.

Then, in 1884, as Miles's aide-de-camp, Allen found himself enroute to Alaska to look for Lt. William R. Abercrombie, another aide whom Miles had sent to explore the Copper River. Allen found the sad and dejected officer near the mouth of the Copper. Because of rugged terrain and moving glaciers, Abercrombie had failed to go any farther than sixty miles up the river.

Reading voraciously on Alaska and quizzing every old-timer, Allen designed a plan to explore the Copper and Tanana rivers—two of the largest uncharted rivers in Alaska.[13] With Miles's blessing, $2,000, and two enlisted men, Allen arrived at the Copper River Delta in the spring of 1885. His plan depended on reaching the headwaters of the Copper on ice. In freezing rain, lacking proper food, and confronting nearly impossible terrain, he pushed north along the Copper. At the Indian village of Taral he picked up John Bremner, who had arrived the previous summer and survived a hard winter, living on rabbits and Indian charity. Despite his dwindling supplies, Allen explored the Copper's major tributary, the Chitina River. On this trip he learned how the Indians built skin boats and, more important, how to navigate them. Back at Taral, he continued upriver using his skin boats but with fewer and fewer provisions. One night they feasted on "a little paste, rotten wormy meat for dinner." The next evening they crawled into an Indian house where the occupant gave them "a dinner of boiled meat from which he scraped the maggots by handfuls before cutting it up."[14]

With new guides, Allen and his party left the Copper and crossed the Alaska Range through a low portal that Allen named Miles Pass. In a notable first, he had charted the rugged Copper and crossed one of North America's highest mountain ranges. Descending one of the Tanana's tributaries, he paused at an Indian village where the children knew the English alphabet and some of the Bible. In fact, the Reverend Vincent Sims had just left this country on the exhausting journey that broke his health.

Allen felt compelled to reach the Yukon via the fastest means

Henry T. Allen. In 1885 General Miles sent 1st Lt. Henry Allen (center), Sgt. Cady Robertson (right), and Pvt. Fred Fickett (left) to explore and map the hitherto unknown Copper, Tanana, and Koyukuk rivers. Allen contributed substantially more to geographical knowledge than any other Yukon explorer. *University of Alaska Archives.*

possible. Because of the improper diet, John Bremner and one of the enlisted men suffered from scurvy. To save his party, Allen decided to forgo exploring the Tanana to its headwaters and instead headed for a trading post at the mouth of the Tanana said to be well stocked with provisions—more than 560 miles away and through territory held by reportedly hostile Indians. Shortly after reaching the Tanana, Allen met one of the supposedly warlike chiefs with thirty followers. Through sign language, he learned that his reputation as "medicine man" had preceded him. The Indians wanted his brightly colored pills. With great relief, he distributed a few to each Indian and then hurriedly launched his boat before the purgative agent and quinine took effect.

When at long last the party reached the mouth of the Tanana, they had been out of food for several days. At the trading post they found only three dozen crackers, three quarts of beans, twenty pounds of flour, and some machine oil. The Indians reported that the Alaska Commercial Company steamer was expected within two weeks. While they waited, the explorers lived on fish fried in machine oil. Scurvy continued to ravage the party. Meanwhile Allen watched as the Natives on the two major rivers converged for their annual trading and pleasure fair.

After the steamer finally arrived bearing ample food, Allen's men improved rapidly. John Bremner had experienced enough exploring, however, and decided to stay at Tanana for the winter. Allen sent his scurvy-ridden enlisted man to St. Michael on the *Yukon*. Guided by Koyukon Indians, Allen and one other man portaged to the Koyukuk River. Although they did not reach the headwaters of the Koyukuk, they succeeded in mapping still another uncharted river. Using birchbark canoes, they floated 556 miles to the Yukon and then on to St. Michael. On September 5, they left St. Michael on a revenue cutter bound for San Francisco.

Allen's achievements rank with the great explorations of North America.[15] In less than seven months and under extreme hardship, he and his small party traveled 2,500 miles. He charted three major rivers for the first time, contributing more than 1,500 miles of original exploration. Although he had little time for scientific observation, he noted the absence of glacial evidence north of the Alaska Range and observed the similarities in language between the Copper River Natives and Apache Indians of the American Southwest.

Allen also addressed Miles's questions regarding the nature of the

Indians. Contrary to rumors of hostility among the Indians of the Copper, Tanana, and Koyukuk rivers, Allen reported a peaceable but destitute group of people. Unlike Schwatka, he thought that the traders took advantage of the poverty-stricken and degraded condition of the Natives on the lower river. He went further to recommend government charity and assistance.[16]

Despite his achievements, Allen lacked Schwatka's flair for the theatrical and failed to gain the widespread publicity that came to his flamboyant fellow officer. Moreover, the government did not print his report for nearly two years, and the initial stir that his trip caused in the press was forgotten. His contributions, however, provided a firm foundation for other explorer-scientists to build on. His greatest praise and hyperbole came from his commander, General Miles, who called it the most remarkable journey since the Lewis and Clark Expedition.[17]

Allen's subsequent career overshadowed his Alaskan exploits. He served as an instructor at West Point, as military attaché in Russia and Germany, and fought wars in Cuba and the Philippines. He organized the Philippine Constabulary and served on Gen. John J. Pershing's Mexican Punitive Expedition. With the outbreak of World War I and the expansion of the army, Allen was made a major general. Following the war he commanded the United States occupation forces in Germany. He retired in 1923 to assume a number of positions with philanthropic and peace-seeking organizations and to toy with politics. In 1930, at the age of seventy-one, he died of a stroke.

As the results of the explorations of Schwatka and Allen reached Ottawa, Canadian government officials inaugurated their own scientific investigations. They chose as leader of a well-equipped government party, known as the Yukon Expedition, a thirty-five-year-old dwarf with a humped back, George Mercer Dawson. Dawson was the oldest son of Sir John William Dawson, an educator, geologist, naturalist, and Canadian Superintendent of Education. George Dawson was educated at Montreal High School, McGill University, and in Edinburgh and London, studying geology, ethnology, and natural history. After work on the British North America Boundary Commission, he joined the Geological Survey of Canada as Chief Geologist in 1875. By 1883 he had become its assistant director and by 1887 had researched Queen Charlotte Islands, the Alberta coalfields, and the Peace River. He welcomed the challenges of the Yukon Expedition.[18]

Joining Dawson on the Yukon Expedition were two other compe-

George Mercer Dawson. Aroused by American exploring parties, the Canadian government selected Dawson to head its Yukon Expedition. In 1887 the expedition mapped the old trading routes of British Columbia and the Yukon district and gathered the first Canadian scientific data on the region. *Public Archives of Canada.*

tent and hard-working geologist-surveyors. Richard George McConnell, thirty years old and with a degree in geology from McGill University, had joined the survey in 1880. William Ogilvie, the oldest of the three at forty-one, specialized in surveying and since 1869 had served as Dominion Land Surveyor. In 1883 he had accepted the rigors of exploratory surveys and mapped the Peace and Athabasca rivers.

Dawson defined the purpose of the expedition as to gather information on the "vast and hitherto almost unknown tract of country . . . referred to as the Yukon district."[19] He divided the assignment into three parts: Ogilvie to survey the Yukon and international boundary near Fortymile, McConnell to map the Stikine River and lower Liard, and himself to continue the line of survey from the Cassiar district in northern British Columbia to the upper Liard and over the uplands to the Yukon Basin.

On April 22, 1887, the three party leaders and their crews left Ottawa for Wrangell, which they reached on May 18. Dawson and McConnell started up the Stikine River while Ogilvie continued to Dyea and Chilkoot Pass. McConnell began his survey of the Stikine, and Dawson made his way up the Stikine to Dease Lake, where once again McConnell joined him. Together they floated the Dease to the Liard. Here McConnell went downriver.

Following the route of Robert Campbell's exploration of 1840, Dawson moved on up to Frances Lake. He found the route fully as difficult and tedious as had Campbell forty-seven years earlier—filled with submerged gravel bars, steep canyons, fast currents, and dangerous rapids. At Frances Lake, Dawson came upon the outline of Campbell's old stockade, abandoned since 1851. Despite Campbell's report and those of other Hudson's Bay Company traders, Dawson failed to find the portage trail to the Pelly. Striking out on his own, he hit the Pelly twelve days later. Here he and his men constructed a canoe. As he floated and mapped the Pelly, he dutifully kept Campbell's place-names. On August 11, Dawson reached the junction with the Lewes—Schwatka's Yukon. He had expected to meet Ogilvie at the ruins of Fort Selkirk or at least find a cache of supplies to see him back to the Chilkoot. Because he lacked adequate provisions to return home, Dawson began construction of a boat to carry him and his crew to the trading post at Fortymile.

Ogilvie's convenient arrival interrupted Dawson's plans. Ogilvie had been delayed at Dyea by his Chilkat packers, who refused to move the seven tons of equipment and supplies he carried for both his and Dawson's crews until paid in advance. (Ogilvie would come to know three of these packers better in the years ahead; they were Skookum Jim Mason, Tagish Charley, and an American married to a Tagish woman—George Washington Carmack.) While Ogilvie and his packers labored over Chilkoot Pass, one of his party, William Moore, explored another portal through the mountains to the south, later to be called White Pass. Once over the Chilkoot, Ogilvie encountered further delay as bad weather slowed his survey of the river—a task that in any event only duplicated Schwatka's work. When Ogilvie and Dawson finally joined, the expedition was far behind schedule.[20]

Within four days Dawson retraced Ogilvie's steps back to the Chilkoot. Although Dawson and Ogilvie found Schwatka reasonably accurate, they expressed annoyance with his disregard for existing place-names. Even so, Dawson retained many of Schwatka's traditional names. Schwatka's decision to rename the Lewes the Yukon, however, came in for severe criticism. Dawson believed that the Pelly, not the Lewes, was the longer and more traditional "mother of the Yukon" and refused to change its name. As a result, confusion reigned until the 1950s, when Canadian officials adopted Schwatka's nomenclature.

Dawson spent four months traveling 1,322 miles. Although he followed old Hudson's Bay Company trails, he was the first scientific observer and surveyor over this tortuous terrain. His report provided Canadian officials with essential information about the Yukon Basin. He defined the navigable rivers, correctly judged the discharge of the Yukon, reported that the Chilkoot Pass was not suitable for pack animals but added that the White Pass might be, believed that hardy crops could be grown but could foresee no market, and stated strongly that Canada's Yukon district surpassed in material resources Alaska and all other country to the north. His report summarized the known facts of the upper Yukon. Descriptions of geological and geographical features and routes of travel provided a sound basis for further exploration.

When Dawson returned to Ottawa in the fall of 1887, Ogilvie and McConnell remained in the West. Leaving Dawson at the ruins of Fort Selkirk, Ogilvie moved down the Yukon to the international boundary. Here he built winter quarters, including an open-roofed observatory. During the winter months he obtained enough astronomical observations to enable him to define the 141st meridian by blazing trees on both sides of the river. Those on the west he marked with an "A" for Alaska, and those on the east with a "C" for Canada. Since he resided not far from Fortymile, miners dropped by to visit. They quizzed him on Canadian mining regulations and laws and complained that they were unreasonable. He also witnessed and reported the bad health of the miners caused by scurvy. Not content with surveying and geology, Ogilvie vividly described the fur trade, mining activity, riverboats, and Indian legends and religious ceremonies.

With the arrival of spring, Ogilvie prepared to continue his survey and moved his supplies down to the mouth of the Tatonduk River. With the help of nine Han Indians from Charley's Village and thirty-six dogs, he traveled up to the Peel River divide. Here, however, his Indian guides and packers turned back in fear of Indians on the other side of the mountains whom they called cannibals. Crossing to the Porcupine because the country toward the Peel was reportedly too rugged, Ogilvie ascended to the Bell and on to La Pierre House. Later he surveyed and mapped a new pass to Rat River that Hudson's Bay Company trader James McDougall found in 1872. It proved lower and easier than the route pioneered by John Bell in 1839. When he reached the Peel River and Fort McPherson on June 20, 1888, Ogilvie's survey was complete.

McConnell, meanwhile, had also been active. After separating from Dawson on June 25, 1887, at the junction of the Dease and Liard, he descended the Liard and wintered at Fort Providence. At breakup in 1888, he descended the Mackenzie to the mouth of the Peel. Here he met Ogilvie, with whom he spent a day. Without waiting for the supply steamer and with only one crew member, McConnell followed Alexander Murray's route across the Peel River Portage to La Pierre House, which he found abandoned. Since he had hired a group of Indians to portage his boat to the trading post via the easier McDougall Pass, he was ready to float to the Yukon. Once there, however, he quickly discovered that the boat was ill-suited for ascending the fast-moving river. Nonetheless, the two men made it to Fortymile, where they built a new boat and continued upriver. They crossed the Chilkoot, went on to Juneau, and then to Ottawa.[21]

All three of the Yukon Expedition leaders gained recognition for their achievements. Dawson won honorary degrees from Queen's University and McGill University. The Royal Society of England made him a fellow, and in 1893 he became president of Canada's Royal Society. In 1895 he was appointed Director and Deputy Head of the Geological Survey of Canada. In 1897 the Royal Geographical Society awarded him its prestigious gold medal. He died suddenly in 1901 of capillary bronchitis. McConnell returned to the Yukon Basin every summer from 1898 to 1905. In 1914 he was appointed Director of the Geological Survey and Deputy Minister of Mines, posts he held until he retired in 1921. He too became a fellow in the Royal Society of Canada. He lived until 1942. Ogilvie returned to the Yukon in 1895 where he was destined to play a major role in the unfolding of the Klondike frontier.

In 1889 the United States government checked Ogilvie's international boundary determinations along the 141st meridian. The United States Coast and Geodetic Survey sent two ten-man parties to intersect the international boundary on the Porcupine and Yukon rivers. J. E. McGrath led the Yukon team and J. Henry Turner the Porcupine party.

Ascending from St. Michael on the *Yukon's* last voyage, the two crews traveled together as far as the ruins of Fort Yukon. The old vessel even entered the Porcupine for the first time and carried Turner and his party to within thirty-seven miles of the boundary before low water forced a retreat to the Yukon. With great effort and hardship, Turner's party pulled a heavy whaleboat and lighter up the river to Rampart House. Much to Turner's dismay, he found through his astronomical observations that the Hudson's Bay Company trading post, moved in 1869 from Fort Yukon, still stood on American domain. Onward twenty miles he pushed to the boundary. During these last few miles, one of the Indians accompanying the expedition drowned. Only the intervention of the Hudson's Bay Company trader prevented Indian hostility, retaliation, and revenge.[22]

Near the border Turner established Camp Colonna, with a large T-shaped house and observatory. Cloudy weather and fog limited his astronomical observations. On March 27, 1890, he, two crew members, the Hudson's Bay Company trader, and three Indian guides began to follow the boundary line northward to the Arctic Ocean. Initially Turner had planned to survey the line, but on the third day both chronometers stopped, so "the exploration degenerated into sort of a rough reconnaissance."[23] On April 10 they reached the Arctic Ocean, made some quick observations, ascertained the meridian altitude of the sun, and started back to Camp Colonna. The whole trip, two hundred miles each way, lasted only eighteen days.

With the arrival of summer, Turner and his party completed the triangulation of the camp area and erected boundary monuments. In mid-July they started downriver, continuing to map the Yukon to its mouth. Storms and other bad weather delayed their arrival at St. Michael until after the last ship had sailed. Disappointed, Turner made the most of his second winter in Alaska through observations for time, latitude, longitude, and azimuth. His party produced three topographic maps and recorded meteorological, magnetic, and tidal observations as well. At last, on July 9, 1891, they left St. Michael for San Francisco.

While the *Yukon* carried Turner and his party up the Porcupine, McGrath and his party surveyed Fort Yukon. When the steamer returned to the Yukon, McGrath continued upriver to Ogilvie's station, which he renamed Camp Davidson. Since the *Yukon* was on its last voyage, McGrath left most of his supplies at St. Michael for the new steamer, the *Arctic*, to bring up later in the summer. Unfortunately for McGrath, the miners on the river, and the Indians, the *Arctic* sank on its maiden voyage, although its cargo was saved. McGrath and his men decided to weather the winter on reduced rations and continue their assignment. He sent two men downriver to guard their supplies and to attempt to hire dog teams to bring as much food back as possible. Meanwhile McQuesten's garden at Fortymile turned out nearly a thousand pounds of turnips, and caribou proved abundant.

Just as for Turner, cloudy weather and late blizzards kept McGrath from fulfilling his assignment. Nonetheless, the men double-checked Ogilvie's observations on the Yukon and at Fortymile. They found him remarkably accurate. Still, McGrath thought he needed another winter to record observations, and this time the resurrected *Arctic* came upriver to deliver the camp's supplies. Weather continued cloudy and rainy, yet the nights allowed observations that the previous year had not. During the summer of 1891 McGrath made a running survey of the Yukon from the border to Holy Cross Mission. Gratefully he and his men reached St. Michael in ample time to board the revenue cutter for San Francisco.

Accompanying the Coast and Geodetic Survey teams was a lone representative of the United States Geological Survey, Israel C. Russell. Traveling at the invitation and expense of the Alaska Commercial Company, Russell gathered notes on the surface geology of the Yukon Valley. He took the steamer as far as Fort Selkirk, where he witnessed Arthur Harper and his Native wife reestablishing a trading post at Campbell's old site. Then with four miners he journeyed over Chilkoot Pass.

Although not as ambitious nor productive as the Canadian Yukon Expedition, the American boundary expedition yielded five articles in popular magazines.[24] Like those before them, these articles excited the American public and revealed some measure of the hardships demanded of visitors to the northland. Popular magazines and newspapers especially relished the adventure story found in Alaska and sent reporter-explorers north to capture the mood and the romance of conquering the last frontier.

First to capitalize on the public fascination was *Frank Leslie's Illustrated Newspaper*. Linking Alaska with Africa, the newspaper hired an associate of African explorer Henry M. Stanley to cover the expedition, which had been placed under the leadership of E. H. Wells. Edward James Glave was only twenty-eight in 1890, but he had spent three years exploring the Congo and one year on the lecture circuit. The Leslie expedition also included scientist-astronomer A. B. Schanz, a photographer, a scout, and three adventurers. Among the last was Jack Dalton, who had grown up on the Cherokee Strip in Oklahoma and worked as a logger and cowboy. He had traveled with Schwatka on his abortive attempt to climb Mount St. Elias and decided that he liked Alaska. He and Glave became good friends. When the expedition reached Kusawa Lake, already mapped by Arthur Krause, Glave and Dalton left the party to cross a divide to a tributary of the Alsek River, which they followed to the Alsek and then to the Pacific. The next year the two men returned to the Alsek with pack horses. They explored as far as the Kluane Lake area, which later became part of the Haines Cutoff of the Alaska Highway. Glave's stories appeared in *Leslie's Illustrated Newspaper* and *Century*.[25] Glave returned to the Congo in 1892 and died there in 1895. Dalton, on the other hand, developed the Dalton Trail in 1895 for driving cattle and other livestock to mining camps on the Yukon.

Meanwhile, in 1890 E. H. Wells and the remainder of the Leslie expedition proceeded from Kusawa Lake to the Yukon. Shortly after reaching the Yukon, A. B. Schanz became violently ill. When the raft carrying the men reached Fort Selkirk, they learned that McGrath's boundary survey included a physician. Pushing on, they reached McGrath's camp at the boundary and left the sick Schanz. The party then retraced its route to the Fortymile to refit before ascending the Fortymile. Because it was early in the season, the trading post lacked provisions. Nevertheless, with inadequate supplies, Wells and his party started off to explore new country. They followed the Fortymile to its head and crossed into the Tanana Basin. Determined to find unexplored terrain, they crossed the Tanana to the Tok River. Running very low on food, they resorted to killing and eating their pet dog and digging for roots. Next they decided to return to the Tanana and float until they reached an Indian village. As Allen before them, the expedition was saved by Indian charity, not once but several times. At last they reached the Yukon, where the *New Racket* carried them to the Unalakleet portage. More disappointment awaited at St. Michael when they arrived after the last ship of the season had sailed for San Francisco. Eventually the party, including A. B. Schanz, returned to the States.[26]

The Leslie expedition contributed little to either cartography or science. Glave added some knowledge of the upper Alsek, Wells gave a new dimension to the Tanana, and Schanz defined and mapped Lake Clark. Still, yielding more than forty articles for *Frank Leslie's Illustrated Newspaper*, the expedition's adventures caught the public imagination and stirred a tempest of publicity. Each week readers avidly read the current episode and anxiously anticipated the next. Alaska was not only as exciting as Africa, but was much closer and American.

Once again, in 1891, Frederick Schwatka returned to Alaska for a fourth exploration, this time in the service of a syndicate of fifty newspapers. Having failed to climb Mount St. Elias in 1886, he now planned to cross the range from the Canadian side via the White River. He asked the United States Geological Survey to assign a geologist to the expedition, and Charles Willard Hayes got the job. Hayes was an assistant to Israel C. Russell, who in 1889 had accompanied the American Boundary Survey Expedition. Forgoing the Chilkoot Pass, Schwatka and Hayes volunteered to examine the Taku River out of Juneau as a possible packhorse trail to the interior. An experienced miner agreed to guide them, and six Indians were hired as boatmen and packers. From the headwaters of the Taku, they portaged to the Teslin River and descended it to the Yukon. At Fort Selkirk the party, with new Indian packers, decided to cross overland to the White rather than ascend the river from its mouth. Along the way Hayes mapped the new country, retaining the Indian names of geographical features. Near the headwaters of the White, where the expedition had to cross a glacier, the Indian packers refused to go any farther. With scant provisions, Schwatka and Hays decided to push on. Within a few days they found themselves over the pass and then pushed on to the Copper River. At Taral they met Nicolai, the Indian chief who had befriended Lieutenant Allen. Nicolai gave them a hospitable welcome and floated with them to the coast. Despite the difficulties of the travel, Hayes had surveyed an unexplored and unmapped country.

During this trip Schwatka explored more of Alaska than he had in 1883, but he was not to publicize his exploits. By 1892 he had ulcers, which he treated himself with laudanum, a tincture of opium. On November 2, 1892, a policeman found him on the streets of Portland in a comatose condition from an accidental overdose. Within hours he was dead, at the age of forty-three.[27] In a series of lectures and articles, however, Hayes contributed to the scientific and popular knowledge of Alaska.[28] He confirmed deposits of copper and detailed the topography, vegetation, geology, and the volcanic and glacial aspects of the country. Hayes went on to become Director of the United States Geological Survey.

In 1892 two solo explorers followed. Warburton Pike, a thirty-one-year-old Englishman, scouted the Pelly River nearly to its source. When he returned home, he wrote of his experiences with considerable flair and spiced his narrative with spirit and adventure.[29] The other adventurer was twenty-seven-year-old Frederick Funston, who would one day gain fame as an army general but now worked for the Department of Agriculture. Funston made some botanical collections in the Yakutat area, then returned in 1893 to spend the summer in the Yukon Basin, descend the Mackenzie River, and travel a distance of more than 3,500 miles. Although Funston explored no new areas, pioneered no new routes, and contributed little to scientific knowledge, his vividly detailed and flowing narratives informed the readers of *Scribner's Magazine* and *Harper's Weekly* of an area soon to take on magical qualities.[30]

In the summer of 1895 the Canadian government once again sent William Ogilvie to the Yukon. This time he was to mark the boundary from the Yukon River south to Sixtymile River. Again he traveled via the Chilkoot, where he renewed acquaintance with Skookum Jim and Tagish Charley. Again bad weather delayed his arrival at Fortymile until late August. Although Ogilvie spent several days with Inspector Charles Constantine of the North-West Mounted Police at Fort Cudahy, the two men did not like each other, professionally or personally. With considerable relief Ogilvie continued to his boundary station. Finding his old camp burned, he spent the fall rebuilding it. He rechecked his work of 1887-88 and discovered it 109 feet too far east. Throughout the winter he and his crew of six men ran the boundary line south nearly fifty-five miles to Sixtymile River. Miners appeared grateful for the boundary, even though some Americans found their claims in Canada and contested Inspector Constantine's authority.[31]

During the summer of 1896 Ogilvie received word that negotiations were under way with the United States for a joint commission to mark the international boundary. Since he would be the Canadian commissioner, he stayed on at Fortymile. While in the gold rush community he surveyed the townsite and that of Cudahy as well. In September he wrote his supervisor of "a most important discovery of gold" on a tributary of a river known as the Klondike.[32] He reported claims earning $100 to $500 per day. A week later word arrived that plans for a joint commission had failed and that he was to return to Ottawa. An early winter, however, brought snow and freezeup before the steamer's last trip.

William Ogilvie. While Dawson retraced Campbell's routes, Ogilvie (seated second from right) surveyed the international boundary near Fortymile. In 1895 he returned to resurvey the boundary, then moved to the new town of Dawson to survey the townsite and associated claims. *Public Archives of Canada.*

Although Ogilvie was eager to return home, he deemed the expense and hardship of a winter sled trip excessive. Instead, he wintered at the new town of Dawson.

Ogilvie's services during the winter of 1896-97 made him unique among the score of explorers and scientists who observed and documented the Yukon Basin. He not only surveyed the townsite of Dawson but the claims of miners as well. Recognized as a friend of the miner, he brought order out of chaos, resolving claim controversies and substituting science for intuition. Equally important, Ogilvie sent word to Ottawa of the dimension of the gold strike so that a gold commissioner and police reinforcements were on hand shortly after breakup. Thus Ogilvie, unlike other frontier observers, actually influenced the evolution of the frontier. From 1898 to 1902 he served as commissioner of the newly established Yukon Territory. Through his books on the Yukon he provided firsthand knowledge and scientific expertise that promoted the development of the area. He died in retirement in 1912.

Despite tradition and folklore, Alaska and the Yukon Basin were not the vast, unknown wasteland until "discovered" with the Klondike gold rush. Since 1860 American, Canadian, and foreign scientists had described the geology, geography, ethnography, and potential resources of the land. Government explorers surveyed and mapped old transportation routes and discovered new ones. Journalists and adventurers titillated their readers with tales of adventure and romance. Scores of articles and books on Alaska poured from public and private presses. Explorers, scientists, and adventurers alike followed the lecture circuit, exciting their audiences with their exploits and the land. Thus by 1896 Alaska and the Yukon had already captured the public's imagination. For a depression-stricken nation, however, the glamour and thrill of a gold rush dwarfed the impact of earlier publicity. Nonetheless, without the background information that these scientists provided, the trails to the Klondike would have been even harder, even more punishing, and even less forgiving.

CHAPTER 6

The Klondike Frontier and Its Backwash

The Klondike gold rush did more to shape the history of the Yukon than any other event. Although never as rich as some other western gold rushes, the Klondike strike resulted in new techniques of mining, subsequent gold rushes, and the development of an isolated country. To the Klondike thousands came as they had fifty years before to California. The Yukon, however, presented a more hostile environment, and many would-be miners lost their lives because of recklessness or carelessness.

The discovery of the Klondike has been credited to George Washington Carmack, who filed the first claim.[1] Canadians, however, boast that Robert Henderson mined the first gold and gave Carmack the tip-off. Native historians now claim that Skookum Jim Mason and Tagish Charley found the gold while Carmack slept. Nonetheless, the discovery occurred and a snow-balling stampede was on. First Fortymile smiled in disbelief but quietly investigated "Lying George's" assertions of gold on the Klondike River. Then letters to Circle City emptied that community within a month. By the winter of 1896 the Yukon's first real gold rush had begun.

The ground proved exceedingly rich by Yukon standards. Individuals claimed up to $800 from a single pan of pay dirt. Others received more than $140,000 for a winter's work. All the best claims had been staked long before the steamboat *Excelsior* arrived in San Francisco bearing the first Klondike gold. Claims changed hands for exorbitant sums. Near the rich finds a boomtown sprang up. Joe Ladue platted it and named it Dawson, for the Canadian geologist who had made the first report on the mineral resources of the Canadian Yukon. Eventually lots in Dawson sold for as high as $5,000 a front foot. But most of the miners,

In 1896 George Washington Carmack (left), Skookum Jim Mason (right), and Tagish Charley (not shown) discovered the gold that led to the Klondike stampede—the last great gold rush of North America.

not wanting to take time to build log cabins, lived in tents. Life was a frantic rush.

Unlike earlier American gold rushes and later Alaskan stampedes, Canadian government officials prevented chaos, anarchy, and violence. William Ogilvie, Dominion Land Surveyor, arrived in the winter of 1896–97 to survey Ladue's townsite. He stayed on to survey the two major creeks, Bonanza and Eldorado. While Canadian law allowed five hundred feet per claim, in the urgent confusion of staking, many miners had haphazardly staked their claims. As a result, some claims were larger than five hundred feet; others failed to abut one another. Ogilvie's survey resolved these irregularities by creating "fractions" or smaller claims between larger ones. Since all other land had been staked, they sold for high prices. Ogilvie's foresight thus prevented endless legal disputes. From Fortymile came the North-West Mounted Police, who imposed law and order. Although life in Dawson was hectic and lively, it was seldom violent or disorderly.

Dawson sprang up near the mouth of the Klondike River. In 1897 tents strung up the picturesque hills still outnumbered permanent structures. *University of Alaska Archives*.

When news of the Klondike gold rush reached Seattle and San Francisco, a nation caught in the throes of depression responded with exuberance. The frontier was not dead. Adventure, romance, and gold still remained in the Far North. Within months Dawson swelled with the influx of stampeders. Many arrived penniless; others had mortgaged everything they owned. Few brought adequate supplies, and even fewer were prepared for the trails to El Dorado.

Like the trails of the California gold rush, which crossed the American West, the Klondike inspired comparable trailbuilders. Each sought an easier route to the goldfields. None found it. Goldseekers with money took the easier but slower steamboat course up the Yukon from St. Michael. The majority of argonauts, however, followed the Chilkoot and White Pass trails.

The shortest but steepest trail, the Chilkoot, began at the Chilkat village of Dyea, where John J. Healy had begun trading in 1886. As thousands poured over the trail seeking gold, others stayed behind to improve

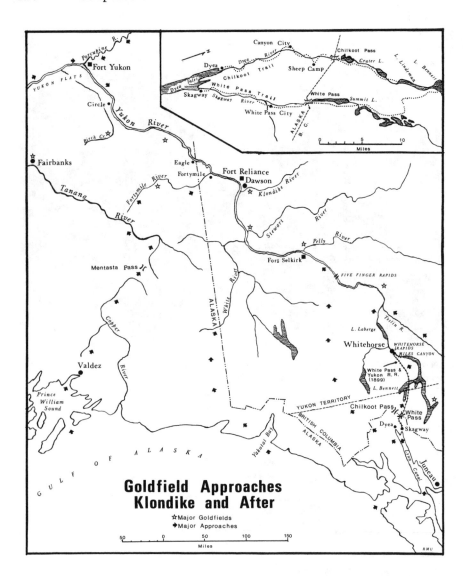

**Goldfield Approaches
Klondike and After**

☆ Major Goldfields
✦ Major Approaches

the route, build toll bridges and tramways, and establish towns, such as Canyon City and Sheep Camp. Nearing the summit, the Klondikers confronted a nearly vertical wall of snow. Undaunted, they cut "Golden Stairs" in the snow to climb to the top. From there to Lake Bennett the trail was downhill.

Three miles south of Dyea, on the Lynn Canal, the city of Skagway marked the trailhead for the White Pass Trail. Although less steep and longer than the Chilkoot, its narrow twisting valleys and roller-coaster

Chilkoot Trail. The shortest but steepest trail to Dawson crossed Chilkoot Pass, where men climbed step-by-step over the summit. After the 1897–98 starvation scare, the Canadian government required a thousand pounds of supplies per person. Thus, before a tram was built, argonauts had to make ten to twenty trips over the "Golden Stairs." *University of Alaska Archives.*

terrain brought death to more than one thousand horses and extreme hardship to their owners. Eventually a wagon road and later a railroad proved the viability of the route, but the stampeders preferred the shorter Chilkoot.

Both the White Pass and Chilkoot trails met at Lake Bennett. From there the hopeful miners whipsawed timber into lumber and hammered out rough boats to float the Yukon to Dawson. Before they reached the Yukon proper, however, they faced Whitehorse Rapids, which shattered many a greenhorn's boat before the North-West Mounted Police established rules for portaging and piloting the rapids. Later a tramway carried the Klondikers' boats and outfits around the rapids. Around it grew a small town—Whitehorse. Five Finger Rapids, looking worse than it proved, was the last obstacle before Dawson.

Factors other than the difficulty of the Chilkoot and White Pass

Miles Canyon and Whitehorse Rapids. After successfully climbing either Chilkoot or White Pass, the Klondikers congregated at Lake Bennett to await spring breakup. Then in whipsawed boats or rafts they tried to negotiate Miles Canyon and Whitehorse Rapids. Because many failed, the Mounted Police required the stampeders to portage around the obstacles, thus giving rise to the town of Whitehorse. *University of Alaska Archives.*

trails motivated stampeders to seek alternate routes. In February 1898, when the Canadian government ordered all newcomers to carry with them a year's supply of food and equipment, thousands of Americans, trying to avoid the requirement, sought all-American routes to Dawson. Thirty-five hundred attempted to cross the Valdez Glacier to the Copper River, then over the mountains through Mentasta Pass to the Tanana River, and on to the headwaters of the Fortymile. Few made it. Other all-American routes proved equally difficult. While Americans tried to avoid Canadian routes and Canadian customs, Canadians favored their own trails, free of American customs officers. All these trails were poorly marked, longer, and slower than the Chilkoot and White passes. One exception was the Dalton Trail, marked out and improved by Jack Dalton. Stretching from Pyramid Harbor on the Lynn Canal to Fort Selkirk on the Yukon, it was the only trail that cattle and horses could safely travel. Dalton charged $250 for its use. Each stampeder learned that there was no easy way to the Klondike.[2]

Regardless of the route followed, few men arrived in time to stake claims. Early Yukoners from Circle and Fortymile had snatched up most of the easy gold claims. Frustration and despair arose as more and more swarmed to the overstaked creeks. The old rules and customs that had made the earlier Alaska-Yukon camps cohesive communities no longer applied: doors were locked, claims were jumped, and men distrusted their partners. Moreover, Americans, accustomed to American law, chaffed at being taxed 10 percent of their gross production. Discontent bubbled near the surface as Alaskan "sourdoughs" and red-blooded Americans trimmed their behavior to Canadian law.

Conflict was not limited to individual Americans and Canadians. The governments of Canada and the United States discovered that both claimed the boomtowns of Dyea and Skagway, and both nations collected customs from the unlucky stampeders. Before the Americans could send troops to the disputed territory, the North-West Mounted Police, led by Col. Samuel Benfield Steele, established posts at the summits of the White Pass and Chilkoot trails. "It was a case of possession being ten points in the law," explained a Canadian official, "and we intend to hold possession."[3] While controlling the two main routes to the Klondike, the Mounted Police could insist that each new arrival bring a year's supply of food—an additional hardship to poorly prepared argonauts. When the American troops arrived at Skagway and Dyea, their commander wisely avoided involving himself in an international boundary dispute. In October 1899 the two governments established a provisional boundary using the summits of the two passes.[4]

The construction of the White Pass and Yukon Railway, however, proved that the two countries could cooperate. In March 1898 the Close Brothers of London purchased an earlier defunct charter to build a railway over White Pass. After obtaining a charter of incorporation for an American railway, the company lobbied the American Congress for a law extending the right-of-way into Alaska, and this finally passed in May 1898.

Meanwhile a company official negotiated and secured a toll road already constructed part way to White Pass, which the company needed for the railroad. With two major obstacles out of the way, the company sent surveyors to Skagway. After preliminary fieldwork, however, they expressed firm conviction that a railroad could not be built over White Pass. Overhearing the discussions, an independent Canadian contractor, Michael J. Heney, injected himself into the conversations. Convinced that the railroad could be built, he volunteered to prove it. And he did. Often the sheer will of his personality overcame seemingly impossible odds. Most of the grade had to be rock supported, nearly every mile of roadbed had to be blasted with dynamite, and local timber proved useless for ties, bridges, and stringers. Huge quantities of supplies, equipment, and labor had to be imported. Heney worked his men around the clock during the long hours of summer, but winter snows and winds imposed limits that even he could not overcome. Nonetheless, Alaskans and Canadians alike supported the line. The governor of Alaska, John G. Brady, even visited the scene of construction. Finally on July 29, 1900, the railroad was complete to Whitehorse—110 miles with a maximum gradient of 3.9 percent and a cost of $10 million.[5]

While thousands poured into Dawson and others flowed out in search of new bonanzas, men overlooked one precious commodity—food. Gold-crazed miners, eager to be among the first, had traveled light, expecting to buy their year's supply at Dawson with the nuggets they would easily mine. But a series of incidents created panic. The two commercial companies owned only six small steamboats, whose design, coupled with an early winter, left them stranded in the shallow water of the Yukon Flats. When this happened in September 1897, Dawson became frantic. The commercial companies had already rationed their supplies because the steamboats had been unable to keep up with the heavy influx of people. Furthermore, because of their inflationary value, the companies had stocked up on liquor and hardware rather than food.[6] As the Yukon began to freeze, the North-West Mounted Police joined with the commercial companies to urge newcomers without proper provisions to leave immediately. The ensuing panic led to the Canadian requirement that each person entering Canadian soil bring a year's supply of food—eleven hundred pounds, or three pounds per day. Hundreds fled downriver toward the marooned boats at Fort Yukon; others returned the way they had come.

Meanwhile, the United States War Department ordered Capt. Patrick Henry Ray and Lt. Wilds P. Richardson to Alaska via St. Michael. They were to investigate and report on whether troops were necessary, whether civil authorities were providing protection to life and property, whether the people were law-abiding, and whether there was food in the country for the population to winter. By this time Ray was already fifty-five years old. He had come up through the ranks during the Civil War, served in the Sioux and Apache campaigns between 1872 and 1876,

The White Pass and Yukon Railway. Because of the rigors involved in reaching Dawson, Canadian contractor Michael J. Heney constructed a narrow-gauge railroad from Skagway to Bennett. On February 20, 1899, the first passenger train crossed the summit of White Pass. *Yukon Archives.*

and commanded the International Polar Expedition to Point Barrow from 1881 to 1883, where he traveled more than one thousand miles by dogsled over unexplored terrain and partially explored the Meade River. His Arctic experience made him a natural choice. Richardson, on the other hand, was thirty-six years old, a graduate of the United States Military Academy at West Point, and had just completed five years there as an instructor in tactics. When the two officers reached St. Michael in August, Ray reported Dawson's food shortage grave. He also observed a "turbulent and lawless" element entering the country lured by the Klondike's gold. As he steamed up the river, he recognized the isolation of the Yukon. There was no law enforcement, no communication, and no government.[7]

At Circle City an astonished Captain Ray confronted his first miners' meeting. More than 180 miners had arrived in Circle from Dawson and Birch Creek only to learn that the commercial companies had by-passed Circle City for the more profitable Dawson market. Thus, the warehouses were empty as winter closed in. Concerned, upset, and even scared, the miners had called a miners' meeting and decided to hold up the next steamboat in order to obtain the necessary supplies. As Ray stared into the shotguns of the miners, he called attention to their "unlawfulness." The miners responded, "There is no law or any person in authority to whom we can appeal."[8] They then cleared the boat of stragglers and posted guards to prevent pilfering. All goods received full payment at Dawson prices. To avoid charges of favoritism, they stopped the Alaska Commercial Company's *Bella* and the North American Transportation and Trading Company's *Portus B. Weare*. Ray criticized the miners for their radical steps in interfering with legitimate business, yet also condemned the commercial companies for their monopolistic practices and poor planning.

When an unseasonable warm spell cleared the river of ice, a mad dash to Fort Yukon ensued. Captain Ray was at the center of the scattered fleet. He was certain that there would be violence when the Dawson hundreds landed at Fort Yukon. His premonition proved correct; in fact he narrowly averted an armed revolution. Immediately the commercial companies turned over their merchandise to him for protection. He then distributed outfits to the destitute in exchange for chopping wood. The companies' exaggeration of their supplies stored at Fort Yukon created additional complications. A group of demanding, belligerent miners called another miners' meeting to take the warehouses by force. Ray and Richardson succeeded in fending off the threat, but the North American Transportation and Trading Company was looted, and $6,000 was stolen. One "destitute" miner obtained an outfit under false pretenses. Although he was apprehended and jailed in Circle City, a miners' meeting voted to release him. Blatantly he auctioned off his outfit and gambled away his proceeds.

By January, Ray reported that neither Dawson nor Circle City remained in danger—the starvation scare had passed. But the miners' meetings convinced Ray that, against the increasing lawless and turbulent element, civil government was totally inadequate. He recommended a semimilitary government with military posts along the Yukon at St. Michael, Tanana, and near the Canadian border at Mission Creek. This military force would have a moral effect on the population, support the civil authorities, control the Yukon River, prevent smuggling, and provide law and order. The striking contrast between Canadian law and government, symbolized by the North-West Mounted Police, and the absence of any government or law enforcement in Alaska filled him with frustration. Furthermore, the country needed exploration surveys, roads, railroads, light-draft steamers, and agricultural development. At the same time Ray made these recommendations, the commercial companies and the few civil officials also requested protection and assistance. Thus, Lieutenant Richardson alone remained throughout the winter to patrol the river, preserve order in mining towns, and extend relief and medical aid.[9]

Although the starvation threat consumed most of Captain Ray's time, he still reported his observations on social conditions, population, and settlement. He estimated that twelve hundred people lived along the Yukon between the Tanana and the Canadian boundary.[10] Observing that the hunger panic had winnowed out the weak and dependent, he noted that the more self-reliant and persevering had spread out to live off the land and had explored, prospected, and staked new areas. Yet more significantly, these miners were Americans returning from Canada. Accustomed to less restrictive American laws, they expressed dissatisfaction with Canadian laws, especially the royalty imposed on their profits. Since no rich new discoveries had been made in Canada, they were returning to the good-paying districts they had abandoned during the Klondike rush. Creeks and rivers such as Fortymile, American, Seventymile, Coal, and Birch drew them back to the west.

Ray did not underestimate the anger that Americans felt over the restrictive Canadian laws and customs. *The Alaska Mining Record* in Juneau ran a poem expressing the miners' sentiments:

Stay on the Yankee Side of the Line

There is gold in Alaska, and plenty of it too,
But don't rush on to Dawson, for surely if you do,
You'll remember what I've told you in the *Record* of this place,
Which has never printed else but truth about this golden race.
Keep on the side of freedom; I mean don't cross the line,
And millions of our countrymen may settle down and mine,
For the Stars and Stripes are free to all, our canyons and our gold,
And ten percent is robbery—and ten percent, I'm told,
Must be paid up in solid cash or else your claim is lost
And confiscated by the crown regardless of its cost,
Infringing rights and all that's dear, your liberty and time;
Dominion law is slavery; let's brand it as a crime.[11]

The miners further demonstrated their disaffection through the patriotic names they gave to their camps and creeks—Eagle City, Star City,

Nation, Independence, Union Gulch, and Fourth of July Creek.

Before Captain Ray left Alaska in February 1898, he estimated the population of some of the Yukon towns: Fortymile 140, Eagle City 200, Star City 250, Charley River (later called Independence) 180, Coal Creek 75, Circle City 250, Fort Yukon 350, Rampart 500, Tanana nearly 250, and St. Michael 250.[12] Ivy City and Nation City were founded within the year. Tied together by the main thoroughfare of the interior, the Yukon River, these small communities kept abreast of developments within their region and the broader mining community.

The development of the Yukon mining camps paralleled those of the American West in nearly every respect. Like the Rocky Mountain mining camps, the Yukon camps represented the cutting edge of the urban frontier.[13] An unstable population and a lack of planning characterized the camps in both regions. Moreover, these camps appeared almost simultaneously with the opening of the region, preceding, even stimulating, general settlement. They attracted a heterogeneous population, generally young and predominantly male. Quickly the young communities grew and expanded, adding newspapers, churches, schools, debating societies, and literary clubs. Common problems developed: creating municipal governments, raising revenue, enforcing laws and ordinances, and controlling sanitation. Their isolation and ready cash made them attractive markets for goods and services—always at inflated costs. Their townspeople expected and demanded government aid and assistance. They wanted mail service, lenient mining laws, military protection, and territorial government, but not federal regulation. Yet the transitory nature of mining and miners led to rapid decline and eventual abandonment. On the whole mining camps, both in the Rocky Mountains and on the Yukon, failed to evolve into permanent urban communities.

Disaffected American miners funneled back to American soil. First they reexplored and reexamined those creeks and camps within view of the Canadian border. Nearly as quickly they bounded back to the proven grounds near Circle and Birch Creek. The more adventurous and less fortunate continued downriver to investigate minor strikes and break new ground.

Mission Creek, just across the international border, welcomed the first wave of discontented Klondikers. Here the mountains fell away from the river, opening a good townsite on a fifteen-foot-high riverbank. American Creek, a tributary of Mission Creek, had produced gold as

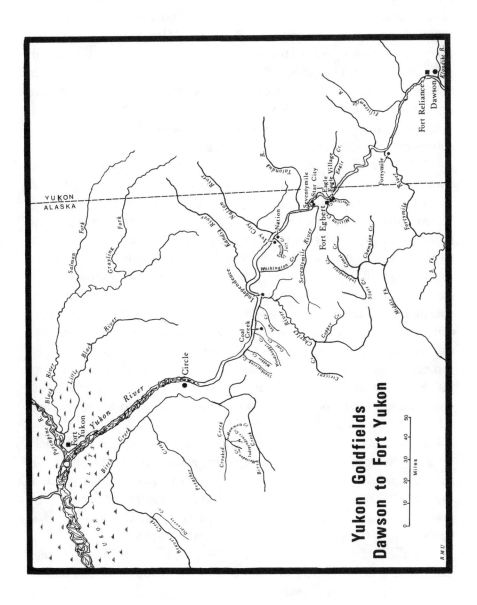

**Yukon Goldfields
Dawson to Fort Yukon**

YUKON
ALASKA

Fort Reliance
Dawson
Klondike R.

Fortymile
Eagle
Eagle Village
Star City
Fort Egbert
Seventymile
Nation
Mission Cr.
Washington
Independence
Charley River
Coal Creek
Circle
Salmon Fork
Grayling Fork
Kandik River
Nation River
Tatonduk R.
Seventymile River
Copper Cr.
State Cr.
Champion Cr.
Crescent Cr.
Woodchopper Cr.
Thanksgiving Cr.
Fort Yukon
Porcupine R.
Black River
Little Black River
Birch Creek
Preacher Creek
Crooked Creek
Mammoth Cr.
Birch Creek
Beaver Cr.
Deadwood Cr.
YUKON FLATS
Yukon River

0 10 20 30 40 50
Miles

R.M.U.

early as 1895. Difficulty in controlling the creek's water, however, had inhibited development, and it was eventually abandoned. When Spurr visited the diggings in 1896, he found a number of men camped at the junction of Mission Creek and the Yukon, not far from François Mercier's abandoned trading post, Belle Isle. Mission Creek had taken its name from an Episcopal mission that Rev. Vincent C. Sims had built next to the trading post but that had been abandoned since 1888. In 1896 the United States Geological Survey estimated that thirty-five miners worked American Creek with an output of $15,000, but the Klondike strike quickly drained this area. In 1897 only the owners of seven claims remained. Each, however, averaged $20 a day.[14]

While American miners worked the Klondike, they discovered and learned new mining methods and adopted old ones that they would later apply to Alaskan creeks. Initially they mined old stream bars, as they had in Fortymile and Stewart rivers and Birch Creek, with gold pan and rocker. Quickly they graduated to gulch diggings that required either the burn-and-drift method or the open-cut and sluicing method. Once these claims had been staked, a few adventurers experimented with bench mining. The gamble paid off. New possibilities for claims arose overnight, and new methods developed. The poorer miner began deeper drift mines, but the miner with capital and labor turned to hydraulic mining, using pressurized water to blast off the deep overburden. When miners returned to American Creek, they noted that the benches were 200 feet deep and that the claims could be 1,320 feet long, which discouraged individual prospecting. Thus, the allowed footage made capital investments worthwhile.

Problems arose, too. The presence of running water at bedrock, even in the coldest weather, made prospecting and drift mining difficult. Moreover, the annual rainfall, eleven inches, and the grade of the creek were not sufficient to create the necessary pressure for hydraulic mining.[15] Despite the drawbacks of American Creek, other Alaskan streams proved not so hostile to Klondike methods.

By the end of the winter of 1897-98, as a result of the discontent and restlessness of American miners, the starvation scare, the lack of unstaked land in the Klondike area, and the growing appreciation for older Alaskan claims, guidebooks reported "a great stampede to American Creek." Finally on May 28, 1898, a group of twenty-eight miners laid out a townsite three miles downriver from a Han Indian village. They called their town Eagle City. Cabin sites were allotted by drawing numbered slips of paper out of a hat and sold for $500 to $1,000. By summer government geologists reported more than 500 cabins and a population of 1,700.[16]

Almost overnight a town sprang forth. A sawmill moved in together with three commercial companies—Alaska Commercial, North American Transportation and Trading, and Alaska Exploration Company, a new firm backed by the Rothschilds of England. As had other mining communities before it, Eagle elected a civil government, consisting of a mayor, councilmen, and police judge. These officials quickly established formal codes for civil, sanitary, and criminal regulation. More than twenty doctors had access to a hospital funded from community donations. Social life included the usual activities associated with saloons and gambling parlors, but also dances, ball games, and a literary club, called the Eagle City Lyceum. The Lyceum sponsored a newspaper, *The Eagle Reporter*, edited by journalist W. D. K. Weimer, with a motto of "Equal rights to all and special privileges to none." An independent and handwritten newspaper, *The Eagle City Tribune*, also provided community news and editorials on the differences between Canadian and American mining laws, customs, and tariffs.[17]

The population boom proved fleeting. Although 140 claims had been staked on American Creek and 71 on Mission, the population dropped to 400.[18] Yet coarse gold, which often determined the quality of the claim, had been found—even a nugget valued at $192.[19] Meanwhile the Secretary of War followed the recommendation of the recently promoted Major Ray and, pending formation of a recognized civil government, included Eagle City within the boundaries of a military reservation associated with the new post Ray had proposed. In late 1899 another gold rush, this time to Nome, almost wiped out the small mining community. Eagle City's location on the Yukon River, supported by services of a military post, government officials, and three of the largest trading companies, saved it from the fate of other gold rush ghost towns.

Simultaneously the spin-off from the Klondike affected nearly every creek and river on the Yukon. Although gold had been discovered in 1887 on the Seventymile River, and men took out fifty dollars a day with rockers, little development occurred. During the summer of 1897 fifteen men averaged $2,500 each on the river, but because of numerous falls and rapids it remained only superficially prospected.[20] During the winter of the starvation scare, 1897-98, miners laid out a townsite, Seventymile City, at the mouth of the Seventymile River. During spring breakup the town flooded, so another was started two miles up the Yukon called Star City.[21] By June 1898 enough people, approximately 250, lived at Star City to qualify for an officially designated post office. In February 1899, when Lieutenant Richardson came through enroute to Eagle, he spent the night at Star City. He thought that it had a good townsite with forty to fifty cabins and a small Alaska Commercial Company store.[22] The population of the towns remained stable at 250 for two years. Then word of the Nome strike hit. By September 1900 Star City and Seventymile City had become ghost towns.

Farther downriver, near the mouth of Fourth of July Creek, another pair of cities began in the summer of 1898. Ivy City and Nation City, founded three miles apart, reflected the optimism on Fourth of July Creek. At Nation City on June 6, 1898, a miners' meeting established the rules for organizing a town: each lot measured fifty by one hundred feet, each block had eight lots, only one lot allowed per person, streets parallel with the river were named and those perpendicular numbered, and streets were forty feet wide. Although sixty-six lots were eventually claimed, by winter Lieutenant Richardson observed only seven or eight cabins. At Ivy City the Arctic Express Company, one of many short-lived commercial companies to spring up during the Klondike rush, built the only commercial building. By 1900 the brief stampede, which had recorded more than one hundred claims on Fourth of July Creek, had proved a disappointment, and the district was abandoned for Nome's greater potential.[23]

When Lieutenant Richardson made his winter trip from Circle to Eagle in February 1899, he met the "emergency relief reindeer herd" near Charley River. During the starvation scare of 1897, Congress had authorized $200,000 for the purchase and shipment of Lapland reindeer herds to provide relief to Dawson. Although experienced Lapp herdsmen were hired, the reindeer's staple diet, caribou moss, did not grow along the route from Haines to Dawson. Only 125 out of 539 reindeer survived to reach Circle two winters later.[24]

While at the mouth of the Charley River, Richardson recorded the beginnings of a small town called Independence. Here eight to ten cabins made up the town, which supplied sixty men mining the Charley River. Todd Creek reported the best prospects, with thirty-cent pans.[25] Although no towns existed, miners described good possibilities on adjacent Sam and Coal creeks.

Disappointed Klondikers also worked their way back to the Birch

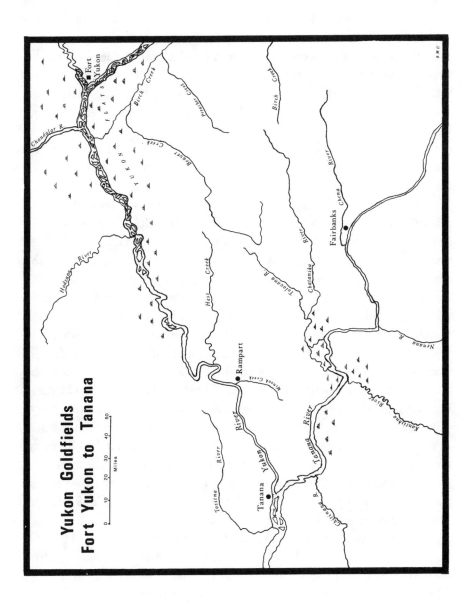

Yukon Goldfields
Fort Yukon to Tanana

Miles
0   10   20   30   40   50

Fort Yukon

Chandalar R.

FLATS

Birch Creek

Preacher Creek

Birch Creek

Beaver Creek

YUKON

Birch Creek

Chena River

Fairbanks

Chatanika River

Hodzana River

Hess Creek

Tolovana R.

Nenana R.

Rampart

Minook Creek

Kantishna River

Tozitna River

Yukon River

Tanana

Tanana River

Chitnia R.

RMU

139

Creek diggings. Samuel Dunham of the Department of Labor predicted that Mastodon and Mammoth creeks would eventually produce as much gold as any ten miles of the Klondike. Because of an even distribution of gold, an output extending over a long period of time, and the employment of large numbers of men, Dunham argued that these mines would produce greater economic benefit to Alaska than the phenomenal production of the Klondike.[26] By January 1, 1899, Circle City had recovered its population of eight hundred people, including Lieutenant Richardson's military camp. But by September all but the army had bolted to Nome.

Miners also returned to the Rampart district still farther downriver. Here in 1882 Edward and Effelin Schieffelin, silver miners from Arizona, may have found some gold. Later, in 1893, John Manook (later spelled Minook) Pavaloff discovered gold on a stream bar on Minook Creek. His discovery followed on the heels of the Birch Creek strike found by his brother, Pitka Pavaloff, and his brother-in-law, Sergi Cherosky. Three years later miners seriously began to work the coarse gold lying in the deeply incised canyons draining Minook Creek. That same year, 1896, the town of Rampart was platted. Small mining operations, using only the shovel and sluice box, worked the surrounding creeks. Little Minook Creek became the major producing stream. Following the backwash of the Klondike, more sophisticated miners arrived and began hydraulic plants on most of the producing creeks. But as on American Creek, the lack of an adequate water supply caused many to fail. From the Minook drainage, prospectors moved across the divide into other drainage systems but never struck productive placers. Meanwhile the community boomed to 923 persons, who lived in 423 cabins. With a development similar to Eagle City, Rampart established a post office, sprouted several commercial companies and saloons, and stimulated two newspapers, *The Alaska Forum* and *The Yukon Valley News*. Like Eagle, the Native village set itself apart from the white community.[27]

Latecomers to the Klondike, in 1898, heard rumors of gold discoveries in the headwaters of the Koyukuk River. More than two hundred men stampeded to the region. Gordon Bettles, an early Yukon sourdough, started a store, and eventually a town named for him evolved around it. Although John Bremner had explored the Koyukuk in 1888 prior to his murder, N. V. Hendrick found the first successful mine for the area. In 1893 Hendrick took a steamer as far as he could go, found color on Tramway Bar, built a ditch, and mined a quantity of gold.

Would-be Klondikers responded enthusiastically to old mining tales of the Koyukuk, but few found enough gold to pay their expenses.[28]

The massive movement of people during the Klondike gold rush had a profound effect on the Han and Kutchin Indians, especially those groups adjacent to the booming communities of Dawson, Eagle, Circle, and Rampart. Not only did the Indians confront white miners on the Yukon but on every stream, valley, and even mountain ridge. No other group of Indians, except those of the California area, experienced anything so intense or so consequential. White men's tools proved more efficient than the aboriginal, most remarkably the fish wheel and the repeating rifle. The traditional shelters—the moss house and the caribou skin house—gave way to log cabins and canvas tents. Furthermore, Indians found their territory governed by two political systems, American and Canadian. The gold rush not only accelerated acculturation but destroyed the few remaining vestiges of traditional culture. Every facet of Han and Kutchin culture suffered serious impact.[29]

Overall the backwash from the Klondike stampede resulted in thorough exploration of the Alaskan Yukon. During the three and a half years of the Klondike rush, the Alaskan Yukon placers produced nearly $2 million.[30] A few settlements flourished briefly until drained by news of the latest strike. This pattern would be repeated several times. After each new stampede, disenchanted miners would return to the old slow but steady diggings of the Alaskan Yukon. These miners of the Klondike frontier had been tempered and trained by it. They learned that the trail to gold in the North was unforgiving and could involve the forfeiture of their lives. They accepted the bitter lesson that the commercial companies were undependable. Paying more than $1,300 yearly in food, shelter, and equipment, they had to pack the 1,500 pounds to the mines on their backs.[31] If the mines failed to produce, the miners were stranded, dependent upon the charity of these same commercial companies. As miners they faced disappointment, starvation, hardship, and isolation. Yet many stayed on to search for the next bonanza and, in so doing, made the country an easier place to live for those who followed.

CHAPTER 7

The Soldier's Frontier

"The lines of the Army have advanced simultaneously with the advance of the settler along our vast frontiers," observed the Senate Committee on Military Affairs in a report of 1900 on military activities in Alaska. "It has been the uniform policy of the Government," continued the committee,

> to foster the development of the country by exploring and opening up trails for emigrants and prospectors, convoying their supplies, aiding in the transmission of their mail, in all things extending a helping hand to them, and in keeping step with the advance of civilization. . . . Wherever [the emigrant] went he found that somewhere or somehow the military branch of the Government had with wise, unerring foresight established posts for his protection and relief.[1]

In truth, the army had not always kept pace even with America's continental frontier, and the prospectors of Fortymile and Circle City would have been astounded by the claim that the army had aided them with exploration, roads, law and order, or anything else. On earlier frontiers an Indian-fighting mission had moved the army to try to keep up with the emigrant and settler, and such services as it provided to civilians were largely a by-product of this mission. In Alaska no Indian threat materialized, and the army, preoccupied as always with preparations for foreign war, made no preparations for a frontier mission in Alaska.[2] Unlike the North-West Mounted Police, which United States military officers admired, the army did not even think of reaching for the goals stated by the Senate Committee until the violence and chaos of the Klondike dramatized the need.

The army could claim only a slight shadow of military presence on the Yukon during the winter of Dawson's "starvation scare." It took the form of two officers, Capt. Patrick H. Ray and Lt. Wilds P. Richardson They arrived on the river in late August 1897 bearing orders from the Secretary of War to investigate and report on conditions created by the rush to the Klondike. Later in the year Lt. Col. George M. Randall established a post at St. Michael with two officers, a surgeon, and twenty-five infantrymen, and two officers were sent to Dyea to look into conditions at the United States end of the Chilkoot Trail; but on the Yukon itself only Ray and Richardson represented United States military authority.[3]

Ray's informative reports to the Adjutant General of the army during the winter of 1897–98 laid the groundwork for the development of military policy toward Alaska. The disorder and lawlessness Ray observed at Circle and later at Fort Yukon, especially as thousands of disappointed Klondikers began to stream back to United States soil, led him to conclude that the civil authorities holding office under the weak provisions of the 1884 Organic Act, which set up Alaska as a civil and judicial "district," could not protect life and property. Ray therefore submitted a series of major recommendations aimed at readying the army to take over the mission, and all gained War Department sanction. Most immediately, he proposed that a detachment of troops be sent to St. Michael to preserve order during the winter of 1897. Less than two months later, Colonel Randall arrived. In addition, Ray recommended the establishment of two posts on the Yukon, one at Mission Creek near the international boundary and one at the mouth of the Tanana. Second, he encouraged the exploration and survey of "all-American" routes to the river, one from Cook Inlet and one from Prince William Sound. Third, he suggested a cutter or gunboat patrol of the river to help maintain law and order. Fourth, he advocated the opening of roads to assist mining and other development. Finally, by February 1898, when he left the Yukon by dog team, he concluded that food stocks were ample to see the miners through the winter, and he therefore urged cancellation of proposed relief expeditions.[4]

Meanwhile, events in Skagway and Dyea drew the attention of the army. Canadian officials had sent the North-West Mounted Police to the summits of Chilkoot and White passes to provide order to the miners and adventurers who crossed the coastal mountains to reach the Klondike. Americans looked on the passes as disputed territory, but the

Mounties not only enforced Canadian law, but collected customs and barred anyone traveling with less than a thousand pounds of provisions.

Below, in clearly undisputed United States territory, the contrast with red-coated law could hardly have been more pronounced. At Skagway and Dyea, steamships landed "gamblers, thugs, and leud [sic] women from the worst quarters of the coast."[5] Exemplifying the lawlessness, one man had organized con artists, pimps, and cutthroats into a powerful syndicate since October 1897. A Georgian in his mid-thirties, Jefferson Smith had a stocky build, square-set jaw, and dark, intense eyes that radiated magnetism. He became known as "Soapy" Smith because of a con game he designed around the selling of soap. When one of his bartenders killed a deputy marshal and another man, Soapy adeptly hid his employee but headed a subscription drive for the deputy's widow. Then he convinced the United States Commissioner, a good friend, to deputize ten guards to escort the accused murder to a steamer ready to debark. To no one's surprise, the man escaped while in their custody.

Outcries from Alaska's Governor John G. Brady and reputable merchants and citizens of Skagway and Dyea poured into the office of the Secretary of War. Because no laws allowed the communities to organize a municipal government and because the federal officials either reeked of corruption, as the United States Commissioner, or felt powerless, as the deputy marshall, the governor begged for federal troops to preserve law and order and at the same time support United States boundary claims. Without further prompting, Secretary of War Russell A. Alger rushed four companies of infantry under Col. Thomas M. Anderson to the Alaska panhandle.[6] During the next six months the army succeeded in establishing amicable relations with Canadian authorities—a cordiality that prevailed until a provisional boundary could be agreed to in 1899. At the same time, the army prevented hostilities between the Chilkats and Jack Dalton and his trail builders. And in July 1898 the army intervened to prevent a full-scale lynching party when the Skagway community rose against Soapy Smith. Killed in a shootout with a vigilante leader, Smith did not live to see the dissolution of his empire and the rise of the first Alaskan city to be incorporated with its own municipal government—an honor it shared with Juneau.

As crises bubbled just below the surface at Skagway and Dyea, the War Department moved to carry out Captain Ray's recommendations. Canceling the planned relief expedition to save starving miners, Maj.

Gen. Henry C. Merriam, commanding the Department of the Columbia at Vancouver Barracks, instead organized three exploring parties. All three were designed to rely for transportation on reindeer initially purchased for the relief expedition. Although the reindeer arrived at Haines Mission in time for the summer exploration season, the lack of reindeer moss for forage left them more dead than alive. Eventually enough recovered to travel the Dalton Trail to the Yukon and down to Circle, but in the meantime the three expeditions found themselves without pack animals of any kind.

Orders for the expeditions included penetrating Alaska's interior and ascertaining practicable routes to the goldfields. The first expedition was to leave Skagway or Dyea along the Dalton Trail to Dawson and from there to Belle Isle near the 141st meridian. This expedition, however, never got started because of the problems with the reindeer, and higher officers eventually determined it to be unnecessary. The second expedition received orders to explore the valley of the Copper River and its tributaries and proceed over the mountains and down to the Tanana River. The third party was to determine the most direct route from Cook Inlet to the Copper River and the Fortymile area.

Capt. William R. Abercrombie led the Copper River Exploring Expedition. In 1884 he had tentatively probed the Copper River Delta but had failed to negotiate the glaciers and the marsh. He learned, however, of a shortcut portage to the Copper via Port Valdez. Leaving Seattle on April 8, 1898, he repaired first to Haines Mission only to discover that the reindeer could not be used and that Colonel Anderson could not authorize use of his pack mules. Pushing on to Valdez, Abercrombie planned to proceed on foot. After a few exploratory ventures, however, he decided that attempting to cross the Valdez Glacier pulling sleds would destroy his command, and he returned to Seattle to acquire forty head of horses.

By mid-June sickness and reassignments had reduced Abercrombie's officer complement to one other, Lt. P. G. Lowe—"a man to be killed but not conquered."[7] With three men and eleven pack animals, Lowe set out to trace an all-American route from Valdez to the Yukon following Lieutenant Allen's trail of 1885 up the Copper River, over Mentasta Pass, up the Tanana, and thence to the Yukon by way of the Fortymile. He reached the Yukon after the last steamer had left for St. Michael. Not wishing to spend the winter in Alaska, Lowe and his men boarded a steamer headed up the river with supplies for Canadian troops at Fort

Selkirk. From there they went on to the summit of White Pass and rode the narrow-gauge railroad to Skagway.

Meanwhile, Abercrombie sent out a number of expeditions to explore the routes across the Valdez Glacier as well as those through Keystone Canyon and on through Thompson Pass to the Copper River Valley. The United States Geological Survey lent the War Department F. C. Schrader to explore and map Prince William Sound and the Copper River tributaries. Although some historians minimize Abercrombie's achievement, contending that miners led the way, by the end of Abercrombie's summer the Copper River was explored and mapped and an all-American route surveyed to the Yukon.[8]

Capt. Edward F. Glenn led the third expedition from Cook Inlet to the Yukon. He left Vancouver Barracks with Abercrombie and arrived at Haines Mission to learn that the reindeer could not be used for transportation and packing. Unlike Abercrombie, Glenn acquired pack animals without official authorization, and at ice-free Resurrection Bay (near the present town of Seward), he assigned a party to explore northward to Cook Inlet. W. C. Mendenhall, on loan from the United States Geological Survey, mapped this route, which the Alaska Railroad later followed. Reaching Cook Inlet, Glenn dispatched other parties to survey the river valley opening on it—the Susitna, Chickaloon, Talkeenta, Chulitna, and Matanuska.[9]

The most difficult task Glenn assigned to Lt. J. C. Castner—to follow the Matanuska River to its headwaters and down the Delta River to the Tanana, then across the Tanana Highlands to the Yukon. Accompanied by only two men and two mules, Castner barely survived. He attempted to ascend the Goodpaster, known then as the Volkmar, without adequate food or equipment. Cutting his men to half rations and killing his last mule, Castner pushed on. After great hardship, he reached the Yukon just as freeze-up began. Waiting until he could travel by dog team, he moved up the Yukon, reaching the White Pass Railroad at Bennett on January 23, 1899. Despite Castner's trials and near tragedies, he contributed little that was not already known of interior routes. His report, nonetheless, glowed with praise for the Indians who time and again saved his life and those of his men.[10]

The significance of the Abercrombie and Glenn expeditions lies not in opening new routes but in officially mapping and recording those that miners and Indians already used. On nearly every river the explorers traced, they met miners and sometimes even geologists of the United

States Geological Survey. For the most part, the military surveyors carried out their mission conscientiously and at risk to their lives. Abercrombie and Glenn made recommendations for trails and even railroad routes, and both commented on agricultural potential, timber and mineral exploitation, and the general state of the Indians. By the end of the field season of 1898, the area south of the Tanana River between the Susitna River and the Wrangell Mountains had been throughly surveyed. The most reasonable routes to the Yukon were clearly mapped and even some elementary trail work begun.

While the two exploring teams worked their way toward the Yukon, the army moved to establish itself more firmly on the river. Colonel Randall had departed St. Michael, leaving Wilds P. Richardson, now a captain, the senior officer on the Yukon. Alarmed by the influx of disappointed and nearly destitute miners, Richardson in July 1898 urged that troops with relief supplies be stationed at Rampart City, Fort Yukon, and Circle City. General Merriam responded at once by sending reinforcements to St. Michael. Richardson strongly believed that soldiers were essential to protect lives and property, and he greeted the new troops with great relief. Still, available steamboats limited the number he could bring up the river. Leaving 76 under a lieutenant at St. Michael, he divided the remainder, about 110, between Rampart City and Circle City. He himself took station at Circle.[11]

As Richardson and his men settled in at Circle, he found the civil law fragile, and miners opposed to the arrival of troops. Miners preferred to dispense law and order through their institutions, chiefly the miners' meetings. Still, Richardson attempted to establish a simple town government. He called a series of town meetings to discuss fire protection, sanitation, and care for the destitute. During the third meeting the town voted overwhelmingly to abolish all forms of government. Discouraged, Richardson unilaterally adopted regulations regarding the sale of liquor to Natives, carrying concealed weapons, and establishing a military patrol to enforce law and order. Of all civil authorities, he approved of only the United States Commissioner. The others—the customs agent, deputy marshal, and land registrar—were corrupt or incompetent. Throughout the winter Richardson succeeded in communicating with his troops along the river and initiating a winter patrol to Eagle near the international boundary.[12]

Meanwhile, the detachment at Fort St. Michael found itself occupied with maintaining law and order on the Seward Peninsula. Following the gold rush to Cape Nome in the late fall of 1898, the military was called there to provide protection against claim jumping, destruction of location notices, lynching, and general chaos. Lt. O. L. Spaulding was sent with five enlisted men to the Nome area to assess the situation and help transport the last of the reindeer from the relief expedition of 1897, sent to shipwrecked sailors at Point Barrow. Meanwhile, the Kotzebue Sound and Koyukuk River gold rushes failed miserably, and St. Michael was besieged with starving, scurvy-ridden, destitute miners. St. Michael's commander, Capt. E. S. Walker, posted notices on all trails to discourage prospective miners. As time passed, the garrison at St. Michael spent more and more time on matters relating to the Seward Peninsula.[13]

While troops struggled to maintain law and order on the Yukon, department headquarters continued to operate on Captain Ray's recommendations of 1897. Thus, despite Richardson's suggestion that Circle be selected for a military reservation, orders arrived in March for him to mark off a tract of land near Eagle. Moreover, following Ray's recommendations for a minimum of three forts in Alaska, the War Department in 1899 established the District of North Alaska and assigned Ray, now a major, as district commander. On July 8, 1899, he arrived at St. Michael to assume command. Accompanying him were three companies of the Seventh Infantry to establish and man a post at the mouth of the Tanana to be called Fort Gibson and one at Eagle to be called Fort Egbert.

As Ray moved north to establish the new district, exploring expeditions continued from Cook Inlet and Prince William Sound. Capt. Edward Glenn again directed operations from Cook Inlet. Although he sent out four expeditions, only one contributed new geographical knowledge. Lt. Joseph S. Herron, with a surgeon, two enlisted men, two packers, and two Native guides, ascended the Yenta, a tributary of the Susitna, crossed the Alaska Range, and descended the Kuskokwim's South Fork. Here his guides abandoned him, and the party wandered lost for weeks. He attempted to float to an Indian village, but the raft wrecked and left the men without rations or equipment. Worn out and nearly destitute, they staggered into an Indian village, whose people fed and cared for them for two months. Guided by these Indians, Herron continued north to a tributary of the Tanana River and arrived on the Yukon on December 11, 1899. Despite tremendous hardship, he had successfully explored the upper Kuskokwim and completed the most original and detailed

Early Fort Egbert. In 1899 the War Department established three forts on the Yukon. Lt. W. P. Richardson began Fort Egbert near the international boundary. For the first several years the soldiers constructed log buildings and lived under rustic conditions. *National Archives.*

exploration of any of those conducted in 1898 and 1899.[14] Glenn's other three expeditions failed to achieve much beyond determining the limits of navigation of the Susitna and its tributaries.

Captain Abercrombie's assignment, unlike Glenn's, differed in scope from his of the previous year. This time his orders included building a military road from Valdez on Prince William Sound to Copper Center on the Copper River and on to Eagle—a response to still another of Ray's initial recommendations. In addition to road building, Abercrombie sent off two exploratory expeditions—one to the Wrangell Mountains and the other to the headwaters of the Slana River. As part of his assignment he selected a location near Valdez for a military reservation and surveyed it; later it took the name Fort Liscum. Landing at Valdez, he met hundreds of destitute miners, scurvy-ridden and some even mentally deranged. These he handled by establishing primitive hospital facilities and cookhouses. Roadwork moved forward, and by October he had completed ninety-three miles for pack horse, thirty-five miles excavated, and sixty-seven miles cleared and grubbed. In addition he had built twenty-six bridges.[15]

Once again Abercrombie sent an expedition north to the Yukon. This time he chose his quartermaster clerk, John Rice, who followed the route pioneered by Lieutenant Allen and retraced by Lieutenant Lowe. Generally without mishap, Rice and his packer, hunter, and cook made it to the Yukon in forty days—nearly half the time it had taken others to cover essentially the same route. After checking in with Major Ray, Rice turned around and followed the same route in reverse, thus successfully making a round trip to the Yukon within one field season. Moreover, he proved that this all-American route was two hundred miles shorter than the Skagway-Dawson route.[16]

Despite some noteworthy achievements, the United States Army's record of exploration and mapping did not measure up to the level of competence and accomplishment set by the United States Geological Survey. Like the army's exploration team in the American West, those in Alaska were doubly hampered by logistics, inadequate training, and lack of expertise. The scientific corps that John Wesley Powell designed in 1878 proved more ideally suited for exploration and mapping. Led by Alaska's own version of Powell, Alfred Hulse Brooks, the Alaskan division of the Geological Survey took the lead in exploration, mapping, and geological reconnaissance.[17]

As Abercrombie and Glenn concluded the final season of army exploration, Major Ray worked his way up the Yukon in the army's sixty-ton sternwheeler, the *Argo*. At the mouth of the Tanana he dropped off two companies of the Seventh Infantry to erect Fort Gibbon while he continued upriver to his headquarters at Fort Egbert with one company under Capt. W. K. Wright and a detachment of the Hospital Corps (but no medical officer). Enroute he posted small detachments at Rampart and Circle. At Fort Egbert he found Captain Richardson and his twenty-five men hard at work constructing a post. Sheltered in tents, the soldiers had laid the foundations for six buildings—barracks, storehouse, hospital, officers quarters, office, and guardhouse. The onset of winter, however, caught the troops still in tents and the buildings far from complete. Not until December could any be occupied.[18]

The officer left to construct Fort Gibbon was Capt. Charles Stewart Farnsworth, an able young officer who played an important part in Alaska's early military history and whose experiences capture the essence of army life on the Yukon at the turn of the century. Born in Pennsylvania in 1862, Farnsworth graduated from West Point in 1887. He served with the Twenty-fifth Infantry in Dakota Territory and Montana and participated in the suppression of the Sioux Ghost Dance—the nominal end of the Indian wars. After teaching military science and tactics at the University of North Dakota, he transferred to the Ninth Infantry and eventually served as Gen. Adna R. Chaffee's aide and quartermaster in Cuba's Santiago campaign of the Spanish-American War. A conscientious, hard-working, and competent officer, Farnsworth read books on Alaska's history, exploration, and ethnography to prepare for his assignment on the Yukon.[19]

Accompanied by his young son, Robert, and his second wife, Helen, Farnsworth arrived at the site of Fort Gibbon on July 28, 1899, to find a fort composed of tents. Few of the enlisted men boasted carpenter or lumberjack skills, yet all were expected to share in the vigorous and hard labor. With barracks incomplete, they spent most of the winter in lean-tos. Farnsworth rented a one-room log shack with a leaky sod roof. Despite its drawbacks, this shack became the center of social activities for the post. Enlisted men and Indians from the village upriver crowded into the tiny room to eat dessert and listen to Helen Farnsworth play the piano while her black cook sang. Meanwhile winter arrived before shipments of winter clothing, and paydays came erratically and months late. Thus Farnsworth contended with low morale, drunkenness, and desertion. Two men died from pneumonia or consumption. In December, led by Indians, Lt. Joseph Herron and his eight men, bedraggled and lice-covered, knocked on Farnsworth's door. They stayed at the fort until breakup, then moved on upriver and out of Alaska.[20]

Because of the Nome gold rush and the influx of thousands of miners to the Seward Peninsula, on January 19, 1900, the War Department established the Department of Alaska and assigned Brig. Gen. George M. Randall to its command. Upon visiting Nome, Randall observed general lawlessness and disorder. Only the military provided law, order, and sanitation. Undoubtedly as a result of his observations, Congress in 1900 amended the Criminal Codes of 1899 to allow the use of the army as *posse comitatus* in Alaska—the only exception in the United States. Randall also urged that a post be built near the booming town of Nome. Establishing his headquarters at Fort St. Michael, he named Fort Egbert headquarters of the District of North Alaska and established Fort Liscum at Valdez. To connect the parts of his widespread department,

Charles and Helen Farnsworth. In 1899 the Farnsworths arrived at Fort Gibbon, near the mouth of the Tanana. In contrast to the near anarchy at Fort Egbert, Captain Farnsworth commanded a tight post. Within a year, he was assigned to clean up Fort Egbert and construct a telegraph line to Canada. *University of Alaska Archives.*

he pushed for telegraph communications and military roads, especially one joining Fort Liscum and Fort Egbert.[21]

Throughout the winter of 1899–1900, at Fort Gibbon, Farnsworth heard disturbing rumors from Fort Egbert. Supposedly Company L of the Seventh Infantry had lost nearly all its men to desertion. Then letters began to come in from Major Ray and others from Captain Wright. Ray accused Wright of misappropriation and insubordination, while Wright countercharged Ray with misappropriation of public funds. The long winter made Ray more severe and domineering, while Wright retaliated with insubordination and attempted to turn his enlisted men against their commander. The men, taking advantage of the disharmony between the officers and the lax discipline, began drinking and squabbling among themselves and with the townspeople, a condition aggravated by the inclusion of the town of Eagle within the boundaries of the military reservation. Although the charges were distorted and petty, the town and the fort split into quarreling factions.[22]

In contrast to Ray, Farnsworth ran a tight post at Fort Gibbon. He urged missionaries of all faiths to perform services and mass at the fort. Dances, skating parties, minstrel shows, stereo-optical shows, lessons in map reading and Spanish, and an expanding library kept his men busy and out of trouble.[23]

Finally on July 30, 1900, Farnsworth received orders to proceed by river steamer with Company E to Fort Egbert and relieve Captain Wright and Company L. The department's inspector found Wright entirely to blame for the chaos, arrested him, and took him downriver. Meanwhile Ray was ordered back to the States.[24] Although the hard and confining conditions of establishing a new post in Alaska compromised Ray's effectiveness as district commander, the War Department implemented all of his recommendations from 1897–98. He continued to the Philippines, eventually retiring a brigadier general in 1906.

When Farnsworth reached Fort Egbert in late August, he found Company L "the most drunken and worthless company I have ever seen." Disgusted and discouraged, he described the mess: "There was not a semblance of discipline among either the soldiers or civil employees. The men of the company were living all around the post in cabins and were mutinous when ordered to work. The supplies had not arrived at the end of August and the hills were already covered with snow." Fortunately for Farnsworth, Company L left within a week. Digging deeper into the disorder, he found the records of the post incomplete, the quarters insufficient, contracts for wood, hay, and coal unapproved, stables for horses nonexistent, and no quartermaster or other officer of experience.[25]

Several events occurred however, to relieve the pressure on Farnsworth. The passage of the Criminal Codes Act in 1899 and the Civil Codes in 1900 had led to a skeleton civil government, and the Secretary of War agreed to exclude Eagle City from the Fort Egbert Military Reservation. In turn, this decision relieved a major cause of friction between the garrison and the townspeople.[26] Moreover, the authorized abandonment of the Circle City subpost allowed Farnsworth to give Fort Egbert his full attention.

With vigor if not enthusiasm, Farnsworth put his men to work. Some began to build an addition to the barracks. Others caught and dried fish or hunted caribou. A fourteen-man detachment started construction of a telegraph line to meet the Canadian line from Dawson. Although kept well disciplined and busy, the garrison suffered six desertions to Canadian wages of ten dollars a day.

Farnsworth pushed to complete the telegraph hookup before winter and in time for the presidential election returns. He reinforced the construction crew to thirty men. Despite rocky mountains and frozen ground in the last three miles to the boundary, he achieved his goal. On October 29, 1900, Fort Egbert telegraphed the States via Dawson and British Columbia. Later, excited listeners heard that William McKinley had carried the presidential election. Canadians allowed military and civilian messages sent for fifty-six cents per word, and a reply could be expected in five days. Previously, messages took at least a month and more often four. Almost as important, the international telegraph line inspired excellent cooperation between Canada and the United States.[27]

With winter came short daylight hours and severe cold. By mid-November, with temperatures of thirty degrees below zero, the soldiers had completed the stables and the addition to the barracks, caulked all log buildings, and sheathed the storehouse with corrugated iron. Farnsworth conducted daily drills in the drill hall of the barracks. Also, he had secured permission to build a post exchange without cost to the government—exchange profits would pay the soldiers for their labor. A kitchen, dining room, billiard room, barroom, and store occupied the building. "The absence of proper places of amusement and the bad character of the saloons near the reservation," Farnsworth explained to his superior, "render it a very important matter that there should be a good building erected for an exchange."[28]

For Thanksgiving the garrison organized a dance. The soldiers planed the drill-room floor smooth. One officer drove a bobsled pulled by four mules to collect the seventeen women of the town and post while another, dressed in livery green, acted as footman. The dance proved a great success, and at the request of the citizens Farnsworth promised two each month.

As time passed, the Farnsworths discovered many appealing and some less appealing aspects of life at Fort Egbert. For one, Farnsworth became an avid sportsman. On one three-day hunting trip he killed five caribou and fifty ptarmigan. Although the snow and ice made a picturesque setting, temperatures as low as seventy degrees below zero forced everyone to remain inside. Fires in every room consumed more than four hundred cords of wood during the winter, and even then barely kept the rooms warm. Mrs. Farnsworth got "disgusted" with the cold because it burned her lungs. Noses and cheeks got a little frozen, but no one seemed to mind too much. Overall, Farnsworth recognized that Alaska was a hard country for soldiers. "As all the men are on fatigue everyday," he wrote, "they are practically nothing more than day laborers." He worried that none would reenlist for service at Fort Egbert.

Although a teetotaler himself, one of the captain's worst fears was the closing of the canteen, a prospect raised by the temperance agitation back in the States. "The men can be kept fairly well amused without drinking much as we sell beer at twenty-five cents per glass," he reported, "but if the canteen is closed the men will go to the horrible whiskey holes downtown, get crazed by the vile stuff they sell, and get into fights and other troubles, and finally desert." An order abolishing the canteen confirmed Farnsworth's apprehension. Within a month a sergeant and a "worthless" enlisted man deserted. Drunkenness increased threefold.

Aside from the saloons, the relationship between the fort and the town emerged as one of compatibility and cooperation. The military allowed officers of the Department of Justice newly assigned under the Acts of 1899 and 1900 to use the post sawmill to prepare lumber to build the town's courthouse and jail, although the department had to supply the logs and labor. Clubs and meetings brought an intermingling of military and townspeople. Farnsworth participated in the "Wise Men's Club," otherwise known as the "Club of Twelve Cranks," whose members wrote and criticized one another's essays and also gave the keynote speech at the opening of the Presbyterian reading room.[29]

Although interested in the construction of the post and the telegraph line, Farnsworth worried about his wife's health and finally requested a change of station. Relinquishing command to his lieutenant, Benjamin Tillman, he left on June 29, 1901. Farnsworth moved first to San Francisco, then on to the Philippines, Montana, Michigan, and Kansas. In 1910 he returned once again to Alaska to command Fort Gibbon and supervised the abandonment of Fort Egbert the following year. Later, in 1916, he commanded a field battalion and supply base under Gen. John J. Pershing on the Mexican border. With the opening of World War I, he assumed command of the 139th Infantry Brigade, Thirty-seventh Division, and joined the American Expeditionary Force in Europe. He retired in 1925 as a major general but continued an active life until his death in 1955 at the age of ninety-three.[30]

Lieutenant Tillman turned out to be less successful than Captain Farnsworth. He had once displayed leadership ability and a delightful sense of humor, but he had recently been jilted by his southern fiancée and had grown morose, melancholy, and self-absorbed. The men of Farnsworth's original company had completed their enlistment and had returned with him to the States for their release from the service. Tillman thus found himself saddled with a company of green recruits, and he did not handle them well. Because of cold, he held few drills and little target practice, and he punished only a few miscreants with the chore of chopping wood. Without sufficient work and guidance to keep them busy, the men drifted into trouble.

One incident came close to tragedy. Some of the soldiers became embroiled in a saloon brawl that landed a number in jail. Indignation swept the company, followed by an impulsive decision to free their comrades. The noncommissioned officers issued arms and ammunition, formed the men into a column of fours, and marched them toward town. Unknown to the soldiers, however, the United States Deputy Marshal had deputized the citizens, posted them on the roofs of the cabins, and ordered them to shoot any soldiers who attempted to break into the jail. As trappers, hunters, and expert shots, the townsmen could have annihilated the recruits. On the outskirts of town, however, Lieutenant Tillman intercepted the column. In a loud, firm voice, he shouted: "Men, you are going back to the barracks. You may kill me, but I will kill four or five of you before you go any further. Column right, march!"[31] The soldiers marched meekly back to the barracks where Tillman severely reprimanded them. He experienced no further disciplinary problems.

Such misconduct among the soldiers moved government officials to doubt the need for the military. Since army policy had been one of assistance to civil authorities and since government had finally come into its own, territorial politicians and government observers felt that the military appropriations or their equivalent should be made available to the civil authority.[32] These critics, however, overlooked a primary purpose of the military—to improve transportation and communication facilities. More and more, the army in Alaska focused on the telegraph.

The Army Signal Corps took the lead. Its chief, Brig. Gen. Adolphus Washington Greely, had won fame as an arctic explorer, and he now made the Alaska telegraph his personal cause. Even after Captain Farnsworth hooked Fort Egbert to the Canadian telegraph, communication with other Alaskan military installations proved cumbersome and time-consuming. Steamers traversed the Yukon at infrequent intervals. The only other means was by couriers. Moreover, friction with Canada and England over the international boundary made rapid communication important for diplomatic purposes as well as military.

Greely therefore conceived the Washington-Alaska Military Cable and Telegraph—WAMCATS—to extend the line from Fort Egbert to other Alaskan destinations and on to Seattle by undersea cable. In Washington the forceful Greely, backed by the politically astute Secretary of War Elihu Root, pressed hard for congressional funding. As a rugged outdoorsman and arctic expert, Greely minimized neither the logistical difficulties nor the cost. On May 26, 1900, Congress responded with an appropriation of $450,550.[33]

With only a handful of skilled Signal Corpsmen led by Captain Frank Greene, Greely exacted from the Alaskan infantry forces the necessary manpower to build WAMCATS. Simultaneously, at Forts Davis (near Nome), St. Michael, Gibbon, and Egbert, commanders ordered exploration teams to survey the telegraph route. Eager to assess the telegraph's progress, General Greely made his way to Fort St. Michael. With his enthusiasm and dynamic personality, he inspired his men and, for his graying double-forked beard, won the nickname "Old Whiskers." Recognizing the difficulties of laying an underwater cable from Nome to St. Michael, he recommended the straighter shot from Port Safety. Polar ice movement, however, kept breaking the cable, so Greely pushed for increased research into the recently developed wireless telegraph installed in Long Island Sound. With authorization for a submarine cable between Skagway and Juneau, Greely began the long and laborious task of keeping it operational. Meanwhile telegraph crews from Fort St. Michael and Fort Gibbon moved toward each other. "the seasons have seemed to conspire against telegraph construction," complained Captain Greene, "the ground being almost impassably boggy in the fall; the cold intense in the winter; the snow soft and deep in the spring; and now in the summer, hordes of appallingly ferocious mosquitoes drive the men of the working parties to the verge of insanity." The absence of trees and the permafrost presented novel problems. But on November 18, 1901, the line between the two forts was completed.[34]

While crews worked to link western Alaskan posts, Greely pushed to connect Fort Liscum, near Valdez, with Fort Egbert, which in turn joined Canada with the United States. After completion of the Canadian-Alaskan segment in October 1900, Captain Farnsworth, tired of waiting for veteran explorer Capt. William R. Abercrombie to blaze a trail north from Valdez, explored the route as far as Kechumstuk Summit himself. Sam Peter, a Han Indian from Eagle, guided him over an Indian trading trail that proved the most practicable route. Upon his return, Farnsworth set forty-two men to work cutting trail over the route he had reconnoitered. To General Greely he reported the logistical problems: bare rock mountains, frozen ground, steep cliffs above rivers, and insufficient and inappropriate tools.[35]

When Farnsworth transferred to another assignment, construction on the Egbert-Liscum portion of the telegraph line stopped. Lieutenant Tillman had all he could handle with a company of unruly recruits. In the summer of 1901, Greely, concerned about progress of the telegraph line, sent an officer to investigate the problems and recommend solutions. He was a twenty-one-year-old veteran of the Philippine Insurrection, Lt. William "Billy" Mitchell, and he was destined to leave his mark not only on Alaska but on his country's military history. To Mitchell, confident and competent yet also impressionable, the construction of the Alaska telegraph system seemed as important as the Lewis and Clark Expedition, Frémont's trip to California, and the opening of the routes along the Mexican border to the Pacific coast.[36]

Alaska's wild and unknown country enchanted the young officer. As he surveyed the route between Fort Egbert and Fort Liscum, he quickly evaluated the problems: primarily those of transporting supplies. Deep moss, swamp, and muskeg in which mules sank to their knees covered the route. Little could be moved during the summer. In winter, however, with the ground frozen, one mule could pull a sled of two thousand pounds. While others may have made similar observations, Mitchell expounded his into a full theory. "Nobody had tried to freight with horses and mules in winter on account of the cold," he later wrote, and as the dogs could pull comparatively little, almost nothing had been accomplished on the telegraph line. . . . It seemed to me the thing to do was to work through the winter getting the materials out: the wire, insulators, poles, food supplies, and forage; then to actually construct the lines in the summer when we could dig holes in the ground and set the telegraph poles." Thus Mitchell shrugged off old-timer's tales of freezing and other myths of winter.

Greely listened to Mitchell's report and recommendations, then ordered him back to Alaska to build the telegraph line. "I was delighted at the prospect," recalled Mitchell. He wasted no time preparing for his winter assignment.

Mitchell quickly learned a few essentials about intense cold. Leather could not be worn. Rubber cracked at temperatures of thirty degrees below zero. Mercury thermometers froze at thirty-five below and thus served little purpose. Kerosene froze at fifty below, when lamps went out. Iron stuck to ice at forty below. Chilled steel and wooden runners slid more smoothly than regular steel. Mitchell devised special clothing for working in temperatures of sixty below. A parka of heavy bedticking with a hood of wolverine tail lined with marten skin broke the wind and prevented the face from freezing. Fleece-lined mittens of moose skin, three pairs of woolen socks, moccasins, fleeced-lined underwear, wool trousers, and smoked goggles completed the outfit. He also recognized the danger that dressing too warmly caused perspiration, which immediately froze and made all clothing useless.

After a winter reconaissance over the trail, Mitchell organized a transportation system. Carefully selecting matched dog teams, he established a series of caches along the route. When the mule skinners refused to follow, he simply paid them off and hired new ones. When he discovered Fort Egbert's inadequate supplies, he bought or made new equipment. When he ran out of funds, he telegraphed Greely for more and received an astonishing $50,000. Rather than wait for the official warrant from the United States Treasury and lose a winter's work, he immediately obligated the funds for equipment, salaries, and services. "An officer who always follows the letter of the Book of Regulations instead of the spirit seldom gets anywhere," he explained. It was a motto he followed throughout his life. In this instance it worked spectacularly. The telegraph transmission had misplaced a comma, and the actual allocation turned out to be only $5,000. Greely had to request a special appropriation from Congress to cover Mitchell's obligations.

Although many horses and mules had to be shot because of improper care in temperatures of seventy degrees below zero, the work went forward. The crew cut the right-of-way, laid out the telegraph line

William "Billy" Mitchell. In 1901, when the military telegraph floundered at Fort Egbert, the army sent Lt. Billy Mitchell to troubleshoot and then to build the line. He inaugurated winter transportation and summer construction schedules. In addition, he explored the Goodpaster route to Fairbanks. *Library of Congress*.

along the route, and attached buzzer instruments that allowed communication with Fort Egbert. Throughout, Mitchell proved a strong and tireless leader. He personally conducted all reconnaissances, led the crews on their first trip, and kept up constant inspection tours. To prevent complaints and discontent while working in subzero temperatures, he prohibited thermometers. He established a wheelwright's shop at Fort Egbert to make specially modified sleds, harnesses, and horseshoes. These modifications prevented the horses and mules from freezing as they had during the early winter. He even worked out a table that showed the load a sled could bear at various specific temperatures.

During the summer of 1902 Mitchell's crew strung the telegraph line on poles, dried salmon for winter dog food, hunted caribou and cached meat, and built stations at intervals of ten to twenty miles, each with a telegraph office, cabin, stable, and storehouse. On August 24, 1902, at Tanacross Junction, the Fort Liscum line linked up with Fort Egbert's line.

The most difficult job, however, lay ahead. Following the Yukon, the telegraph system from Fort Gibbon to Fort Egbert had mired in the swamps of the Yukon Flats near Circle. Mitchell determined that the better route would be up the Tanana and Goodpaster rivers to Kechumstuk Summit, there to link into the Fort Liscum–Fort Egbert line. Once again with an Indian guide, Chief Joseph, a Kechumstuk Indian, Mitchell personally reconnoitered the trail—the first white man to traverse the Goodpaster. The route was hardly perfect. Portions of the trail had to be blasted, bridges erected over warm water springs, and boats constructed from whipsawed lumber. Still the trail pushed along on schedule. When news of the Fairbanks gold rush reached Dawson and Eagle, the winter telegraph trail became a highway for stampeders.

Summer 1903 brought hordes of mosquitoes to plague both crew and animals. The chopping crews Mitchell remembered as composed of "great bearded fellows in blue denim clothing, high horsehide boots and slouch hats, with remnants of mosquito netting around the edges. Their faces were running sores from the terrible assaults of the mosquitoes and black flies. As they attacked the spruce trees, the forest seemed to fall in front of them."[37]

Time ran tight when the Tanana crew working east failed to meet Mitchell at the appointed spot. Since appropriations were to run out on June 30, 1903, the remaining sixty-five miles had to be surveyed, the right-of-way cut, and the line stretched and erected in only thirty

Pack Train carrying wire for the Trans-Alaskan Telegraph

Construction of the military telegraph system. Mitchell learned that mules and horses could carry more supplies than dogsleds. In winter, pack trains (above) carried wire and other equipment to camps. In summer, the soldiers lived in canvas tents and fought constant battles with mosquitoes (center). Permafrost demanded a novel tripod arrangement to keep the telegraph poles upright (below). *University of Alaska Archives*.

days. The mosquitoes became a terrible scourge and demanded constant smudge fires. Caribou and bear replenished the exhausted meat supply. If a supply boat were to capsize in the rapids of the Tanana, completion of the line would have to be postponed indefinitely. To prevent such a catastrophe, Mitchell personally guided each boat through the rapids. Before the builders reached the Salcha River, a forest fire flamed directly in the path of the line. Nevertheless, on June 27, 1903, with three days to spare, Mitchell himself made the last connection on WAMCATS. Nearly fifteen hundred miles of wire stretched from Ft. St. Michael to Fort Egbert and Fort Liscum at a cost of $617 per mile. "America's last frontier had been roped and hogtied," Mitchell remembered exuberantly.[38]

Despite Mitchell's calm, modest confidence, the construction of the telegraph line had been a monumental achievement. "It is doubted whether in the peaceful annals of the Army," General Greely praised, "there have been met with nobler fortitude by the enlisted men equal conditions of hardship and privation. It is to be understood that the line of the Army has displayed in this work the same energy and endurance as the Signal Corps."[39] Battling unexplored terrain, extremes of climate, and clouds of mosquitoes, inventing new equipment and methods of construction, organizing efficient transportation and supply lines, Greely, Mitchell, and all the other officers and enlisted men conquered the "wedge which cleft open the country to communication."[40]

Billy Mitchell had completed his assignment. He returned to the States and spent time in Cuba and along the Mexican border. During World War I he participated in fourteen major engagements, rose to the rank of brigadier general, and won medals of honor from the French, British, Italian and American governments. In the postwar years he served with the Air Service of the United States Army. From the beginning he perceived the military potential of strategic bombing, airborne forces, and polar air routes. Promoting a stronger air corps, his aggressiveness, self-confidence, and public attacks on the War Department alienated his superiors. Although court-martialed for insubordination, he correctly predicted the Japanese attack on Pearl Harbor and the role of air power in World War II. In 1946, ten years after his early death, the Senate voted him a special medal of honor.

While the army in Alaska focused on the telegraph, on September 30, 1901, the War Department decided to discontinue the Department of Alaska, after only twenty-one months of existence. General Randall returned to Vancouver Barracks and assumed command of the Department of Columbia. The Trans-Alaskan Military Road, the project begun by Captain Abercrombie in 1899 working north from Valdez-Liscum, was turned over to the Signal Corps.

The main occupation of the Regular Army in Alaska became maintenance of the telegraph line. The crews at remote trail stations found life either arduous and dangerous or monotonous. The telegraph line needed constant care: storms, floods, vandals, and avalanches broke it repeatedly and thus necessitated repair in every kind of weather. During its first year of operation, telegraph transmissions were interrupted 206 times. Meanwhile the submarine cable between Valdez and Seattle, finished on October 5, 1904, furnished the last link in the Washington-Alaska Military Cable and Telegraph System. Annual costs for the maintenance of the land line averaged $90,000, whereas the submarine cable, which included the cost of its maintenance ship, the *Burnside*, averaged more than $200,00 yearly. Nonetheless, charges for commercial messages paid for the upkeep of WAMCATS. In fact the telegraph line carried five times more commercial messages than military.[41]

The high cost of maintenance and the success of wireless stations at Fort St. Michael and Safety Harbor brought changes for the military in the rest of Alaska. Initially the army perceived the primitive wireless stations as auxiliaries to the faster land line. But as the wireless developed and land line maintenance costs continued, the army began in 1908 to experiment with wireless stations at Forts Gibbon and Egbert and at the communities of Fairbanks and Circle. The military quickly found that wireless telegraphy was especially adapted to Alaska's topographical and climatic conditions, which made upkeep of land lines so onerous. Within a few years wireless operation proved itself more reliable—less than one day of interrupted service as compared with a total of four to twenty-four days a year for the land lines.[42] Wireless experts and experienced Signal Corpsmen relieved the troops at the posts of the hard labor of maintaining land lines.

With the installation of wireless stations, the military posts settled into quiet routines. Drilling, training, target practice, and other pastimes brought the common peacetime army complaint of alcoholism. One enlisted man at Fort Egbert even "blew his brain out in a fit of desperation because he could not get whiskey." On the other hand, the new leisure led to the expansion of the posts to include gymnasiums, which relieved the sense of isolation and loneliness. The buildings contained basketball courts, shooting galleries, bowling alleys, and other athletic

Fort Egbert, 1907. After completion of the telegraph line, the soldiers kept busy maintaining it. Eventually, wireless telegraph stations eliminated that onerous task, and life slipped into quiet routines. *University of Oregon Special Collections.*

facilities. The main floors accommodated winter field meets and semi-monthly dances. Daily, officers conducted drills followed by lectures. The remaining time men spent perfecting their skills in the gymnasiums. Free time allowed indulgence in practical jokes and pranks, yet also time to appreciate nature's wonders.[43]

The army also played other roles in developing Alaska. The Alaska Road Commission, established by Congress in 1905, was composed of army officers, including Maj. Wilds P. Richardson as its chairman. The commission initiated plans for three hundred miles of wagon roads and twelve hundred miles of trail, designed to open up new areas to mining and to increase production. Still another branch of the army, the Corps of Engineers, dredged St. Michael Canal to provide a sheltered passage for river boats from St. Michael to the mouth of the Yukon.[44]

As Alaska developed, the impact on Alaskan Natives became more and more pronounced. Nearly every annual military report graphically described the deplorable condition of the Natives: "They are exploited by the traders, are debauched by the lower class of whites, and are gradually fading away through disease, dissipation, and starvation."[45] Each commanding officer through to the Secretary of War recommended legislation to provide permanent and adequate relief for the destitute Alaskan Native.

By 1910 changed conditions in Alaska's interior prompted the War Department to reassess its role. Gold development in the mining districts of Fairbanks and the Seward Peninsula had eclipsed the Yukon. The replacement of the land lines with wireless stations required less maintenance. General conditions throughout Alaska had stabilized, and civilian government proved effective. Meanwhile the high cost of supplying Alaskan posts and the shortage of officers forced the commanding general for the Department of the Columbia to recommend the abandonment of the most isolated post, Fort Egbert. Both Fort Davis and Fort Egbert were reduced to a Signal Corps detachment to operate the wireless station. As the years passed, the Chief Signal Officer urged that commercial telegraph companies take over from the military. He could no longer justify military responsibility for the system and requested relief. Finally, in 1922, with the completion of the Alaska Railroad from Seward to Fairbanks, the army abandoned the Yukon, and Forts Gibbon, St. Michael, and Liscum were closed. WAMCATS eventually became the Alaska Communications System, but the Signal Corps continued its operation.[46]

Between 1925 and 1940, the military presence in Alaska was minimal. Fort Seward, constructed near Haines in 1904, housed two hundred men, and two hundred more operated the Alaska Communication System. In 1935 Brig. Gen. William Mitchell, in his last public appearance before his death, pleaded at length in hearings before the House Committee on Military Affairs for recognition of the strategic importance of Alaska. "I believe [that] in the future he who holds Alaska will hold the world," Mitchell declared, "and I think it is the most important strategic place in the world."[47] Not until 1940, however, did Congress appropriate funds for another military installation—not for a base, but for a cold-weather testing station for aircraft near Fairbanks, called Ladd Field.

Finally, when Hitler invaded Norway and Denmark, Congress authorized an army airfield at Anchorage and expanded Ladd Field into a full base. Then as pilots ferried planes to the Soviet Union by way of

Alaska, the necessity for airfields, weather stations, and radio communication networks became obvious. Later, as World War II gained momentum, the army constructed the Alcan Military Highway, which joined Alaska with the rest of the nation. By 1943 the military had more that 152,000 men in Alaska. After the war, the Cold War with the Soviet Union placed even greater strategic importance on Alaska in terms of the national defense, and by 1960 the number of military men had reached 226,127. In total, the Department of Defense had invested billions of dollars in Alaska and boosted the local economy greater than any single industry. Alaska's military value was never questioned again.[48]

Although the American military admired their Canadian counterparts, the North-West Mounted Police, the latter were not without their problems. In contrast to the Americans on their side of the boundary, the Canadians exerted a strong governmental presence. It was so strong in fact that the various federal authorities quarreled and countered each other. The first commissioner, a former officer of the police, resigned within a few months after arriving in Dawson. Shortly thereafter Inspector Charles Constantine, who with shrewd foresight had moved his police force from Fort Cudahy to Dawson in time to prevent disorder, left the country with the emphatic diary entry, "Thank God for the release."[49]

Superintendent Samuel B. Steele, an aggressive, competent administrator, replaced Constantine and expanded the police force from 96 to 288 officers and men. Steele organized his force in two divisions, one in Dawson and the other in Whitehorse, with patrols checking the outlying territory. In addition, he commanded the passes on the Chilkoot and White Pass trails, required a year's supply of provisions for each traveler on the trails, and controlled the recklessness of running the rapids of Miles Canyon. In September 1898, a contingent of 203 men from the Canadian Regular Army joined Steele's police to form the Yukon Field Force. The Canadian government feared that the large number of Americans in the Klondike would attempt to take it over in the name of the United States. All threats and even rumors of threats died with the arrival of the troops.

Like the American army, the responsibilities of the North-West Mounted police extended beyond maintaining law and order. They carried mail and valuable shipments of gold between Dawson and Skagway. Their duties included investigating breaches of federal and territorial laws, making arrests, arranging for trials, supervising prisoners, and

North-West Mounted Police. The Mounted Police were designed as a police force, not an army. Thus they continued to maintain law and order into the twentieth century. They exerted a strong governmental presence and performed a variety of duties. *Yukon Archives*

patrolling all parts of the territory. They looked after the indigent and the Indians. They served as game wardens, fire wardens, custom and tax collectors, coroners, and justices of the peace. Most important, they controlled travel in and out of the Yukon. Registers at ports of entry listed undesirables, who were refused authorization to continue. In short, the police wielded the widest discretionary powers possibly but without abuse. Between 1898 and 1904 three hundred policemen enforced the laws and institutions of Canada—developed not on the Yukon, as in Alaska, but in Ottawa.

The collapse of the Yukon gold economy brought a similar decline in the number of government officials. In 1904 the recently renamed Royal North-West Mounted Police continued with their nearly universal functions. Under orders to build a wagon road from Fort St. John through the Rockies to Dawson, Charles Constantine struggled for two years to no avail: the trail was hardly used. The government reduced the Yukon police force each year until it numbered only seventy-four in 1909. Still, nine permanent detachments patrolled the territory by riverboat, wagon, and dog team.

Despite the hardships, few policemen died in the line of duty. The one tragic exception occurred in the winter of 1910–11. On the annual mail patrol between Dawson and Fort McPherson, four hundred miles apart, an inexperienced officer and three constables set out without a guide. When they encountered bad weather, they lost their trail and wandered lost until they starved to death.

Unlike the American military on the Yukon, the Royal North-West Mounted Police did not lose its function as civil authorities and institutions developed. Designed as a police force, not an army, the Canadian unit continued to enforce law and order throughout the twentieth century. In 1920 it became the Royal Canadian Mounted Police, but its responsibilities remained unchanged.

Thus, the military frontier on the Yukon differed markedly from the earlier frontiers of the American West in one important respect. There were no Indians to subdue. Instead of fighting the invading white man, the Indian embraced his culture, even joined in the pursuit of gold. When supplies ran short or disease struck, Indians as well as miners sought the assistance of the military. Although no major clashes occurred, the army's presence, not unlike that of the North-West Mounted Police across the boundary in Canada, lent a stability and security to the hectic life of the gold rush era. More important, military occupation required improved communication and transportation. The completion of the telegraph line and a few connecting roads and trails alleviated the isolation of the interior and encouraged further settlement.

CHAPTER 8

The Missionary's and Settler's Frontier

Just as the military frontier differed substantially from its counterparts in the American West, the missionary movement also differed and for essentially the same reason—a different native people. Because no Indian group forcefully resisted white intrusion on its land, no federal Indian policy evolved in Alaska. In the American West, on the other hand, the missionary movement and federal Indian policy grew increasingly intertwined. Between 1869 and 1876 President Ulysses S. Grant actively sought the advice of religious leaders on methods for controlling and "civilizing" reservation Indians.[1] But Grant's Peace Policy, as it became known, lacked relevance for Alaska. No reservations contained, controlled, or "civilized" Alaskan Natives. No Indian agents pushed civilizing programs. No religious entity sought to influence a virtually nonexistent federal government. And few churches and schools evangelized Alaskan children.

Missionaries to Alaska during this period were few in number and followed a simple formula. Covering hundreds of miles a year, they focused on converting as many Natives as possible to Christianity rather than emphasizing the more permanent institutions that missionaries in the American West called "civilization." Some, like William Kirkby and Fathers Isadore Clut and Charles Seghers, spent only a few months ministering to Alaska's spiritual needs. Others, like Anglicans Robert McDonald, William Bompas, and Vincent Sims, made itinerant preaching their lifework. Although they established day schools in association with missions at Rampart House and Fortymile, they journeyed throughout the interior, learning the Athapaskan languages and translating common prayers and hymns. But as in the American West, interdenominational rivalry kept the religious fevers high as the Russian Orthodox, Anglican, and Catholic churches competed for Native souls.

From its base at Russian Mission, established in 1845, the Russian Orthodox Church strove to reach as many Natives as possible on the lower river. In 1850 a school taught basic religious tenets, but sporadic and inconsistent instruction limited the church's impact on Natives and whites alike. When the United States acquired Alaska, the Orthodox Church, fearing supply problems, reduced the number of clergymen and parishes there. Zachary Belkhov, a Creole lay reader and protégé of Alaska's first archpriest, serviced the Yukon from 1868 to 1896. Ordained a priest in 1876 and later accused of engaging in "trade and speculation," he followed orders from San Francisco and shifted his headquarters back and forth between Russian Mission and St. Michael. His superiors felt he could be better supervised at St. Michael, but religious competition demanded his presence on the river. Thus he continued to visit each Native village on the lower river at least once a year.[2]

Meanwhile, on the upper river the serious and determined William Carpenter Bompas ministered to the Kutchin Indians. Arriving on the Yukon in 1865 to relieve the gravely ill Robert McDonald, he found him nearly well. Nonetheless, Bompas stayed in western Canada and traveled occasionally to the Yukon. Here, at Fort Yukon in 1869, he met United States Army Capt. Charles W. Raymond, who determined that the English post stood on American soil. Although unable to deny that Fort Yukon was American, neither Bompas nor McDonald could desert the Yukon Indians. They moved their base of operations across the border to Rampart House but continued to tour the Yukon, conducting services and rituals.

In 1873 the Church of England bestowed upon Bompas in London the bishopric of the Selkirk Diocese. At the same time, in addition to his new administrative duties, he acquired an English wife, Charlotte Selina Cox, who followed him back to Canada. Always short-handed, Bompas tackled the impossible. The Fortymile gold rush immediately complicated his work. Accustomed to handling Natives, he found the miners disruptive to the mission he had started in 1891 at Fortymile. He watched in alarm as they introduced alcohol and other baneful influences to "his" Natives. "The advent of white population strengthens the call for missions to the natives," he asserted. With increasing dismay he scrutinized the miners' behavior. When George Matlock shot Washburn in the thigh, Bompas joined with John Healy to solicit

William Carpenter Bompas. In 1865 the Church of England sent Bompas to
Fort Yukon (in Russian territory) to minister to the Kutchin Indians.
Although he later moved to Fortymile and Dawson, he always considered the
Natives, not the miners, as his first responsibility. *University of Alaska
Archives.*

help from the North-West Mounted Police. Although the miners condemned the Canadian laws the Mounties imposed and resented Healy's niggardliness, they respected and admired the devout bishop and his wife. The attitude of the Indians, however, became alarming. Bompas felt they were "only too apt to imitate the careless whites in irreligion and debauchery."[3]

Nevertheless, Bompas tried to minimize the damage to "his flocks" and, at the same time, restrain the conduct of the miners. Because the American Missionary Society of the Protestant Episcopal Church had yet to send missionaries to the upper river, in 1895 Bompas assigned Rev. R.J. Bowen to the new community of Circle. Bowen held Sunday School and religious services in the schoolhouse. He also opened a two-bed hospital financed by local contributions and the Church of England. The discovery of the Klondike gold upset any long-range plans Bompas might have had for his diocese. Despite his difficulty relating to miners, he requested permission to move his Fortymile mission to Dawson. He used as his justification not the thousands of godless miners but the unfortunate and deprived Indians. During the remaining years Bishop Bompas, whose health had never been good, suffered scurvy twice. After the decline of Dawson in 1901, he moved to Caribou Crossing, which later under his influence became Carcross. There in 1906, while Archdeacon Robert McDonald still preached in Winnipeg, Bishop Bompas died.[4]

Word of Protestant activity on the Yukon reached the receptive ear of the Archbishop of Oregon City—Charles John Seghers. Since his return from Alaska in 1877, Seghers had lectured widely on his experiences, visited the southeastern panhandle, and longed to fulfill his dream of an Alaskan mission. But his appointment as archbishop in 1881 removed him physically and ecclesiastically from Alaska. In 1884, when the Catholic church failed to find willing missionaries for the Yukon, Seghers journeyed to Rome. In a special audience with Pope Leo XIII he offered to surrender his archbishopric and return as bishop of Vancouver Diocese. The pope accepted his offer. "I'm going back to Alaska," Seghers joyfully reported.[5]

Although Seghers returned to Victoria in 1885, it was a full year before he found two Jesuit missionaries and a handyman to accompany him. Fifty-year old Pascal Tosi came from a mission in northern Idaho. His heart was weak but his energy and vitality great. Younger and stronger but no less devout, Aloysius Robaut came from Colville, Washington. Rounding out the party was Frank Fuller, who had applied to the Society of Jesus but had never been ordained. Now he served as teacher and handyman. Skilled in mechanics, hunting, and fishing, intelligent and strong, he gained the complete confidence of Seghers. Tosi, however, believed that Fuller was unstable and tended to be suspicious of everyone, and he cautioned against his inclusion in the missionary party.

As bishop and later as archbishop, Seghers had developed a strong personality. Not the least of his characteristics was stubbornness. Moreover, he proved impractical, impetuous, opinionated, and peremptory. Like all complex men, his personality manifested contradictions: meek and humble yet bold and direct; gentle and amiable yet driving and zealous. He refused special privileges and could be a disciplinarian with an iron will. Nonetheless, the forty-seven-year-old bishop was dearly beloved throughout his diocese. And before he departed for Alaska, Pope Leo XIII gave him the personal title of archbishop for his sacrifice. "I leave for Alaska," Seghers wrote an old friend in 1886, "and God knows when, and whether I shall ever return."[6]

Nearly from the beginning Frank Fuller displayed fits of insanity. He maintained that someone was trying to kill him. Several times Tosi had to remove a gun from his possession, but Seghers stubbornly refused to abandon him. As problems and hardships multiplied, Fuller acted more and more paranoid. At Lake Lindeman a Juneau miner, who had accompanied them over the Chilkoot and whom Fuller had disliked intensely, disappeared, never to be seen again. As the party slaved away whipsawing lumber for a boat, Robaut wrote a friend: "Fuller was the worst man in the world to have been our companion, he was good only to disgust everybody."[7] Tensions mounted as Seghers continued to defend Fuller, and Tosi grew impatient and even contemptuous with Seghers's impracticality and frailty. Storms and near disaster at Whitehorse Canyon rubbed tempers raw. At last on September 4 the party reached Arthur Harper's post at the mouth of the Pelly River.

Here Harper reported Protestant competition on the lower Yukon. The news upset Seghers, and the competitive drive urged him to proceed with all haste to Nulato. Meanwhile, personality conflicts reached their peak. Seghers decided to split the group. Tosi and Robaut would establish a mission in the virgin country around Stewart River while Fuller and he would continue to Nulato. The two Jesuits had had their fill of Fuller. Nevertheless, he was practical, handy with a boat, and a good hunter—all the qualities that Seghers lacked. Thus, the decision appeared sound.[8]

With some difficulty, Fuller and Seghers reached Nuklukayet, where they waited for the Yukon to freeze. Seghers began to record in French his observations of Fuller and his increasing insanity. As Fuller grew more and more paranoid, the two, with three Indians, left by dog team for Nulato. Near the mouth of the Koyukuk River, on the morning of November 28, 1886, Fuller shot Seghers with a .44 caliber Winchester rifle. The archbishop died instantly.

The Indians accompanying the Catholic missionaries and the Alaska Commercial Company traders took Fuller, together with Seghers's body, to St. Michael. There the body rested in a temporary grave until permits and permission could be obtained from the Secretary of the Treasury for its further transportation. Not until two years later was the body buried in a permanent grave in Victoria, British Columbia.

In July 1887 a revenue officer escorted Fuller by cutter to stand trial in the Sitka district court. Fuller's defense attorney pleaded insanity, but Fuller insisted he had killed in self-defense. Because of the high cost of transporting witnesses, the government's case was weak. Only one Indian, who spoke no English, and an Alaska Commercial Company trader testified. After a long deliberation the jury found Fuller guilty of manslaughter. Following eight and a half years of imprisonment, he was released and established residence in Portland, Oregon. Later, in a violent quarrel with his neighbor, he was killed.

Because of Seghers's death, the Catholic church made a firm commitment to the Yukon to ensure that he had not died in vain. Tosi had brought word of the murder to San Francisco and urged church authorities to make Seghers's dream a reality. Robaut, meantime, had moved to Anvik and was one of the first to establish Catholicism on the lower Yukon.

Even before Seghers and Catholicism intensified interdenominational rivalry on the Yukon, religious competition throughout the American West increased. In 1881 the government opened Indian reservations to all religious groups. In 1882 leading Protestants founded the Indian Rights Association to work for the welfare and "civilization" of the American Indian. One year later at Lake Mohonk in New York, an annual conference of Protestant reformers met to determine the most expedient means to "Americanize the American Indian."[9] In gen-

Charles John Seghers. In 1877 the Roman Catholic Church assigned Seghers to Alaska for a year. He left so enchanted that he longed to return. Finally in 1886, despite his archbishopric status, he came back to establish a series of missions. En route to Nulato, he was murdered by a companion. *Oregon Province Archives of the Society of Jesus, Gonzaga University.*

eral most Protestants agreed that education, especially agricultural and industrial, provided the key to making the Indian self-supporting. Once the reservations were open to Catholic missionaries and federal funds allocated for Catholic contract schools, religious tensions grew. Despite differences in religious doctrine, Protestant and Catholic missionaries sought identical goals of civilizing and Christianizing the American Indian.

With the passage of the Organic Act of 1884, this religious intensity and competitive drive spread to Alaska, bringing religious rivalry to a new peak. The act provided an appropriation of $25,000 for the education of Alaskan children. Since Natives constituted more than fifteen-sixteenths of the population, responsibility for implementing the provision fell to the Secretary of the Interior and initially to the Office of Indian Affairs. Commissioner J. D. C. Atkins compared Alaskan Natives to Indians of the American West:

> The Alaskan Indians, so called, are hardly to be looked upon as Indians in the sense in which the word is applied to the tribes on our western reservations. They are Alaskans, the native people of the land, who know how to support themselves by the resources of the country and the industries naturally arising there from, are ready to engage in any other industries which may be established there and to assimilate the customs of those who come to settle among them, and are anxious to be educated. They are the laboring class, which needs neither corralling nor feeding nor agencies nor any of the machinery which has sprung up in connection with our Indian service, and to attempt to foist upon them this machinery would be to ignore all the lessons which the last half century of dealings with Indians should have taught this nation, and to repeat over again the old blunders and errors in Indian management.[10]

Nonetheless, with the distance being so great and the appropriation so small, the Office of Indian Affairs felt it could not send a representative to Alaska. Instead, in 1885 the Secretary of the Interior gave responsibility to the Bureau of Education "to establish a public school system, not for the whites and not for the Indians, but for the *people* of Alaska." Immediately the Commissioner of Education looked around for a knowledgeable missionary to whom to delegate the trust. He found Presbyterian Dr. Sheldon Jackson, who had made three trips to Alaska's southeast panhandle and had publicized Alaska's needs through his columns in the *Rocky Mountain Presbyterian*, a book, and countless letters and lectures. The choice was a good one. The man had boundless energy, great political acumen, and tremendous enthusiasm for Alaska. Through his solicitations, other denominations ventured an interest in providing government contract schools in Alaska.[11]

In Indian affairs the separation between church and state had never been fully effected. Since 1819 the federal government had provided religious organizations with subsidies to instruct American Indians. In 1873 Congress abolished subsidies and instituted a concept of government contract schools wherein a fixed sum was paid for each Indian pupil.[12] With Sheldon Jackson's appointment as General Agent for the Bureau of Education, Alaska joined the mainstream of federal Indian policy. Consistent with the precepts of the Indian reform movement, Protestant organizations in Alaska firmly linked Christianity to "civilization" and Americanism. Education provided the medium just as it did in the American West. In addition, contract schools in Alaska attempted to teach agriculture and trades to Native boys and domestic household skills to Native girls.

First to seize the challenge to establish government contract schools on the Yukon was the Protestant Episcopal Mission Board. They selected the Rev. Octavius Parker of Oregon as teacher and first American missionary on the Yukon. He arrived in St. Michael in 1886, expecting the Alaska Commercial Company to provide housing for his family and a building for a school. After a miserable winter, spent sharing the agent's quarters and competing with Russian Orthodox priest Zachary Belkhov for the children, Parker admitted failure. Then in the spring of 1887 a group of Indians from Anvik met Parker at St. Michael and urged him to establish a mission there. Parker liked the Indians and made plans to comply.

To St. Michael in 1887 came Episcopalian John Wight Chapman. The son of a Vermont sheep farmer, Chapman had wanted to become an artist but instead attended New York's General Theological Seminary. Quiet, soft spoken, and modest, the twenty-nine-year-old man left his new fiancée, Mary Seely, to work with the Eskimos of the Bering Sea. Octavius Parker, however, convinced him to join him at Anvik. Since Chapman had never been west of the Green Mountains, he was greatly relieved to share his first missionary assignment with a more experienced colleague.[13] Accompanying Parker and Chapman on their trip to Anvik was Seghers's Jesuit companion, Aloysius Robaut. Although Sheldon Jackson had contracted with both denominations, competitive tensions made travel and early settlement at Anvik uncomfortable. These tensions continued throughout the existence of both missions.

As the Episcopal missionaries established their mission in the former trader's buildings, Robaut greeted Tosi, who had returned to the Yukon with two other Catholic missionaries. Lay Brother Carmelo Giordano stayed with Robaut in Anvik while Tosi set forth to reestablish Seghers's mission at Nulato. Aloysius Ragaru agreed to attempt a mission at Nuklukayet. Although the Anvik Indians had invited Parker to their village, they had thought that he was a trader and did not take readily to Christianity in any form. Furthermore, neither mission had adequate supplies, and hostilities lay just below the surface. In addition, Robaut spent most of the winter of 1887–88 sick with typhoid fever complicated by pneumonia.

In February 1888, the villagers of Koserefsky, forty miles downriver, invited the Catholic missionaries to settle near them. By May Robaut and Giordano began to clear land and set up a mission across the Yukon from the village. The mission later became known as Holy Cross. In September Father Tosi met three sisters of St. Ann in St. Michael and escorted them to Holy Cross, where they agreed to start a boarding school for Native children. This quickly became the most important activity of the mission. By this time Ragaru had abandoned Nuklukayet and settled at Holy Cross. The missionaries decided to concentrate their energies on Holy Cross and Nulato, where Tosi had just built a church.[14]

By 1889, the mission had expanded to three large log buildings. The church measured a spacious thirty feet by twenty feet. The sisters' house stood a story and a half high but seventy-five feet long and twenty feet wide. It functioned as the school as well. The men's house was forty-six feet by twenty-four feet. The mission boasted twenty-seven boarders, who were physically separated from the day school designed for the children and adults of Koserefsky.[15]

During the same year, the sisters began the first experimental large-scale gardening on the Yukon. "On our knees, we tore up the sods with our hands," recalled one sister, "shook out the soil from the roots, and burrowed as deeply as we could, until, little by little, slowly, very slowly, the garden-patch grew to be twenty-two feet square."[16]

Meanwhile, their Episcopal rivals grew more conservatively. Chapman and Parker found their cabins poorly located—too far from the vil-

Anvik. In 1887 Episcopalian John Chapman started a mission and boarding school among the Ingalik Indians. Always short of money and staff, he served until 1931. *University of Alaska Archives.*

lage and undercut by the two rivers. Thus they moved across the Anvik River, opposite the village, and built a cabin that served as home, church, and school. Chapman prided himself on his linguistic skills and spent his first winter learning Ingalik. As the years passed, he translated the Apostles' Creed, prayers, and gospel into Ingalik and Native folk tales into English for the American Ethnological Society.

As other missionaries before him, Chapman had difficulty accepting the Ingalik culture, especially polygyny, shamanism, and semisubterranean houses. "I sometimes wondered," Chapman despaired,

> whether I was destined to spend my life crawling these
> narrow tunnels on my hands and knees, choking in the

smoky interiors . . . where disheveled creatures—hair
uncombed, eyes bleared from . . . smoke . . . and snow
blindness—sucked their fingers after eating their meal of
boiled fish, tucking away the remnants . . . under the
wooden platform upon which they sat by day and slept by
night . . . I saw many things of which I do not care to tell.[17]

When Parker resigned and left Alaska in 1889, Chapman continued alone. Like the Catholics, Chapman believed that isolating a child
from his home through boarding schools was the only effective way of
acculturating and Christianizing him. Lack of funds, however, prevented
Chapman from emulating his more richly endowed rivals. At best, he
could board only three or four students. During the summer of 1891
Chapman had to confront the success of the Catholics. The Holy Cross
Mission sent its steamer, the *St. Michael*, upriver as far as Nulato to
collect boarding students. Three of the oldest mission girls were taken
along as examples.

In every village the sisters were objects of the greatest
interest, [reported a mission priest] while the "samples"
displayed their knowledge of English, civilized deportment
and magnificent costumes with the most admirable
complacency. The result of this expedition was very
satisfactory. Twenty children were collected, and these poor
little creatures, full of vermin and half-naked, were
delighted at the prospect of going down to Holy Cross.[18]

With great frustration Chapman reported the contrasts between
the two missions to his Board of Missions. Not given to despair, before
he left for his first furlough in 1893, Chapman began to build a permanent church.

When Chapman returned to Anvik in the fall of 1894, he brought
his new wife, Mary Seely, who had waited six years for her fiancé; a
medical missionary, Dr. Mary V. Glenton; and a woman schoolteacher.
Dr. Glenton was the first physician on the Yukon and during her three-
year stay contributed to the mission's influence on the lower river.
Nonetheless, the Indians resisted conversion and followed the Russian
Orthodox Church, which tolerated many of their Native traditions and
practices.

While the Catholics at Holy Cross faced similar problems, their
operation contrasted greatly with Anvik's. Their physical plant had
expanded to seven buildings with extensive gardens growing potatoes,

timothy, turnips, cabbage, cauliflower, radishes, carrots, and onions. Moreover, to attract more Natives, the missionaries added a trading post. In 1894 the Roman Catholic Church raised Alaska to a Prefecture Apostolic with its own ecclesiastical jurisdiction, and Father Tosi was appointed as prefect apostolic. Assisting him, Tosi had three other priests, four lay brothers, and ten sisters, compared to a staff of four at Anvik. More than eighty students boarded at Holy Cross while thirty villagers attended the day school.[19] Like Indian children on reservations in the West, the boys at both missions learned carpentry, blacksmithing, gardening, English, reading, and mathematics while the girls learned English, reading, sewing, cooking, gardening, and other domestic skills.

Nulato, upriver from Anvik, was considerably smaller than Holy Cross. While Holy Cross received all the praise, Nulato had a resident priest who may have contributed more to Alaskan ethnology and linguistics than any at the larger mission. In 1898 a thirty-four-year-old Canadian Jesuit, Julius Jetté, arrived in Nulato from training in France. Already a distinguished scholar and able linguist, he set out to become an authority on Native language, manners, beliefs, and traditions. Patient yet enthusiastic, he visited the Koyukons throughout the area. Eventually he translated much Catholic thought into Koyukon. Knowingly, he wrote his superior: "I am indeed very much like a Native on the point of sensitiveness, and this gives me a wonderful facility to understand them and get along with them, for I have only to treat them as I would be treated myself." Even so, he too fought shamans. During his ten years at Nulato he collected data for a Koyukon dictionary, which grew over the next twenty years to 2,344 pages. Although he published a few of his translations, the bulk of his prolific writings remained unpublished as he spent years refining and polishing. He left Nulato in 1906, but his teachings and rapport with the Natives left Catholicism with a firm foundation.[20]

The Bureau of Catholic Indian Missions, established in 1874, pumped money not only into Alaska's missions but throughout the nation. Because the bureau expended larger sums constructing school buildings that could accommodate more Indian students, Catholic contract schools came to outnumber Protestant schools. The conflict between Holy Cross and Anvik illustrated in microcosm the increasing religious competition throughout the West. Assured that basic Protestant values would be taught in public schools, Protestant organizations, such as the Indian Rights Association, began to lobby for abolition of contract schools. They railed against "the Romanizing process" and "the aggression of the Roman Catholic church." Pushing for a separation of church and state, the Protestant missionary societies, in 1892, withdrew from the contract school system and promoted government schools. Congress continued Catholic contract schools with reduced appropriations until 1900 when it terminated the practice altogether.[21]

In Alaska in 1900 appropriations for education ceased with the passage of the act providing for civil government. Now, instead, schools were allowed 50 percent of all taxes and license fees collected from businesses outside incorporated towns. License fees inside incorporated communities stayed there for use in public schools. Then again in 1905 came further change. Congress allocated the entire license fund for roads, schools, and care of the insane. But the act specified that the schools were for "white children and children of mixed blood who lead a civilized life," and responsibility was transferred from the Bureau of Education to the governor of Alaska. Native schools received only $50,000 in contrast to the $145,000 of prior years.[22] These changes created a segregated school system, which continued until mid-century.

Other national and Alaskan events affected the two missions. With the abolition of contract schools, government teachers became part of the staffs at both missions. Then between 1901 and 1904 Sheldon Jackson extended his pet project, reindeer herding, to Holy Cross and Nulato. For the same reasons that reindeer herding failed elsewhere, it failed on the lower river—poor management and uninterested Native herders. At the same time that reindeer herding reached Nulato, the Army Signal Corps established a telegraph station there, and communication with other parts of Alaska and the nation became possible. Not until 1914, however, did Holy Cross acquire a wireless station.

The increase in the number of whites had great influence on the evolution of the missions. The Klondike and Nome gold rushes initiated the white influx, but the last stampede—in 1910 to the Iditarod River, a tributary of the Innoko River—had more immediate impact than the earlier rushes on the Ingalik and Koyukon Natives and the missions of the lower river. Because of its location near the mouth of the Innoko, Holy Cross became the transportation and communication center for the gold fields. Woodcutting for the steamboats provided new wages for Natives and eliminated the need for subsistence activities and trapping. In an effort to control the influence of this new vocation on the Natives, the missions secured woodcutting contracts and used students to fulfill

Holy Cross. In contrast to Protestant Anvik, Roman Catholic Holy Cross grew from a scattering of log cabins (above) to an established community of two-story frame buildings (below). While Anvik reached a peak of only eight staff, Holy Cross boarded 170 children with a staff of twenty or thirty. In the 1930s, the extensive gardens and physical plant were showplaces. *University of Alaska Archives.*

the obligations. Nonetheless, the Iditarod rush exerted a strong secularizing influence over the missionized Ingalik and Koyukon Natives.

Despite nearly twenty years of evangelizing, the success of the missions was slow, with erratic church attendance and continuation of Native cultural traditions, such as dances and ceremonies. By 1900 acrimony, especially between Holy Cross and Koserefsky, had not abated, whereas at Anvik the entire Native village had moved to mission land. Between 1898 and 1914 a wave of epidemics of mumps, measles, whooping cough, diptheria, and influenza devastated the Native population and undermined the missions. Twenty to fifty percent of the Natives succumbed.[23] Then in 1912, to the dismay of the missionaries, the eruption of Mt. Katmai further increased the shamans' power.

The missions, however, persevered. By 1931 Anvik had reached its peak. With an eight-member staff, it was the largest Episcopal mission in Alaska. In that year John Chapman retired after nearly forty-four years on the Yukon. Resigned to the impossibility of Christianizing the Natives, he admitted that "they still remain at heart very much heathens."[24] Chapman's son, Henry, carried on the family tradition. Although the Depression forced the closing of the boarding school, the mission continued until 1948.

By 1931 Holy Cross boarded 170 children and consisted of newly constructed buildings. With the abandonment of the village of Koserefsky, the mission dominated the area. Throughout the 1930s and 1940s it remained a showplace. But by 1955 the old wooden buildings had deteriorated, the Yukon had intruded into the mission gardens, and a large sandbar had cut off Holy Cross from the main channel. The mission closed in 1957, and the children transferred to a new school at Copper Center near Glenallen. Thus, after nearly seventy continuous years, the missionary frontier of the lower Yukon had passed.[25]

Despite the tremendous competition and differences in size between the two denominations, they shared more in common than either cared to admit. Dedication and long-term commitment marked the staff, especially Chapman, Tosi, Jetté, and Robaut. Like their counterparts elsewhere, they subscribed to the dual processes of Americanizing and Christianizing the Natives. Both encountered similar obstacles in overcoming Native resistance and developing local support. Problems with adjacent villages plagued them, especially Holy Cross. The emphasis on boarding schools over day schools proved more effective at Holy Cross, but Anvik and Nulato established greater rapport and influence with nearby villagers. Despite the slow changes, acculturation did occur. Eventually the villages of Koserefsky and Anvik moved to mission land and gave up their semisubterranean dwellings for log houses. Slowly the Natives learned to trust the white man's medicine rather than the shaman's. Like acculturation on the reservations of the West, the process was never complete. Native cultures adjusted, adapted, and accepted certain aspects of the alien culture, but in the end the traditional cultures continued to exist, changed but viable, like the land itself.

On the upper river, the missionary movement differed considerably from the lower river and from the model set on the reservations of the American West. First, mission boards established missions not for Christianizing the Natives but for miners and townspeople in the burgeoning communities created by the Klondike gold rush. Second, few missions were long-term institutions, nor were the missionaries committed to one location but followed parishioners to wherever they were needed. Finally, the upper river missions did not emphasize education but rather spiritual guidance, stability, and solace for lonely men. Thus, the upper river consisted of several competitive denominations scrambling for dominance among the largely white population.[26]

The early gold strikes at Fortymile and Circle stimulated the first American religious impulses on the upper river. In 1894 Father Superior Tosi sent Jesuit William H. Judge from Nulato to Fortymile. A series of accidents prevented him from spending more than a few months there during the next three years. He ended up dividing his time between Holy Cross and the gold camp. In December 1896 he shipped all his supplies, including an organ and a church bell, to Circle, but an early river closing kept him in Fortymile. While the winter waned, he learned of the Klondike strike and moved there instead. He secured a site for a church and a hospital and provided badly needed health care to the boomtown's population. Overworked and poorly clothed, he fell victim to pneumonia and died on January 16, 1899.[27]

Responding more to the Catholic threat than to the spiritual needs of the miners, the American Episcopal Church in 1895 elected Peter Trimble Rowe as bishop of Alaska and charged him with the responsibility of fulfilling the church's religious obligations in Alaska. Born in 1856 to poor Canadian parents, Rowe grew to manhood with an avid interest in the church. After ordination he spent thirteen years on the Michigan frontier. Rugged, robust, broad-shouldered, he enjoyed the trials of frontier living. Intense energy drove his two-hundred-pound frame relentlessly. A keen sense of humor and a sincere feeling of human compassion tempered his drive and ambition. His athletic strength held him in good stead in 1896 as he climbed over Chilkoot Pass, whipsawed a boat, and faced the Yukon rapids. Visiting Fortymile and Circle, he admitted that "our mission here is to the whites and is the only mis-

Peter Trimble Rowe. As Episcopal bishop of Alaska, Rowe journeyed to Alaska in 1895. He believed his duty was to the miners, not the Indians, and so established missions in most of the mining communities. From Thomas Jenkins, *The Man of Alaska: Peter Trimble Rowe.*

sion to the white population in this part of Alaska." However, he respected and appreciated Bishop Bompas's work among the Indians.

When he reached Circle, Rowe concluded that a single mission could serve both the miners and the small population of Indians. He expressed surprise that the Indians had their own Bibles, prayer books, and hymnals—translated years earlier by Robert McDonald. Lacking a church, he held his services in Beaven's Saloon. At this time he heard rumors that a Catholic priest and three nuns from Holy Cross were coming to Circle to start a mission. "Being first on the ground, I determined to occupy it," he declared.[28] Next he convinced the miners to pledge themselves to the Episcopal Church. After five weeks in Circle, Rowe obtained Beaven's Saloon for his mission at the reasonable price of $1,300. Upon his urging Bishop Bompas agreed to send the Reverend Bowen to serve the mission until Rowe could find an American missionary.

Rowe continued downriver, delighting in his wondrous opportunity to bring God to Godless miners. He established St. James Mission three miles upriver from Fort Gibbon. The Reverend Jules Prevost ran the mission and began the Yukon's first newspaper. Rowe floated to Anvik, where the Chapmans entertained him, and he naively contrasted their lives to those of the "filthy pagan polygamists" across the river.[29]

On Rowe's second tour to Alaska in 1898, he met a seriously ill Bompas, whose scurvy, the result of the "starvation" winter, testified to the cleric's dedication to his mission. Indeed, Dawson impressed Rowe only for the quantity of whisky consumed.[30] Back on American soil, he staked out two mission lots at the new tent town of Eagle City. At Circle, he found only 300 men who had forgone the elusive search for gold at the Klondike. Here his minister from St. James Mission, Jules L. Prevost, had replaced Bowen. Prevost brought with him the first printing press on the Yukon, with which he continued to publish the newspaper, *Yukon Press*, that he had begun at St. James.[31] Rowe and Prevost felt certain that Circle would become permanent and that the miners would inevitably return from Dawson. Prevost opened a reading room and fought a losing battle against the making of "hootch."

As long as Rowe was bishop, he had an inviolate rule that he would never establish a mission among the Natives where one of another denomination already existed. Thus, when the Catholic priest Father Judge, who had initially planned a hospital at Circle, moved on to Dawson, Rowe decided that Circle miners required a hospital. Within a year Dr. James L. Watt and Sister Elizabeth Deane, deaconess and nurse, had charge of the new Grace Hospital. The edifice now accommodated seven beds with room for two more. Medical supplies, however, were always scarce. Although the hospital was full, patients had no money. In one year Dr. Watt hospitalized 42 patients, recorded 4 deaths, and treated 167 outpatients. More than half his patients were Indians.[32]

During these first four of his forty-seven years as bishop of Alaska, Rowe saw not only the establishment of his own twenty-four missions, but the spread of missions of other churches. He started hospitals at Valdez, Ketchikan, Fort Yukon, Rampart, Tanana, and a large one at Fairbanks. Tirelessly he journeyed throughout his diocese, offering encouragement, moral support, and even increased funding. He prided himself on being able to speak most of the Native languages and usually preached without interpreters. Though his pace slowed, he continued his trips to Alaska. Finally, on June 1, 1942, after nearly half a century of dedicated religious service, he died of throat cancer.

Among those Rowe enticed to Alaska was Englishman Hudson Stuck, who replaced Jules Prevost and became the Episcopal archdeacon of the Yukon from 1904 to 1920. A brilliant, articulate, and refined gentleman, Stuck also loved the outdoors. He traveled thousands of miles by dog team in the winter and nearly as many during the summer in the church-owned gasoline launch, the *Pelican*. In 1913, despite a slender frame, sunken chest, and persistent cough, he and three other men, including a Native, were the first to climb the highest summit of Mount McKinley.[33]

Despite a short temper and abrupt manner toward whites, Stuck felt compassion and sincere concern for Alaskan Natives. He founded several missions among them and vociferously championed the retention of their language, clothes, and housing. Unlike his religious contemporaries, he worried that missionized Natives were left without the wilderness skills required to make a living, and he criticized efforts to wipe out Native culture. For years he battled the salmon canneries whose fishery on the lower river deprived Natives of their subsistence. In 1908 he established a hospital at Fort Yukon, staffed by Dr. Grafton "Hap" Burke, which provided vitally needed health services to Natives for more than thirty years. In three major books he described his sixteen years among the Alaskan Natives and his other Yukon experiences.[34]

Always pushing his body beyond its endurance, Stuck developed high blood pressure. In 1919, planning to become a professor, he left Alaska. Bishop Rowe, however, was also ill and asked Stuck to take over the diocese. Despite failing health, Stuck returned on the last ship of 1920 only to die within months at the age of fifty-seven, of a stroke and cerebral hemorrhage.

Although Stuck's and Rowe's energetic roamings provided a forceful Episcopal presence, Catholic missionaries had not neglected the upper Yukon. With the death of Father Judge of Dawson, the Father Superior at Holy Cross sent another Jesuit upriver—Father Francis P. Monroe. He was a logical choice. Born in 1855 in France, he came to America in 1888. Immediately he found himself on the western frontier at Fort Benton, Montana, and later as a missionary to the Crow Indians. In 1895, after spending three years on the lower Yukon, he requested permission to make a preliminary excursion into the gold rush area. He visited Fortymile and the few scattered tents that would later become Eagle. At Circle he found more than six hundred miners with whom he celebrated mass.[35] Even then he expressed a desire to establish a mission on the Alaska Yukon.

On August 19, 1899, Father Monroe arrived at the new community of Eagle and rented a cabin for $10 a month. "The water is pouring freely through the roof when the rain is heavy but this is a very common thing here," he wrote stoically. A Catholic family leaving the area offered him a lot with two cabins for $300. The larger cabin became the chapel of St. Francis Xavier. As Monroe settled in, he recorded a number of observations. He recognized that Eagle had been booming in 1898, but the coming of the soldiers and the discovery of Nome had killed the boom. He perceived that the army was not seen favorably, nor was Maj. Patrick H. Ray liked by his fellow officers.

Within three weeks of Father Monroe's arrival, a Presbyterian minister, James W. Kirk, and his wife, Anna, arrived. The austere Jesuit looked with scorn on their money, piano, and luxuries. "They will very likely become a success in town," he reported dourly, "if not in the religious sense at least in some others." With only fifty Catholics, all poor, Monroe expressed little optimism of being able to meet his expenses, let alone match his rivals.

As winter came, Eagle shrank to one hundred people and was destined to shrink further. Nevertheless the Jesuit reported:

> It would seem that Eagle will soon count nobody but the
> storekeepers, the saloon people, and the soldiers. Yet the
> Alaska Commercial Company has just put up a very large
> store and warehouses, and no place on this side of the line,
> St. Michael included, has larger stores, nor is better supplied
> for many things. At least this would tend to prove that
> business people believe in the future of Eagle.[36]

Francis P. Monroe. The Roman Catholic church sent Father Monroe first to Fortymile, then to Eagle, and finally to Fairbanks. He opened hospitals for the miners and visited remote mining camps. *Oregon Province Archives of the Society of Jesus, Gonzaga University.*

Major Ray also promoted the town with plans for a road to Valdez, mail and telegraph service, and eventually a railroad. Father Monroe's Sunday mass, however, drew fewer than ten people. Since the mission resided within the military reservation, Father Monroe sought the army's approval to occupy six more lots. Approval was granted.[37]

As Monroe had predicted, spring breakup coupled with the Nome stampede emptied Eagle of its miners. Despite the declining population, he felt more confident than ever of Eagle's future, primarily because of the telegraph line and the expected railroad. Since his congregation was so small—only three baptisms in the whole year—he began visiting and caring for the poor and the sick. In 1900 civilians could not be admitted to the military hospital, so Monroe opened a small hospital in Eagle. He treated eight, but two died. Since only a few could repay the hospital, the military doctors volunteered their services. The small hospital continued until 1903, when civilians were allowed admittance to the army hospital. Altogether, he cared for 30 people for a total of 730 patient-days. In addition to his weekly mass and hospital work, Father Monroe spent eight weeks of each summer visiting Catholics in Fortymile and Circle.[38]

In the winter of 1902 gold was struck in the Tanana Valley. Everyone rushed along the trail beside the telegraph line to the new town of Fairbanks. Father Monroe requested permission to follow the rush. Finally, in the spring of 1904, he closed St. Francis Xavier. Even after establishing a Catholic church in Fairbanks, however, Father Monroe made occasional visits to minister to the few Catholics in Eagle. He spent twenty years in Fairbanks and another thirteen serving Catholic missions in the panhandle. He died in 1940 at the age of eighty-four.

Meanwhile, Monroe's Protestant rivals in Eagle, James and Anna Kirk, adjusted to the shocking change from city life in Philadelphia. Unlike mission boards of other denominations, the Presbyterian Mission Board often sent to Alaska novice missionaries who had never experienced the trials of frontier living.[39] The Kirks' home had been built of unpeeled logs and unseasoned lumber, but unlike most cabins it boasted a rough board floor. Yet as Monroe observed, the Kirks came prepared to make a home. They brought silver, china, linen, napkins, piano, organ, sewing machine, and washing machine. In contrast to Monroe's opinion, Anna Kirk insisted, "We brought only necessary articles—there is nothing in all those boxes we do not need."[40] Even a church bell called the community to the services, which for a time were held in a saloon.

The Kirks' home became a center for most of the community's social life. Before the summer was out, they had hosted the governor of Alaska, John G. Brady, as he toured the Yukon. Friday evening singing practice, or "musicales," became one of the major events of the week. For miners and soldiers alike, readings, story writing, and refreshments relieved the tedium of winter. Once a military ball was also scheduled for Friday night. The community equivocated over whether attendance would hurt Mrs. Kirk's feelings. Finally Capt. Charles S. Farnsworth recognized the dilemma and changed the date of the ball. Homesick soldiers and wayward miners often found their way into the warmth and hospitality of the Kirks' cabin.

Although idealistic and socially accepted, the Kirks were aware that there was very little money in camp and little permanence to the population. They sadly watched as their best members dashed off to Nome. On the other hand, like Bishop Rowe, they were impressed with the devout and religious Indian services and remarked frequently on Archdeacon McDonald's achievements. Eventually the Kirks met Bishop Bompas, who encouraged them to take charge of the Indian services while he would furnish the books and the interpreter.

Fascinated with the life-styles around them, the Kirks and others of the time described their frontier existence. Moose, caribou, bear, and grouse supplemented a diet of canned or "evaporated" foods that included potatoes, eggs, onions, fruit, and even vinegar. Because the Yukon River contained excessive mud during the summer, water had to be obtained from a nearby spring, bought from a delivery man, or caught from rain by large barrels under the roof. During the winter, the river water became sufficiently clear that holes could be cut in the ice and water hauled by sleds to nearby houses. The high price of fresh vegetables coupled with the long summer days encouraged small kitchen gardens of potatoes, cabbage, turnips, beets, carrots, and lettuce.[41]

More than twenty women followed their husbands to Eagle, which helped to relieve the loneliness and discomforts of frontier living. The customary piles of tin cans and refuse that marked the bachelor's cabin were replaced by kitchen gardens. Drapes, pictures, and oilcloth tablecloths changed the appearance of the rough-hewn cabins. Yet a class of women bore Mrs. Kirk's scorn: "[I] was often heartsick when I saw those bold, degraded persons calling themselves women who were in the place bent on lowering all standards of morality. I never before saw iniquity in its unblushing hideousness, for wickedness does not stalk abroad in

James and Anna Kirk. In 1899 the first Presbyterians arrived on the upper Yukon. After adjusting to Alaska's primitive life-style, the Kirks made their home the social center for the community of Eagle. From James and Anna Kirk, *Pioneer Life in the Yukon Valley, Alaska.*

Life-style at the turn of the century. Most of those who came to the Yukon settled in log cabins such as this. Unlike the earlier miner's lodging, this cabin shows refinement—glazed windows, an oilcloth for the table, a kerosene lamp with shade, and photographs and pictures on the wall. *University of Alaska Archives.*

the big city where law protects the safety and morality of its citizens. I trembled to think of the perils before our young men on the frontier."[42] Fortunately Mrs. Kirk did not observe the gambling in the saloons or on the military post.

For three years the Kirks sponsored much of the community's social life and religious ceremonies. Then in 1902 they were called back to Philadelphia, where Mrs. Kirk became seriously ill and died within a few days. The Presbyterian Board of Home Missions sent the Reverend Charles F. Ensign and his wife, Mary, to replace the Kirks. By this time the population in Eagle had shrunk to fewer than one hundred people. Although the creeks had been staked, there was no mining. Mary Ensign, to help occupy her time, opened a day school for Indian children.[43]

Finally in 1902 the Episcopalians moved into Eagle. Although Bishop Rowe had staked the lots in 1898, not until the Reverend A. R. Hoare arrived did the Indians have their own church. No longer did they have to wait for the biannual meetings sponsored by the Church of England or attend services administered by Presbyterian ministers. In 1905, with a shrinking congregation hardly worth battling over, the Presbyterians surrendered their church in Eagle City to the Episcopalians. This church became known as St. Paul's, while the one in Eagle Village was known as St. John's.[44]

The Klondike and subsequent gold rushes spurred thousands to the Yukon, followed by ministers and priests of nearly all denominations. For the most part, those who came before the Klondike stampede sought to Christianize the Natives and those after to service the whites. While missionaries on the lower Yukon closely paralleled the policies and practices of Protestant and Catholic missionaries on western Indian reservations, those of the upper Yukon shared more in common with the priests and ministers assigned to newly developing western towns and mining camps. Except for the distance from church hierarchy, missions of the upper Yukon were more representative of the parish and town church than the true mission.

Thus, missionaries up and down the river provided stability and basic institutions. They built churches, schools, and hospitals imitative of those on earlier frontiers. They guided spiritual development but often directed and dominated social and cultural activities as well. Frequently missions offered the basis for town settlement. When the Natives on the lower river abandoned their traditional villages, the missions at Holy Cross and Anvik became their communities. Although Nulato remained a Native community, it adapted to a mission on one side and a Signal Corps reservation on the other. The fluctuating towns of the upper river evolved similarly to western mining camps under the influence, if not the direction, of righteous, church-going townspeople.

At the beginning of the twentieth century, semipermanent missions and mining camps developed permanent foundations with the passage of the Criminal and Civil Codes for Alaska. In 1900, after years of lobbying by Alaskan politicians and commercial interests, the new acts provided taxation, licensing, incorporation, and three judicial districts. For the first time Civil Codes allowed Eagle, Nome, Skagway, and Juneau to organize city governments and to collect fees.[45]

Following the Klondike and the passage of the Criminal and Civil Codes, Eagle and Circle proved characteristic of developing communities on the Yukon. Closely tied to Eagle's development was one dynamic man, destined to play an even larger role in the development of Alaska—James Wickersham. On July 15, 1900, within six weeks of the passage of the Civil Codes, he arrived in Eagle as the first judge of the third district. As an aggressive and ambitious young lawyer from Tacoma, Washington, he had attracted the attention of the Republican party. After campaigning hard for the party, he won appointment to the Alaskan judgeship and proved himself an efficient, competent, and prudent judge. As time passed, he kept in touch with politically powerful persons, and eventually politics, not law, became his true love. In Eagle he rented a furnished cabin at Fort Egbert and began to establish a court system. His district stretched from the Arctic Ocean to the Aleutians, a distance of 2,000 miles—half of Alaska and 300,000 square miles. Initially a lack of trained lawyers hampered court settlements. Moreover, the miners had become accustomed to miners' meetings and, as jurists, stubbornly fought the court. Finally, Wickersham adroitly manipulated the miners into accepting the court system by pointing to innate weaknesses in the archaic miners' meetings.[46]

The Civil and Criminal Codes required saloons to pay a $1,000 annual license fee. Other stores paid a fixed percentage of their annual sales. With this money Judge Wickersham built a courthouse and jail. He drew up the plans and specifications, let the contract out to bid, and negotiated with the military officers to use their sawmill. These first public buildings, completed on April 22, 1901, cost a total of $8,000. Wickersham then drew up rules of procedure for cases heard in the Third Judicial District. During 1900–1901, he traveled to other parts of his district, usually by dog team or steamer. In the dead of winter he journeyed to Rampart, more than 520 miles away, and spent 40 nights on the trail.[47]

Meanwhile, with three hundred permanent residents on record, the City of Eagle submitted to Judge Wickersham a petition for incorporation. The petition allowed the establishment of a city council empowered to tax. Fearful of tax burdens, commercial companies fought the election. Of the thirty-three ballots cast, however, only seven opposed incorporation.[48] Thus Eagle became the first incorporated city in interior Alaska, and third only to Skagway and Juneau in all Alaska. Once elected, the seven-man City Council established six standing committees: Streets, Public Lights, and Wharfage; Health, Sewerage, and Police; Taxes and Licenses; Fire Protection and Water Supply; Public Schools, Grounds, and Buildings; and Elections and Claims. These committees dealt with problems confronted by any developing frontier community.[49]

The Indians at Eagle Village found life somewhat more precarious.

James Wickersham. With the passage of the Civil Codes of 1900, Wickersham arrived as the judge for the new third judicial district. Through long travels and constant battles with miners' meetings, he successfully established a court system. Later he moved to Fairbanks and entered politics. *University of Alaska Archives*.

Indians and acculturation. Nearly every explorer and missionary to the Yukon remarked on the deteriorating state of the Natives. Desire for white trade goods permanently changed their economically independent life-style. Disease, cloth clothing, and insufficient food kept them in poor health. This is Chief Joseph and his entire Fortymile band. *University of Alaska Archives.*

With dire results, diseases of tuberculosis and pneumonia attacked the acculturated Indians. The clothing and partial diet also borrowed from the white man kept them in chronic poor health. They caused no trouble; in fact, out of fifty cases of crime on the docket of the Third Judicial District, not one involved an Indian.[50] Nonetheless, Wickersham visited the village regularly as he attempted to compile an Indian dictionary. Otherwise, despite only a mile separation, there was little intermingling between the two communities.

Meanwhile, in Circle City the large store of the Alaska Commercial Company burned down, despite the efforts of soldiers, steamboat crews, and citizens. The loss was more than $17,500. As a result, the Arctic Hook and Ladder Company formed with a twelve-foot fire sleigh. The Nome gold rush caught the fancy of nearly all the miners of Circle, and by the end of 1899 only fifty-five remained. Reverend Prevost had even returned the printing press to Tanana.[51]

Although Circle never became an incorporated city, social and political institutions existed: a United States Commissioner, a United

States Deputy Marshal, a government-supported school for Indians, an Episcopal church for the Indians, and a United States Signal Corps wireless station. Also a few businesses persevered—a jewelry store, three saloons, three commercial companies, and a restaurant.[52]

As civilian institutions established law and order on the Yukon, Wickersham, in 1900, held the first jury trials in a district court in interior Alaska. Prior to 1900 the law required that a jurist be a taxpayer but provided no authorization for taxation until the Civil Codes were passed. A grand jury in Circle brought forth three different indictments of murder, rape, and larceny. The trial juries followed, and the man charged with murder was found guilty of manslaughter. While the larcenist pleaded guilty, the rapist was acquitted.[53]

But the boomtown of Fairbanks attracted the ambitious Wickersham as it had many others along the Yukon. Even before officials in the Department of Justice granted permission to move the Third Judicial District headquarters, Wickersham shifted his base to the dynamic city on the Tanana.

Fairbanks owed its existence to Elbridge Truman "E. T." Barnette. In August 1901, he sought a means around Bates Rapids on the Tanana by steaming up its tributary, the Chena River. Within eight miles of its mouth, however, the steamer went aground, and the captain forced Barnette to unload his supplies. Lacking any choice, Barnette built a log cabin and supply caches and wintered there. Coincidentally, an Italian immigrant seeking a lost creek obtained a grubstake from the happenstance trading post. The following summer, while Barnette left to find additional financial backing, the miner Felix Pedro struck gold.[54]

The stampede during the winter of 1902–3 spawned two rival towns—Fairbanks, named at Wickersham's suggestion for Indiana Senator Charles W. Fairbanks, and Chena, at the junction of that river and the Tanana. In April 1903 Wickersham arrived in Fairbanks and located the government offices there, giving the appearance of "official approval." Next, hoping to win political favors, he recommended that the two major streets be named for congressmen. By this time Fairbanks had five hundred people, its own newspaper selling for five dollars an issue, and a major trading company. During the summer of 1903, miners struck gold on Cleary Creek, the richest stream in the Fairbanks district, and strikes followed on Fairbanks and Ester creeks. Total gold output from the three streams by 1910 amounted to $30 million.[55]

By fall 1903 the town boomed. More than 1,200 people lived in more

Circle, 1910. After the Klondike stampede, Circle settled into a quiet frontier community. A few frame houses contrasted with those of logs, and a few businesses persevered. *University of Alaska Archives.*

than 500 houses. With sufficient population, the town incorporated and elected Barnette as mayor. His new city government developed a school, a volunteer fire department, and a sanitation system. While the City Council granted franchises for utilities and telephone, Barnette opened a bank. Later other businessmen completed a railroad to the mines. Travelers from Dawson in 1904 remarked that Fairbanks resembled the great boomtown itself. By 1905 Fairbanks claimed distinction as the largest city in Alaska. A devastating fire struck in 1906, but the city rebuilt. Even the collapse of Barnette's bank in 1911 failed to upset the booster mentality of its townspeople. Later, with roads to Circle and Valdez and the first government-owned railroad to the sea, the destiny of Fairbanks was secured.

Another secure community, Whitehorse, in Canada's Yukon Territory, differed greatly from mission communities of the lower Yukon and mining supply camps of the upper Yukon. The White Pass and Yukon Railway created Whitehorse. By 1900 the railroad had successfully circumvented the horrors of Miles Canyon and White Horse Rapids. After this difficult accomplishment Whitehorse, at the lower end of White Horse Rapids, became the primary access to the Yukon and largely eclipsed St. Michael as the major Yukon port of entry. Serving as the terminus for the railway and the head of steamer navigation, Whitehorse rapidly grew into a major transportation center and did not fluctuate with the boom-and-bust-cycles of mining stampedes.

As the Klondike boom faded, Whitehorse continued to grow. In 1905 nearby copper deposits came under development, followed by coal and silver-lead. By 1911, when Dawson had fallen on bad times, White-horse boasted eighteen stores, ten hotels, three churches, a newspaper, government offices, and a steady population of eight hundred.[56] Because of the railroad, adjacent mining developments, and government offices, Whitehorse thrived as a viable city while Dawson played on past glories for tourists weaned on the poems of Robert Service and the novels of Jack London and Rex Beach.

As the missionary and early settlement period drew to a close, the Yukon had passed through one more frontier. The missionaries, most of whom had previously experienced frontier life, provided a stabilizing influence on a restless and changing population. At the same time, they observed and recorded the evolution of mining boomtowns and mission villages settling into permanent communities with established institutions. As these communities became more stable and consolidated, religious competition grew less intense and eased into a comfortable coexistence. The missions as a whole contributed immeasurably to the permanence of the communities.

CHAPTER 9

The Transportation Frontier: Riverways

Transportation across the American West had evolved a sophisticated technology built on nearly a hundred years of frontier experience. The rugged, mountainous, forested land of Alaska and western Canada, however, did not lend itself to patterns developed elsewhere. Although traders and miners blazed overland trails in Alaska and Canada, these pathways, unlike the California-Oregon Trail, Santa Fe Trail, and other western trails, bore light traffic. Separated from the rest of the nation by Canada, Alaska's isolation decreed a slower development than that on continental frontiers. Forests, rivers, and mountains posed transportation problems that, coupled with supply problems, prevented the immediate growth of the wagon roads so crucial to the settlement of the American West.[1] Consequently exploration and migration followed navigable rivers, a pattern that resembled the earliest frontiers along the East coast. In fact, the evolution of water travel proceeded step by step along the Yukon just as it had on the lower frontier—only fifty years later. As dependence on river transportation increased, technology and innovation provided a wide range of river crafts, from one-man canoes to multiple-passenger steamboats.

Early English and Russian traders used rough, whipsawed scows, sometimes even rafts, to transport trade goods and furs. Later, as trade increased, poling boats, skin boats, and Indian birchbark canoes took their place on the river. Because the Russians believed that rapids above the mouth of the Tanana made the Yukon impassable, they stayed on the lower river and conveniently avoided confrontation with British interlopers. When the Mackenzie-Porcupine river route became firmly established, Hudson's Bay Company traders used thirty- and forty-foot *bateaux,* or York boats. The company men traded the Indians for fur, which was packed into ninety-pound bales, loaded into the bateaux, and slowly tracked up the Porcupine River. Typically, seven years intervened between the time a shipment of trade goods left England and the arrival of the furs for which it had been bartered.[2]

Lack of supplies caused great problems for Yukon traders, British and Russian alike. Not until American capitalists of ample means invested in Yukon commercial companies were these problems alleviated. With the introduction of the *Yukon* in 1869, Parrott & Company, which later merged with the Alaska Commercial Company, proved that the Yukon River was navigable for more than one thousand miles. Subsequently each spring ocean steamers left their commercial supply base, usually San Francisco, and carried trading goods to St. Michael. From there shallow-draft river steamers continued the journey up the Yukon to trading stations. In late summer the pattern was reversed. The longer and more dangerous routes fell into disuse. The length of time from investment in trading goods to the return in furs shrank to one year, or at the worst two.

Like the early sternwheel steamboats on western rivers, those on the Yukon—the *Yukon, New Racket,* and *St. Michael*—were basic in design and function. They averaged only 70 feet in length but towed three or four barges to carry the cargo and traders. In contrast, contemporary boats on the Mississippi and Missouri rivers in 1870 averaged 150 feet in length with a tonnage of 210.[3] Despite the fact that sophisticated technology existed, steamboating on the Yukon began with technologically simple machinery. Moreover, each frontier—the trans-Appalachian, the trans-Mississippi, and the Yukon—evolved through a similar history, but the innovations and modifications gained from the earlier frontiers expedited and shortened the later ones.

Although accommodations, technology, and crew skill on steamers on western rivers reached their peak in the decade following the Civil War, those on Yukon steamers of the same period were primitive to nonexistent.[4] The accommodations were so limited that at meal times Yukon steamers stopped while the crew and traders took turns eating at a small table. Crews were Indians or Eskimos, and the captain served also as the engineer. As a novice pilot and captain, Jack McQuesten wrote: "It is a wonder to me that we didn't blow her up or sink her as I didn't know anything about steamboating."[5]

The Yukon presented the usual hazards of low water, shifting chan-

Scow. Early miners and traders used log rafts or rough-sawed, flat-bottomed boats called scows to transport themselves and their belongings. Usually they pulled ashore to eat and sleep. *University of Alaska Archives.*

nels, and submerged sand bars. As on other rivers too, machinery break-downs, boiler explosions, and destructive storms occurred frequently. But the Yukon harbored its own unique perils. A sandbar near the entrance to the Apoon channel of the river's mouth, for example, caused chronic steamer groundings. Steep rock outcroppings, ledges, boulders, and rapids in the Ramparts region called for practiced navigation skills. Worst of all, the innumerable shallow channels and dead-end sloughs of the Yukon Flats put all captains to the severest test. Because the main channel changed during breakup, a new shipping channel had to be plotted each spring and Native guides, familiar with the flats, taken on as pilots.

The hard climate of the Yukon added to the problems. Ice closed the river for seven to eight months each year. An early freeze could prevent cargo from reaching the upper river or catch steamers without a proper winter haven. Because the whole length of the Yukon River froze, there was no harbor truly safe from crushing ice. Breakup in the spring produced floating ice and flooding tributaries, threatening wintering vessels. In addition, the frozen Bering Sea kept the mouth of the Yukon locked by ice nearly a month longer than the rest of the river, catastrophically aggravating the upstream flooding. Storms contributed to fluctuating water levels, but spring thaw and glacier melt added other dimensions and concerns. Only for four summer months was river navigation possible.

With the discovery of gold on the Fortymile, activity on the upper river increased, and the Alaska Commercial Company responded with a larger vessel, the *Arctic*. The earlier and smaller crafts had been brought to Alaska aboard ocean steamers, but the Alaska Commercial Company built the *Arctic* in San Francisco, then knocked it down and reassembled it at St. Michael. One hundred twenty-five feet long and thirty feet wide, the *Arctic* was not only the largest boat on the river but the fastest. Routinely each season it made four round trips between St. Michael and Fortymile, and once it made five. In 1889, on its maiden voyage, it hit a snag or a rock and lost most of the provisions for Fortymile. As a result, most of the miners faced starvation rations or found their way to St. Michael. The *Arctic* was the first steamer into the new city of Dawson, but during spring breakup in 1897 it was caught in an ice jam. During efforts to blast it free with gunpowder, workmen accidentally blew up the boat. The salvaged machinery was later installed in a square-nosed barge that became the steamboat *Margaret*.[6]

Meanwhile, in 1892, competition from the North American Transportation and Trading Company appeared with the 175-foot *Portus B. Weare*, which was even larger than the *Arctic*. Portus B. Weare, president of the company, had traveled the Missouri and Mississippi as a fur trader and knew the capabilities of the captains and pilots there. He thought they would be equally good on the Yukon. Weare sent one of them, Capt. E. D. Dixon, to take charge of the river business, freeing John Healy for the commercial establishments. Dixon introduced the Mississippi system of lashing barges ahead or along side of the steamer and pushing them forward instead of pulling them by long hawser.[7] The two strong personalities of Healy and Dixon immediately clashed, resulting in the Alaska Commercial Company snatching up the competent captain. Soon Mississippi, Missouri, Columbia, and even Puget Sound captains and pilots handled all the steamers of the Alaska Commercial Company.

Although the North American Transportation and Trading Company patterned itself after the Alaska Commercial Company, there were some differences. Capt. John C. Barr, a former pilot on the Missouri River, designed the company's steamboats with two boilers, engines, and smokestacks. These powerful steamers pushed barges of even greater tonnage than the Alaska Commercial Company—initially 350 tons but later nearly 900 tons. Moreover, except for a Native pilot, the company hired all white crews. Each company tried to outbuild the other, and steamers grew larger and swifter.[8]

Yet in times of crisis, the two companies could pull together. When miners at Circle City "held-up" steamers from each company during the starvation crisis of 1897, both commercial companies lobbied hard for military protection.[9] They gained not only protection but large profits for transporting military supplies. At the same time the starvation panic also focused the attention of America on the inadequacy of the two commercial companies to supply the Klondike's needs. Almost instantly, in response, new companies sprang up.

During 1897–98 more than thirty transportation companies organized to capitalize on the gold rush trade. Many did not survive the throes of organization, or were merely "paper companies" selling stock to a gullible public without following through on the utilization of the capital. Other companies innocently tried to move the river vessels under their own power from San Francisco to St. Michael. If they arrived at all, they were either unfit for the river or in partially wrecked condition. Still others found themselves totally out-classed by the older and more experienced companies. A few, however, formed under careful and shrewd managers, succeeded in obtaining a foothold in the profitable business of transporting and selling supplies to the argonauts. The most successful of the new companies were the Alaska Exploration Company, the Seattle-Yukon Transportation Company, the Empire Transportation Company, the Canadian Pacific Navigation Company, and the British American Steamship Company.[10]

Two companies formed during the early Klondike illustrate the range in organization and management—the North British American Trading and Transportation Company and the Seattle-Yukon Company. The founder of the North British Company, Pat Galvin, left his job as city marshal of Helena, Montana, during the Panic of 1893 and wandered into the Fortymile country. Capitalizing on George Carmack's discovery on Bonanza Creek, Galvin made a fortune. He planned a trading and transportation company with riverboats, ocean steamers, trading posts, banks, and hotels to break the monopoly of the old-time fur-trading companies, which had not "treated the boys right." Hastening to London with enthusiasm and a silver tongue, he sparked interest among a number of English businessmen, who agreed to provide the capital for the North British Company. In exchange, Galvin put up his Klondike mines and his experience.

With unlimited credit at the Bank of England, Galvin purchased goods in Seattle and contracted for the building of the *Mary Ellen Galvin*. Designed by Galvin, the boat proved a total failure and caused the loss of the best part of the summer. Consequently, his outfit did not leave San Francisco until the end of August, and with only the hope of buying a boat in St. Michael. There he purchased the *Yukoner*, which had made the fastest round trip on record between Dawson and St. Michael, and a barge, the *Maud*.

Galvin enjoyed sharing his wealth and royally scolded an employee who tried to "economize": "Don't show your ignorance by using that cheap outside word. We don't use it here. . . . You must learn the ways of Alaska. That word is not understood in the North. If you have money, spend it; that's what it's for, and that's the way we do business."[11] As a result, he spent or gave away all his cash and headed up the Yukon without a cent for cordwood.

Galvin's outfit started late in September. Groundings and boiler explosions slowed progress. When reaching Dawson that season began to look hopeless, Galvin left the expedition to report to London. Just above Russian Mission, as ice filled the river, the *Yukoner* went into winter quarters. The crew built a warehouse, winterized the vessel, and prepared for a long winter. The choice of food was characteristic of Galvin's personality—fruit, chicken, turkey, roast beef, shrimp, crab, oysters, *paté de fois gras*, anchovies, ham, bacon, fancy crackers, and champagne.

Finally, on June 1, 1899, the *Yukoner* once again emerged on the Yukon and eventually limped into Dawson. Here the crew found Pat Galvin, but also discovered the Dawson market already well stocked, their own goods spoiled or rancid, and the Galvin mines failed. Pat Galvin's whole enterprise had crumbled, and the English businessmen declared bankruptcy. After spending every cent he had, Galvin slipped out of Dawson and later died of cholera in Manila.

In striking contrast to the Galvin fiasco, the Seattle-Yukon Transportation Company expanded to a business with a gross profit of more than a million dollars a year. Founded in 1897 by W. D. Wood, a Seattle lawyer, probate judge, mayor, and state senator, the Seattle-Yukon Company did not wait in winter quarters but pushed on to Dawson by dog team. Developing a fleet of four steamers and as many barges, Wood competed successfully with the Alaska Commercial Company. Instead of Mississippi River captains, he recruited competent Columbia River captains, such as James T. Gray. Others, however, proved less reliable, and some had chronic alcohol problems. During the winter Wood planned ahead and sent an advance agent to contract for 2,200 cords of wood for $15,000 for the summer season. Although Wood had a considerable stock of supplies, he found that business was done primarily by credit, and collections were hard to make.[12]

Wood also found the competition extreme, especially from Canada. In July 1900 the White Pass and Yukon Railway, connecting Skagway and Whitehorse, was completed. Registered as a general transportation company, the railway built wharfage and docking facilities at Whitehorse and placed steamboats on the upper river under the flag of the British Yukon Navigation Company. Because the upper river broke up nearly a month earlier than the lower, and because Skagway was an ice-free port, American transportation companies could stay in the competition only by offering lower rates. As the gold-rush economy collapsed, transportation companies on the lower river responded as their predecessors had on western rivers: they consolidated. In the spring of 1901, Wood and his Seattle-Yukon Company merged with the Alaska Commercial Company, the Alaska Exploration Company, and the Empire Transportation Company to form two companies: the Northern Navigation Company for the river transportation business and the Northern Commercial Company for the mercantile business. Only the North American Transportation and Trading Company remained intact and competitive. Likewise on the upper river, the British Yukon Navigation Company acquired the fleet of its largest competitor.[13]

During the peak years of the Klondike gold rush, 1897 to 1900, no fewer than 137 steamers, tugs, barges, and launches plied the Yukon transporting supplies and passengers.[14] Three steamers suggestive of the palatial packets of the Mississippi marked the peak development of the Yukon sternwheelers. The *Susie, Sarah,* and *Hannah,* built in 1898, measured 223 feet long, 42 feet wide, with a depth of 6 feet, and a gross tonnage of 1,211. They pushed three barges each at a speed of 15 miles per hour. They also catered to the comforts of their passengers with electric lights, steam heat, cold storage plants, and well-ventilated staterooms.[15] Passengers included prospectors, traders, and a few soldiers. Initially gambling, chiefly faro and poker, amused the men until com-

Hannah. During the peak years of the Klondike three sister ships—the *Susie, Sarah,* and *Hannah*—compared with the palatial steamboats of the Mississippi. They measured 223 feet long and 42 feet wide and pushed three barges at a speed of fifteen miles per hour. The photograph shows the great quantities of firewood needed to power the large boats, especially in contrast to the few passengers. *University of Alaska Archives.*

Steamboats such as the *Hannah* catered to the comfort of their passengers with electric lights, steam heat, cold storage plants, and large dining halls such as this. *University of Alaska Archives.*

pany officials banned it. Occasionally a talented dance-hall woman told stories, danced, sang, and joked to while away the time.

During the heyday of the steamboat, the Treasury Department assigned a vessel of the Revenue-Cutter Service, the *Nunivak*, to the Yukon River to enforce customs and navigation laws. Although Capt. Patrick H. Ray recommended in 1897 that a cutter or gunboat be stationed on the river during its open season, not until April 24, 1899, did 1st Lt. John C. Cantwell receive orders to take the *Nunivak* to the Yukon to ensure law and order. He was to assist destitute miners, aid civil and military authorities, establish astronomical stations, compile charts of the Yukon and its tributaries, and collect data on the flora, fauna, and Indians of the area. His ship resembled other steamers on the river—209 feet long, 35 feet wide, and 6 feet deep with two tandem engines. While most were built in San Francisco and reassembled in St. Michael, an ocean steamer towed the *Nunivak* from San Francisco. As soon as Cantwell reached St. Michael, he began to board steamers and found nearly all lacking some requirements of the law. For two summers, limited by his orders to stay within one thousand miles from the Yukon's mouth, Cantwell powered between St. Michael and Rampart. He assisted stranded miners, provided health care for Natives, charted the Yukon, and ensured compliance with laws. During the winters of 1899–1900 and 1900–1901, he placed the *Nunivak* in winter quarters on the Dall River, upriver from Rampart. Here from October to mid-May he kept his men occupied with drills, wood-cutting, hunting parties, and reconnaissances up the Dall and Koyukuk rivers. Finally in September 1901, following orders, Cantwell took the *Nunivak* to St. Michael, hauled it out on the beach, and placed it in winter quarters with a small force of caretakers. He returned to San Francisco, and the federal government's only official Yukon steamer ended on the auction block.[16]

Like their predecessors on other large rivers, the captains frequently raced their steamers up and down the Yukon. On July 12, 1900, when the *Rock Island* blew a cylinder head within a few miles of Dawson, it lost 110 passengers to the *Sarah*. But one of the more exciting races tested the two fastest boats of the North American Company—the *T. C. Powers* and the *John Cudahy*. They raced from Dawson to St. Michael loaded with five hundred stampeders for Nome. Strangely no newspaper recorded this wild and exciting race, but steamboat men talked of it for years.[17]

Since the Yukon River's channel changed frequently, with innumerable submerged sandbars, each steamboat came equipped with heavy spars and tackle on the forward deck. With this outfit a vessel could almost lift itself over a sandbar or "crutch" itself into deeper water. Navigation, particularly through the Yukon Flats, where the river widens into several narrow, tortuous, and swift-flowing channels, demanded special skill by captain, crew and pilot. Often the captain hired a Native pilot at Fort Yukon to guide the boat through the flats to Circle.[18]

The increase in steamer traffic brought a number of improvements. Tract charts, documenting the shipping channel, sandbars, and other tricky navigation problems, became more explicit and useful. The United States Coast and Geodetic Survey mapped the delta of the Yukon River and located the main channel. By 1899 the survey had charted the river from St. Michael to Dawson. Between 1908 and 1911 the Army Corps of Engineers, under the provisions of the Rivers and Harbors Act of 1905, dredged a safe channel from St. Michael to the mouth of the river. On the upper river in 1899–1900, the Canadian Department of Public Works constructed a breakwater at the head of Lake Laberge. The department also widened the channel at Five Fingers and laid a cable to assist steamers moving upriver. And in 1908 the government removed the rock and reef obstructions at Rink.[19]

The size and makeup of crews also changed. A large steamer's crew now consisted of nearly sixty men, including a master or captain, two mates, one chief engineer, one assistant engineer, one purser, one freight clerk, one steward, two pilots, eight firemen, twenty-five deck hands, three cooks, and seventeen waiters. All were white. The smaller vessels required the same number of officers but fewer subordinates for a total of thirty men. The salaries were liberal enough to entice the best men in the field.[20]

One of the best captains on the river was James T. Gray. Born in 1852 in Oregon, Gray was master of a Columbia River sternwheeler at age twenty-one. He married the daughter of Oliver O. Howard, a general during the Civil War and subsequent Indian wars. Her extravagance and desire for society life pushed Gray into a number of shaky business schemes. The Panic of 1893 left him bankrupt. By 1898 he had found his way over the Chilkoot Pass and into Dawson, where he secured a captain's position with the Seattle-Yukon Company. Here he won the praise of its treasurer as "an excellent man, a perfect gentleman and thoroughly reliable."

James T. Gray. One of the best known Yukon captains was Gray of the Northern Navigation Company. In addition to operating steamboats seven months a year, he designed and constructed shallow-draft boats for the Tanana and Koyukuk rivers. *University of Oregon Special Collections.*

At forty-seven, Gray stood five feet, ten inches and weighed 175 pounds. He prided himself on his strength and endurance, proving he could lift 850 pounds. He expected high performance from his crew and maintained an immaculate boat. Although he never used profanity or alcohol around his family, on the Yukon he was known as the "Master of Impressive Profanity." When the Northern Navigation Company merged with the Seattle-Yukon Company, Gray became Assistant Superintendent of Transportation.

To take advantage of gold rush stampedes on smaller tributaries, the Northern Navigation Company assigned Gray the task of building shallow-draft steamers. With help from Portland ship builders, Gray designed and constructed the *Koyukuk*, 120 feet long, 24 feet beam, with a draft of 9 1/2 inches. As the shallowest draft steamer on the Yukon, the *Koyukuk* carried freight up the Koyukuk River to supply miners near the community of Bettles. Gray also took the *Koyukuk* up the Tanana to service the boomtown of Fairbanks and later up the Porcupine, Chandalar, and Iditarod rivers. In 1904 he supervised the building of a second shallow-draft steamer, the *Tanana*, and in 1905 the *Delta*.

While Gray operated riverboats in Alaska from April to October, his family stayed in Oregon. Each winter he returned to Oregon to prepare for the next season. In 1918 he retired to a small fruit farm, and at the age of seventy-five died of stomach cancer.[21]

Steamboat captains contended with more than merely supervising their crews and running a tight ship. One captain, J. E. Chilberg, found his steamboats with lienable claims of $35,000 that he had to absolve. He collected enough fares at $75 per person to pay his creditors. In fact, the problem proved not the scarcity of passengers, but the surplus. More than three hundred passengers crowded aboard the medium-sized *Monarch*. His crew of twenty-five were unable to control the miners, and Chilberg philosophically allowed them to do as they pleased. More men pushed on board at Circle and Rampart, and most refused to pay. With an unruly mob on his hands, he did not try to force his authority. Another complication Chilberg faced was scheduling meals during the nightless summer. He finally gave up and ran continuous board. Rancid butter provoked a miners' meeting, which he handled with a sense of humor that disarmed the angry protesters. Despite his hassles, he completed three trips between St. Michael and Dawson in 1899. The midsummer trips took between fifteen and twenty days, but the late summer trips took longer because of the shorter days.[22]

Costs and profits for transporting supplies and passengers ran high. Although the steamboat season averaged 120 days, by the time the boilers were cleaned, cargo loaded and unloaded, wood purchased and loaded, and allowances made for storms, darkness, wind, fog, groundings, and maneuvering the mouth of the Yukon, only 50 days remained for actual river travel. Government inspection occurring during the summer also consumed shipping days.[23] Nevertheless, the following table shows that during the Klondike rush the average steamboat made money despite the short season:

Expenses	
Cost of steamboat	$ 60,000
Cost of barge	10,000
Cost of crew—round trip	3,000
Cost of meals for passengers	15,000
Cost of cordwood	13,000
Total	100,000

Income	
300 fares at $220	$ 66,000
600 tons freight at 5 cents per lb.	60,000
70 fares on down trip	15,000
Total	$ 141,000

Profit for first trip—$41,000; profit for second trip—$131,000.[24]

These calculations, however, do not consider the life-span of the steamers. Even the Missouri steamers lasted an average of only three years.[25] Yukon boats confronted harder winters and, in some instances, poorer maintenance. Thus the life-span for Yukon steamers, compounded by lack of business for steamer traffic, proved even shorter. In 1906 alone the Northern Navigation Company lost three steamers.[26] Given the risks, replacement costs, and steep competition, transportation companies could not always be assured a profit.

Although most steamer losses occurred without fatalities, in 1906 the worst disaster in Yukon river history transpired. The *Columbian*, carrying a cargo of explosives and a crew of twenty-five, rounded a bend on the upper river and scared up a huge flock of ducks. A crew member took his gun and stepped forward for a shot. He tripped and discharged his gun into the blasting powder. Suddenly the captain found himself without steering or engine controls, the front end of his steamer, and six crew members. By skillfully reversing the paddle against the current, he succeeded in getting the wreck ashore, saving the rest of the crew.[27]

Since the average steamer burned nearly twenty-five cords of wood daily, fuel was one of the biggest expenses and problems transportation companies faced. The companies used wood predominantly, but occasionally, especially in the Yukon Delta, they resorted to coal. Thus the steamers' furnaces were designed to burn either wood or coal to make steam. In the beginning the steamer stopped every six hours for the whole crew to get off and chop wood. By the gold rush era the commercial companies maintained their own woodyards, where an ample supply could be relied upon. Company wood buyers contracted with woodchoppers for a predetermined price. The price averaged $8 per cord but could jump to $15 or even as high as $45. The contract also required wood five inches in diameter and four feet in length. It was stacked on a sill no higher than six feet tall at a safe distance from the river but not more than fifty feet. A company agent measured the cordwood on the first trip downriver and paid the woodchopper. In 1902 the Northern Navigation Company had thirty-seven wood camps of various sizes along the river.

Some timber was cut on steep hillsides and corded where it fell. By removing the supportive props the whole pile thundered down to the riverbank like an avalanche. It was then carried on board log by log. Other woodchoppers, not fortunate enough to live near hillsides, waited for winter and then sledded their wood to the riverbank. One company

Woodchopper's cabin. Wood was the main fuel for steamboats. As a result, they consumed hundreds of cords each summer. Woodchoppers spent long hours meeting the demand. They never lived lavishly. *University of Alaska Archives.*

wood camp owned a logging engine to transport the wood. This camp hired six woodchoppers. If twenty cords a day were sold, the camp made a profit of $80.[28]

The woodchoppers themselves were hardy outdoor individualists who had come to Alaska to search for gold. When they failed to strike a bonanza, they had to earn a livelihood. Typifying this breed was George Pilcher, who arrived on the Yukon in July 1898.[29] He may have intended to head for the Klondike but decided instead to sell cordwood to steamers. Stopping just above Russian Mission, he built his cabin. He gathered and stacked driftwood, sawed and split spruce wood, and sold his wood for $10 a cord. As he chopped and hauled, he recorded the thousands of disappointed Klondikers passing his cabin. With his wood money he purchased provisions from steamers. To supplement his diet, he built a fish trap and picked raspberries, currents, and cranberries. Taking the raw materials, which he had bought or gathered, he made his own bread, cranberry jelly, and canvas mukluks and mittens. During the winter he trapped for marten and continued to chop, sled, and stack wood. Since these were the bonanza days of the Klondike, a number of steamers and Klondikers wintered near him, providing company and a regular social life of dances, visits, and practical jokes. During the summer he cursed thieving steamboaters who robbed him of his wood while he slept. Each year he moved to another wooded area, built a cabin, and started the process all over again.

On Thanksgiving Day 1899, Pilcher recorded his enjoyment and satisfaction with his life-style:

> I am at peace with all the world and am undisturbed by the sound from another living mortal in my quiet home. I am simply supplied with every necessary comfort and have six grouse besides, yes, a basketfull of eels—my health is perfect not a pain, ache, or woe. I eat like a wolf, sleep like a babe, and work like a tiger from dawn until dusk. My evenings are spent 'if at leisure' in either reading David Copperfield or else writing. . . . The world is beautiful and Providence has my heartfelt thanks.[30]

After four years, however, the hard labor of woodchopping pushed him into trading with the Indians. Eventually he tried being a steamboat engineer, a trapper, artist, bridge builder, and inventor.

A later woodchopper, Frank Charles "Heine" Miller, established a wood camp, which he patented as a homestead in 1925, at the mouth of Tatonduk River. He hired six to seven Natives to cut, haul, stack, and load wood for the steamers. Stories abound about the small, beer-barreled man whose well-built cabins served as stopping places for winter travelers. He had trained his horse, Maud, to haul wood unattended from the hills to the beach. Eventually in 1930 Miller sold his horses and shipped in a caterpillar tractor. This modern innovation allowed him to drag greater quantities of wood from areas even farther away, and he was not compelled to move every year. In the great Yukon flood during the breakup of 1937, Miller was in the house when the river picked it up and carried it twenty feet downriver while also washing away more than six hundred cords of cut and stacked wood. This defeat broke the little man, and he left the area.[31]

Because of the high cost and logistical problems involved with cordwood, steamboat companies searched for coal deposits. In 1897 the Alaska Commercial Company mined and sledded two thousand tons from a bituminous deposit on the Nation River. In order to be profitable, however, coal had to sell at no more than $15 a ton. Since the deposit was found only in pockets, the company abandoned the mine.[32]

Another ambitious attempt to mine coal occurred on Washington

Creek near the Charley River. In 1897 N. B. La Brie found coal on the creek twelve miles from its mouth. He turned his claims over to the Alaska Coal and Coke Company and became its manager. The company built a good trail to the coal beds along which dog teams and horses sledded the coal. Meanwhile, across the creek, a group of four independent miners staked a mine from which they sledded five tons of coal to the Yukon. During the winter of 1905-6 one of the companies, probably the Alaska Coal and Coke Company, brought a 100-horsepower steam tractor in by steamboat. It pulled five sleds, each of ten tons capacity, from the mines to the Yukon. This coal was tested in the Northern Navigation Company's *Sarah* and proved better than most Yukon River coal. At some point the two companies became embroiled in a court case that ended on the steps of a San Francisco courthouse in an inconclusive gun battle.[33]

Companies also mined lignite coal at Nulato and more extensively at Rampart. Although some steamers used the lignite coal in the delta area, where wood was scarce, it crumpled when exposed to air. Also, it contained excessive sulphur, which caused harmful clinkers that in turn could start serious fires when burned by the steamboats. In the end, therefore, these coal mines proved uneconomical and were abandoned.[34]

Finally in 1903 the Northern Navigation Company experimented with one other fuel possibility—imported California crude oil. At heavy expense, the firm erected large storage tanks and modified the furnaces of its steamers. The absence of dirt and cinders, the elimination of tedious delays to "wood-up," and the increased steaming capacity appeared to offer great advantages. By 1907 more than fifty thousand barrels were imported annually.[35] Nevertheless, because wood was cheap and abundant while oil was expensive to ship and store, wood continued to predominate as the fuel of choice.

Although the Northern Navigation Company dominated the lower river steamboat business, it never had a monopoly. The North American Transportation and Trading Company held about one-third of the business. With the slump that followed the Klondike rush, in 1903 the North American Company ran in the red nearly $400,000. Thus in 1904 the company closed its stores at Rampart, Fort Yukon, and Fortymile and leased its vessels to independent captains. But with the Fairbanks boom the struggling company momentarily revived. Following two years of marginal profits, in 1906 a group of Fairbanks merchants, called the Merchants' Yukon Line, acquired the company but retained the North

American Company's name. Finally, with further declines in traffic, the company sold its steamers or left them unrepaired and rotting on ways at St. Michael. In 1912 the North American Company closed its last store at Dawson.[36]

On the upper river the British Yukon Navigation Company enjoyed a virtual monopoly. With the growth of capital-intensive mining in 1903 and later the boom with silver-lead mining, the firm prospered. In 1905 it secretly agreed not to compete for Fairbanks, and in return the Northern Navigation Company stopped operating in Dawson. But business on the lower river contracted, and in 1912 Northern Navigation moved back to Dawson. Although the Northern Navigation operated larger boats at lower rates and owned some of the largest stores in Dawson, the British Yukon Navigation Company organized an American subsidiary, the American Yukon Navigation Company, and tapped the Fairbanks market. The Canadian firm built two swift water steamers, the *Alaska* and the *Yukon*, patterned after those on the Snake and Willamette rivers. These were designed to carry heavy freight downstream and run light upstream.[37]

Finally, as the ruinous rate war threatened mutual bankruptcy, the two companies went to the bargaining table. On April 10, 1914, the American Yukon Navigation Company paid the Northern Navigation Company $1.5 million for its fifty-three steamboats and barges.[38] The years of waning gold production and the prospect of a railroad to Fairbanks had prompted Northern Navigation to unload at a profit. Although the Canadians controlled the Yukon, their control proved a hollow victory. Most of Northern Navigation's vessels remained on the ways at St. Michael, and after 1923 only one steamer, the *Yukon*, operated between Dawson and Fairbanks.

The death knell for the Yukon steamboats was the same as elsewhere—the railroad. In 1914 the American Congress chartered a federally owned and operated railroad, the Alaska Railroad. In 1923, when the railroad joined the coast with the interior, freight moved quickly and cheaply. It arrived from Seattle at either Seward or the new port of Anchorage, was transferred to railroad cars and shipped to Nenana, and there loaded on steamboats owned by the railroad to be shipped anywhere along the Tanana and Yukon rivers. In 1922, the Alaska Railroad's River Boat Service acquired two aging sternwheelers from the deactivated Fort Gibbon, the *Gen. Jeff C. Davis* and the *Gen. J. W. Jacobs*. Later, in 1927, the railroad purchased another old steamer, *Alice*, from the Alaska Yukon Navigation Company to replace the deteriorated and unreliable *Davis*. Because of the marginal equipment and competition from the White Pass Railway, the river operation steadily lost money. Since the Alaska Railroad, solely owned and operated by the United States government, did not demand a profit, the riverboats continued to provide service for miners, trappers, and small communities along the Yukon and its tributaries. Competition with the American Yukon Company ceased with a quid pro quo whereby the Alaska Railroad refrained from running boats into Yukon Territory in exchange for a suspension of the Dawson–St. Michael route by the American Yukon Company.[39]

In February 1930 the Alaska Railroad, to replace the ancient steamers, requested bids for the grandest sternwheeler of them all—the *Nenana*. Two hundred thirty-five feet long and forty-four feet wide, it cruised at twelve knots and far surpassed all steamboats on the Yukon. The boat accommodated eighty passengers in deluxe staterooms with hot and cold running water and electricity. A large social hall with plate glass windows and a promenade protected from mosquitoes by copper mesh screens provided amenities not seen since the Mississippi era. The increased barging and carrying capacity of the *Nenana* augmented the freight revenues dramatically—from $36,826 in 1933 to $64,894 in 1937.[40]

But even as the railroad launched the *Nenana*, the time of the steamboat was fading. World War II curtailed Yukon mining operations but also increased traffic by cargo planes. The sternwheelers became outmoded and uneconomical. In 1948 the riverboats lost $76,338. The managers of the Alaska Railroad urged the Interior Department to allow the company to remove the steamboats. Finally, in January 1953, two new steel towboats replaced the palatial wooden sternwheelers. These were nonpassenger, shallow-draft, 120-foot-long boats with 600-horsepower diesel engines. The *Nenana* continued for a time, but her size defeated her—she was unable to maneuver the winding bends as easily as the smaller steel boats.[41]

Despite the profitable silver-lead industry on the Stewart River, Canadian sternwheelers also fell into decline. The British Yukon Navigation Company designed special vessels to meet the low-water demands of the Stewart: the *Keno*, *Canadian*, and *Nasutlin*. The company and the Canadian government made other navigational improvements to support the Mayo industry, such as dredging channels, hastening the

Poling boat. Although steamboats carried most of the passengers and freight on the Yukon, poling boats supplied the smaller streams. The long, narrow craft allowed two men to push it upstream at a rate of twenty miles per day. *University of Alaska Archives.*

melting of Lake Laberge, and constructing a dam below Marsh Lake. Yet in the 1930s the collapse of the silver-lead industry led to drastic declines in steamer revenues. World War II prevented proper maintenance, and the sternwheelers fell into disrepair. The completion of the Whitehorse-Mayo highway in 1950 and the Stewart Crossing-Dawson road in 1955 killed the last use for the Canadian riverboat. On August 18, 1955, the last sternwheeler on the Yukon River steamed into Dawson for the last time.[42] Another era, even a frontier, had passed.

Although the steamboat captured most of the glory and all of the romance of river travel, smaller craft also plied the river. The Yukon poling boat, adapted from boats on earlier western rivers, allowed small groups to travel inexpensively but with hard labor up rivers and streams that were inaccessible to larger steamers. The poling boat was a long, narrow, tapering craft that allowed two men to carry a ton of supplies upstream at a rate of ten to twenty miles a day. Sometimes the men had to "track" or drag it from the shore. Explorers and geologists of the

United States Geological Survey introduced the Peterborough canoe. This canoe could carry half a ton but was light enough to be portaged by one man if necessary. Before 1900 the poling boat and Peterborough canoe provided the greatest bulk of travel along smaller rivers.[43]

The introduction of the internal combustion engine changed local travel. Small engines of four and six horsepower pushed boats, called gas launches. Later larger engines propelled even larger boats up shallow, swift rivers. By 1907 the Northern Navigation Company ran thirty- to fifty-foot gas launches as mail boats. From 1909 to 1912 such boats also played an important role in supplying the International Boundary Survey teams. During the next forty years other launches and barges evolved to supply isolated river communities and camps, totally replacing poling boats and the Peterborough canoe.[44]

Thus, the rivers and streams of Alaska and Canada allowed the country to be developed. Watercraft of all kinds moved people and supplies into remote areas for exploration and settlement. Navigable water defined the limits for Yukon development prior to overland transportation. Like communities on western rivers, Fairbanks, Dawson, and Whitehorse owed their existence to water transportation. For more than eighty years the sternwheelers characterized and dictated a lifeway dependent on the water. Even late in the twentieth century, water travel remained the major way to reach most of the Yukon valley. Despite improvements in road and air transportation, settlements on the Yukon still perceived the river as their artery of life.

CHAPTER 10

The Transportation Frontier: Trails and Roads

During the Klondike stampede and the critical years of the Yukon Valley's development, the river itself probably bore the largest share of Yukon freight and passengers. But eight months of the year the river was frozen. People still wanted to travel, mail had to be delivered, and freight needed to be transported. Thus other methods of travel came into use.

Horses, so vital to the westward movement on the continental frontier, initially proved unsatisfactory on the Yukon. Horse feed was one problem. Native grass was believed to lack nutrition, and imported hay was too expensive. The severe cold was another problem, requiring special winter care and housing. In 1899 one early mail contractor attempted to use horses on the all-American route from Valdez to Eagle, which Capt. William Abercrombie had recently explored. The first mail trip killed eleven horses, cost $3,000, and delivered only three letters.[1] While horses reached the Yukon on the Dalton Trail, thousands of others died on the White Pass Trail.

Dogsleds afforded the best method of winter transportation. The native breeds of dogs were ideally suited for the harsh environment. They were well boned, deep chested, strong in the back, fore, and hind quarters, with thick outer and inner coats of hair, and paws with fur between the pads and toes. They were easily fed dried salmon, which was cheap, or a concoction of bacon and oatmeal. They required no housing. After feeding they curled up in a ball that withstood all but the heaviest snow and deepest cold. Because the Yukon River froze unevenly and wind along the open river exacerbated the cold, dog team drivers preferred to travel established winter trails that followed along the banks of the Yukon and its tributaries rather than on the rivers themselves.[2]

Almost immediately, mail carriers began to use dog teams in the winter. By 1901, a mail trail ran nearly the whole length of the Yukon River. The United States Post Office divided the route into districts, or "runs," of fifty to seventy-five miles in length and contracted with the Northern Commercial Company and individual mail carriers to carry the mail and maintain the trail. Generally the trail followed the river, but sometimes it crossed a wooded portage that reduced the distance and afforded shelter for the trail from drifting snow. Stakes or tree branches marked the trail where it crossed the river or a lake. Occasionally, where the distance between roadhouses was greater than twenty-five miles, mail contractors erected cabins stocked with provisions and equipped with stoves.[3]

If any one occupation won the admiration and praise of the sourdoughs, it was carrying the mail. Mail carriers traveled in all weathers and temperatures. Under contract to deliver the mail a certain number of times each year, they also had to keep a rigid schedule; any delay would hold up carriers all along the line. Travel in the spring, when the ice rotted, and again in the fall, before it solidified, was dangerous. Risks were taken. In compensation, the mail carrier always had the right of way and stood out as the most important person on the trail or at the roadhouse.[4]

Representative of mail carriers was Max (Ed) Adolphas Biederman. Born in Bohemia in 1870, Biederman talked his father into helping him find passage on a steamship bound for the United States. At the age of only thirteen, he found himself in Philadelphia apprenticed to a baker. Later, he traveled about the country doing odd jobs and wound up in San Francisco when word broke of the Nome strike. During the summer of 1900, he left for Nome only to find, as had thousands like him, that all the ground had been staked. He then wandered down to the Yukon River and got a job with the Northern Commercial Company. After cutting cordwood for a while, he became a winter mail carrier for the company between Tanana and Rampart. Remaining on the company's payroll all year round, in the summer he boarded dogs and functioned as a troubleshooter for company repair jobs.[5]

Eventually, when the Northern Commercial Company subcontracted with its drivers to carry the mail, Biederman received the contract between Eagle and Circle. In 1918, approximately halfway between

The Yukon mail at Eagle, Alaska

Yukon mail. Mail carriers quickly adopted dog teams as the fastest and most effective means of winter transportation. They averaged twenty-five miles a day and traveled in all weather and temperatures. *University of Oregon Special Collections.*

the two towns and across from the mouth of the Kandik River, Ed built a home. Here he and his family fished and boarded dogs in the summer. On the last steamer before the freeze, Ed moved his family to Eagle so the children could attend school.

During the winter, with only one dog-sled team, Ed carried the mail. He spent one week on the trail between Eagle and Circle. The first night out of Eagle he stayed at Miller's Camp, then Nation, home on the third night, Woodchopper on the fourth, either Twenty-Six-Mile Way Station or Twenty-Two-Mile Roadhouse on the fifth night, and finally into Circle. Resting only one day, he started back. Thirteen trips a season he averaged. During the spring and fall, mail became irregular, but with the first hard snow Biederman made a good trail with a toboggan. Thereafter he used specially designed sleds. One year he lost his contract to a mail carrier with horses, but the following year he had it back.

In 1925 tragedy struck. A steamboat accident killed Biederman's well-trained dogs. With green and unfamiliar dogs, he accidentally drove through a creek that had overflowed—thick layers of ice had pushed

Ed Biederman. Characteristic of the mail carriers was Ed Biederman, shown here with his Native wife, Bella. For nearly twenty years, between 1918 and 1938, he or his sons carried the mail between Eagle and Circle. *George Beck Collection, Eagle, Alaska.*

warm flowing water on top of the ice, where it had remained insulated from freezing by the protective snow. He was only four miles from Twenty-Two-Mile Roadhouse, and he thought that he could drive that far safely. His judgment proved wrong, and his toes froze and had to be amputated.

For the next four years, the Northern Commercial Company sub-contracted with another carrier. By this time, Ed's oldest son, Horace, had taken over the route, and Ed contracted with a master sled builder to design him two special mail sleds. Horace used the sleds once, and his younger brother, Charlie, used them the last three years. In 1938 the Biedermans lost the mail contract permanently to airplane pilots.

Ed continued to maintain Biederman Camp until after World War II. He boarded dogs during the summer for miners and trappers who did not want the problems of caring for dogs in the off-season. In addition, he caught, smoked, and dried fish. Most of his fish went to dog food, but he also provided a quality product for the table. In 1945, when Ed died at the age of seventy-five, the family moved permanently to Eagle.

Another major user of the trails was the freighter. Generally, freighters used dog teams, although occasionally horses. Like the mail carrier, the freighter preferred malemutes—dogs native to Alaska—whose strong, short, stocky build favored pulling heavily loaded sleds. Because of the narrow trails, the dogs were most often hitched tandem rather than in pairs, and with padded leather collars and harnesses similar to horse rigs. The leader responded to verbal calls of "gee," "haw," and "whoa."

The weight of the load depended upon the condition of the trail, the terrain, and the number of dogs. While mail carriers made 25 miles a day with 50 pounds per dog, freighters loaded three sleds with 600, 400, and 200 respectively, or about 150 pounds per dog.[6] By using three sleds the load was distributed over twenty-one feet of bearing surface instead of twelve. Moreover, the three sleds allowed winding through narrow forest trails and up and down hills. Rather than give a single dried fish to each dog, good dog handlers preferred to cook rice or oatmeal mixed with tallow to stretch the diet and warm the dog.

Freighters earned seven cents a pound per trip but had to deduct the cost of their dogs, their year-round maintenance, and the sleds. During the peak of the Klondike, freighters made more than $100 per day. Mail carriers, on the other hand, earned only $125 per month after all costs were deducted.[7]

By the turn of the century, horses began to take their place in the evolution of land transportation. In 1897-98, some freighters kept twelve horses working all winter on a diet of native hay and sheltered in heated tents. The following year, the North-West Mounted Police successfully wintered a number of horses. With the development of small farming operations, more and more horses could be fed and sheltered. Horses, unlike dogs, proved their worth all year round. Moreover, a horse carried more than five times the load of a dog. Each horse in Dawson during the gold rush earned its owner $4,500 per season.[8] Almost immediately, passenger stagelines, packtrains, and mail carriers began to use horses. In contrast to the judgment of some freighters in 1899, by 1901, the horse had largely superseded the dog for all functions except on unbroken and remote trails.

To accommodate winter travelers, roadhouses sprang up. Supplied by steamers during the summer, these roadhouses were often self-sufficient entities throughout the winter. Some, while doubling as roadhouses, functioned mainly as home bases for trapping, woodchopping, or mining. Others depended on and catered to winter travelers. Most roadhouses had associated outbuildings—a stable or corral for the dogs, additional bunkhouses, and sheds. Each meal cost two dollars, and so did a bunk or a place to throw a bedroll.[9]

Judge James Wickersham immortalized an early roadhouse known only as Webber's. The ten-by-sixteen-foot cabin and adjacent dog stable typified roadhouse accommodations. Dirt floor spattered with grease and rough-hewn table, bunks, and three-legged stools provided only minimal furnishings. The meal, however, could hardly be regarded as typical. "In fact, we begrudged our animals the hot pan of rice and bacon we had prepared for them," bemoaned Wickersham. The landlord prepared rabbit stew in a large kerosene can that perpetually simmered on an ancient Yukon stove. As the guests reduced its contents, more water, rabbit, caribou, bear, or lynx were added. "The odor and steam from this ragout of wild meats permeated the tavern," reported the judge, "glazed the half-window with beautiful icy patterns, and filled the two-inch air-hole above the door with frost." Other roadhouses, however, won Wickersham's praise. In fact any winter traveler and the few summer walkers enjoyed and appreciated the hospitality furnished by these Yukon institutions.[10]

In December 1905, a famous winter traveler mushed a dog team along the Yukon mail trail. He was Norwegian Roald Amundsen, the first man to negotiate the Northwest Passage, and he was wildly eager to telegraph his achievement to the world. From the beginning the tall, gaunt, arctic scientist had shown strong determination and faith in his project. At thirty years of age he had given up a medical career in favor of polar exploration. Methodically, thoroughly, and seriously, he set out to become an expert in all aspects of travel and survival in the Arctic.

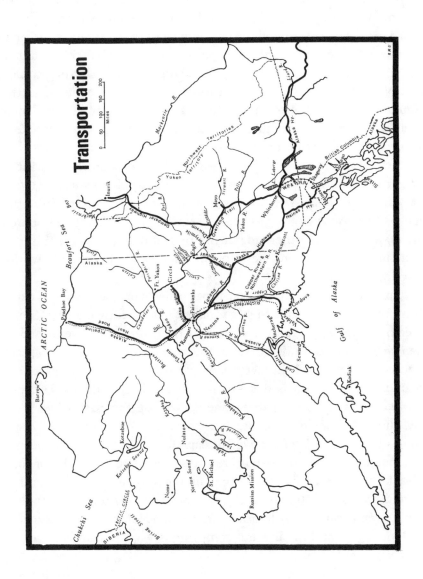

Transportation

He was a dedicated, capable, tough, but patient explorer and leader.

Amundsen's adventure had begun more than two years earlier, on June 1, 1903. With a crew of eight and supplies for four years, he had set sail in a stoutly built walrus sloop, the *Gjoa*, powered by a small gasoline engine. With great navigational skill and without blasting any ice, he had made his way around the northern coast of Greenland and Canada, and had achieved both his principal aims—to establish the existence of a Northwest Passage, and to determine the exact location of the magnetic North Pole. During his two years in the northern Canadian Arctic, Amundsen lived close to the Eskimos and learned and adopted their living and survival techniques. Then he moved on to put in at Mackenzie Bay to pass the winter of 1905–6.

Several American whaling ships, caught unexpectedly by winter, found themselves locked by ice in Mackenzie Bay along with the *Gjoa*. The captain of one, William Mogg of the *Bonanza*, offered to outfit an expedition to the nearest telegraph station, more than five hundred miles away, on the other side of the rugged Brooks Range. Without funds but anxious to get news of his success to the outside world, Amundsen agreed.

Unfortunately for Amundsen, Mogg insisted on going along as expedition commander. While highly regarded as a whaling master, Mogg's three-hundred-mile trip by dog team in 1892, from Herschel Island to Rampart House, did not in Amundsen's opinion qualify the captain for the journey ahead. In fact, according to Amundsen, Mogg's poor judgment greatly increased the peril. Nonetheless, with two Eskimos and two dog teams, the party made its way up the Firth River, over nine-thousand-foot mountains, and down the Coleen and the Porcupine to the Yukon. The overweight captain demanded that he be carried aboard the sled and also decreed that men and dogs rely for food on sacks of cooked beans rather than on the nutritious pemmican that Amundsen wanted to take. Fighting their way over unbroken trail in subzero temperatures with rations wholly inadequate for the exertion, the Norwegian and his Eskimo companions wasted away and verged on exhaustion.[11]

At Fort Yukon, the travelers learned that the telegraph office was at Fort Egbert, more than two hundred miles up the Yukon. Parting with the Eskimos, Amundsen and Mogg took one team and started up the Yukon mail trail. Suddenly, Mogg decided the two would forgo the midday meal in order to make better time. At that, Amundsen rebelled and

Roald Amundsen at Eagle. In 1905 Amundsen became the first man to negotiate the Northwest Passage. After an arduous journey over the Brooks Range to Eagle, he telegraphed word of his accomplishment to the world. *University of Alaska Archives*.

threatened to leave the dictatorial captain to his own devices and take refuge in a roadhouse. Mogg promptly backed down. Finally, after a six-week journey in temperatures as low as sixty below zero, the two men arrived at Fort Egbert, and word of Amundsen's deed flashed to the world.[12]

From around the world, telegrams swamped Fort Egbert station. Scientists proclaimed Amundsen's expedition as one of the most important scientific achievements of the century. Explorers of three centuries, with the resources of wealthy nations, had failed to find the Northwest Passage. The world was captivated by the modest, unassuming man. The State Bank of Seattle wired him $500, the *Seattle Post-Intelligencer* telegraphed a three-year condensation of Norway's news, and the Norwegian government offered all the aid he might require.

While Amundsen waited for the mail, his two-year voyage, topped by the exhausting dogsled trip, demanded a two-month recuperative period. During that time he lectured to the citizens of Eagle and the officers and soldiers at Fort Egbert and attended balls in his honor. Finally on February 13, 1906, with medicines for the stranded American whalers, Amundsen left Eagle. Without Mogg the return trip to his ship proved uneventful and considerably easier. When the ice broke up, the *Gjoa* continued its voyage to San Francisco. Here it remained as a monument to a historic exploration until 1972, when the City of San Francisco returned it to Norway.

Amundsen meanwhile went on to achieve even greater fame. He became the first to reach the South Pole in 1910, and in 1926 the first to cross the North Pole in the airship *Norge*, from Spitsbergen, Greenland, to Nome, Alaska. In 1928, Amundsen left retirement, borrowed a seaplane from the French government, and entered a search for a missing arctic explorer. His plane disappeared, and Amundsen was never seen again.

The mail trail had proved its value, even though it ultimately gave way to faster means. In 1931 the United States Post Office contracted with pilot C. Harold Gillam to carry the mail by airplane from Cordova to Eagle. Some uproar resulted from people who resided away from settlements with airstrips: how would they be serviced? Furthermore, computations showed that the government spent $275,000 annually on mail contracts. Not only mail carriers expressed concern but all those who benefited from the $275,000—fishermen, drivers, supply towns, and roadhouses. Even so, by 1939 airplane pilots had taken over mail contracts for most of the Yukon. Roadhouse owners and mail carriers turned to trapping, mining, freighting, and fishing. Slowly the roadhouses closed up, and the mail trail fell into disrepair. The large number of winter travelers dwindled to an occasional drifter. By 1939, Dawson's population stood at seventy-two people, and Eagle City elections could turn out only twenty-six voters.[13] The hurry-scurry of the Klondike era had subsided to a quiet shuffle.

Although life had slowed, the need for more efficient travel had not lessened. Wagon roads such as helped settle the American West touched the Yukon only lightly. Very few roads or trails existed anywhere in the interior. Because of the cost, the difficult terrain, and the independence of the individual travelers, private toll roads failed. Moreover, the Secretary of the Interior historically claimed insufficient power to grant franchises and thus discouraged private charters for toll roads. Even after pioneer road builder George Brackett succeeded in acquiring the appropriate legislation and constructing a toll road from Skagway to White Pass Summit, he spent a fortune battling trespassing packers and freighters in court. The one major exception was the Dalton Trail, from the Lynn Canal to Fort Selkirk. Because Jack Dalton patrolled the trail with rifle and pistol, he routinely collected his toll. Few cattle drivers cared to confront the tough and uncompromising Dalton.[14]

In 1899, upon the recommendation of the gold commissioner at Dawson, the Canadian government built the first public road in the territory to connect the major gold-bearing streams. The following year the government linked Dawson with Grand Forks. In 1901, the United States Congress followed suit and appropriated $100,000 to the War Department for roads and trails in Alaska. Between Eagle and Valdez, following the WAMCATS telegraph line, the army laid out a crude pack trail with a few bridges over the swifter and deeper rivers. Lack of funds curtailed additional development.[15]

As early as 1899 the Canadian government tried to improve the postal service to the Klondike by contracting for a wagon and sleigh road between Lake Bennett and Dawson. But not until 1902, when the White Pass and Yukon Route secured the government mail contract for its sternwheelers and agreed to construct a winter road between Dawson and Whitehorse, did the Yukon have an "Overland Trail." Built for $129,000 in six months, the trail did not follow the Yukon and thus cut seventy miles from the river route. With a twelve-foot right-of-way cleared, a few culverts for drainage, and a graded surface, the Overland

Trail accommodated horse-drawn stages and sleighs. Triweekly runs carried passengers and freight and became, as one Dawson resident called it, "the winter link with civilization."[16]

The United States government responded more slowly than the Canadian to transportation needs in the north country. In 1904, Congress directed the United States Commissioners in Alaska to appoint a road overseer in each district. Instead of appropriating funds, however, Congress decreed that every man in the district work two days on roads each year or pay a head tax of eight dollars. Although no massive road system developed, smaller road projects did succeed. Trappers, miners, and townspeople worked on roads and trails, such as roads from supply towns to mining areas and trails between supply towns. They built bridges, cleared trees, brushed out trails, blasted through canyons, and did a small amount of grading. The men took pride in their work. As one remarked: "The work was done well and will stand for years."[17]

Meanwhile, Alaskans rallied to promote a more effective and efficient road system. The Eagle and Valdez city councils lobbied strongly for a connecting wagon road. Miners, however, pushed for a shorter connective road with the Fortymile to allow Eagle rather than Dawson to supply the miners in that area. A proposed railroad joining the Yukon with the coast caught everyone's fancy. And the greatest dream of all was a permanent, year-round road linking the rest of the United States with its orphan land.[18]

In 1905, Congress passed a law providing for a Board of Road Commissioners for Alaska, to consist of three army officers, one from the Corps of Engineers.[19] Their task was to locate, lay out, construct, and maintain wagon roads, winter sled roads, and pack trails. The first commissioner in charge of what came to be known as the Alaska Road Commission was none other Maj. Wilds P. Richardson, who had patrolled the Yukon during the "starvation crisis" of 1897. At forty-four, his girth had expanded greatly, and he tipped the scales at more than three hundred pounds. A long-time Alaskan, he won the devotion and loyalty of his subordinates. His colleague Thomas C. Riggs described him as "a huge man in every way and with a capacity of liquor which has seldom been equaled. . . .[and] an overwhelming hatred for James Wickersham." The animosity toward Wickersham arose from the territorial delegate's continuing barrage of mostly unfounded accusations of corruption in the commission.[20]

Initially, funds for road construction were to come from the Alaska

Wilds P. Richardson. Major Richardson served as first commissioner of the Alaska Road Commission, which was mandated to build trails and roads. Despite his three hundred pounds of excess flesh, he planned and built the first Alaskan roads. *University of Alaska Archives.*

Fund, created from vocational and trade licenses collected outside of incorporated towns. Although allowed 70 percent of the fund (later reduced to 65 percent in 1913), Richardson found the sum inadequate and recommended additional appropriations. Throughout the next several years, special acts of Congress defined the scope of work and provided additional funding.[21]

The Alaska Road Commissioners designed a broad plan. Roads and trails would form part of a connected system covering all of the developed areas of Alaska. Although expensive, surveys preceded any road or trail construction. Next came the evolutionary development of trail, sled road, and finally wagon road. Each stage built on the foundation of the previous one. Richardson's basic plan emphasized the trail overland from Valdez on the coast to Fairbanks, with linking trails to military posts and communities on the Yukon. Although dog teams had used the trail as early as 1902, the Alaska Road Commission did not formally consider the trail adequate for sled travel until 1907. In 1910, named the Richardson Highway, it accommodated horse-drawn wagons and in 1913 allowed the first automobile, one year after the first on the Canadian Overland Trail. Also in 1913, the Alaska Road Commission collected data that proved that the direct savings in the cost of transportation of freight for one year because of the improved road system were $2,144,667.[22]

Road building in the Yukon Basin presented unique problems. Engineers, like the early miners, found the subsoil permanently frozen. Moreover, the long hours of summer daylight encouraged thick vegetation and underbrush. When this died and combined with a heavy moss, it formed a heat-resistant blanket, called "muck," that prevented further thawing. Once the muck level was cleared, however, the subsurface began to thaw, shrink, and become water-soaked, with no place for the water to drain. Roads at this stage became impassable until a subgrade of corduroy—scrub logs placed side by side across the width of the road—was constructed. To prevent the permafrost from thawing, early engineers laid corduroy directly on the mossy surface without disturbing the insulating blanket. This action, however, foreclosed any future leveling or grading. Eventually the Alaska Road Commission learned that the frozen subsoil would thaw and drain in three years, and these calculations were programmed into the work schedule. The road builders also discovered that native timber was not strong or durable enough for bridges, and more suitable timber had to be imported. The gradual increase of automobiles and light trucks required expensive gravel roads, which came to replace the traditional earth-packed ones, and more costly maintenance. Moreover, Alaska's high cost of wages and supplies depleted the meagerly funded road projects. Because of these problems, costs ran between $1,500 and $3,300 per mile for wagon roads, and the commission confronted unsubstantiated charges

Early road builders in both Canada and Alaska used horse teams to remove the heavy vegetation from the permanently frozen ground (top). They learned that, as the ground thawed, the road became impassable. The only remedy was to corduroy—to lay logs across the width of the road—before then spreading gravel (bottom). *University of Oregon Special Collections* and *University of Alaska Archives.*

of malfeasance and corruption from the district's nonvoting, but highly political, delegate to Congress, James Wickersham.[23]

In contrast to the wagon roads, sled roads and summer trails proved cheaper and easier to build. Sled roads could be located on low, swampy ground along streams or lakes. Construction required only that the timber be cleared, the stumps removed, and bridges built. Some of the steeper grades occasionally needed grading. Not only were the sled roads 70 to 90 percent cheaper to construct, but the average cost of transporting one ton of freight one mile by bobsled on winter sled roads was thirty-seven cents. Transporting the same weight during the summer by light truck cost fifty cents, and by wagon $1.23. Summer trails, on the other hand, required the driest ground available and the lowest grades.[24]

In 1917 Richardson's momentum came to a standstill as world war required the full attention and all the resources of the United States. Although Alaskans pressed wagon roads to serve as feeder lines for the Alaska Railroad, slowly wending its way to the interior, the Alaska Road Commission could barely maintain major roads. Because of high prices, scarce labor, loss of expert personnel, and reduced funding, miles of established roads and trails fell into disrepair.[25] Richardson, meanwhile, served during World War I as brigadier general in command of the American forces in northern Russia. He retired from the army in 1920 and died nine years later at the age of sixty-eight.

In 1920 new life and appropriations came to the Alaska Road Commission, now headed by Col. James Gordon Steese. At thirty-eight, the solidly built West Point graduate had gained engineering skills in Panama and administrative experience on the general staff during World War I. As a lifetime bachelor, he devoted his full energy and time to the road commission and other duties assigned to it. Thus the next ten years were ones of expansion and improvement. During this period the commission reopened old roads and trails, constructed heavier roads for autos and trucks, adjusted to the needs of the Alaska Railroad, procured mechanical equipment, and developed a new ten-year program. This program required careful study of the topography and assessment of economic return prior to initiating new construction, a goal of seventy miles of new road a year at a cost of $10,000 per mile, construction to newly discovered mineral areas and potential agricultural lands, and maintenance of the existing road system. The Yukon District maintenance alone demanded $50,000 per year. In 1929, after twenty-five years of service, the Alaska Road Commission boasted 1,623 miles of wagon road, 1,375 miles of sled road, and 7,044 miles of trail. Because of the road network, the commission calculated an annual savings of $32 million in the transportation of freight.[26]

Meanwhile, Canadian road construction had not stood still. By 1914 Canadians had built more than fourteen hundred miles of road in Yukon Territory. Canadian road builders concentrated first on the Klondike area, then on the new silver-lead district of Mayo, and then on White-horse. An informal cost sharing between the territorial and central governments provided the funds. The formula proved comparable to Alaska's, where the federal government picked up more than 60 percent of the cost. Canadian road builders also claimed that road construction paid for itself through reduced costs of transportation. Like their American counterparts, Canadian engineers felt that road construction greatly facilitated the territory's development. Roads allowed the importation of dredges and encouraged greater use of mechanized equipment. Roads also assisted in the growth of communities and provided the means for greater population mobility after the exhaustion of a mineral resource. As in Alaska, world war reduced Canada's Yukon road funds, and the full effort went toward maintaining existing roads. During the 1920s, the Overland Trail was rerouted to include the Mayo district. In contrast to Alaska's Richardson Highway, the Overland Trail was viewed as a winter substitute for water transportation and was not maintained during the summer. When air mail service began in the 1930s, the Overland Trail fell into virtual abandonment. But in 1950 the Canadian government completed a road connecting Whitehorse with Mayo and in 1955 extended it to Dawson. At last, a road linked the two major communities of the upper Yukon.[27]

Meanwhile, the Alaska Road Commission pursued its ten-year program. In 1929 Alaskans finally had their wagon road from the coast to the Yukon. The Steese Highway, which like the Richardson took its name from the one who initiated it, joined Fairbanks with Circle and thus with the coast at Valdez. Later, the Taylor Highway linked Eagle with Fairbanks via the Fortymile district and extended on to Dawson. The commission also accepted responsibility for constructing new airfields in remote communities.

In 1932, the Alaska Road Commission left the War Department to become part of the Department of the Interior. Following the extension of the Federal Aid Highway Acts to Alaska in 1956, the commission transferred to the Department of Commerce and merged into the Bureau of Public Roads, ending a fifty-one-year service. At that time, it had completed more than 5,152 miles of road, including 1,959 miles of hard-surfaced highway, which linked interior cities and military posts with all-weather, ice-free ports. After Alaska gained statehood in 1959, the Bureau of Public Roads yielded most of its responsibilities to the newly created Alaska State Department of Public Works, and thus ended the frontier period of road construction.[28]

Between 1904 and 1913, one major overland project could not utilize the established roads and trails—the International Boundary Commission. Although the Anglo-Russian Treaty of 1825 clearly identified the 141st meridian as the eastern boundary of Russian America, imprecise wording regarding the southeastern panhandle produced conflict as Canada claimed the heads of the larger inlets that cut into the coastal area. In 1903 four of the six "impartial jurists of repute" of the Alaska Boundary Tribunal ruled in favor of Alaska. Thus, while the diplomats of the United States and Great Britain debated the terms of formal agreements, joint U. S.-Canadian teams, part of the International Boundary Commission, began the task of surveying and marking the boundary.[29]

Since 1869, numerous teams had surveyed portions of the boundary. In 1904, however, the United States and Great Britain concluded a formal agreement for the definitive survey of the boundary in the southeastern panhandle, where many difficult problems gave rise to constant uncertainty. Headed by O. H. Tittman, Superintendent of the United States Coast and Geodetic Survey, and W. F. King, Canada's Chief Astronomer, the International Boundary Commission began its labors at once. Survey teams resolved points of conflict, rechecked and often rerouted the line, and established boundary monuments at each river and stream crossing and wherever there was mining activity. Disagreements over the boundary in White and Chilkoot passes were definitively resolved in 1905 and 1906, respectively. Because of the rugged, mountainous terrain, covered with ice and snow, the survey of the panhandle continued piecemeal until 1920.

Because the 1904 agreement did not deal with the 141st meridian, a new convention between the United States and Great Britain in 1906 applied the provisions of the 1904 accord to the 141st meridian. With the legal and diplomatic technicalities resolved, the boundary survey

Surveyors for the International Boundary Commission. Between 1906 and 1912, American Thomas Riggs (left) and Canadian J. D. Craig (right) led their respective surveying teams along the 141st meridian. On July 18, 1912, they celebrated the completion of the boundary survey by swimming in the Arctic Ocean. *Provincial Archives of British Columbia.*

moved ahead. Next, time signals to and from Vancouver transmitted along the American-Canadian telegraph line established the exact longitude at Boundary, the initial point for the survey, more accurately than the astronomical methods of Ogilvie in either 1887–88 or 1895–96 or McGrath in 1889–91. With this preliminary but essential step completed, surveying began in earnest in 1907.[30]

Americans led by Thomas Christmas Riggs, Jr., reached Boundary, on the south bank of the Yukon, in June. At thirty-four, Riggs had already completed a degree in civil engineering at Princeton, worked as a newspaper reporter in Tacoma, and participated in the Klondike and Nome gold rushes. Prior to joining the commission, he had surveyed portions of Utah, Montana, and Idaho. His outdoor life left him with a florid and weather-beaten complexion. Known for being a "little impetuous," he admitted to flying "off the handle quickly."[31] Because the Canadians lacked adequate appropriations, Riggs and his American crews had the first season largely to themselves. Later, however, American and Canadian teams worked together and moved in coordinated units along the line.

During that first season, Riggs established the basic method and the work schedule that governed for the next six years. He divided the men into six major teams. The projection party marked the boundary line at points on ridges about ten to twenty miles apart. These projections turned out to be within a foot of the line as it was finally surveyed. The reconnaissance team selected the triangulation stations and erected signals for use by the triangulation party, which carefully measured the base lines. The topographical parties followed, mapping a belt along the boundary four and a half to five miles wide at a scale of 1:45,000, with contours of one hundred feet. Then came the vista and stadia team, which cleared timber for ten feet on either side of the line. Last came the monumenting parties, erecting permanent monuments on sites selected by the stadia team, usually about three miles apart.[32]

For most of the 550 miles of the boundary, the teams relied on pack trains for transportation. The terrain, alternating between ridge and valley, was not suited for horses, but no alternative existed. Stream crossings were often dangerous, trails on permafrost thawed and became impassable, and natural feed was scarce. Moreover, horses had difficulty carrying supplies and the awkward surveying instruments. Although the teams tried to winter the horses, they seldom succeeded without great loss. When the boundary crossed major rivers, such as the Kandik, Porcupine, and Fortymile, poling boats and even steamers supplied many needs.[33]

The teams endured other travails. Their monotonous diet consisted largely of flour, sugar, bacon, ham, beans, butter, cereal, and evaporated milk. Wild game afforded a welcome diversion. Only at night, in specially designed tents, could the men escape the eternal scourge of mosquitoes. Even so, some men and a few cooks found the mosquitoes so unbearable that they quit. Only smudges provided relief for the horses, and that very little. Temperatures fluctuated from freezing to the nineties, and some men even suffered sunburns. Despite all the hazards and hardships, however, no man lost his life.[34]

During the seven years of the project, a number of incidents disrupted the surveying. In 1910, described as the year when "everything which could go wrong went wrong," hoof rot killed more than half the horses. Other times the parties failed to find food cached in advance and ran short on rations. In 1911 an American physician traveling with the teams diagnosed smallpox among the Indians, and the surveyors found themselves enforcing a quarantine. Also in that year, the steamer *Tanana*, servicing the survey, hit a rock on the Porcupine River and sank in a few feet of water, but was refloated and repaired.[35]

Finally on July 18, 1912, the teams reached the Arctic coast. Here Riggs and his Canadian counterpart celebrated the occasion by swimming among the ice floes in the Arctic Ocean. "It was with rather a lost feeling," Riggs wrote, "that we arrived at the shore of the Arctic Ocean and saw the practical completion of the work on which we had been engaged for so many years." The following year Riggs focused on the line south of the Yukon. After unsuccessfully attempting to climb Mount St. Elias, and weathering the drain of the gold strike at Chisana, in the Wrangell Mountains near the boundary line, Riggs telegraphed the completion of the survey and sadly reported, "Regret my work completed."[36]

While the boundary survey teams pushed northward, two geological teams fielded jointly by the United States Geological Survey and the Canadian Geological Survey studied the land between the Yukon and the Arctic Ocean. American A.G. Maddren worked north of the Porcupine River, Canadian DeLorme Donaldson Cairnes south of the river. These surveys helped to correlate the geology of Alaska with that of Yukon Territory, British Columbia, and the North-West Territories. For the first time, geologists reported Pre-Cambrian rocks in which the placer gold may have originated.[37]

On December 15, 1918, the International Boundary Commissioners reported to their respective governments. Not only had the international boundary been surveyed, mapped, and marked, but the project had cemented cordial relations between the two nations and promised future cooperation. Though competition remained, many of the bad feelings from forty years of boundary conflict faded. Men of two different but neighboring countries resolved their differences and confronted the rigors of the environment together.

The international boundary represented more symbol than substance. Traffic flowed back and forth across the line as if it did not exist. Although government agents collected customs from steamboats, most land travelers, who avoided the river corridor, failed to acknowledge the change of national sovereignty. Trails and roads, like the mighty river itself, intimately tied Canadians with their Alaskan neighbors.

CHAPTER 11

The Transportation Frontier: Railways, Highways, Airways

Although roads and trails carried the bulk of the Yukon's supplies and equipment, the area did not entirely lack railroads. The White Pass and Yukon Railway had proved its value to the development of the river, but Alaskans and Canadians found its rates steep and unnegotiable. High rates had also diminished the appeal of the Copper River & Northwestern Railway, built to connect the coast at Cordova with the rich copper mines at Kennecott, in the Wrangell Mountains. Neither railroad, however, linked Fairbanks, the Yukon Basin's largest city, with an ice-free seaport.[1]

A number of small but ambitious companies sprang into being to capitalize on the rich gold strikes of Nome and Fairbanks and the potentially valuable agricultural land of the interior valleys. In 1902, businessmen with more vision than money formed the Alaska Central Railroad to tap the undeveloped but diversified resources of inland Alaska. After establishing the townsite of Seward on the tip of the Kenai Peninsula, the company built a terminal, wharf, dock, and fifty miles of track. In 1909 the Alaska Central reorganized as the Alaska Northern Railway and pushed on for a total of seventy-two miles before folding. Meanwhile, thirty-four miles of narrow-guage railroad tied new mining camps with Fairbanks and called itself the Tanana Valley Railroad. Like the Alaska Central, its founders envisioned a powerful railroad, this one joining Nome and Haines. As Fairbanks gold production declined, so did the railroad. By 1916 it was virtually bankrupt.[2]

Thus, by 1911, a privately constructed railroad from Fairbanks to the coast seemed unprofitable and remote. Yet the need and pressure for an all-American route to facilitate development of the interior persisted. President William Howard Taft requested that Congress provide for a federally constructed and owned railroad in Alaska. In the Home Rule Act of August 1912, formally establishing Alaska as a territory with a territorial legislature, Congress responded by authorizing the President to appoint a commission to study and recommend possible railroad routes.[3]

Although the commission made a number of recommendations, the major issue was government ownership. Several congressmen feared socialism, precedent, and continuing subsidies. Even so, in March 1914, Congress granted President Woodrow Wilson the power to locate and construct a railroad at a cost of no more than $35 million. To assist him in this task, Wilson created the Alaskan Engineering Commission. As chairman he chose a calm and patient fifty-eight-year-old, William C. Edes, who had graduated from the Massachusetts Institute of Technology and had made a name as locating engineer for the Southern Pacific Railroad. The most aggressive commissioner, Frederick Mears, had worked for the Great Northern Railroad and risen through the army's ranks from a private in the Philippines to chief engineer of the Panama Railroad. Tall, strong, and opinionated, he commanded respect and loyalty. The third member was the highly popular Thomas Riggs, late of the International Boundary Commission.

Immediately the commission fielded survey teams. Because the commission wanted to tap the Matanuska coalfields, they focused on the Seward-Fairbanks route of the defunct Alaska Northern. This route also supported the belief of the three men that long-range and diversified economic development of Alaska—coal, gold, stock-raising, and truck farming—should be encouraged, even subsidized. Despite their heavy debts, Wilson supported the purchase of the Alaska Northern and the Tanana Valley railroads. The Alaska Railroad was begun.[4]

The three commissioners divided the route into three divisions, and each assumed responsibility for one. Each division had its problems. The southernmost consisted of the old Alaska Northern, which the commission attempted to operate while also reconstructing its shoddy work. Crews laid new and heavier rail, filled gorges or replaced trestles, widened cuts, built a tunnel, and reduced curvature. The middle section moved north from the new town of Anchorage. The crews, international in composition, worked round the clock, clearing, grubbing, and grading the hundred-foot right-of-way, often with only hand tools. Horse-drawn sleds, supplemented by some boat transportation, carried men

The Alaskan Engineering Commission. In 1914 President Woodrow Wilson appointed this commission to locate and construct the first federally owned railroad in the United States. From left to right, Frederick Mears, William C. Edes (chairman), and Thomas Riggs. Each commissioner took responsibility for the construction of one-third of the Alaska Railroad. *National Archives.*

and supplies. On the route south from Fairbanks, the third division, the commission confronted permanently frozen ground covered with its insulating blanket of moss and muck. Workmen used steam to thaw the ground for trestle pilings and watched as the roadbed sank out of sight into the thawed muck. Weather caused many delays as floods washed out roadbeds, buildings, and bridge footings.[5]

In addition to constructing the railroad, the commission was responsible for the new railroad townsites of Anchorage and Nenana, as well as smaller construction camps along the way. In the two towns, the commission had to provide telephone, telegraph, commissary, fire protection, water, sanitation, and law enforcement services, as well as schooling for the children.

Labor proved a continuous problem. The railroad paid a dollar a day less than the Alaska Road Commission and thus could not effectively compete in a labor-scarce market. In 1916 the workers struck for higher wages and won.

World War I brought more disruption. The railroad lost more than half its labor force. Mears, the power behind the construction, resigned to join the army, and Riggs left to become governor of Alaska. Wartime inflation escalated prices and wages. The Industrial Workers of the World (IWW) instigated a strike at Nenana, and the commissioners obtained more than fifty soldiers to protect federal property from militant workers. Finally, the influenza epidemics of 1918 and 1920 swept along the right-of-way, wiping out nearly one-tenth of Nenana's population and eventually claiming the lives of seventy-seven railroaders.[6]

Following the war, now officially the Alaska Railroad, the enterprise rushed to completion. In poor health, Edes resigned, but Mears returned and took over. The two greatest engineering tasks—bridges over the Susitna River and Hurricane Gulch—were accomplished in 1921. Hardly less an achievement was the near-record span over the Tanana River at Nenana—a simple truss 700 feet long.

Acquiring two army steamers, the *Gen. Jeff C. Davis* and the *Gen. J. W. Jacobs*, the railroad launched boat service on the Yukon. Potentially ruinous competition with the White Pass and Yukon Route was averted by a "gentlemen's agreement." Alaska Railroad sternwheelers operated on the Tanana and the lower Yukon. In exchange, the sternwheelers of the White Pass controlled the upper Yukon and carried silver-lead ore from Mayo to Nenana for shipment to the ocean on the Alaska Railroad.[7]

Finally, on July 15, 1923, at Nenana, President Warren G. Harding drove the golden spike that marked completion of the first government-owned railroad in the United States.

Operation of the Alaska Railroad created a host of new problems. The leftover rolling stock from the Panama Railroad required constant maintenance and wore out quickly. Year after year, maintenance requirements pushed the railroad into the red. In an effort to streamline the bureaucracy, the Alaskan Engineering Commission was merged with the Alaska Road Commission under Colonel Steese. The merger only complicated problems and caused severe demoralization, and after nine months it was rescinded. Critics attacked the railroad and its commissioners, charging mismanagement, waste, and even corruption. Unfortunately, Thomas Riggs had trusted some of his sourdough buddies, and a series of scandals rocked the railroad management and his governorship. Because of basic policy and premise, the railroad strove to generate development, not income. Consequently, its rates were lower than comparable railroads, and it simply subsidized development.

As deficits mounted and efficiency measures depressed morale, two

Construction of Alaska Railroad. Like road builders, railroad engineers and crew confronted permafrost. Here thawing permafrost has caused ragged rail lines. *University of Alaska Archives.*

men over the next twenty-one years succeeded in forging a profitable railroad. First to arrive, in 1924, was Noel Smith, with thirty years of experience on Pennsylvania railroads. Politically and economically conservative, the quiet but stern general manager changed a number of the railroad's practices. He opposed subsidizing development, such as constructing spur roads to assist prospecting and agriculture. On the other hand, he insisted on long-range, permanent improvements, such as steel bridges, fill rather than trestles, and new rolling stock. Moreover, he closed unprofitable enterprises like the Anchorage dock. His biggest problem, however, lay in labor relations: he never gained the loyalty or support of his men. Nonetheless, in 1927, for the first time, the railroad showed a surplus.

When Smith left to return to Pennsylvannia in 1928, his successor, Otto F. Ohlson, continued many of his policies. Ohlson stayed seventeen years and created an efficient and effective railroad. At fifty-eight years of age, he was a native Swede who had more than thirty-four years of railroad experience. Known for his flashy dress and large nose, the heavy-set manager was personable, hard working, and loved by his men. More popular with Alaskans than Smith, Ohlson succeeded in closing the former Tanana Valley Railroad to save money and in competing, sometimes unfairly, with truck freighting on the Richardson Highway.

Otto F. Ohlson. Ohlson became general manager of the Alaska Railroad in 1928. During the next seventeen years, surviving a congressional investigation, the Depression, and World War II, he created an efficient and effective railroad. *Alaska Railroad Photograph Collection, Anchorage Historical and Fine Arts Museum.*

He survived a critical congressional investigation, the Depression, and World War II.

By 1944, under Ohlson's management, the Alaska Railroad's surplus was $5 million—though artificially inflated by the army, which provided labor, guard duty, longshoring, and extensive shipments. Even so, it had proved its value by carrying more war-related material than any other form of transportation in Alaska. At war's end, however, the railroad was battered, worn, and deteriorated. So was the seventy-five-year-old Ohlson, who retired in 1946.

Following World War II, the United States military establishment recognized the strategic value of Alaska and supported the management of the Alaska Railroad in its appropriation requests for rehabilitation. Between 1948 and 1952, the road was largely rebuilt with the profits gained from war shipments and activity. The railroad managers purchased new rolling stock and built new track and roadway. Steel bridges replaced wooden ones, and crushed rock, instead of tamped earth, provided solid and stable bases. During this period, the railroad shifted from steam to diesel locomotives. Although revenues increased, so did expenditures. By 1952, the books had slipped once more into the red.[8]

New methods and technology brought the Alaska Railroad back into profitable operation. In the 1950s, it inaugurated containerized shipments and piggyback truck trailers—already in use in the southern forty-eight states. Next came car ferries and seatrains, which brought loaded rail cars from the other states to Alaska. New technology and machinery improved maintenance and lowered labor costs. Meanwhile, the military continued its support by lending diesel locomotives and providing nearly 60 percent of freight tonnage.

On the other hand, new pipelines, highways, and docks eliminated existing and potential revenue. In 1964, the Alaska earthquake nearly destroyed Seward, parts of Anchorage, and long stretches of the railroad. Three and a half minutes wiped out $27 million worth of railroad property. More than two years were required to recover and rebuild the railroad.

As the United States government expanded, changes came to the Alaska Railroad. By executive order in 1963, the Interstate Commerce Commission acquired the responsibility to assign rates. Always a misunderstood entity in the Department of the Interior, the railroad found a new and more sympathetic home with the creation of the Department of Transportation in 1966. While railroads in the lower forty-eight saw consolidation and government operation of passenger trains under AMTRAK during the 1970s, the Alaska Railroad remained untouched. In fact, with construction of the Alaska Pipeline, the railroad carried its greatest tonnage since World War II. The loss of revenue after 1975, however, stimulated Congress in 1982 to pass a law creating an independent commission to assess the value of the railroad for possible purchase by the oil-rich state of Alaska.[9]

From the beginning Congress hoped that the Alaska Railroad would stimulate development, but the result is difficult to assess. More than 70 percent of Alaska's population resides along the railbelt. Without the railroad, it is unlikely that the population centers would have developed. Moreover, Alaska's largest and most important city, Anchorage, began with the railroad. In addition, the development of mines, especially in the Fairbanks area, profited from the railroad. During and after World War II, the military built five of its six largest bases adjacent to the railroad and relied heavily on it. Though the state government touts expansion of mining and agriculture as justification for acquiring the railroad, its greatest current value lies in tourism. Politicians and businessmen have even promoted extension of the railroad through Canada to join with transcontinental railroads at Prince George, British Columbia.[10] Yet like railroads elsewhere, the Alaska Railroad continues to lose money, and its equipment and tracks have deteriorated. The future value of the railroad is unknown, but it is unlikely to fulfill the dreams of Alaskans.

Meanwhile, the privately owned White Pass and Yukon Railroad followed a similar evolution. In 1946, the United States Army relinquished the lease it had acquired to ensure delivery of the supplies required for constructing the Alcan Military Highway. Within a few short years the railroad found itself $2.5 million in debt and with worn-out equipment. In 1951, a new company acquired the railroad and began extensive modernization. Like the Alaska Railroad, the White Pass purchased new rolling stock, including diesel locomotives, and built new shops and offices. Next, it moved into containerization, in which one large metal box contained many small ones. Instead of loading and unloading several hundred boxes, only one large container was moved. Unlike its Alaska counterpart, however, the White Pass integrated containerization into every aspect of its transporation—coastal vessels, railroads, and highway trucks. With the mining of silver-lead around Whitehorse, the railroad operated at a profit until 1978.[11]

Radical change after 1978 jeopardized the future of the White Pass and Yukon Railroad. With the completion of the summer road between Whitehorse and Skagway, trucking firms effectively and ruinously competed for freight and containerized traffic. The silver-lead mines of Yukon Territory, which produced 70 percent of the firm's revenue, declined and brought a subsequent decline to the railroad. With the closure of the mines in 1982 and the failure of the Canadian government to extend a subsidy to the railroad, the officials for the White Pass announced in January 1983 that the railroad would close unless a coalition of Alaskan city, state, and railroad union officials could work out a lease on the line. Since much of the economy of Skagway and White-horse depended on the railroad, its closure would affect both communities heavily. Rosy predictions made in 1974 for the Alaska and White Pass railroads proved wrong and short-sighted. Both railroads appeared to have outlived their usefulness. The high cost of maintenance and limited mobility when compared to highways inhibited their flexibility and adaptability.[12]

While the Alaska Railroad met one of Alaska's basic transportation needs, Alaskans had to wait another twenty years to have a land link with the rest of the United States. Initially, in 1897 and 1905, Canada led the way with two abortive North-West Mounted Police expeditions that tried to build wagon roads to her remote territories. Next, Fairbanks businessmen formed a national lobbying association to promote a connective highway. With pressure from the Alaska Territorial Legislature, Congress in 1930 authorized the President to cooperate with Canada in a study of a highway to Alaska. Despite the positive recommendations of this study, the Canadian government lost interest. Fearing that such a highway would compromise Canada's neutrality in case of war between Japan and the United States, the Canadian military strongly opposed a joint highway venture.[13]

As war pressure mounted, however, both nations agreed, in 1938, to investigate potential routes for a highway. After assessing three major routes for cost, engineering feasibility, tourist potential, and agricultural and mineral possibilities, an international commission concluded that a route through Canada's Rocky Mountain Trench best met the criteria.

Japan's attack on Pearl Harbor on December 7, 1941, exposed America's west coast and emphasized Alaska's strategic value. Essential for the defense of North America and as a base for material support to Russia, Alaska critically needed a linking highway. After languishing for decades, the concept of an Alcan (Alaska-Canada) Military Highway was approved within two months. The earlier Rocky Mountain Trench route was thrown out in favor of one that linked a series of airfields between Edmonton and Whitehorse. Not only could these airfields protect the highway from attack, but they could serve as supply depots as well.[14]

The United States War Department took the lead in constructing the highway. It was conceived as a two-phase project. First, the Army Corps of Engineers would build a pioneer road. Then civilian firms under contract to the Public Roads Administration would follow with a finished gravel road twenty feet wide.

In March 1942, construction began. Eleven thousand men in seven regiments, including three black regiments, worked six separate sectors simultaneously. Within each sector, six construction crews moved forward rapidly. First, locating parties marked the right-of-way. Then came the advance tractors, which cut a fifty-to-hundred-foot swath. Bulldozers followed, leveling and grading the right-of-way. Ditching and culvert crews provided critical drainage. Grading teams established finished grades. And last came the bridge-building crews.

Within three months the two-phase program crumbled. The massive flow of men and equipment devastated the pioneer road. In August, the civilian contractors began work on the final road, even before the pioneer road was completed.

Problems plagued the project. Locating the highway required the dual efforts of aerial reconnaissance and trapper and Indian guides. In the end, field surveyors determined the final right-of-way and generally followed the path of least resistance. River crossings slowed progress until ferries and portable pontoon bridges could be devised.

Like miners, the Alaska Road Commission, and the Alaskan Engineering Commission, engineers on the Alcan Military Highway had to learn the hard way about permafrost and muskeg. Muskeg, they learned, had to be removed prior to constructing a stable roadbed. But if the insulating blanket of muck was removed from permafrost, the once-stable surface became a quagmire as the sun thawed the frozen ground. Only by trial and error did the army resolve the problem and adopt a method similar to that of the territorial road engineers—retaining the cover on permafrost.

The greatest problem, however, was supply. The principal burden fell on the White Pass and Yukon Railway and on Whitehorse as the operational headquarters for the project. When the small railroad could not meet the army's demand because of lack of manpower, the army leased the railroad and pushed the railroad's equipment to handle more than two thousand tons a day. The army also built a massive new railhead outside Whitehorse to house the shipments.

In addition, working conditions were less than ideal. Men put in eleven-hour days—the civilian laborers without overtime pay. Some lived in semipermanent camps made from insulated plywood, others in tents or shacks mounted on skids. The cold weather took its toll as several soldiers froze to death when their equipment broke down. Poor mail delivery brought low morale, and unlike men at the front, no entertainment existed for the soldier-engineer.[15]

On November 20, 1942, eight months after it was started, the pioneer Alcan Military Highway was completed. More than fifteen hundred miles of road opened to military traffic. The War Department removed all but two regiments as the Public Roads Administration pushed to finish the road. Eighty-one contractors employing more than fourteen thousand civilians struggled with a task nearly as momentous as the pioneer road. The army's road was substandard and lacked consistent quality. Drainage was inadequate, the road poorly located, and bridges washed out with spring breakup. The natural insulation of permafrost had been disturbed in places, and all corduroy had to be replaced. Thus, the Public Roads Administration relocated and reconstructed much of the pioneer road. In addition, more than one thousand miles of road were built to connect the highway to the all-weather port at Haines.[16]

In July 1943, the Alcan became the Alaska Highway, and the United States maintained it until six months after the war ended. Isolation, however, continued supply and maintenance problems. Spare parts for all equipment had to be stockpiled. While snow made the highway more serviceable in the winter, the thaw made it impassable in the spring. Many of the same problems that the Alaska Road Commission confronted had to be resolved anew. Finally, on April 1, 1946, the United States ceded the Canadian portion of the Alaska Highway to Canada. But not until 1948 did the Canadian government open the highway to general traffic.

Ironically, the Alaska Highway proved less useful militarily than initially hoped. While it provided an alternative to ocean transport in case of Japanese attack, it never seriously competed with the White Pass and Yukon Route or the Alaska Railroad. Because of the advancement of aircraft and communication technology, airports along the route grew obsolete before war's end. After the war, because the military highway had bypassed the producing areas of Dawson and Mayo, it failed to attract local traffic and took no part in exporting minerals. Moreover, freight transported along the highway cost ten cents per mile in 1948, barely adequate to ensure a minimum return to the carriers. Only in the movement of high-revenue commodities, such as meat, produce, and petroleum products, did the highway live up to expecta-

The Alaska Pipeline. The largest and most costly private project in history stretched more than eight hundred miles from the Arctic coast to the Gulf of Alaska. Here the large diameter pipe strings out over the tundra. *Joe Standart, National Park Service.*

tions. Despite the gravel road, oppressive dust, and sometimes monotonous terrain, tourism along the highway boomed. As thousands of tourists follow the low-cost route, new industries blossomed along the highway. Motels, gas stations, and restaurants provide additional income to local economies. Maintenance and improvements, though costly, stimulated Yukon and Alaska communities. The highway also contributed greatly to the development and growth of its two major cities, Whitehorse and Fairbanks.[17]

In contrast to the Alaska Highway, two other major roads were developed principally to tap resources north of the Yukon River. Canada began its Dempster Highway in 1957 to assist in the search for oil and gas. When the government changed, the highway project fell dormant for seven years until the discovery of oil in 1968 at Prudhoe Bay on the North Slope of Alaska. The government then pushed the road from Dawson northward 453 miles to the government-created town of Inuvik, near the mouth of the Mackenzie River. Completed and opened to the public in 1979, the road cost $103 million with a projected annual cost for maintenance of $2 million. Because thirty-four of the thirty-five wells drilled proved dry, petroleum exploration slowed. But freight costs remained high, with the road used only slightly by mining companies and curious tourists and the long-term value yet to be realized.[18]

Unlike the Alaska Highway and the Dempster Highway, private funding constructed the Alaska Pipeline and its associated haul road. With the discovery of more than ten billion barrels of oil and trillions of cubic feet of natural gas at Prudhoe Bay, a consortium of companies undertook the largest and most expensive private project in history. The pipeline stretched more than eight hundred miles from the Arctic Ocean to Valdez and cost more than $8 billion. From Fairbanks northward, the pipeline company built a haul road nearly four hundred miles long to carry supplies and equipment. Begun in April 1974, the road was completed in 154 days. Major river crossings, such as the Tanana and Yukon, took an additional year. In October 1975 the first and only bridge spanning the Yukon River was completed. Although the oil companies turned the highway over to the state of Alaska in October 1978, not until 1980 was it opened to the public.[19]

The pipeline and haul road confronted major problems and left long-term impacts. In order to obtain the necessary government permits, the Alaska Native Claims issue had to be resolved. The unlikely alliance of oil companies and Native groups lobbied for and in 1971 obtained a fair settlement for the Natives of forty million acres of land and $962 million. This act gave promise of greater impact on Alaska and its Native people than any act since statehood. Not only did it create new Native profit-making corporations, but it provided for more than 100 million acres of national parks and wildlife refuges. The American Congress in one omnibus law tried to erase the mistakes of two hundred years of Indian policy. Provisions allowed for the traditional, subsistence-oriented Natives and the acculturated profit-oriented Natives. Only time would assess the success of the new policy.[20]

Detailed environmental impact statements and extensive scientific testing aimed at minimizing the damaging effects of the pipeline. Environmentalists feared the consequences of a hot-oil pipeline running across permafrost and through caribou migration routes. Learning from the mistakes of early road builders and the Alaska Highway of the unpredictability of thawing permafrost, the design engineers insulated the pipeline and haul road with tons of gravel. Despite all precautions, however, the pipeline and road appeared to have permanently divided the caribou herd, just as the transcontinental railroad a hundred years earlier divided the buffalo herd of the American West. The project also appeared to have caused some erosion and siltation problems. Yet all the tests and research associated with the pipeline greatly expanded the knowledge of Alaska soils and the mechanics of permafrost. In addition, provisions for Native hire and local hire enhanced the skills and increased the earnings of Native and non-Native Alaskans. Short-term negative effects also occurred. None of the Alaskan communities, least of all Fairbanks, was equipped to handle the influx of people. Public utilities became overloaded, housing was impossible to find, high pipeline wages left businesses and community services short-handed, and the cost of living skyrocketed. When seen in context, however, no other construction project in history had ever been designed with such concern for the environment and the local people. Whether the Alaska Pipeline would become the model for future construction and development remained to be seen.[21]

Unlike the generally anonymous builders of the Alaska Highway and the two Arctic highways, the pioneers of Yukon aviation displayed dynamic and colorful personalities. As latecomers to the transportation field, these pioneers and early capitalists exploited the exploding technology of their time. In no other aspect of transportation did technology have greater impact.

Initially, however, the machines and the men who flew them were simple, even experimental. For example, in 1913, as part of the Fourth of July entertainment, Capt. James Martin made several flights at Fairbanks. The First World War, however, left both the United States and Canada with a surplus of planes unsuitable for intercity traffic but readily adaptable to conditions in the north. With skis and floats, planes could use lakes, rivers, and snow-covered terrain instead of expensive airstrips.

Not until 1920 did the first airplanes flown from the lower forty-eight touch down in the far north.[22] Gen. Billy Mitchell, who had helped construct the military telegraph line in Alaska in 1901-2, coupled his campaign to demonstrate the effectiveness of air power with his belief in the strategic value of Alaska. In July 1920, Mitchell sent the Black Wolf Squadron of the army's Air Service from New York to Nome to show the feasibility of establishing an air route between Alaska and the rest of the United States. Along the way, the four biplanes stopped at Whitehorse, Dawson, Fairbanks, and Ruby, enchanting many Yukoners with the prospect of future aviation. Despite the publicity of the round-

Yukon River Bridge. Pylons set hundreds of feet deep to withstand the crashing forces of spring breakup take shape to support the only bridge that spans the Yukon River. With the construction of the bridge, the haul road—later named the Dalton Highway—took motor vehicles to the Arctic coast. *Joe Standart, National Park Service.*

trip flight, the army and other federal interests never embraced the concept of northern aviation.[23]

The promises of flight excited many would-be pilots. The first to dream of an Alaskan air service was New Yorker Clarence Prest. In 1922 he tried to fly from a beach near Juneau over the coastal mountains to the Yukon River, which he hoped to follow into Alaska. After four engine failures, he made it as far as Dawson, but one final failure left him to walk out of the wilderness near Eagle. Discouraged, he returned home to New York.

When the Black Wolf Squadron landed in North Dakota, Carl Ben Eielson watched them take off for Alaska and decided to follow. He had learned to fly in preparation for World War I, but the war ended before he completed his training. After the war he became a barnstormer, performing circus stunts and carrying passengers for joy rides. Although he tried law school, the romance of Alaska pulled him northward—but as an unromantic high school science teacher in Fairbanks. Within less than a year, however, in 1923, he had convinced some Fairbanks businessmen to bankroll him, form the Farthest North Airplane Company, and order a plane. When the parts arrived, he threw the plane together and took off from a baseball field. For a year, he flew passengers and mail to the mines around Fairbanks—the first commercial payload in the Yukon Basin. A year earlier an Anchorage aviator, C. O. Hammontree, took up sightseeing passengers and then flew supplies to nearby canneries.

Unlike other Yukon bush pilots, Eielson was never comfortable in a plane. He had the uncanny ability of getting lost no matter how many times he traveled a route. Of restless and impatient nature, he seldom slept before a flight. Despite his fears, he exhibited great courage and determination in overcoming his failings. Prior to a forced landing, he had never deigned to learn the mechanics of the airplane. But again, like other bush pilots who would follow him, he dug in and learned the airplane inside and out.

After flying mail between Fairbanks and Nenana, Eielson convinced the United States Post Office Department to grant him a contract to fly the mail between Fairbanks and McGrath, on the Kuskokwim River. On February 21, 1924, he successfully flew cross-country and returned an instant hero. President Calvin Coolidge even sent him a congratulatory letter. Considering the uncertainty of both the plane and the pilot, on his eighth trip in May, the inevitable happened. His plane crashed,

Ben Eielson. On February 21, 1924, Eielson flew the first mail between Fairbanks and McGrath and returned an instant hero. The photographer caught the contrast of the old and the new—dog team and airplane. *University of Alaska Archives.*

and the Post Office canceled his contract. Angry, bitter, and impatient, he left Alaska to fight the Post Office. Unable to convince the department of its mistake, he rejoined the Army Air Service.[24]

In 1926 Eielson returned to Fairbanks to help explorer George Hubert Wilkins fly over the Arctic Ocean to the North Pole. A series of plane crashes ended that dream and even required the amputation of a frostbitten finger. The following year, the two men succeeded in flying from Barrow, Alaska, over the North Pole to Spitzbergen Island, Greenland. Later, Eielson became the first pilot to fly in Antarctic. Winning awards, accolades, and praise, he returned to Alaska to set up his own flying service. Despite the risks, the courageous if sometimes foolhardy pilot accepted the assignment of removing valuable furs from an icebound ship off the Siberian coast. Too impatient to wait for better weather, he and his mechanic took off in a blizzard on November 9, 1929. Searchers found their bodies two months later. Alaska had lost a hero.[25]

While Ben Eielson brought publicity and glamour to Alaskan aviation, others, more cautious and conservative, propelled it into a trustworthy and profit-making business. Most characteristic of this breed was Noel Wien. Born in 1899 in Lake Nebagamon, Wisconsin, he began flying in 1921. From the beginning, he and his plane became as one. Without instruments, he flew by the sound of the wind in the wires of the early biplanes. He barnstormed for two years, then in 1924, at twenty-five years of age, he went to Alaska. Here the quiet, calm, cautious, honest Wien briefly met Carl Eielson. No two men could have been more different, yet each shared the dream of Alaskan flying. Wien began bush flying immediately and was the first pilot to fly between Fairbanks and Anchorage. He developed bush-flying techniques that others copied. He flew to Fort Yukon and elsewhere on the Yukon and the Koyukuk. After being forced down, he began to carry emergency gear to make his ground stays more survivable. Unlike Eielson, Wien possessed a tremendous sense of direction and almost never got lost, even on his first flight over unfamiliar terrain. Thus he became the archetypical bush pilot and racked up more "firsts" than any. In 1925 he was also the first to fly between Fairbanks and Nome. After he convinced his brother Ralph to join him as an airplane mechanic and sometime pilot, the Wien brothers began to draw more and more attention. Finally, in 1927 Noel Wien went into business for himself in Nome.[26]

Unlike Eielson, Wien passed up opportunities to gain fame and publicity and instead worked hard to develop his business. In 1929, only four years after he had pioneered the route between Fairbanks and Nome, he set up a branch in Fairbanks. Within a matter of months, however, Alaska Airways Inc., led by Ben Eielson, bought him out, and he returned to the states. After brother Ralph died in a plane crash, Wien returned to Fairbanks in 1932 to start a new business.

The 1930s were the heyday of Alaska aviation. Every year the number of planes increased, from twenty-two in 1931 to forty-two in 1933. These planes flew more than a million passenger-miles and carried more than 700,000 pounds of freight and mail.[27] Pilots remained with Wien until they could save up enough money for their own planes. Thus competition grew tough and, without regulations to ensure safe operations, ruthless.

Although the industry burgeoned, all companies faced similar problems. Because permafrost made level and stable airstrips difficult to obtain, there were few good landing strips in either Alaska or northern Canada. Aircraft technology was also stretched beyond its limits. Engines pushed too hard often quit, landing gear ripped off in rough landings, fabric tore, and propellers bent or splintered easily. Moreover, weather conditions complicated every pilot's life, especially since

Noel Wien. Wien brought early aviation the stability required for
profit-making corporations. Forging an airline from surplus military planes,
he merged his company with others to become one of the giants of Alaskan
aviation. *University of Alaska Archives.*

weather reports were nonexistent. Competition, nonetheless, often forced pilots and companies to fly in unsafe weather. In addition, the lack of radio communications and poor aircraft instruments coupled with inadequate maintenance made the aviation business a high-risk investment. Finally, in 1933, the inevitable happened—the first commercial passenger death occurred near Livengood, on the Yukon River.[28]

Beginning in 1925, Congress passed a series of laws that provided new incentives to aviation entrepreneurs. The Air Mail Act of 1925 authorized contract air mail routes for new airlines. In 1926, the Air Commerce Act made the Department of Commerce responsible for aviation and in 1928 created the first accident review board. Not until 1938, however, did these laws affect Alaskan aviation. With the passage of the Civil Aeronautics Act, government regulation came to Alaska and essentially brought an end to dog-eat-dog bush flying. The Civil Aeronautics Board assigned airlines specific routes based on prior usage. This forced a number of consolidations and mergers. More important, however, the board began enforcement of government regulations and sent inspectors to evaluate planes and pilots. While some Alaskan companies tried to fight government regulation, the most progressive fell into step and delivered a higher quality and more consistent service to Alaskans.

The greatest boon to northern aviation was World War II. Because of Alaska's strategic value, thousands of tons of equipment and supplies had to be flown to newly established military bases. Important contracts and charters for military personnel and goods boosted the profits of airline companies. On the negative side, the war caused a great shortage of pilots, as most resigned from civilian companies to join the military. Maintenance also created great problems, with acute shortages of skilled labor and spare parts. The ferrying of planes from the states to Alaska for Russian pilots to fly to the European front led to creation of new airstrips and better radio communications. Better aircraft, more accurate instruments, and improved weather forecasting and reporting came out of the war. At the conclusion of the war, surplus planes once again found prolonged longevity in service on the Alaskan frontier. Helicopters proved their value in prospecting and exploring for minerals in remote and isolated areas. The large cargo planes from the war could finally compete with railroads, ocean steamers, and highways.

Meanwhile, Noel Wien and his company survived a number of crises and mergers. Despite personal setbacks—polio in 1935 and loss of an eye in 1939—Wien continued to fly commercially until 1955. At the same time his airline grew and merged with smaller lines to become one of the two major airlines in Alaska. The University of Alaska gave him an honorary doctorate in 1962 in recognition of his achievements and his contributions to Alaskan development. The deregulation of the airlines in 1978 created conditions not unlike those of Wien's early bush-flying days. The ability of the Alaska-bred airline to survive still another era of intense competition, however, depended on new and younger executives.

Of all modes of transportation, air travel marked the wave of the future for the Yukon. Despite improvements in other means of transportation, primarily roads, every bush community remained dependent on the airplane for mail and fast freight. While dog team and snow-machine allowed winter access to remote locations, neither could compete with a plane on skis—except in cost of operation. Thus, unlike transportation in the American West, early modes of transportation—the raft, poling boat, and dog team—existed side-by-side with the most recent and sophisticated technology—aircraft.

Transportation in general resembled the patterns of the trans-Mississippi frontier with exceptions caused by climatic conditions. Like the early frontier, Yukon travelers followed rivers, using increasingly larger boats. But settlers along the Yukon and its tributaries confronted the reality that more than half the year the rivers were frozen. From this dilemma arose a network of winter trails that connected settlements. Roadhouses and way stations accommodated hardy winter travelers. Initially, the trail system contrasted with western trails in the Yukon use of dog teams instead of horses for freighting and carrying the mail. Later, however, Yukoners too found horses more effective and efficient if they could be wintered safely.

Technology brought radical change to the Yukon as it did across the United States and Canada. Although the Alaska Railroad and Alaska Highway terminated in Fairbanks, hundreds of miles from the Yukon proper, both changed the river immensely. Like western railroads and highways, greater quantities of supplies were available more quickly and cheaply, allowing opportunity for greater development. Aviation linked remote communities and provided greater and easier mobility.

But improved transportation also provided avenues to escape the demanding Yukon. Other areas lured miners, trappers, and townspeople. Eventually, the river could no longer afford the luxury of steamboats. Steel tugboats replaced the wooden sternwheelers, and airplanes replaced dog teams. Only nostalgia remained to feed on memories of the glorious "good old days."

CHAPTER 12

The Twentieth-Century Miner's Frontier

At the same time that the embryonic transportation system evolved, the Yukon's primary industry, mining, progressed slowly. The great Klondike gold rush created gold fever throughout a nation recently hit by financial depression. The lure of instant wealth drew thousands to the Yukon. Only a few found fortune. Others fanned out to explore, prospect, and discover their own bonanza. The severity of the Yukon's environment, coupled with the discouraging mining results, forced many to leave the country. Others augmented their income with additional jobs—woodchopping, trapping, freighting, fishing, or special services. Thus post-Klondike miners fell roughly into three categories: the stampeder who followed new gold strikes hoping to cash in on good luck, the prospector who stubbornly sought his own elusive bonanza, and the miner who settled for a claim that allowed him, with hard work and perseverance, to eke out a livelihood.

Although numerous gold strikes fueled stampedes until the Iditarod rush of 1910, the last great bonanza was the Tanana discovery near Fairbanks in 1902. Its close proximity drained the upper Yukon region of all but its most determined miners. For example, the heavily prospected area between the Canadian boundary and the Yukon Flats, which once had every creek staked and boasted six supply communities within 250 miles, quieted to two, Eagle and Circle, and a few stalwart miners and prospectors.

Typical of those who stayed on the upper Yukon was C. A. "Bert" Bryant. A farm boy from New York attracted to the Yukon by the Klondike gold rush, Bryant arrived in Eagle in 1899.[1] At first he worked as a packer for the army at Fort Egbert, then shifted over to his own business of freighting supplies to the Fortymile miners. Finally, in 1901, he staked his first claim on the Seventymile River and bought another claim on nearby American Creek. During the winter he contracted with the army to haul cordwood to the fort. This provided money to prospect and mine.

Bryant's first mining venture occurred on Jack Wade Creek in the Fortymile country. Here he freighted his supplies by dog team and began a drift mine. He sank a mining shaft, without timbering but, because of the permafrost, without danger of cave-ins. Using wood fires to thaw the ground, he drove his first drift mine down twenty-two feet, then drifted along bedrock to a width of seventy-five by thirty-five feet. All the dirt he hoisted to the surface and dumped to await spring breakup. When enough water flowed, he washed the gravel, only to learn that, after expenses, he had earned a meager $2.50 per day.

In the summer of 1903, Bryant prospected Copper Creek, a tributary of the Charley River, which he named when he located and claimed a copper ledge. Although he spent several months of the next two years developing the mine, his main income came from freighting and logging contracts. A mining expert cast a "cold draft" on his hopes when he assayed the specimens as good but counseled that the location was too remote to be mined profitably. Discouraged, Bryant went "outside" to Minnesota, where he met an old flame from school days. "Married her in March," he recalled, "that was the beginning of my bad luck." Together they returned to Eagle.

Bryant next tried his luck on a quartz lode mine on Flume Creek of the Seventymile River. With his partners, he constructed a water-powered arrastra to grind the gold from the quartz rocks and completed sixty-six feet of tunnel, but the vein did not prove rich enough to develop without better transportation. Bryant turned once again to freighting. For a couple of months he even served as Eagle City's jailer. Finally, in 1910, he established a camp at Alder Creek on the Seventymile. Here, several old-timers dating from Fortymile days worked mines along with Bryant. Among them was George Matlock, a holdover from earlier rushes but still a tough, self-reliant individualist.

Bryant decided to mine Alder Creek by ground sluicing. He constructed two dump gates on the creek to control the water. Then he made a cut, approximately twelve feet wide and one hundred feet long. Through this cut he sluiced the overburden and much of the gravel, thereby concentrating the gold in the remaining gravel. Finally, he shoveled this remaining gravel into sluice boxes for a final clean-up of sixty-five ounces. The succeeding years saw floods that filled his mining cuts with debris and hot, dry summers that produced no water at all for mining.

When mining failed, Bryant prospected. Prospecting consisted not of aimless wandering and searching for easy surface finds but of a systematic approach. First, the history of a creek was researched and old-timers' tales pieced together. Second, United States Geological Survey Bulletins were consulted. Finally, since few prospectors could afford expensive drilling methods, a line of prospecting shafts was sunk to bedrock to assess the pay dirt. On Barney Creek one winter, Bryant sank sixteen prospecting holes to bedrock, with indifferent results.[2] His resigned comment typified the feeling of the average prospector: "We melted ice for water, had caribou meat. . . . We put in a pleasant winter. No financial results but a lot of valuable experience."

In 1917 Bryant joined thirty-five other men at the Alder Creek mine, which he had leased to men planning to mine by hydraulic methods. They built a six-mile ditch to provide additional water and pressure to remove the overburden and push the gravel into sluice boxes. During the winter he returned to Eagle and chopped wood. The following spring he bought an interest in the hydraulic plant. The subsequent dry summers barely paid off. Later a few good years stimulated him to travel to New York to look for financing to dredge the Seventymile River, but without luck. For the next twenty-five years Bryant continued working his Alder Creek mine during the summer and freighting, chopping wood, or trapping during the winter. In 1933 he left Alaska, only to return in 1941. He died in an automobile accident in 1945 at the age of eighty-three.

C. A. Bryant's life typified the experiences not only of the miners along the Yukon but throughout Alaska and western Canada. Few ever struck it rich, but more than an elusive hope of wealth kept them at their claims. After years of pouring labor and money into developing a mine, they grew reluctant to part with it. At best, it provided a livelihood and, at the very least, an appealing independence.[3] Thus they returned to their claims year after year. In addition, as the years of the lucky bonanza receded, the United States and Canadian Geological surveys surveyed, studied, and produced detailed reports on the economic geology of the Yukon and the most appropriate mining methods. Miners merged their experience and background with this theoretical knowledge and slowly evolved efficient and profitable operations on low-grade placer claims.

The geologists traced the Yukon gold placers back to the mineralization of the area during the middle Mesozoic era, or approximately one hundred million years ago. Subsequent erosion broke up and removed the gold from the granite intrusions. Millions of years later, time and pressure cemented gold-bearing gravel into rock known as Tertiary conglomerate.[4] Identification and recognition of this process supplemented the prospectors' intuition of where gold might lie. Folding and faulting, however, further disturbed the horizontal attitude and contributed to the irregular distribution of the gold. Later, streams and rivers cut through these Tertiary placers, scattered the gold-bearing gravel, and created new placers. Chance, then, played an important role in discovery of placer deposits.

Still, chance could be minimized by careful and scientific prospecting. Warnings throughout the U. S. Geological Survey's bulletins cautioned miners to study an area thoroughly before committing large capital toward its development. As more knowledge accumulated on the geology of placer deposits, the more sophisticated and efficient operations became. Initially the bonanza miners of the Klondike period had focused on river bars, creeks, or beaches where only a gold pan or rocker supplied a daily wage. Finding an environment totally different from past mining experience, miners developed drift-mining to take advantage of the permanently frozen ground. Later they modified the other three basic mining methods—open-cut, hydraulic, and dredging—to conform to their special circumstances. Not only did they explore, survey, and research, but they innovated and adapted as well.

Like the road builders, early Yukon miners struggled with permafrost and muck. Every miner faced the problem of removing the muck or burrowing through it to the permafrost.[5]

For small-scale operations, drift mining in the permafrost offered the easiest approach, for in the frozen ground no timbering or pumping was needed. Furthermore, drift mining perpetuated the miner's independence. One man could run the operation, and so no large capital, complex organization, or expensive machinery was required. Unfortunately, drift mining only mined the bedrock, and any gold in the overburden was irretrievably lost.[6]

As the bonanza strikes made the less-fortunate miners restless, the time-consuming method of melting the permafrost with wood fires led

Open-cut and sluice-box mining. One of the most prevalent mining methods involved stripping the overburden, excavating the gold-bearing gravel, and finally running water and gravel through long sluices. Clean-up collected gold that fell behind. *Alaska Sportsman.*

to another innovation—steam thawing. In 1898 C. J. Berry of Dawson noticed that steam from his engine exhaust had thawed a hole in the muck.[7] He connected a rubber hose to the exhaust and channeled it directly into the ground. Next he attached a rifle barrel with a small hole bored in the side and hammered it into the frozen ground. The steam point was thus invented. By this process, steam under high pressure from a portable steam boiler passed through rubber hoses and into hollow steam points driven into the ground. Once the points were heated, the pressure was reduced and they were left to thaw the surrounding ground slowly. Since thawing for drift mining could now be easily directed and channeled, shafts could be sunk more quickly, though at greater expense.

While drift mining progressed with the introduction of steam points, open-cut mining—the mining of a large area from the surface to the bedrock—adapted a myriad of western mining techniques. Although

Klondike miners had practiced open-cut methods, deep placers and frozen overburden had presented seemingly insurmountable problems. They found that, by removing the protective moss and allowing the muck to thaw naturally, shallow placers could be mined. Standard manual methods used by Bryant typified these small operations—ground sluicing or booming followed by shoveling in.

Open-cut mining also adapted itself to large-scale modifications. Mechanical methods such as steam scrapers, bottomless scrapers, cableway excavators, and dragline excavators were employed.[8] The high cost of transportation, however, discouraged the use of bulky and heavy machinery. The choice of method, manual or mechanical, depended upon the topography, the bedrock grade, the depth of the overburden, the abundance of water, the quantity of frozen gravel, and the amount of capital to be invested. All methods ended at the sluice box and worked only with enough water to sluice down the excavated gold-bearing gravel. Unfortunately, by 1910 shallow deposits were rare. Furthermore, the bedrock grade of the Yukon seldom proved steep enough to dispose of the tailings adequately.

The shallow bedrock grade also prevented the full exploitation of hydraulic mining as it had developed in California. In 1852, in California, Edward E. Matteson had invented the process that channeled water under high pressure into pipes that shot it out in jets of great velocity against the face of a gravel bank.[9] When the bank fell, the gravel was then disintegrated and carried by force into a sluice.

On the Yukon the process was modified to include any operation that applied water under pressure. Hydraulic mining could be used to excavate, transport, sluice, or dispose of the tailings. Most commonly, the process was used to strip overburden and muck.[10] Often hydraulic mining supplemented open-cut, dredging, or even drift mining and, unlike in California, was seldom the sole method employed.

In addition to steep bedrock grade, hydraulic mining depended on an abundance of water under high pressure together with adequate dumping room for disposal of the tailings. The Yukon environment supplied none of these advantages. The annual precipitation was less than twelve inches, and few natural reservoirs impounded the available water. Thus reservoirs, ditches, and wooden flumes had to be built to increase the water supply, with resulting high initial cost and continuing maintenance expense. The gentle slopes of the mountains and the low grade of the creek valleys prevented high pressure from developing

Hydraulic mining. Hydraulic mining channeled water under high pressure into pipes that shot it out in jets of great velocity against the face of a gravel bank. When the bank fell, the gravel was then disintegrated and carried by force into a sluice. *University of Alaska Archives.*

naturally and allowed no sufficient grade for sluicing or dumping the tailings. Moreover, the short season, from June to September, made large investments risky and scarce. Unlike California gold, that of the Yukon was not distributed throughout a bench bank but rather concentrated in the lower 15 percent near bedrock.[11] Also in contrast to California's large-scale industry, hydraulic plants of the north country were small, with low capital investment. Although a number of mines used hydraulic methods in some part of the process, true hydraulic mining occurred only in shallow placers where soft bedrock cleaned readily and other environmental requirements were met.

As the bonanza deposits that allowed inefficient and wasteful practices became exhausted, miners began to improve their methods and reduce costs, thus enabling them to exploit the lower grade gravel. Meanwhile, improvements and modifications lifted the steam point from a simple tool of poor miners to a component of large-scale mining. Now steam thawing required boilers, machinery, and additional men. Eventually miners applied the technique to large areas of overburden and muck that could be washed away. Then the whole area, from surface to bedrock, could be worked. Once the steam point made thawing of large areas practicable, other and more elaborate methods also became practicable, chiefly dredging.

New Zealand miners invented the dredging process, but Californians quickly adopted and improved on it. In 1899, hard on the heels of the bonanza diggings, the first dredge arrived in the Klondike. The bucket-ladder-and-stacker-type dredge developed in California became the most widely used. Typically, the dredge consisted of a bucket elevator placed on a barge averaging thirty-five feet wide and one hundred feet long. Constructed in a pit below the water level of the creek, the barge floated once water was readmitted. The dredge then dug its way forward by means of a chain of steel buckets upon a lowering ladder. The buckets in turn dumped the gravel through a screen and into a revolving washing apparatus at the rear of the barge. After the gravel was washed and the heavy gold fell into sluice boxes, the tailings traveled by conveyor belt to the stacker forty feet or so beyond the barge. Here they were dropped out of the way of the dredge. The dredge advanced forward and sideways by means of winches moored to posts on shore and powered by hydroelectricity or wood or coal boilers. Later, diesel engines served as effective power sources.[12]

Early dredges on the Yukon proved costly failures. Inadequate prospecting propelled operations into expensive investments and mistakes. Moreover, poor construction coupled with grandiose plans for large dredges contributed to the failures. Finally, unforeseen high costs in construction, transportation, labor, and maintenance added unusual

Dredge mining. The most efficient method of mining—dredging—required a broad valley with shallow and even distribution of gold. A mechanical bucket ladder (above) dug up the gravel and dropped it into a revolving washing apparatus. The gold fell out, but the gravel continued to the stacker (below) for dumping. *Melody Webb, National Park Service.*

expenses. The chronic problem of frozen gravel dealt the lethal blow to the early ventures.

Thus the same problems that faced drift miners, open-cut miners, and hydraulic engineers confronted dredge operators—frozen gravel and muck. Hydraulicking and ground sluicing stripped the muck and opened the gravel to natural thawing that often took two to three seasons to complete. Dredge owners turned to steam points to thaw the gravel in advance of their dredges.

In 1912 the high cost of using steam points led to experiments with hot water. The Yukon Gold Company of the Klondike commissioned two men, Henry M. Payne and W. L. Churchill, to investigate the temperature, nature, and depth of the frozen material. The commencement of World War I disrupted their studies. In 1917, however, John H. Miles startled the placer industry by announcing the superiority of cold-water thawing over hot water and steam. Not only was it cheaper because the water did not have to be heated, but it produced a superior thaw pattern. Miles recommended a minimum temperature of thirty-six degrees; but the warmer the water, of course, the more heat available for transfer to the frozen ground.[13]

Although the problem of thawing frozen gravel had been resolved, other factors had to be considered before profitable dredging could commence. Extensive prospecting and drilling were absolute necessities in order to learn the character and depth of the bedrock, the dimensions of the deposit, its gold tenor, and the distribution of boulders. The climate, length of season, water and fuel supplies, power possibilities, labor, and transportation costs had to be considered. Finally, the valley to be dredged had to be broad, with an even distribution of gold and deposits no deeper than thirty-five feet and no shallower than two. Once these factors were considered, the operator faced the task of ordering and installing the dredge, followed by organizing and maintaining a camp of not less than twenty men.[14]

Although mining methods improved and evolved chronologically, their application occurred in a haphazard manner. The least efficient, drift mining, happened simultaneously with the most efficient, dredging. Nonetheless, the development of the placer industry followed the basic pattern established in California. Eclipsed by the romance and excitement of the early gold rushes, the history of north country placer mining centered on the persevering and innovative miner.

Throughout the history of the placer industry, Yukon miners con-

Steam thawing. All mining necessitated the thawing of the permanently frozen ground. Techniques evolved from steam points to hot and cold water thawing. Once the lines were driven into the ground, the warmth of the water thawed the permafrost enough to allow mining. *University of Alaska Archives.*

fronted the same problems: short working season, lack of suitable grade in the streams, poor water supply, poverty of timber resources, high cost of labor and transportation, concentration of gold on or in bedrock, great thickness of overburden, frozen gravel, lack of wagon roads, high cost of fuel, inadequate police protection, and ineffectual laws and mining regulations. Although conditions improved with time, these problems were never fully solved. In fact, as miners of lower grade deposits inched their way into profits, dry seasons or erratic transportation catapulted them back into shoestring operations. Thus the placer mining industry moved forward, but also slid backward as far as it advanced.

The first period of Alaskan placer mining reflected the bonanza mentality. From 1897 to approximately 1906, miners either followed the moving frontier of gold-rush towns or prospected for their own bonanza. Those who remained on the Yukon sought the most expedient means to reach bedrock. The development of bonanza deposits led to wasteful methods—the gold pan, rocker, and sluice box. With capital, experience, or ability, miners lucked into rich shallow deposits. The lure of this poor-man's mining attracted thousands of ill-equipped and inexperienced men, each unwilling or uninterested in consolidating claims, investing large capital, or organizing long-range plans. This era found claims on every creek.

Fairbanks became the biggest bonanza. The gold discovered in 1902 proved rich and deep but covered with more than a hundred feet of heavy overburden and muck. Thus, deep mining or drift mines developed. By 1905, however, the Fairbanks area accounted for more than one-half of the gold produced in the territory. Cleary Creek alone added $4.5 million. In 1906, despite water supply problems, Fairbanks contributed more than $9 million. For Fairbanks the bonanza years continued until 1909, when the Iditarod rush and the exhaustion of rich placers occurred simultaneously.[15]

Meanwhile, a few hardy souls experimented with California's more advanced techniques. While miners on Seventymile started a hydraulic mine, others on Fortymile applied steam points to their drift mines. Since steam boilers required at least two men, greater technological development in turn forced greater cooperation. The miners on American Creek built a flume and tried to use the ineffective method of hydraulic elevators. Because the USGS had just begun its yearly reconnaissance and survey reports, miners could learn only by trial and error what methods would work in the unusual Alaskan environment. On Mammoth Creek, near Circle, they attempted mechanical methods of open-cut mining and introduced the steam shovel.

Although some machinery had been brought in and searches for suitable dredging ground had begun, most Yukon miners ignored the low-grade gravel and capitalized on the smaller but richer placer deposits. For example, twenty individual miners or small operators of Fourth of July and Woodchopper creeks produced the largest quantity of gold in the area. Moreover, more than half the claims used drift-mining methods. In 1906, Woodchopper alone, largely through winter drift mines, produced more than $18,000. These miners were not unique; more than 85 percent of Alaska's gold production came from placers.[16] Only in southeastern Alaska and Prince William Sound did gold lode mines develop extensively.

General discontent prevailed across the territory. The lack of roads and trails and the inadequate steamboat service hampered the development of good mining claims. Abuse of the power-of-attorney provision in federal mining law provoked further complaints. With this power,

Alfred Hulse Brooks and the U.S. Geological Survey. From 1895 through World War II, the USGS pioneered geological studies, which led to more efficient mineral extraction. More significant and less known, the USGS staff chronicled the growth of the Yukon's most important industry—mining. *United States Geological Survey.*

one individual could tie up a creek, prevent any new bonanza seeker from staking a claim, and contribute to rampant speculation.[17]

Slowly the bonanza seekers recognized that the rich deposits were rapidly becoming exhausted. The few small gold rushes that occurred evoked only a bit of nostalgia for a past era. Although the Yukon had been a holdout against outside investment, by the end of 1906 several groups of claims had passed into the hands of strong companies that promised improvement in mining technology. As the bonanza period ebbed, a transitional period, from 1907 to 1914, resulted in a decline in gold production. During this transition from bonanza mining to low-grade mining, miners experimented with dredges, ditch systems, and hydraulic plants. Careful prospecting and planning, however, did not precede these large developments. Thus, when the cycle of drought years began in 1910, all mines suffered heavily.

Characteristic of the transitional years, Iditarod boomed with production of $2 and $3 million per year while Fairbanks placers declined. At the same time, mining operators began experimenting with small dredges in Fairbanks and Iditarod, tried new mechanical scrapers for moving gravel, and opened a few failed drift mines to open-cut mining methods. Representative of the transitional period was an increasing number of open-cut mines. In addition, four steam-powered dredges moved into the Fortymile area using steam-point thawing. Still another dredge was built on Mastodon Creek, and new steam scrapers mined open cuts on Fourth of July Creek. Miners on American Creek, Seventy-mile River, and Mammoth Creek attempted hydraulic plants and ditch systems, but the shortage of water forced them to close. Even though gold production declined in this period, the effort to improve mining methods drew praise from both the USGS and the editors of *The Mining and Scientific Press*.[18]

During the transitional period, miners throughout Alaska confronted similar problems. For instance, an overall business stagnation that followed the financial panic of 1907 prevented large amounts of capital from being invested in large-scale placer mines.[19] Lack of capital also meant inadequate transportation systems. Cries for improved transportation culminated in a singular demand for a railroad.

Because of the problems and lack of knowledge and experience, low-grade deposits remained almost untouched, and the placer-mining business fluctuated. Mining companies recognized that only with the exploitation of lower grade material would stability arrive.[20] Yet at the same time, the pioneer miner, who discovered and opened new districts, could take little part in the development of large enterprises.

The years 1915 and 1916 saw conditions improve considerably, except in the Fairbanks area. As Fairbanks mines shifted emphasis from bonanza to lower-grade mining, Iditarod gold production surpassed that of Fairbanks. In the upper Yukon, only a new dredge on Mammoth Creek

survived to the end of the doldrums. Hydraulic plants, however, prolif-
erated on Alder, Crooked, Fourth of July, Mastodon, Eagle, Switch, and
Butte creeks. In 1916 more than 70 mines in the Eagle-Circle area employed 265 men and produced in excess of $375,000. The tendency
toward large-scale mining increased. On the other hand, drift mining,
especially in Fairbanks, where miners perfected it to its ultimate peak,
still occurred. The great production, however, came from the larger
operations.[21]

With the onset of World War I, the improvement in mining conditions ceased abruptly. A gold depression set in that lasted from 1917 to
1923. The war depleted the labor supply and raised the cost of materials and equipment. Dry summers plagued those who attempted to mine.
Mines such as Alder and Woodchopper closed. Less than half the placers endured as one after another of the small-scale, high-cost operations
succumbed to the adverse conditions. With the exhaustion of the bonanza deposits, the production of gold shrank to new lows. No longer did
gold rank as the territory's leading export. Prospectors in large numbers,
discouraged by the continuing depression and attracted by good business opportunities elsewhere, left the territory altogether.[22]

Hard times hit both the large and small miner, but the small miner
lacked stamina and resources to last out the gold depression. In 1920
the average annual return to the small miner was $398, whereas his
yearly provisions cost $420. Thus he had to find remunerative occupa-
tions, such as trapping or woodcutting, in addition to mining. Yet at
the same time owners of the large dredges and hydraulic plants could
not allow them to lie idle, and thus continuous improvement in mining methods and economic management occurred. A general consen-
sus in the USGS was that the day of profitable small operations had
passed. Almost as important was the recognition that large operations
could not support the settlements built on bonanza mining and that
some were bound to decline or die.[23]

Although prospects on placer mining appeared bleak, one bright
hope became reality. The Alaska Railroad neared completion. Improved
transportation now offered an opportunity to exploit the low-grade
deposits that previously could not be profitably mined. Slowly the
placer-mining industry struggled back to a stable base.

The following period, 1924 to 1929, marked the consolidation of
claims and a peak for the production of low-grade deposits. Nevertheless,
mineral production continued to rank second to fisheries in monetary

value. During these years, rainfall and water supply proved sufficient, and thus hydraulic mining grew in popularity. Careful planning, efficient management, extensive experimentation, and the replacement of obsolete machinery also signaled a new approach to low-cost mining. The completion of the Steese Highway, moreover, allowed new and heavy equipment to be transported by railroad and then by road to the Yukon mines. Despite these improvements, gold production in the Fairbanks district continued to decline. To compete with newly consolidated and automated mines, the Fairbanks Exploration Company began consolidating claims, building ditch lines, constructing dredges, and drilling to learn the extent and tenor of its goldfields.[24]

During these years of consolidation, placer mining evolved from the mine of the poor man to the mine of the engineer and the capitalist. Technical training, large capital, and labor-saving machinery replaced the old-timer's intuition and back-breaking labor. Consequently, the number of prospectors decreased. Responding to the strong mining lobby, the territorial legislature passed the Prospector's Aid Act. Under this legislation, Alaska prospectors received monetary assistance to meet some of their transportation expenses.[25]

The next period, 1929–34, found the world in business stagnation and depression. Unlike the gold depression of 1917–23, however, this period did not bring a slump to placer mining. In fact, the constant price of gold, coupled with large unemployment, revived an interest in prospecting. Yukon placers, stimulated by a number of new miners and plentiful supplies of water, produced greater quantities than before 1918.[26]

Fairbanks's mines led the way. The year 1929 marked the first full year of production for Fairbanks Exploration Company's three dredges in the Fairbanks area. The following year the company added two more and worked into January—the longest dredging season in history. Gold production climbed to nearly $3 million. The USGS cited Fairbanks Exploration's extensive mining operations as "the outstanding placer-mining enterprise not only in the Fairbanks district but throughout the territory."[27]

The Great Depression, however, limited the capital available for development and increased the value of machinery and supplies. Thus small operations enjoyed a revival. At the same time, miners recognized the effectiveness of hydraulic and open-cut methods, and drift mining became an anachronism. In 1932, when the price of gold rose from

Changes in technology. While modern technology did not eliminate the prospector, his prospect hole, or ever-present steam boiler (above), sophisticated drilling rigs (below) made prospecting more scientific, cost effective, and reliable. *George Beck, Eagle, Alaska and University of Alaska Archives.*

$20.67 to $35.00 an ounce, the appeal of placer mining intensified. With this boost, in 1934 Ernest Patty began prospect drilling of Coal Creek with contingency plans for a dredge.[28]

Although the global depression continued until World War II, the

Yukon saw its peak production and development between 1935 and 1942. The year 1940 registered the greatest year in placer mining. The Fairbanks area alone climbed to a peak of $7.3 million, Circle district came in with $1.5 million, and Iditarod brought just under $1 million. Fairbanks Exploration had extensive operations throughout the Fairbanks area, including eight dredges and numerous small hydraulic plants. Dredges also worked Deadwood, Mammoth, Mosquito, Walker Fork, and Jack Wade creeks. Dragline, bulldozer, and other hydraulic operations capitalized on the boom. Despite the flourishing conditions, strikes in 1941 closed most of the Fairbanks Exploration dredges, and production fell more than $2 million.[29]

While Fairbanks and Circle boomed, Ernest Patty and Gen. A. D. Mc-Rae bought and consolidated the claims on Coal and Woodchopper creeks in the Eagle district. During the next few years, their mining company built ditch systems, two camps with frame structures mounted on skids, a road joining the two camps, and two dredges. With hydraulic nozzles, they stripped the muck to the gravel, then, using the ditch water, applied cold-water thawing. An airstrip improved transportation of supplies, men, and equipment. Other camps in the area progressed as well.[30]

Because of the Depression, interest rates were low, and the government offered limited subsidies as well as tax deductions on unprofitable enterprises. Nevertheless, the territorial legislature placed a license tax of 3 percent on mineral production in excess of $10,000.[31]

The boom shuddered to a halt with the entry of the United States into World War II. Wartime industrial planners declared gold mining nonstrategic, and operations shut down.

After the war, rapidly rising costs forced many mines to stay closed. To cut costs, Patty discontinued hydraulic stripping of muck overburden in favor of ground sluicing, allowing the creek water to erode the muck. He also abandoned cold-water thawing for solar or natural thawing. In spite of all new techniques adopted, soaring labor and material costs forced profits lower and lower. Finally, in 1957, Patty closed the dredges. They were leased for five years, then sold in the early 1970s to Joe Vogler, a politician and developer, and Ernest Wolff, a mining engineer and professor at the University of Alaska, and his partner, Dan Colben.

Thereafter high costs prevented much profit despite the inflated value of gold. Operations other than Patty's fared as poorly. A few miners worked the old deposits around Circle and Eagle, but only marginal operations continued at Coal and Ben creeks, and both were mined by open-cut methods.[32]

In 1967 the federal government removed the fixed standard for the price of gold and allowed it to float on the market. In 1980 gold reached its peak of $800 per ounce and then fell to an average $300 per ounce. The high price of gold, however, sparked renewed interest in placer mining. Mining companies reexamined old goldfields, novice miners leased tailing piles, and prospectors and mining engineers searched for new fields. Despite the spurt of enthusiasm and interest, most miners and mining engineers recognized that most of the placer deposits were exhausted. Moreover, the high cost of petroleum fuels, equipment, and labor discouraged extensive operations on marginal fields.[33]

Mineral development on the Canadian side of the border followed a pattern similar to Alaska's. Although the gold-rush economy collapsed in 1902, the period between 1900 and 1914 became known as the Golden Age of Dawson. Of the $250 million that the Klondike ultimately produced, more than 75 percent came out after 1900. Like the Alaska Yukon, the period before World War I produced stability and security through capital-intensive mining, sophisticated machinery and technology, and the acquisition and consolidation of individual claims. By 1914 gold production reached more than $5 million with producing mines at Mayo as well as on the Klondike. Moreover, copper mines near Whitehorse opened the territory's first productive base-metal industry.[34]

World War I had a wide-reaching impact on gold mining. It raised production costs, maintained rigid gold prices, depleted the labor supply, and caused inflation. Thus, the Canadian gold-mining industry, like the Alaskan, came to a virtual halt.

Development of the Canadian mining industry confronted one major obstacle not present in Alaska—Arthur Newton Christian Treadgold. An Oxford graduate and former schoolmaster, the budding entrepreneur arrived in Dawson in 1898 determined to control the area. Within three years he did. Although he initiated the process of consolidation and introduced novel methods of mining frozen gravel, his ruthless goal to own the Klondike undermined the whole industry. Using the investment capital of various companies that he controlled, he bought claims and more claims. As a result, between 1918 and 1932, gold mining, both in Mayo and Dawson, stagnated.[35]

Meanwhile, in 1919 silver-lead ore was discovered on Keno Hill, near Mayo. Despite Treadgold control, the area boomed in 1924 with

Canadian mining. After the ebb of Klondike, silver-lead ore deposits near Mayo and lead-zinc near Faro brought new life to Yukon Territory. Just as Dawson faded into memory, the exhaustion of these ores devastated dependent communities. *Yukon Archives.*

the installation of a concentrating mill. By 1925 silver-lead production surpassed Klondike gold production. Exhaustion of one ore body, in 1932, forced the closing of the mines and concentrator. Meanwhile, the worldwide depression caused gold mining to boom. Hounded by creditors, Yukon Consolidated Gold Corporation reorganized and removed Treadgold from control. Almost immediately the industry began full-scale production with efficient reworking of known reserves. Each year between 1937 and 1942 mineral production exceeded that of 1917.[36] World War II, however, forced most of the mining industry to suspend operation.

Not until after 1950 did mining industries in Yukon Territory once again begin effective production. The national government stimulated the depressed industry with cost-sharing programs in road construction and exploration grants worth 40 percent of the total exploration cost. The Canadian government also provided geological services, airstrips, and mineral access roads. These boosts assisted the development of new deposits of tungsten and asbestos and encouraged reopening copper and silver-lead mines.

During this time, the largest mining project on the Yukon began. In 1953 a prospector found a large deposit of lead-zinc 120 miles northwest of Whitehorse. As exploration commenced in 1966, a minor rush resulted in more than sixteen thousand claims being staked. Backed by an American firm and subsidized by the Canadian government, the Cyprus Anvil Mining Corporation constructed the townsite of Faro in 1968 and began production in 1969. By 1978 the mine was the greatest producer of Canada's lead and provided 40 percent of the revenues of Yukon Territory. Faro had become the territory's second largest city.[37]

The Canadian mines, however, bottomed out in the 1980s. In 1982 the Cyprus Mine shut down, the Keno Hill mine near Mayo closed its silver-lead operation, and the Whitehorse copper mine depleted its ore body.[38] The closing of the mines left thousands unemployed, suspended operation of the White Pass and Yukon Railway, and devastated the communities of Faro, Whitehorse, and Skagway. The mining frontier appeared ended.

The Yukon experienced the drama and excitement of gold-rush bonanzas, saw experiments with various mining methods, suffered through droughts and depressions, realized full potential, and slumped with the exhaustion of its deposits. Faced with a unique environment and its related problems, twentieth-century miners adopted or modified the methods of earlier mining frontiers and, in several instances, invented new techniques to conform to unusual environmental demands. But as in the exploitation of any mineral deposit, exhaustion always occurred. Although the placer industry waned, a few miners continued to live as had C. A. Bryant in the early days. The mining frontier did not vanish altogether, and a handful of prospectors hoped that other minerals might foster still other mining horizons.

CHAPTER 13

The Enduring Frontier

Two of Turner's frontiers—ranching and farming—never fully developed in the Yukon Basin. The short growing season, rough terrain, peaty soil, permafrost, uncertain market, high freight costs, and inadequate land laws discouraged agricultural ventures. Although local farmers in the Tanana Valley produced vegetables, hay, and grain for Fairbanks and for mining camps, farms remained small. By 1917, after liberalization of the homesteading laws and development of agricultural experiment stations, Alaska claimed only fourteen hundred homesteaders. While in 1959 the Tanana Valley had six hundred patented homesteads, and nearly all the accessible land had become private through the homesteading process, the valley could boast only one large dairy farm, a few smaller ones, and some potato farms. Most of the homesteads became rural or second homes for people employed in Fairbanks. Others stimulated the real estate industry as the valley population grew after World War II. Despite hardy hybrid crops developed for the North's severe environment, potential farmers never overcame the enormous transportation and marketing problems of the region.[1]

Instead of developing agricultural frontiers, latter-day frontiersmen harvested the natural bounty. In keeping with the mystique of the last frontier, entrepreneurs pursued the historic occupation of the nineteenth century—trapping. During the twentieth century, trapping and mining became the only industries to endure in the rural areas of the Yukon Basin. While the U.S. Geological Survey has documented the development of mining, no scholar has probed the significance of trapping to Yukon economy and lifeways.

The story of Evelyn Berglund Shore portrays the nearly anachronistic life of the modern fur trapper.[2] She was born on July 30, 1917, on American Creek near Eagle. Typically, her father mined and did a little trapping. Two years after her birth the family moved to Nation City, where they shared their "city" with six old-timers and twelve or fourteen Indians. Here they tried to earn a living by catching salmon to dry and sell, supplemented by backyard trapping. They left Nation City in 1921 and for the next seven years trapped the Sheenjek River, a tributary of the Porcupine. In 1928 Evelyn's father, crippled with arthritis, entered the Fort Yukon hospital while his wife and three daughters, aged nine, eleven, and twelve, joined an old trapper on the Salmon River, a tributary of the Black River 280 miles from Fort Yukon. For the next thirteen years these women, with a self-reliance typical of the occupation, trapped and hunted to support themselves in a remote and demanding country far from schools and friends.

Each summer they bought on credit a year's supply of food and necessary equipment, which they loaded into hand-built scows and poling boats, equipped with a motor to help over the rough spots. Cases of canned goods and sacks of flour went on the floor of the boat with sugar and perishables on top. Then dogs and kids were added. The upriver trip took six weeks to two months as they poled and tracked the boats, fighting snags, riffles, and drift piles. They kept mosquitoes at bay, in the days before effective insect repellent, with hats, gloves, bandannas, and smudge fires.

Once at the home cabin, the women set to work fishing. Twelve dogs demanded great quantities of salmon, grayling, and pike. Gill nets and fishing poles provided sixty to seventy fish a day. They also cut dry grass to serve as winter bedding for the dogs. Repair work commenced on the home cabin while the picking of currants, cranberries, raspberries, and blueberries offered diversions not only in diet but also from tedious labors. With September came the hunting season. Since there were only three weeks before ice formed on the river and moose grew too thin from rutting, the women spent long, hard hours poling, stalking, killing, and packing the two moose and four or five caribou needed to last through the winter.

In November the trapping season began. With it came the hardest work of the year—setting out the traplines. They cut new trails, cleared old trails, killed additional game for the line cabins, built meat caches, and erected trail tents or line cabins. The latter were small log structures often built without windows and containing only two pole bunks,

Evelyn Berglund Shore. Between 1928 and 1941, Evelyn Berglund with her mother and two sisters trapped and hunted in a remote area of the Yukon Basin. Their self-reliant but debtor life-style typified that of the last frontier. *University of Alaska Archives.*

a pole bench, campstove, and green spruce boughs for the floor. Yet these simple structures required eight days of hard labor. In addition, adjacent dog shelters, usually made from the boughs and tops of trees, consumed more time and energy. Finally, wherever they saw tracks, they built trail sets for wolf, fox, wolverine, lynx, marten, mink, and ermine. Eventually they had three hundred miles of trapping trails, ten line cabins, several line trails, twelve tent camps, and a number of permanent caches. The hours were long and the work hard, but as Evelyn wrote: "We never stopped to think what was girl's work and what was men's work. It was all work, and if it needed to be done, we had to do it."

Winter work entailed running the traplines. After each new snow, trail had to be broken by packing the trail in front of the toboggan with snowshoes. Each toboggan carried approximately three hundred pounds. These supplies included rations for thirty days, which were twenty loaves of frozen bread, one hundred frozen doughnuts, thirty pounds of dried beans, half a slab of bacon, thirty pounds of sugar, thirty to forty

pounds of flour, two pounds of tallow, six pounds of butter, ten to fifteen pounds of frozen cranberries, fifty pounds of frozen mooseburger
patties, five pounds of dried milk, two to three pounds of dried eggs, six
cans of tomatoes, a little macaroni, cheese, baking powder, and salt.
The utensils consisted of a big kettle, two frying pans, two small pots,
and a plate, knife, fork, spoon, and cup for each person. A caribou skin
mattress and feather sleeping robes and pillows provided bedding. The
first trip each year included tents, campstoves, and five hundred traps
plus snares. Finally 200 to 250 pounds of cornmeal and dried fish for
dog food and game rifles, evenly distributed, completed the load. Once
they had set the traps and established the trail camps, the toboggan carried home the harvested fur.

The trails were run every few weeks, depending on the weather
and how remote they were. The large animals caught—lynx, wolf, and
fox—stayed frozen until early spring, when trapping season closed. The
smaller animals—marten, mink, and ermine—were skinned as soon as
caught. The women got three to fifteen marten each trip. One successful winter they trapped forty wolves.

Between trapping runs, life at the sixteen-by-eighteen-foot home
cabin was busy. Clothes were washed and dried while meals of beans,
bread, pies, and doughnuts were cooked in quantities large enough to
be frozen for trips. They used the less valuable skins for a number of
purposes: rabbit for lining mittens, caribou and bear for mattresses, and
untanned caribou strips for mending dog harnesses and threading snowshoes. During the long evenings, they played checkers, knitted, or listened to the radio.

Spring ended the trapping season, but not the work. All traps, tents,
and campstoves had to be collected. The larger animals had to be skinned
and stretched. Any left-over meat was cut in strips and smoked dry. For
two weeks in April, the women trapped beaver until they reached the
limit of ten each. If time allowed, they planted a small garden of lettuce,
turnips, and other hardy vegetables. At long last, they loaded the scow
and poling boat with the furs and floated to Fort Yukon. Here, each year
for eleven successive years, they learned that their $1,600 to $2,000
worth of supplies cost more than their furs had brought.

The twelfth year, an exceptionally good year for fur and fur prices,
the women finally worked themselves out of debt. The following year,
in February 1941, Evelyn, now twenty-three years old, left the trapline
to marry a man she had met in Fort Yukon—another trapper. Almost

contentedly she wrote: "Four of my five children were born, as I was born, on snowshoes. It would not surprise me at all if some of them, at least, spent most of their lives wrestling loaded toboggans out from between niggerheads, lighting fires in the icy stoves of snowed-in cabins, making camp in cold, dark, lonesome tents way out in the timber with the northern lights pulsing from horizon to horizon and the wolves howling far away. They will never get rich, but they could do worse."[3]

Although the seasonal cycle described by Evelyn Berglund Shore applied to trappers of both the nineteenth and twentieth centuries, several differences set them apart. The greatest arose primarily with the increased number of white trappers. Previously, only Natives had trapped fur-bearing animals for trade at white trading posts. In 1899 Congress amended the Customs Acts of 1868 and 1879 to allow non-Natives to trap. The gold rushes brought an increase of white miners and new summer occupations such as steamboat work, prospecting, and single-man gold claims, which could be coupled with trapping for winter income. Thus, in contrast to the Native trapping families of the nineteenth century, many of the twentieth-century trappers were either bachelors or men whose families remained behind in neighboring communities. The desire for schooling for their children forced both Native and white trappers into abbreviated seasonal cycles and modified life-styles.

In addition, modes of transportation had changed radically. Trappers— white and Native—now used dog teams more frequently than they walked their traplines. Eventually technology introduced the "iron dog," the snowmobile, which proved much faster, more powerful, and in the long run more effective than the dog team. Although steamboats brought more supplies closer to the traplines, poling boats and scows were still utilized to a great extent. During the first quarter of the twentieth century, motorboats slowly replaced poling boats and scows and eased summer transportation. Thus trappers working the Yukon and Tanana corridors, unlike the Berglund family, had their summers free because their home cabins were closer to a supply base. Finally, the last transportation improvement, the airplane, allowed trappers to exploit even more remote and isolated areas than ever before.

Trapping technology also differed between the two centuries. Because of the Yukon's isolation and transportation limitations in the nineteenth century, supplies were either scarce or prohibitively expensive. Thus, without labor-saving equipment, the early Yukon trapper spent more effort and time on his trapline than modern trappers. Typical was the deadfall. Using a natural confinement or creating one from logs, the early trapper designed a door or killing log, manufactured from one big log or a series of smaller ones. A trigger stick propped up the door, and bait was carefully placed beneath it. When an animal entered the confinement to get the bait, it knocked over the trigger stick and was struck and killed by the door or killing log. The deadfall required no imported equipment except an axe, but demanded considerably more labor than a metal trap or snare.

As twentieth-century technology improved transportation, supplies became more plentiful. Metal traps and snares replaced deadfalls. The most popular was the Newhouse trap, but Blake and Lamb, Victor, Oneida, and later Conibear were also used. These required less labor but cost money and added weight to a trapper's outfit.

Like deadfalls, traps needed occasional repair. Some trappers boiled their traps in water with spruce tips and alder bark added, then hung them in a dry, sheltered place away from human odor. Others went so far as to wax their traps to prevent rust. Various sizes were used for different animals: No. 1 for ermine, marten, and muskrat; No. 1 1/2 for marten, mink, and fox; Nos. 2 and 3 for lynx and fox; No. 4 for beaver and wolverine; and No. 4 1/2 for wolf.

Snares, on the other hand, were inexpensive, easy to transport, and easy to set. They could be handmade, as they were in the nineteenth century, from a roll of nineteen-strand wire. Those commercially made in the twentieth century, however, came with a locking slide on double-twisted cable. Both came in different sizes for different animals. Trappers from both centuries snared lynx and beaver and occasionally wolves.

Other technological improvements made twentieth-century trapping more effective. Repeating rifles supplanted muskets, and nylon fishnets, fish wheels, and chain saws contributed to a more efficient exploitation of the resources with considerably less effort from trappers. Technology, however, had its price. Trappers lost self-reliance and independence. They now depended on the uncertainties of machinery and the ability of other people to supply fuel, parts, and repairs. Furthermore, the introduction of engines demanded a greater capital outlay than the more labor-intensive equipment of earlier days.

Despite the differences in trapping technology between the two centuries, many aspects remained the same. Trapping methods changed little over the centuries. Skill in trapping still required knowing more than how to set a trap or snare. Trappers studied the behavior and habits of the animals, then adapted the best lures and trapping sets to exploit this behavior. Familiarity with the land—its hills, gullies, lakes, streams, meadows, and forests—coupled with knowledge of the animals, increased the annual take. Whereas some trappers learned a few basic techniques to supplement their income, the expert trappers spent years perfecting their knowledge and skills.

Trapping lures changed little from those of the nineteenth century. They consisted of scents and baits that enticed the animal into the traps or snares. Trappers regarded the scent as more valuable because it lasted longer and created greater curiosity in the victim. Occasionally, however, trappers used bait in addition to scent. Bait most often was the entrails or skin of moose or caribou but could also be fresh or frozen salmon. Although some trappers used commercial lures, most had their own personally invented favorites, which they often kept secret from their competitors. All agreed, however, that different lures attracted different animals; thus no one lure served all. Sometimes the urine, feces, or glands from animals served as lures. Most used beaver castor as an important ingredient, but others had lynx liver, fish oil, muskrat musk, aniseed oil, and fancy commercial additives. Before setting the trap or snare, the trapper smeared the lure onto rabbit fur, bird wings, flat pieces of wood, or moose skin. To keep the trap set attractive, trappers replaced scent and bait each time they ran the trapline.[4]

Intimate knowledge of the animals of the Yukon Basin meant not only success but often survival. Most novice trappers recognized mink, beaver, bear, fox, and wolf. Marten, lynx, and muskrat, however, required further identification. Marten resembled mink but was longer and heavier, with an orange patch under its neck. Lynx, similar to the bobcat of the American West, lacked a tail and had long legs and large paws that helped keep it on top of deep snow. Muskrat was much smaller than beaver and had a tail flattened vertically rather than horizontally.

The habits of each group of animals differed. Knowledge of the diet and the behavior of each was important. Marten, for example, were very mobile and would leave a region without warning or reason. Thus a trapper did not set traps for marten except where he found their tracks. Lynx, on the other hand, were extremely curious and dieted exclusively on snowshoe hares, which fluctuated on a ten-year cycle. Therefore lynx

Trapping muskrats. Trapping required skills in traps and lures, but also knowledge of the land and its animals. Here, because the trapper knew the muskrat's habits, he successfully set a trap in its "push-up," or lodge. *University of Alaska Archives.*

could be easily attracted into traps, but their numbers varied proportionally to the quantity of snowshoe hare.

Few expert trappers from either century skillfully utilized extensive or widespread traplines. Knowledge of the land was nearly as essential as knowing the animals themselves, and trapping areas were thus relatively small. Traplines averaged twenty-five miles in length and radiated from a base or home cabin. A trapper needed to know which rock outcroppings would funnel lynx trails, which spruce-covered hills contained marten, and which beaver lodge contained harvestable quantities. In addition, the placement of trails and cabins required knowledge of creek floodings, wind direction, and animal activities.

The trapper's traps, lures, and knowledge of the land and its animals culminated in the planning, placement, and building of the trap set. Each animal and geographic location required a different set. Sometimes the lay of the land dictated the form of the set, at other times the habits of the animal. The care taken in designing the set often determined the success of the trapper.

The trap set of the lynx, for example, demanded knowledge of the land and the habits of the lynx as well as skill with lures, scents, and traps or snares. First, the trapper identified a lynx trail by knowing that

Baling skinned and stretched fur. After skinning an animal, the trapper turned it inside out and scraped off the fat. Next he stretched the skin as wide as possible and left it to dry. Before shipment, the trapper turned the fur right side out and baled the skins tightly. *University of Alaska Archives.*

lynx inhabited forested river valleys and by recognizing its tracks. Next, he followed the lynx trail to a natural funneling caused by rock outcroppings, steep banks, or heavy underbrush. Then, depending on the surroundings, he selected either a snare, which would be secured to a large branch that dangled along the trail, or a trap, which would be tied to a heavy log. Sometimes the trapper narrowed the trail further with cut branches or small sticks stuck into the snow on either side of the trap or snare. To take advantage of the lynx's curosity, the trapper occasionally attracted its attention with a piece of rabbit skin, a bird's wing, or brightly colored ribbons. Finally, to ensure capture, a scent of beaver castor smeared on something in back of the trap lured the lynx into the trap.

Once the trapper brought in an animal from the trapline, he skinned, stretched, and dried it. Cutting across the anus from foot pad to foot pad of the hind legs, he pulled the skin back from the legs and stripped the carcass out of its tail. Then, cutting around the ears, eyes, nose, and mouth, he drew the skin over the head, inside out. Next he took a stretcher, two tapered boards hinged together at the pointed end, and slipped the cased skin over it. By sliding a wooden peg between the two boards towards the hinge, he could stretch the skin as wide as desired.

Next, with a dull table knife, he scraped off the fat. Finally, he hung the pelt from the cabin ceiling to dry overnight. When it was fully dried, the trapper removed the stretcher and turned the skin right side out so the fur buyer could examine the quality of the fur.

The value of the fur was usually related to its durability. The fur that wore the best brought the highest price. Excluding the fur of the endangered sea otter, beaver and mink offered durability without heavy weight, thereby often bringing high prices. Rabbit, squirrel, and ermine, on the other hand, weighed less, wore out easily, and brought lower prices.[5]

During late winter or early spring, trappers sold their fur to a local fur buyer or shipped it to a fur auction. Auction houses, such as West Coast Fur Sales and Seattle Fur Exchange, operated on straight commission. They accepted the furs, graded the pelts, put them in lots of similar size and quality, and then offered them for sale at widely publicized auctions. The results of the auction, minus the commission, were then mailed to the trapper. While fur auction prices averaged 20 percent higher than local prices, most trappers, especially Natives, lacked the capital required for shipping costs and export taxes.

Historically, the auction houses had very little control over the price of fur. Fashion and the quality and quantity of fur harvested determined the market value. As with any product, the market rose and fell, responding to international economic forces such as war and depression. These fluctuations affected the Yukon trapper and his quality of life.[6]

During the early 1900s, the fur market remained fairly stable. Then in 1914 the market fell until stimulated by the First World War's demand for fur. Prices rose again in 1917. At the same time, the hare and lynx reached their maximum population cycle. One trapper observed that the "country was alive with lynx"; he had trapped 225 lynx selling for eight dollars each.[7]

After the war, fur, like many other products, suffered a recession until approximately 1923, when the market recovered. The years from 1923 until 1929 marked the real boom of twentieth-century trapping. The United States replaced England as the raw-fur marketing center and Russia as the purchasing center for expensive, finished furs. During that time, lynx brought trappers up to one hundred dollars each. Meanwhile, the Alaska Game Commission, established in 1925, feared that marten might be trapped into extinction and thus closed the season in many areas of Alaska. From the winter of 1916 to the spring of 1929, the sea-

Fur harvest. Between 1915 and 1917, fur prices and yield peaked. In 1915, at New Rampart House on the Porcupine River, the bountiful fur harvest included lynx, wolf, marten, and fox. *University of Alaska Archives.*

son on marten was open only during three winters. Moreover, the season on beaver trapping was also closed during 1925, 1926, and 1929. Thus the price on marten and beaver crept from six dollars each to twenty-six dollars for beaver and thirty dollars for marten and sometimes much higher. Regardless of the closed seasons, the greatest peak in trapping occurred during 1928–29 with a total value of fur worth more than $4.5 million.[8]

During the Great Depression, fur prices declined. Either from overtrapping during the high fur prices or from scarcity of food for the furbearer, the fur catch also diminished. Game wardens blamed the decline on unscrupulous trappers using such illegal trapping methods as poisoning, trapping after the season had legally ended, poaching from Canadian trappers, and trapping more than the limit allowed. Furthermore, the high prices of the 1920s had tripled the number of trappers exploiting the fur resources—in 1929 more than 5,265 made their entire living from the fur business, not including 2,500 unlicensed Native trappers. The poor season of 1929–30, however, discouraged trappers throughout Alaska. For several of the seasons during the 1930s, the shortage of fur precipitated measures limiting marten and beaver to ten per trapper.

In addition, the lynx population cycle started a downward swing. Thus local conditions contributed to the fur depression as well as the international business failure and the scarcity of money.[9]

By 1936 the number of trappers had increased, the quantity of fur had improved, and prices had begun to climb. In 1937–38 above average prices coupled with increasing numbers of furbearers produced the best harvest return for the Depression era. In 1939 the value of the fur exports exceeded those of the fisheries and minerals.[10] Thus during the hard times of the Depression, the fur market provided trappers a low but steady and secure income.

The Fort Yukon area offered one of the richest trapping localities in Alaska. Unlike areas in which trapping augmented other income, Fort Yukon's trappers depended entirely on trapping for a livelihood. Because the majority of trappers were Natives with a cultural tie to the land, they trapped the same lines for years. This practice encouraged conservation and maintenance of adequate breeding reserves of furbearers. Seldom did game wardens complain of overtrapping, except by Canadians who poached on the American side of the boundary and stripped the region of fur. Indeed, game wardens found the Natives more attentive to game regulations than transient white trappers. It was not unusual for Natives to request that areas be closed to marten and beaver trapping. One warden reported that some Natives had personally warned some unscrupulous trappers and "threatened them with more severe penalties than those imposed by the Alaska Game Law."[11]

Game wardens had a nearly impossible assignment. For several decades, only two or three men patrolled the area north of the Kuskokwim River to the Arctic coast. They lacked government boats, cars, dog teams, or airplanes. One warden purchased his own personal aircraft, which he used solely for game patrols. In the first fifteen years of operation, the Alaska Game Commission reported an average of twenty thousand miles covered per year in patrol. These miles included three thousand by dog team, one thousand by snowshoe, as well as the easier miles by automobile, railroad, and steamer. In addition, trappers resisted government regulation and easily avoided confrontation with overworked wardens.[12]

In 1941 the Alaska Game Commission and the Northern Commercial Company began an active program of education for the trappers. Slide shows, bulletins, and on-site lectures covered the proper methods for handling fur. In addition, the Game Commission discouraged the

Lynx and wolf. The two largest animals trapped for fur were wolf (left) and lynx (right). Initially, trappers hunted or trapped wolf only for the state bounty. Later, because wolf fur did not freeze, clothing manufacturers used it for coat collars. On the other hand, the quantity of lynx varied on a cycle with the hare population—its primary source of food. *George Beck, Eagle, Alaska.*

wasteful shooting of beaver, which contributed to increasing losses of the animal, and encouraged trapping, which was more difficult but brought greater market value without wasteful losses. When encouragement failed to produce results, the commission required that all bea-

ver skins be tagged or sealed within thirty days and closed the season
earlier. These actions, which prevented shooting and required trapping,
decreased the take of beaver on the Yukon.[13]

World War II, however, created another boom in fur prices. Fur par-
kas for soldiers in northern theaters contributed to the boom. In addition, the scarcity of lynx and the closed seasons on marten brought high
prices for these furs. Although fur prices were high and fur appeared in
abundant supply, the number of trappers decreased. The high wages of
defense work and the Selective Service drew trappers away from their
traplines. The resultant void was partially filled by untrained novice
trappers, who moved into the vacant cabins and traplines to the anger
and helpless frustration of their absent owners. Nonetheless, the fur
catch for 1941 amounted to $2.25 million. Because of the few trappers
and the closed season on marten, the 1942 fur harvest dropped to the
lowest since 1935.[14]

Immediately after the war, in 1946, more trappers in the field and
high market prices resulted in intensive trapping. As in the years following World War I, the fur market fell and remained low throughout
the 1950s and 1960s. Initially, trappers claimed that the high price of
the finished furs discouraged the public from buying them. These high
prices, which in turn were caused by a federal tax on fur, inflated labor
and other costs in processing and manufacturing fur. High markups by
retail furriers also brought hardship to the trapper and raw fur traders.
But these reasons failed to explain altogether the continued doldrums
of the fur industry. Even though airplanes could be chartered to fly supplies and trappers into previously inaccessible areas, trappers lost interest in the unprofitable and demanding occupation and sought other jobs
in the developing territory.[15]

Conditions affecting the Alaskan trapper also shaped the life-style
of his Canadian counterpart. Market prices and the quality and quantity of furbearers dictated the standard of living. But there were some
differences. For example, the Canadian Game Department required fur
buyers to have a store to conduct business. This prevented traveling fur
buyers from presenting unfair competition to local buyers as they did
in Alaska. Another difference arose in 1950 when the Yukon Territorial Government began to register individual traplines. This measure
encouraged conservation practices and also prevented quarrels and illegal use of traplines and cabins. Still another difference lay in the compo-

sition of the trapping fraternity. In Yukon Territory most of the trappers were Indians who resented white trappers with registered traplines near transportation corridors and supply communities. More than 65 percent of the white trappers lived in Dawson, Whitehorse, and Watson Lake, whereas only 25 percent of the Indian trappers lived adjacent to towns or roads.[16]

Although one-third the size of Alaska, Yukon Territory contributed only about one-sixth as much fur. Its best year was the winter of 1927–28 with $610,348 worth of fur taken. Alaska, by contrast, trapped $3,699,707 worth of fur, more than six times that of Yukon Territory. In 1942, when trapping in Yukon Territory ranked second in earnings to mining, Yukon furs brought only $400,000 while Alaskan furs brought nearly $1.7 million and ranked near the top in value of exports.[17]

Like Alaska, Yukon Territory lost its trappers during the low fur prices of the 1950s and 1960s. Trappers moved into vocations of regular employment. Many of the registered traplines became underutilized. Although the Yukon Game Department and the Royal Canadian Mounted Police disapproved of unused traplines, no economic pressure existed to force the trapper to use or release the trapline. Moreover, in 1962–63 the average income of white trappers was only $342 as compared to $556 for Indians similarly located. Indians distant from transportation corridors, such as Old Crow, averaged only $480. These figures contrasted greatly with the relatively high costs for transportation, supplies, licenses, and shipping, as well as the extensive labor and severe hardship involved in trapping.[18]

Only in the early 1970s did trapping throughout the Yukon Basin experience a resurgence. Prices were high, but not compared to wages. Trappers came for values other than profit. These latter-day trappers represented a "return-to-the-land" syndrome, resulting from an environmentally conscious society and a recognition of the lost values of self-sufficiency and rugged individualism. Although many, if not all, "trespassed" on federal or Native land, they rationalized their presence as part of the traditional and historic use of the land, traced from the early fur trader to the profitable trapper of the 1920s and 1930s.

In 1977 fur prices boomed. The hardy individualist became a viable entrepreneur. In 1978 trappers saw the highest prices ever paid for wild fur. The value of Alaskan fur jumped from $860,000 in 1971–72 to more than $6 million in 1977–78. Mink prices leaped from ten dollars to more than sixty, muskrat from one dollar to five, and lynx from nine to nearly two hundred dollars. In addition, more than eleven thousand trapping licenses were sold.[19]

Regardless of the increase in novices and plunderers, the committed trapper, like the prospector and miner, maintained the values of the country. Knowledge of the land and its animals became increasingly important. Trappers took pride in knowing the ridges, benches, creeks, and rivers of their traplines. The construction of trails and cabins grew from expediency to craftsmanship. More important, most trappers recognized that a country trapped too hard took too long to recover, and conservation in harvesting furbearers became policy.

For these people, trapping became a lifelong occupation that offered its own seriousness and knowledge. They learned to read the land, understand its animals, and survive its climate. For some, like John Haines of Fairbanks, such a life became philosophical, even metaphysical. "It was a strange, mixed enjoyment," he meditated,

> the smell of something victorious, to have worked that hard in the cold and gotten something for my labor. To have outwitted that creature, set the trap or snare, and caught it. To discover by morning light something that lived and moved by night, and of which I had known nothing before but a footprint left in the snow. . . . It was far, far back in time, that twilight country where men sometimes lose their way, become as trees confused in the shapes of snow. But I was at home there, my mind bent away from humanity, to learn to think a little like that thing I was hunting. I entered for a time the old life of the forest, and became part fur myself.[20]

Such trappers felt no inclination to apologize to a modern world whose values eschewed the killing of wild animals. They intuitively knew the land and its history and accepted it.

For the most part, modern trappers recognized the debt owed to earlier frontiersmen. Not only did they use trails, cabins, and traplines of previous residents, but they sensed a bond with the mountain men of the American West. The hostile and unforgiving northern wilderness resembled the unknown and rigorous West of their forebears. The Yukon's unusual environment and isolation, however, created differences that forced reflection of and comparison with earlier northern frontiers and experiences. While romance and nostalgia may have colored their interpretation of history, these modern Yukon frontiersmen owed much of their life-style and collective history to the evolution of the westward movement that took place in the north country.[21]

Trapping thus became the principal alternative to Turner's successive frontiers—the Yukon's last and perhaps enduring frontier. Unlike mining, trapping does not—or need not—exhaust its resources and therefore need not come to an end as did Turner's other frontiers. Trapping is a Turnerian frontier in another sense too: it attracts or develops character traits Turner thought typical of frontier people. The "river people" of today—the trappers of the Yukon's last frontier—accurately fit Turner's description of a century ago, for they possess in ample measure:

> That coarseness and strength combined with acuteness and
> inquisitiveness; that practical, inventive turn of mind,
> quick to find expedients; that masterful grasp of material
> things, lacking in the artistic but powerful to effect great
> ends; that restless, nervous energy; that dominant
> individualism, working for good and for evil, and withal that
> buoyancy and exuberance which comes with
> freedom—these are traits of the frontier.[22]

Because trapping represents a throwback to Turner's early scenario of conquering the wilderness, the romanticization of that occupation has helped perpetuate the myth and mystique of "the last frontier." Alaskans, especially, relish and commercialize the motif. Travel posters and brochures excite potential tourists with images of "the last frontier." Memoirs from the early twentieth century nostalgically recall life on the last frontier. In the 1970s the cliché became the official state motto. Those who most often take up the refrain reside in cities and resort to rural excursions as vacations or hobbies rather than as committed life-styles. Ironically, statistics show that more than two-thirds of the population reside in the six largest communities.[23]

The perception of the last frontier is also used to further or hinder greater development. Ernest Gruening, former Alaskan territorial governor and U.S. senator, summoned it to dramatize neglect under American administration. Alaskans blame the lack of development of their state on frontier colonialism. On the other hand, environmentalists strive to keep Alaska as a frontier so that all Americans can enjoy the flavor and spirit of America's frontier past. During debate of the Alaska National Interest Lands issue of the 1970s, both sides raised the banner of "last frontier"—one side as a reason to save it, the other as reason for development. Finally, American authors express fascination with the last frontier and characterize its people in colorful vignettes rather than explore the more commonplace concept of urban settlement.[24]

Today this mythic "last frontier" of the popular imagination co-exists with a true last frontier represented by the river people who trap the Yukon and exemplify Turner's frontier character traits. They stand in ironic contrast to the Natives: once land users, they are now, as a result of the Alaska Native Claims Settlement Act, land owners. Profit, not harmonious land use, confronts and dilutes and sometimes even destroys their traditional cultural values. At the same time, white trappers have returned to the land to seek the mythical values of self-sufficiency and self-reliance.

Only the land seems static. It has been constant throughout the successive frontier waves that rolled over the Yukon. Although the army and the steamboat companies nearly deforested the land, it has now essentially returned to its appearance before the gold rush. Recent forest fires appear more destructive than the exploitive activities of miner, trapper, and townsperson. Historically, game populations rise and fall, nearly as much in response to natural forces as human pressures. Today, the same historic and dynamic cycles of nature and man continue, and the land and its animals fluctuate accordingly.

However apparently timeless, even the land could change, slowly or abruptly. Already the concept of free land so central to Turner's thinking has receded from the Yukon scene. Much of Alaska's 365 million acres remained open to homesteading until 1974, contributing to the persistence of the last frontier. Now, because of the Alaska Statehood Act of 1959, the Native Claims Settlement Act of 1971, and the Alaska National Interest Lands Conservation Act of 1980, free land no longer exists.

Resource exploitation could loose forces of change threatening to the last frontier. If strategic minerals or petroleum deposits prove worth developing, the valley could be changed swiftly and drastically. Exhaustion of nonrenewable resources, however, would release the Yukon to recover just as the collapse of the Klondike rush did nearly one hundred years ago. If the Alaska Highway were paved, the Alaska Pipeline haul road and Dempster Highway commercially exploited, and additional feeder roads constructed, new development and more rural homes could be initiated. If new technologies allow people to adapt to the extremes in temperature, as has occurred in the Sun Belt, the Yukon could change slowly and permanently.

However reparable such changes, irreparable change cannot be ruled out. Pressures for hydroelectric power from metropolitan areas or the lower forty-eight could resurrect the Rampart Dam proposal. This dam, the largest ever proposed anywhere in the world, would impound the river waters for 280 miles up the valley to the Canadian border, have a maximum width of 80 miles, and inundate more than 10,600 square miles. The reservoir would destroy significant fisheries, waterfowl nesting, wildlife habitat, and several Native villages.[25] The Yukon could never recover.

Yet the Yukon encompasses a truly vast land. Despite excursions into it by the modern world, it remains virtually untouched by permanent intrusions. It still provides a setting that nourishes the last frontier, and also one that illuminates patterns of history and environment that make each frontier unique but that are likewise common to all. Because of the timeless quality of the Yukon, the last frontier could turn out to be an enduring frontier.

Abbreviations Used in Notes

Compilation	*Compilation of Narratives of Explorations in Alaska*, Senate Reps., 56th Cong., 1st sess., no. 1023 (1900) (Serial 3896).
EARC	Eagle, Alaska, City Record Collection with copies in State Division of Parks, Anchorage, Alaska, and on microfilm at the University of Alaska Archives, Fairbanks.
GPO	Government Printing Office.
HEH	Henry H. Huntington Library, San Marino, California.
Minerals of Alaska	*Mineral Resources of Alaska: Report on Progress of Investigations*.
NA	National Archives, Washington, D.C.
OPA	Oregon Province Archives of the Society of Jesus, Gonzaga University, Spokane, Washington.
RG	Record Group.
UAF	University of Alaska Archives, Fairbanks.
UOE	University of Oregon, Eugene.
USGS	United States Geological Survey.
UWMC	University of Washington Manuscript Collection, Seattle, Washington.

Notes

Chapter 1

1. Frederick Jackson Turner, "The Significance of the Frontier," *The Frontier in American History*, 3rd ed. (New York: Holt, Rinehart, and Winston, 1963), p. 12.

2. The Turner thesis is probably the most controversial of any American historical theory; thus the historiography is massive and complex. For a full bibliography, see Ray Allen Billington's and Martin Ridge's detailed and annotated bibliography in *Westward Expansion: A History of the American Frontier*, 5th rev. ed. (New York: Macmillan Publishing Co., 1982), pp. 703–8.

3. Black Box No. 8 (152–54) and File Drawer 14B, Folder 9, Frederick Jackson Turner Papers, HEH.

4. Frederick Jackson Turner, "The West—1876 and 1926: Its Progress in a Half-Century," *World's Work*, 52 (July 1926), 327.

5. Turner, "Significance of the Frontier," p. 14.

6. These are revised figures from the Army Corps of Engineers quoted in *The Alaska Almanac: Facts About Alaska* (Anchorage: Alaska Northwest Publishing Company, 1981), p. 117. Leo Mark Anthony and Arthur Tunley, *Introductory Geography and Geology of Alaska* (Anchorage: Polar Publishing, 1976), p. 160, and Alfred Hulse Brooks, *Blazing Alaska's Trails* (Fairbanks: University of Alaska Press, 1973), pp. 16–24, provided earlier figures that the Yukon was 2,300 miles long and drained an area of 350,000 square miles.

7. Brooks, *Blazing Alaska's Trails*. Clyde Wahrhaftig, *Physiographic Divisions of Alaska*, USGS Professional Paper 482 (Washington, D.C.: GPO, 1965). Howel Williams, ed., *Landscapes of Alaska: Their Geologic Evolution* (Berkeley: University of California Press, 1958). Anthony and Tunley, *Introductory Geography and Geology of Alaska*.

8. R. D. Guthrie, "Paleoecology of the Large Mammal Community in Interior Alaska During the Late Pleistocene," *American Midland Naturalist*, 79 (1968), 346–463. David Hopkins, ed., *The Bering Land Bridge* (Palo Alto: Stanford University Press, 1968).

9. Charles W. Hartman and Philip R. Johnson, *Environmental Atlas of Alaska* (Fairbanks: University of Alaska, 1978), pp. 21–22.

10. Turner, "The Significance of the Frontier," p. 15. The best work on Turner and the Indians is David Nichols, "Civilization Over Savage:Frederick Jackson Turner and the Indian," *South Dakota History*, 2 (Fall 1972), 384–405. Compare Jack Forbes, "Frontiers in American History and the Role of the Frontier Historian," *Ethnohistory*, 15 (Spring 1968), 203–35, and Howard Lamar and Leonard Thompson, "Comparative Frontier History," in *The Frontier in History: North America and Southern Africa Compared*, ed. Howard Lamar and Leonard Thompson (New Haven: Yale University Press, 1981), 3–13. Similiar is Robert F. Berkhofer, Jr., "The North American Frontier as Process and Context," also in *The Frontier in History*, 43–75, and his *The White Man's Indian: Images of the American Indian from Columbus to the Present* (New York: Alfred A. Knopf, 1978).

11. To differentiate native-born white Alaskans from Alaskan Aleuts, Indians, and Eskimos, it is customary to capitalize Native as one does Indian.

12. Although numerous scholars and observers have written ethnographies of different groups of Eskimos, only Wendell H. Oswalt's *Alaskan Eskimos* (San Francisco: Chandler Publishing Co., 1967) handles all of the Eskimos. For specific details for the Eskimos along the Yukon River and Delta, see Edward W. Nelson, *The Eskimo About Bering Strait*, Bureau of American Ethnology, Eighteenth Annual Report, pt. 1 (Washington, D. C.:GPO, 1899); Kathryn Koutsky, *Early Days on Norton Sound and Bering Strait: The St. Michael and Stebbens Area*, vol. 8, Anthropology and Historic Preservation Occasional Paper No. 29 (Fairbanks: University of Alaska Cooperative Park Studies Unit, 1982); and Dorothy Jean Ray, *The Eskimos of Bering Strait, 1650–1898* (Seattle: University of Washington Press, 1975). In large measure, however, the Eskimos of the Yukon Delta have never captured the imagination of scholars or the public compared to their Eskimo relatives to the north.

13. The best interpretive book on the Athapaskan Indians is James W. VanStone, *Athapaskan Adaptations: Hunters and Fishermen of the Subarctic Forests* (Chicago: Aldine Publishing Co., 1974). The best general coverage of all subarctic groups is June Helm, ed., *Handbook of North American Indians: Subarctic*, vol. 6 (Washington, D. C.: Smithsonian Institution, 1981). For Alaskan Athapaskans, see William E. Simeone, *A History of Alaskan Athapaskans* (Anchorage: Alaska Historical Commission, n.d.). For specific boundaries of Athapaskan groups, see "Map of the Native Peoples and Languages of Alaska," designed by the Alaska Native Language Center, University of Alaska, Fairbanks, 1975. An older but still valuable source is Cornelius Osgood, *The Distribution of the Northern Athapaskan Indians*, Yale University Publications in Anthropology No. 7 (New Haven: Yale University Press, 1936).

14. The precontact population of Athapaskans is unknown. VanStone, *Athapaskan Adaptations*, p. 11, provides population figures during the late nineteenth century. By that time, however many of the Native people had succumbed to European diseases.

15. Compare Richard K. Nelson, *Hunters of the Northern Forest* (Chicago: University of Chicago Press, 1973), VanStone, *Athapaskan Adaptations;* Nelson H. H. Graburn and B. Stephen Strong, *Circumpolar Peoples: An Anthropological Perspective* (Pacific Palisades, California:Goodyear Publishing Co., 1973); and Helm, *Handbook of North American Indians: Subarctic.*

16. Every Athapaskan group of the Yukon Basin has had its ethnographer. For concise ethnographies, see *Handbook of North American Indians: Subarctic.* For greater detail, see the major works of the following anthropologists. The best synthesis on the Ingalik is James W. VanStone, *Ingalik Contact Ecology*, Fieldiana Anthropology No. 71 (Chicago: Field Museum, 1979). For the Tanana Indians see Robert McKennan, *The Upper Tanana Indians*, Yale University Publications in Anthropology, No. 55 (New Haven: Yale University Press, 1959). For the Han and Kutchin, see Cornelius Osgood, *The Han Indians: A Compilation of Ethnographic and Historical Data on the Alaska-Yukon Boundary Area*, Yale University Publications in Anthropology, No. 74 (New Haven: Yale University Press, 1971); Osgood, *Contributions to the Ethnography of the Kutchin*, Yale University Publications in Anthropology No. 14 (New Haven: Yale University Press, 1936); and Robert McKennan, *The Chandalar Kutchin*, Arctic Institute of North America Technical Paper, No. 17 (Montreal: Arctic Institute of North America, 1965). For the Koyukon, see Annette McFadyen Clark, *Koyukuk River Culture*, Canadian Ethnology Service Paper, No. 18 (Ottawa: National Museums of Canada, 1974), and William John Loyens, "The Changing Culture of the Nulato Koyukon Indians" (Ph.D. diss., University of Wisconsin, 1966). For the Tagish, Tuchone, and Inland Tlingit, see Catherine McClellan, *My Old People Say: An Ethnographic Survey of Southern Yukon Territory*, 2 vols., Publications in Ethnology, No. 6 (Ottawa: National Museums of Canada, 1975).

17. Osgood, *The Han Indians*, p. 32, and *Ethnography of the Kutchin*, p. 15.

18. VanStone, *Athapaskan Adaptations*, presents a thesis on environment and culture similar to the hypothesis of Frederick Jackson Turner.

19. Osgood, *Ethnography of the Kutchin*, pp. 110–13, paints a rosy and complacent picture of the precontact Kutchin.

20. Russell Sackett, *The Chilkat Tlingit: A General Overview*, Anthropology and Historic Preservation Occasional Paper, No. 23 (Fairbanks:University of Alaska Cooperative Park Studies Unit, 1979), synthesizes all that is known of the Chilkat culture. For a broader study of all Tlingits, see Aurel Krause, *The Tlingit Indians*, trans. Erna Gunther (Seattle: American Ethnological Society, 1976).

21. Turner, "Significance of the Frontier," pp. 37–38.

Chapter 2

1. Dorothy Jean Ray, *The Eskimos of Bering Strait, 1650–1898* (Seattle: University of Washington, 1975), pp. 97–98.

University of Washington Press, 1977), defines the purposes behind Bering's voyages.

3. Svetlana G. Fedorova, *The Russian Population in Alaska and California, Late 18th Century–1867*, trans. Richard A. Pierce and Alton S. Donnelly, Materials for the Study of Alaska History, No. 4 (Kingston, Ontario: Limestone Press, 1973), p. 105.

4. Ibid., pp. 106–18.

5. Ibid., pp. 62–64. Alexander Mackenzie, *Voyages from Montreal through the Continent of North America to the Frozen and Pacific Oceans in the Years 1789 and 1793, with an Account of the Rise and State of the Fur Trade* (New York: G. F. Hopkins, 1802), p. 60.

6. G. I. Davydov, *Two Voyages to Russian America, 1802–1807*, trans. Colin Bearne, ed. Richard A. Pierce, Materials for the Study of Alaska History, No. 10 (Kingston, Ontario: Limestone Press, 1977), pp. 200–202.

7. John S. Galbraith, *The Hudson's Bay Company as an Imperial Factor, 1821–1869* (New York: Farrar, Straus and Giroux, 1977), pp. 113–76, includes a comparison of the two trading companies and their personnel.

8. Throughout this narrative the Anglicized and more easily recognizable place-names will be used instead of their Russian equivalents, such as Sitka for New Archangel or Novo-Arkhangel'sk and St. Michael Redoubt for Mikhailovskii Redoubt.

9. P. A. Tikhmenev, *A History of the Russian-American Company*, trans. and ed. Richard A. Pierce and Alton S. Donnelly (Seattle: University of Washington Press, 1978), p. 183. Tikhmenev's book was published in two volumes in 1861–63. Although a company history, it was compiled from primary documents now lost.

10. A Creole in Russian America was the offspring of a Russian father and a Native mother. Russian Creoles generally had the same privileges and opportunities as those born in the colonies of pure Russian blood.

11. Two Russian sources describe the journey: Tikhmenev, *History of the Russian-American Company*, pp. 183–84; and Henry N. Michael (ed.), *Lieutenant Zagoskin's Travels in Russian America, 1842–1844: The First Ethnographic and Geographic Investigations in the Yukon and Kuskokwim Valleys of Alaska*, Arctic Institute of North America, Anthropology of the North: Translations from Russian Sources No. 7 (Toronto: University of Toronto Press, 1967), p. 209. James W. VanStone, *Ingalik Contact Ecology:An Ethnohistory of the Lower-Middle Yukon, 1790–1935*, Fieldiana Anthropology Volume 71 (Chicago: Field Museum, 1979), pp. 49–51, provides one of the best syntheses of the Russians on the lower Yukon.

12. Three translations of Glazunov's journal have the date 1833–34:James VanStone, "Russian Exploration in Interior Alaska: An Extract from the Journal of Andrei Glazunov," *Pacific Northwest Quarterly*, 50 (April 1959), 37–47; VanStone, *Ingalik Contact Ecology*, pp. 51–55; and Ferdinand Petrovich Wrangell, *Russian America: Statistical and Ethnographic Information*, trans. Mary Sadouski, ed. Richard A. Pierce, Materials for the Study of Alaska History, No.

15 (Kingston, Ontario: Limestone Press, 1980), pp. 69–79. Two Russian authorities, however, set the date at 1835: Zagoskin, *Travels in Russian America*, p. 93, and Tikhmenev, *History of the Russian-American Company*, p. 184.

13. VanStone, "Russian Exploration," p. 44.

14. Zagoskin, *Travels in Russian America*, pp. 10, 81. Barbara Smith, *Russian Orthodoxy in Alaska: A History, Inventory, and Analysis of the Church Archives in Alaska with an Annotated Bibliography* (Anchorage:Alaska Historical Commission, 1980), p. 6. VanStone, *Ingalik Contact Ecology*, pp. 56–57.

15. Zagoskin, *Travels in Russian America*, pp. 252, 337. Smith, *Russian Orthodoxy*, p. 6. Wendell H. Oswalt, *Kolmakovskiy Redoubt: The Ethnoarchaeology of a Russian Fort in Alaska*, Monumenta Archaeologica Vol. 8 (Los Angeles: Institute of Archaeology, University of California, 1980), p. 12.

16. Zagoskin, *Travels in Russian America*, pp. 146–47. Fedorova, *Russian Population in Alaska*, p. 246.

17. Zagoskin, *Travels in Russian America*, pp. 146–47. Fedorova, *Russian Population in Alaska*, p. 140.

18. Robert Campbell, *Two Journals of Robert Campbell, 1808 to 1853* (Seattle: John W. Todd, Jr., 1958). Clifford Wilson, *Campbell of the Yukon* (Toronto: Macmillan of Canada, 1970).

19. Above quotations come from Campbell, *Two Journals*, pp. 61, 68–69, and 75.

20. Allen A. Wright, *Prelude to Bonanza: The Discovery and Exploration of the Yukon* (Sidney, British Columbia: Gray's Publishing, 1976), pp. 43–48. Wright provides the best synthesis of early exploration on the Yukon.

21. Ibid., pp. 48–49. Alan Cooke and Clive Holland, *The Exploration of Northern Canada: 500 to 1920, a Chronology* (Toronto: Arctic History Press, 1978), p. 171.

22. Cooke and Holland, *Exploration of Northern Canada*, pp. 173–74.

23. Zagoskin *Travels in Russian America*, p. 15.

24. All quotations in the above paragraphs came from Zagoskin, pp. 159, 162, 187.

25. Quotation and population figures come from Tikhmenev, *History of the Russian-American Company*, pp. 383–84. See also Smith, *Russian Orthodoxy in Alaska*, which details the records in the extensive Kvikhpak Mission Collection, the greatest depository of Alaska Russian Orthodox Church records.

26. Wright, *Prelude to Bonanza*, pp. 50–53. Nan Shipley, "Anne and Alexander Murray," *Beaver*, 298 (Winter 1967), 33–35.

27. Murray, *Journal of the Yukon*, p. 35. There is no documented evidence that Russians traded this far upriver.

28. Ibid., p. 45. This Native account of Russian explorations may be an exaggeration of Zagoskin's expedition. The Natives were fascinated with his pistols.

29. Above quotations come from Murray, pp. 66 and 43

30. Ibid., p. 69. Zagoskin also complained of inadequate trading supplies and high prices charged in outposts. These descriptions of Russian goods are

apparently examples of Indian bargaining—playing one nation against the other.

31. Shipley, "Anne and Alexander Murray," p. 36.

32. In 1936 Cornelius Osgood analyzed the Kutchin and divided them into eight groups, depending on culture and dialect. Thus, Murray was extraordinarily astute, *Contributions to the Ethnography of the Kutchin*, Yale University Publications in Anthropology No. 14 (New Haven: Yale University Press, 1936), p. 13.

33. Quotations from Campbell, *Two Journals*, pp. 78–88.

34. Wright, *Prelude to Bonanza*, p. 66.

35. Murray, *Journal of the Yukon*, p. 76.

36. Campbell, *Two Journals*, p. 98.

37. Letter quoted in Wright, *Prelude to Bonanza*, p. 69.

38. Jules Jetté, "Jottings of an Alaskan Missionary," pp. 12–15, on Microfilm #33 of the Jesuit Alaska Mission Records at the UAF, from originals at OPA. Jetté collected oral history from the Natives of Nulato fifty years after the event. His version and that of the Natives differ substantially from that of the Russians. Jetté thought that the Russians feared British reprisals and, thus, made Barnard to blame for peremptorily summoning the Natives on the Koyukuk. Jetté's version is more believable—that Barnard was an innocent victim of Native retaliation for Russian cruelty.

39. The main source for the Nulato Massacre is William H. Dall, *Alaska and Its Resources* (Boston: Lee and Shepard, 1870), pp. 48–61, which relates the traditional Russian version that Barnard's tactlessness provoked the massacre. Other Americans repeat his and the Russians' story. Frederick Schwatka, *Report of a Military Reconnaissance in Alaska Made in 1883*, Senate Ex. Docs., 48th Cong., 2d sess., no. 2 (1885), p. 103, repeats Dall's story as does Ivan Petrov, "Population and Resources of Alaska," *Compilation*, pp. 199–200. Contrast these stories with Jetté's version in "Jottings."

40. Quoted in Thomas C. B. Boon, "William West Kirkby: First Anglican Missionary to the Loucheux," *Beaver*, 295 (Spring 1965), 36.

41. Quoted in Wright, *Prelude to Bonanza*, p. 87. See also W. W. Kirkby, "A Journey to the Youcan, Russian America," *Annual Report, Smithsonian Institution, 1864* (Washington, D. C.: GPO, 1872), pp. 416–20; and Cook and Holland, *Exploration of Northern Canada*, pp. 216–22.

42. Gerard George Steckler, "Charles John Seghers: Missionary Bishop in the American Northwest, 1839–1886" (Ph.D. diss., University of Washington, 1963), p. 64. Cooke and Holland, *Exploration of Northern Canada*, pp. 221–32. Jetté, "Jottings," pp. 16–18.

43. F. A. Peake, "Robert McDonald (1829–1913): The Great Unknown Missionary of the Northwest," *Canadian Church Historical Society Journal*, 17 (September 1975), 54–72.

44. Dall, *Alaska and Its Resources*, pp. 276–77, reports the date as 1863 and confuses the achievements of Ivan Lukin with those of his father. Oswalt, *Kolmakovskiy Redoubt*, p. 82, uses the Russian-American Company, Communications Sent, to correct the date to 1860.

45. Dall, *Alaska and Its Resources*, p. 276. Jetté, "Jottings," p. 18, has 1863 as the date that Jones went to Nuklukayet.

46. The best interpretation of the Alaska purchase is Ronald J. Jensen, *The Alaska Purchase and Russian-American Relations* (Seattle: University of Washington, 1975). See also David Hunter Miller, *The Alaska Treaty*, Studies in Alaska History No. 18 (Kingston, Ontario: Limestone Press, 1981). Less useful in this regard is Paul S. Holbo, *Tarnished Expansion: The Alaska Scandal, the Press, and Congress, 1867–1871* (Knoxville: University of Tennessee Press, 1983).

47. Alaska does not mean "great land." The specific Aleut word, *Alaxsxaq*, means literally "where the sea breaks its back," or the Alaska Peninsula as perceived from a sea-oriented people. Jay Ellis Ransom, "Alaxsxaq—Where the Sea Breaks Its Back," *Alaska Journal*, 8 (Summer 1978), 199. David Richardson, "The Geoghegan Brothers of Alaska," *Alaska Journal*, 6 (Winter 1976), 24.

48. Oswalt, *Kolmakovskiy Redoubt*, pp. 89, 107–13, believes that the Russian impact was not that strong. Further, he viewed the Russian-American Company not as a money-making corporation but rather an arm of Russian foreign policy. Thus trading posts were mere symbols of Russian sovereignty over the interior, and no real effort was made to exploit economic potential. Compare Osgood, *Ethnography of the Kutchin*, pp. 170–74; Cornelius Osgood, *The Han Indians: A Compilation of Ethnographic and Historical Data on the Alaska-Yukon Boundary Area*, Yale University Publications in Anthropology No. 74 (New Haven: Yale University Press, 1971), pp. 127–37; and VanStone, *Ingalik Contact Ecology*, pp. 97–100.

49. Frank H. Sloss and Richard A. Pierce, "The Hutchinson, Kohl Story:A Fresh Look," *Pacific Northwest Quarterly*, 62 (January 1971), 1–6. Frank H. Sloss, "Who Owned the Alaska Commercial Company?" *Pacific Northwest Quarterly*, 68 (July 1977), 120–30. William Ogilvie, *Early Days on the Yukon* (Ottawa: Thorburn and Abbott, 1913), p. 64. Lois D. Kitchener, *Flag Over the North: The Story of the Northern Commercial Company* (Seattle: Superior Publishing Co., 1954), pp. 32–34.

50. Charles W. Raymond, *Report of a Reconnaissance of the Yukon River, Alaska Territory, July to September, 1869*, Senate Ex. Docs., 42nd Cong., 1st sess., no. 12 (1871), p. 9. B. D. Lain, "The Fort Yukon Affair, 1869," *Alaska Journal*, 7 (Winter 1977), 13. Clifford Wilson, "The Surrender of Fort Yukon One Hundred Years Ago," *Beaver*, 300 (Autumn 1969), 47–48.

51. Quotation from Raymond, *Report of the Yukon*, p. 14. Although four years earlier the Western Union Telegraph Expedition had two small stern-wheeler steamboats, the *Wilder* and the *Lizzie Horner*, there is no specific documentation that either made it on to the Yukon itself.

52. Lain, "Fort Yukon Affair," p. 16. Wilson, "The Surrender of Fort Yukon," pp. 50–51.

53. The British withdrew up the Porcupine River and built Rampart House. In 1889, J. H. Turner of the International Boundary Survey found the post still on American soil. Once again the Hudson's Bay Company moved the post

upriver and erected New Rampart House "within rifle shot" of the boundary marker.

Chapter 3

1. General works that place the fur trade in perspective with other frontiers are Ray Allen Billington and Martin Ridge, *Westward Expansion: A History of the American Frontier* (New York: Macmillan Publishing Co., 1982), pp. 386–408, and Ray Allen Billington, *America's Frontier Heritage*, (Albuquerque: University of New Mexico Press, 1974), p. 40. The two classic works on the fur trade are Paul C. Phillips, *The Fur Trade*, 2 vols. (Norman: University of Oklahoma Press, 1961), and Hiram Martin Chittenden, *A History of the American Fur Trade of the Far West*, 2 vols. (Stanford, California: Academic Reprints, 1954). The more popular story is told in Bernard DeVoto, *Across the Wide Missouri* (Boston: Houghton Mifflin Co., 1947).

2. Kennicott's journal for this trip was initially published in the first volume of the *Transactions of the Chicago Academy of Sciences* in 1869, but the original manuscript and most of the printed copies were destroyed in the Chicago fire of 1871. Excerpts of his journal appear in James Alton James, *The First Scientific Exploration of Russian America and the Purchase of Alaska* (Chicago: Northwestern University, 1942), pp. 46–135. Secondary sources include Allen A. Wright, *Prelude to Bonanza* (Sidney, British Columbia:Gray's Publishing Ltd., 1976), pp. 77–86; William H. Dall, *Alaska and Its Resources* (Boston: Lee and Shepard, 1870), p. 4; and Morgan B. Sherwood, *Exploration of Alaska, 1865–1900* (New Haven: Yale University Press, 1965), pp. 17–18.

3. Charles Vevier, "The Collins Overland Line and American Continentalism," *Pacific Historical Review*, 28 (August 1959), 237–53. H. F. Taggart, ed., "Journal of William H. Ennis, Member, Russian-American Telegraph Exploring Expedition," *California Historical Society Quarterly*, 33 (March 1954), 1–12; and ibid., 33 (June 1954), 147–68. Sherwood, *Exploration of Alaska*, p. 16.

4. George R. Adams, a member of the expedition, believed that Kennicott committed suicide by taking strychnine, *Life on the Yukon, 1865–1867*, ed. Richard A. Pierce, Studies in Alaska History No. 22 (Kingston, Ontario: Limestone Press, 1982), p. 91. Others, however, discounted suicide and blamed poor health and the harassment he was enduring. See Dall, *Alaska and Its Resources*, pp. 5, 70, and quotation cited in Sherwood, *Exploration in Alaska*, p. 24.

5. Although James, *First Scientific Exploration*, p. 45, credits the expedition with providing information that helped move the Alaska purchase legislation through Congress, Sherwood, *Exploration of Alaska*, pp. 35–56, sets forth a more valid interpretation: the information was too limited to be useful until several years after the purchase. Sources arising from the expedition include: Dall, *Alaska and Its Resources*; Frederick Whymper, *Travel and Adventure in the Territory of Alaska* (London: John Murray, Albemarle Street, 1868); Adams, *Life on the Yukon*; C. S. Bulkley, "Journal of the U.S. Russo-American Telegraph Expedition, 1865–1867," microfilm, UAF; Ferdinand Westdahl, "Interview

at Anderson Island, Puget Sound, June 7, 1878," manuscript, Bancroft Library, University of California, Berkeley.

6. François Mercier, untitled manuscript found in Father Francis Monroe Papers, OPA, translated from French by Linda Yarborough. Richard Mathews, *The Yukon* (New York: Holt, Rinehart, and Winston, 1968), p. 77. The Alaska Commercial Company's records were destroyed in the San Francisco earthquake and fire of 1906. Furthermore, in correspondence with the company, the author was told that the company's definitive history is L. D. Kitchener's *Flag Over the North: The Story of the Northern Commercial Company* (Seattle: Superior Publishing Co., 1954), p. 147. This source is a great fund of information but is poorly organized, has no footnotes, index, or bibliography, and contains enough inaccuracies to question all data that have no corroboration in other sources.

7. Mercier manuscript. Robert L. Spude, "Navigability Study for the Upper Yukon Region, Alaska," draft manuscript (Anchorage: Bureau of Land Management, 1980); printed in 1983 under the same title but with James Ducker listed as author.

8. Mercier manuscript. Ivan Petrov, *Population and Resources of Alaska*, House Ex. Docs., 46th Cong., 3d sess., no. 40 (1881), pp. 67–69. William Ogilvie, *Early Days on the Yukon* (Ottawa: Thorburn and Abbott, 1913), pp. 64–65.

9. Gerald George Steckler, "Charles John Seghers: Missionary Bishop in the American Northwest, 1839–1886" (Ph.D. diss., University of Washington, 1963), p. 96. Walter R. Hamilton, *The Yukon Story: A Sourdough's Record of Goldrush Days and Yukon Progress from the Earliest Times to the Present Day* (Vancouver, Canada: Mitchell Press, 1964), p. 151.

10. Mercier manuscript. Kitchener, *Flag Over the North*, p. 148. Steckler, "Seghers," pp. 96–98. Hamilton, *Yukon Story*, pp. 151–52. James VanStone, *Ingalik Contact Ecology*, Fieldiana Anthropology Vol. 7 (Chicago:Field Museum, 1979), pp. 138–39.

11. There are many accounts of McQuesten, Harper, and Mayo. There are only three primary sources: Mercier manuscript; Leroy N. McQuesten, *Recollections of Leroy N. McQuesten of Life in the Yukon, 1871–1885* (Dawson City: Yukon Order of Pioneers, 1952); and Erinia Pavaloff Cherosky Callahan, "A Yukon Autobiography," *Alaska Journal*, 5 (Spring 1975), 127–28. Most of the following details derive from these three primary sources. The best secondary sources include: Ogilvie, *Early Days*, pp. 87–91; Mathews, *The Yukon*, pp. 84–97; Kitchener, *Flag Over the North*, pp. 149–55; and Alfred Hulse Brooks, *Blazing Alaska's Trails* (Fairbanks:University of Alaska, 1973), pp. 312–30.

12. McQuesten, *Recollections*, p. 3.

13. Mercier manuscript.

14. See Mercier manuscript and Billington, *Westward Expansion*, pp. 386–408.

15. Petrov, *Population and Resources of Alaska*, pp. 67–68.

16. Dates throughout this chapter should be viewed with caution. The three primary sources were written years after the experiences recounted. As

determined through careful cross-checking, the dates given are probably accurate within a year or two.

17. McQuesten, *Recollections*, p. 6.

18. McQuesten, *Recollections*, p. 8, has the name spelled Kosevnifoff. Steckler, "Seghers," p. 159, is probably more correct because Seghers knew Russian.

19. McQuesten, *Recollections*, p. 8. Callahan, "A Yukon Autobiography," p. 127, provides a more sympathetic portrait of Korgenikoff as "a kind, jolly old man," but she was only sixteen years old at the time of the shooting and greatly traumatized. McQuesten's interpretation is probably more valid as neither the company nor the traders attempted to punish the Indians.

20. Mercier manuscript. William H. Gilder, *Ice-pack and Tundra: An Account of the Search for the 'Jeannette' and a Sledge Journey through Siberia* (London: Sampson Low, Marston, Searle & Rivington, 1883), also reprinted as "St. Michael, 1881" in *Alaska Journal*, 3 (Spring 1973), 122–24.

21. Mercier manuscript. McQuesten, *Recollections*, p. 9. Secondary sources and local tradition have placed the building of Belle Isle in 1874 and on the island off the present town of Eagle. McQuesten and Mercier specifically state that neither of these are true.

22. Although legends tell of a red-haired Scot, an employee of the Hudson's Bay Company, who supposedly traveled overland from the Yukon to the coast at an early date, George Dawson investigated the story and dismissed it. Other stories had Michael Byrnes of the Western Union Telegraph Company on the upper Yukon in 1867, but those stories cannot be proved.

23. George Holt's trip was recorded in customs records and *The Alaskan*, a Sitka newspaper, on October 2, 1897. Secondary accounts include: Sherwood, *Exploration of Alaska*, p. 146; George M. Dawson, *Report on an Exploration in the Yukon District, N.W.T. and Adjacent Northern Portion of British Columbia* (Ottawa: Queen's Printer, 1887), p. 179; R. N. DeArmond, "A Letter to Jack McQuesten: 'Gold on the Fortymile'," *Alaska Journal*, 3 (Spring 1973), 114; and Brooks, *Blazing Alaska's Trails*, pp. 321–22.

24. All quotations come from L. A. Beardslee, *Reports of Captain L. A. Beardslee, U. S. Navy, Relative to Affairs in Alaska*, Senate Ex. Doc., 47th Cong., 1st sess. (1882), p. 60.

25. McQuesten, *Recollections*, p. 11. For references to Faulkner, Bell & Company, see *The Alaska Appeal* (San Francisco), March 6, 1879, p. 3, and June 17, 1879, p. 6.

26. Edward Schieffelin, "Edward Schieffelin's Trip to Alaska," manuscript, Bancroft Library, University of California, Berkeley, pp. 1–7. Spude, "Navigability Study."

27. Frederick Schwatka, *Along Alaska's Great River* (Chicago: George M. Hill Co., 1898), p. 268. Frederick Schwatka, *Report of a Military Reconnaissance in Alaska, Made in 1883*, Senate Ex. Doc., 48th Cong., 2d sess., no. 2 (1885), pp. 44–46.

28. The following quotations come from Steckler, "Charles John Seghers," pp. 4, 155–59, and 175.

29. Letters and journals of Rev. Robert McDonald found in *Letters and Papers of the Church Missionary Society*, London, and on microfilm at the Public Archives of Canada, Ottawa, reels A-103 and 110, 1878–81.

30. Sims to C. C. Fenn, September 20, 1883, V. C. Sims Papers in *Letters and Papers of the Church Missionary Society*, London, and on microfilm at Public Archives of Canada, Ottawa, reel A-112.

31. Canhan to Wigram, May 21, 1885, ibid.

Chapter 4

1. The mining frontier seen in perspective with other frontiers is best addressed in Ray Allen Billington and Martin Ridge, *Westward Expansion: A History of the American Frontier* (New York: Macmillan Publishing Co., 1982), pp. 555–72. Among the first and best on the California gold rush is Rodman W. Paul, *California Gold: The Beginning of Mining in the Far West* (Lincoln: University of Nebraska Press, 1947). Often overlooked as less romantic than the bonanza miner was the professional mining engineer, who was essential to the development of any mining frontier. Clark C. Spence corrects this oversight with *Mining Engineers and the American West: The Lace-Boot Brigade, 1849–1933* (New Haven: Yale University Press, 1970). The best overall interpretive history of the mining frontier is Rodman W. Paul, *Mining Frontiers of the Far West, 1848–1880* (New York: Holt, Rinehart, and Winston, 1963). For details of mining methods, see Otis E. Young, *Western Mining: An Informal Account of Precious-Metal Prospecting, Placering, Lode Mining, and Milling on the American Frontier from Spanish Times to 1893* (Norman: University of Oklahoma Press, 1970).

2. J. E. Chapman, "Interview," *The Alaskan* (Sitka), October 30, 1886.

3. W. H. Pierce, *Thirteen Years of Travel and Exploration in Alaska, 1877–1889*, ed. and updated R. N. DeArmond (Anchorage: Alaska Northwest Publishing Co., 1977), p. 75. Pierce also fabricated a story of cannibalism among the Tanana Indians that has no basis in fact. Even so, he represents the typical prospector of the era.

4. Alfred Hulse Brooks, *Blazing Alaska's Trails* (Fairbanks: University of Alaska Press, 1973), p. 328.

5. The best synthesis is Robert N. DeArmond, "A Letter to Jack McQuesten: 'Gold on the Fortymile,' " *Alaska Journal*, 3 (Spring 1973), 114–21. For contemporary accounts see Frank Buteau, "My Experiences in the World," in *Sourdough Sagas*, ed. Herbert L. Heller (New York: Ballantine Books, 1967), p. 91; and Will H. Chase, *Reminiscences of Captain Billie Moore* (Kansas City: Burton Publishing Co., 1947), p. 173.

6. Buteau, "My Experience in the World,'', pp. 88–90. Henry Davis, "Recollections," in *Sourdough Saga*, ed. Herbert L. Heller (New York:Ballantine Books, 1967), pp. 24–77.

7. Participants described the murder and subsequent retribution. See Erinia Pavaloff Cherosky Callahan, "A Yukon Autobiography," *Alaska Journal*, 5 (Spring 1975), 127–28; Davis, "Recollections," pp. 48–51; Gordon C. Bettles, "Some Early Yukon River History," in *Sourdough Sagas*, pp. 109–12; and Jim Bender, "Early Days in Alaska," in ibid., pp. 80–81.

8. Davis, "Recollections," p. 51.

9. The sole source for this story is James Wickersham, *Old Yukon: Old Tales, Trails, and Trials* (St. Paul, Minnesota: West Publishing Co., 1938), pp. 138–39. Gerard George Steckler, "Charles John Seghers: Missionary Bishop in the American Northwest, 1839–1886" (Ph.D. diss., University of Washington, 1963), pp. 562–63, repeats the story nearly verbatim from Wickersham.

10. Tappan Adney, *The Klondike Stampede* (New York: Harper and Brothers, 1900), p. 241.

11. Early mining experiences on the Fortymile can be found in Buteau, "My Experiences in the World," pp. 86–108.

12. For life in Fortymile see Allen A. Wright, *Prelude to Bonanza: The Discovery and Exploration of the Yukon* (Sidney, British Colombia: Grays's Publishing Ltd., 1976), p. 248; William Ogilvie, *Information Respecting the Yukon District* (Ottawa: Department of the Interior, Government Printing Bureau, 1897), p. 52; and Charles Constantine, "Report of Inspector Constantine, 10th October 1894," in *Report of the Commissioner of the North-West Mounted Police Force, 1894* (Ottawa: The Queen's Printer, 1895), p. 77.

13. Josiah Edward Spurr, *Through the Yukon Gold Diggings: A Narrative of Personal Travel* (Boston: Eastern Publishing Co., 1900), p. 133.

14. Wright, *Prelude to Bonanza*, pp. 256–57. Virginia S. Burlingame, "John J. Healy's Alaskan Adventure," *Alaska Journal*, 8 (Autumn 1978), 310–14.

15. Constantine, "Report of October, 1894," pp. 75–81. Wright, *Prelude to Bonanza*, pp. 263–65.

16. McQuesten's generosity was legendary, and nearly all observers commented on it: Davis, "Recollections;" Brooks, *Blazing Alaska's Trails*; Adney, *The Klondike Stampede*; and William Ogilvie, *Early Days on the Yukon* (Ottawa: Thorburn and Abbott, 1913).

17. Chase, *Reminiscences of Captain Billie Moore*. Capt. William D. Moore, "From Peru to Alaska," typescript in UWMC.

18. The date is difficult to pinpoint, but gold was probably found in 1892 and Circle founded the following spring of 1893. See Callahan, "A Yukon Autobiography," p. 128; Joseph Vlmer, "History of the Circle Mining District, Alaska," manuscript in UAF; and Samuel C. Dunham, "The Alaskan Goldfields and the Opportunities They Offer for Capital and Labor," *Bulletin of the Department of Labor*, ed. Carroll D. Wright, House Doc., 55th Cong., 2d sess., no. 206, pt. 3 (1898), p. 359.

19. Callahan, "A Yukon Autobiography," p. 128.

20. Spurr, *Through the Yukon Gold Diggings*, p. 173. Davis, "Recollections," p. 67. Vlmer, "History of Circle Mining District," however, has freight costing twenty-five cents a pound.

21. Alfred Hulse Brooks, "The Circle Precinct," in *Report on Progress of Investigations of Mineral Resources of Alaska in 1906*, USGS Bulletin 314 (Washington, D. C.: GPO, 1907), p. 188. Adney, *The Klondike Stampede*, p. 458.

22. The development of early Circle is told in several primary accounts: Adney, *The Klondike Stampede*, p. 458; Spurr, *Through the Yukon Gold Diggings*, p. 161; Dunham, "The Alaskan Goldfields," p. 350; and Harold B. Goodrich, "History and Conditions of Yukon Gold District to 1897," *Eighteenth Annual Report of the United States Geological Survey to the Secretary of the Interior, 1896–97*, pt. 3 (Washington, D. C.: GPO, 1898), p. 118. The best secondary accounts are: Vlmer, "History of Circle Mining District"; Hudson Stuck, *Voyages on the Yukon and its Tributaries: A Narrative of Summer Travel in the Interior of Alaska* (New York: Charles Scribner's Sons, 1925); and L. D. Kitchener, *Flag Over the North: The Story of the Northern Commercial Company* (Seattle: Superior Publishing Co., 1954), p. 188.

23. Life at the Birch Creek mines is told in Goodrich, "History and Conditions of Yukon Gold District," p. 118; Adney, *The Klondike Stampede*, p. 458; Davis, "Recollections," p. 67; and Spurr, *Through the Yukon Gold Diggings*, p. 176.

24. Arthur Treadwell Walden, *A Dog-Puncher on the Yukon* (New York: Houghton Mifflin Co., 1928), pp. 42–43.

25. Henry De Windt, *Through the Gold-Field of Alaska to Bering Straits* (New York: Harper and Brothers, Publishers, 1898), p. 160.

26. Goodrich, "History and Conditions of the Yukon Gold District," p. 119. Brooks, *Blazing Alaska's Trails*, p. 332.

27. For the role that mercantile establishments played in the development of Circle, see Dunham, "The Alaska Goldfields," p. 358; Buteau, "My Experiences in the World," pp. 107–8; William Douglas Johns, "The Early Yukon, Alaska, and the Klondike Discovery As They Were Before the Great Klondike Stampede Swept Away the Old Conditions Forever By One Who Was There," typescript, UWMC.

28. Spurr, *Through the Yukon*, p. 196. Others also describe dances:Johns, "The Early Yukon," p. 171; Davis, "Recollections," p. 68; De Windt, *Through the Gold-Field*, pp. 161–62; and C. S. Hamlin, *Old Times on the Yukon: Decline of Circle City; Romances of the Klondyke* (Los Angeles:Wetzel Publishing Co., 1928), p. 4.

29. Miners' Association of Circle, Alaska, Vol. 1—Constitution, By-Laws, and Membership of the Miners' Association; Vol. 2—Minutes, Nov. 16, 1895, in Historical Library, Juneau, Alaska. See also Davis, "Recollections," p. 14; and Johns, "The Early Yukon," p. 137.

30. Compare Paul, *California Gold*, pp. 210–39, with observers of the Yukon's judicial system, such as Dunham, "The Alaskan Goldfields," p. 363; Walden, *A Dog-Puncher on the Yukon*, pp. 49–53; Johns, "The Early Yukon," p. 148; *Conditions in Alaska*, Hearings Before Subcommittee of Committee on Territories, Senate Reps., 58th Cong., 2d sess., no. 282, pt. 2 (1904), p. 95; Good-

rich, "History and Conditions of Yukon Gold District," p. 127; and Buteau, "My Experiences in the World," p. 83.

31. Goodrich, "History and Conditions of Yukon Gold District," p. 127. Walden, *A Dog-Puncher on the Yukon*, p. 48.

32. Walden, p. 49.

33. Anna Fulcomer, "The Three R's at Circle City," *Century Magazine*, 56 (June 1898), 223–29.

34. Johns, "The Early Yukon," pp. 127, 135, 141, 142.

35. *Alaska Mining Record*, October 26, 1898, p. 3. *Alaska Weekly*, August 10, 1923, p. 3. Kitchener, *Flag Over the North*, p. 153. Ogilvie, *Early Days*, pp. 101–19. Wright, *Prelude to Bonanza*, pp. 292–94.

Chapter 5

1. See Morgan B. Sherwood, *Exploration of Alaska, 1865–1900* (New Haven: Yale University Press, 1965) and William H. Goetzmann, *Exploration and Empire: The Explorer and the Scientist in the Winning of the American West* (New York: Alfred A. Knopf, 1966).

2. Frederick Whymper, *Travel and Adventure in the Territory of Alaska* (London: John Murray, Albemarle Street, 1868). Robert Kennicott, "Biography of Robert Kennicott and Extracts from His Journals," in *Transactions of the Chicago Academy of Sciences*, vol. 1 (Chicago, 1869). Robert Kennicott, "The Journal of Robert Kennicott, May 19, 1859–February 11, 1862" in *The First Scientific Exploration of Russian America and the Purchase of Alaska*, ed. James Alton James (Chicago: Northwestern University, 1942). William H. Dall, *Alaska and Its Resources* (Boston: Lee and Shepard, 1870). For a full bibliography of Dall's publications, see Sherwood, *Exploration of Alaska*.

3. Edward W. Nelson's work includes: *Report upon the Natural History Collections Made in Alaska, 1877–1881*, Senate Misc. Doc., 49th Cong., 1st sess., no. 156 (1887) (Serial 2349); and *The Eskimo About Bering Strait*, Eighteenth Annual Report of the Bureau of American Ethnology, pt. 1 (Washington D. C.: GPO, 1899). Those who have written biographical sketches include: Sherwood, *Exploration of Alaska*, pp. 93–97; James W. VanStone, *Ingalik Contact Ecology: An Ethnohistory of the Lower-Middle Yukon, 1790–1935*, Fieldiana Anthropology Vol. 71 (Chicago: Field Museum, 1979), pp. 107–8; Margaret Lantis, "Edward William Nelson," *Anthropological Papers of the University of Alaska*, 3 (December 1954), 5–16; Anna E. Riggs, "E. W. Nelson: Unpaid Collector," *Alaska Journal*, 10 (Winter 1980), 91; and Morgan Sherwood, *Big Game in Alaska: A History of Wildlife and People*, (New Haven: Yale University Press, 1981).

4. Sherwood, *Exploration of Alaska*, pp. 57–69, has done a masterful detective job in exposing the true character of Petrov's autobiography, which long was taken at face value.

5. Ivan Petrov, "The Population and Resources of Alaska, 1880," in *Compilation*, p. 61.

6. VanStone, *Ingalik Contact Ecology,* p. 108, questions Petrov's data on Natives.

7. Ivan Petrov, *Population and Resources of Alaska,* House Ex. Doc., 46th Cong., 3d sess., no. 40 (1881), pp. 60–62.

8. Aurel Krause, *The Tlingit Indians: Results of a Trip to the Northwest Coast of America and the Bering Straits,* trans. Erna Gunther (Seattle: University of Washington Press, 1956). Sherwood, *Exploration of Alaska,* pp. 82–83. Allen A. Wright, *Prelude to Bonanza* (Sidney, British Columbia: Gray's Publishing Ltd., 1976), pp. 139–40.

9. Johan Adrian Jacobsen, *Alaskan Voyage, 1881–1883: An Expedition to the Northwest Coast of America,* trans. Erna Gunther (Chicago:University of Chicago Press, 1977), p. 91.

10. Sherwood, *Exploration of Alaska,* pp. 98–99.

11. Frederick Schwatka, *A Summer in Alaska* (St. Louis: J. W. Henry, 1893), p. 11.

12. Frederick Schwatka, *Report of a Military Reconnaissance in Alaska Made in 1883,* Senate Ex. Doc., 48th Cong., 2d sess., no. 2 (1885), p. 43.

13. Heath Twichell, Jr., *Allen: The Biography of an Army Officer, 1859–1930* (New Brunswick: Rutgers University Press, 1974), is a highly readable full biography. Sherwood, *Exploration of Alaska,* pp. 107–18, provides a good thumbnail sketch of Allen's experiences in Alaska.

14. Quoted in Twichell, *Allen,* p. 50. See also Henry T. Allen, "A Military Reconnaissance of the Copper River Valley, 1885," in *Compilation,* p. 444.

15. Sherwood, *Exploration of Alaska,* pp. 115–16. Twichell, *Allen,* p. 58.

16. Allen, "Reconnaissance of the Copper River," p. 481.

17. *Alaskan* (Sitka), November 28, 1885. Sherwood, *Exploration of Alaska,* p. 117.

18. Wright, *Prelude to Bonanaza,* pp. 162–210, provides the best synthesis of this expedition. See also J. C. Barkhouse, *George Dawson: The Little Giant* (Toronto: Clark, Irwin and Co., 1974).

19. George M. Dawson, *Report on an Exploration in the Yukon District, N.W.T. and Adjacent Northern Portion of British Columbia* (Ottawa: The Queen's Printer, 1887), p. 1. Also found in F. Mortimer Trimmer, ed., "Extracts from the Report on an Exploration Made in 1887 in the Yukon District N.W.T. and Adjacent Northern Portion of British Columbia by George M. Dawson," in part 2 of *The Yukon Territory* (London: Downey & Co., 1898), p. 245.

20. Ogilvie describes this trip in several accounts: "Exploratory Survey from the Pelly-Yukon to Mackenzie River by Way of Tat-on-duc, Porcupine, Bell, Trout and Peel Rivers," *Department of the Interior Annual Report, 1889,* part 8, section 3 (Ottawa: Brown Chamberlin, 1897); *Information Respecting the Yukon District* (Ottawa: Department of the Interior, Government Printing Bureau, 1897); and *Early Days on the Yukon* (Ottawa:Thorburn & Abbott, 1913).

21. R. G. McConnell, *Report on an Exploration in the Yukon and Mackenzie Basins, N.W.T.* (Montreal: William Foster Brown & Co., 1891).

22. Lewis Green, *The Boundary Hunters* (Vancouver: University of Brit-

ish Columbia Press, 1982), p. 31. J. H. Turner, "The Alaskan Boundary Survey: III. The Boundary North of Fort Yukon," *National Geographical Magazine*, 4 (February 8, 1893), 190.

23. Quoted in Green, *Boundary Hunters*, p. 32.

24. T. C. Mendenhall, "The Alaska Boundary Survey: I. Introduction," *National Geographical Magazine*, 4 (February 8, 1893), 177–80. J. E. McGrath, "The Alaska Boundary Survey: II. The Boundary South of Fort Yukon," *National Geographic Magazine*, ibid., 181–88. J. Henry Turner, "The Alaska Boundary Survey: III. The Boundary North of Fort Yukon," *National Geographic Magazine*, ibid., 189–97. Israel C. Russell, "A Journal up the Yukon River," *Journal of the American Geographical Society*, 27 (1895), 143–60. Alfred Brunot Schanz, "The Alaskan Boundary Survey," *Harper's Weekly*, 35 (September 12, 1891), 699–700.

25. E.J. Glave. "The Leslie Expedition," *Frank Leslie's Illustrated Newspaper*, November 15, 22, 29 and December 6, 13, 20, 27, 1890, and January 3, 10, 1891. E.J. Glave, "Pioneer Packhorses in Alaska," *Century*, 44 (September 1892), 671–82; and 44 (October 1892), 869–81. Richard D. Tero, "E.J. Glave and the Alsek River," *Alaska Journal*, 3 (Summer 1973), 180–88. Sherwood, *Exploration of Alaska*, p. 141. Wright, *Prelude to Bonanza*, pp. 228–39.

26. E. H. Wells, "The Leslie Expedition," *Frank Leslie's Illustrated Newspaper*, July 4, 11, 18, 25; August 1, 8, 29; September 5, 19, 1891. A. B. Schanz, "The Leslie Expedition," *Frank Leslie's Illustrated Newspaper*, September 26; October 3, 10, 17, 24, 31; November 7, 28, 1891. Ro Sherman, "Down the Yukon and Up the Fortymile," *Alaska Journal*, 4 (Autumn 1974), 205–13, and Sherman, "Exploring the Tanana River Region," *Alaska Journal*, 5 (Winter 1975), 41–48. Sherwood, *Exploration of Alaska*, pp. 141–42.

27. Morgan Sherwood, "The Mysterious Death of Schwatka," *Alaska Journal*, 9 (Summer 1979), 74.

28. Charles W. Hayes, "An Expedition Through the Yukon District," *National Geographic Magazine*, 4 (May 15, 1892), 117–62. Sherwood, *Exploration of Alaska*, p. 143. Wright, *Prelude to Bonanza*, pp. 221–28.

29. Warburton Pike, *Through the Sub-Arctic Forest* (New York: Arno Press, reprint for the Abercrombie and Fitch Library, 1967). The book was originally published in 1896.

30. Frederick Funston, "Over the Chilkoot Pass in 1893," reprinted from *Scribner's Magazine*, November 1896, in *Alaska Journal*, 2 (Summer 1972), 16–24; Funston, "Along Alaska's Eastern Boundary," *Harper's Weekly*, 40 (February 1, 1896), 103; and Funston, "Frederick Funston's Alaskan Trip," *Harper's Weekly*, 39 (May 25, 1895), 492.

31. Green, *Boundary Hunters*, pp. 40–42. William Ogilvie, "Extracts from the Report of an Exploration Made in 1896–1897," in *The Yukon Territory*, ed. F. Mortimer Trimmer (London: Downey & Co., 1898), pp. 393–94. Ogilvie, *Early Days*, pp. 245–48.

32. Ogilvie, "An Exploration Made in 1896–1897," p. 401. Also quoted in Green, *Boundary Hunters*, p. 43.

Chapter 6

1. The story of the Klondike gold rush has been told countless times. The best primary account is Edwin Tappan Adney, *The Klondike Stampede* (New York: Harper and Brothers Publishers, 1900). The best secondary narrative is Pierre Berton, *The Klondike Fever: The Life and Death of the Last Great Gold Rush*, rev. ed. (Bloomington: Indiana University Press, 1972). David Wharton, *The Alaska Gold Rush* (Bloomington: Indiana University Press, 1972) and William R. Hunt, *North of 53°: The Wild Days of the Alaska-Yukon Mining Frontier, 1870–1914* (New York: Macmillan Publishing Co., 1974) handle the rush in a more interpretive manner.

2. Berton, *Klondike Fever*, pp. 146–288, 356–57. Edwin C. Bearss, *Proposed Klondike Gold Rush National Historical Park Historic Resource Study* (Washington, D.C.: National Park Service, 1970). Robert L. Spude, *Chilkoot Trail: From Dyea to Summit with the '98 Stampeders*, Cooperative Park Studies Unit, Anthropology and Historic Preservation, Occasional Paper No. 26 (Fairbanks: University of Alaska, 1980).

3. Lewis Green, *The Boundary Hunters: Surveying the 141st Meridian and the Alaska Panhandle* (Vancouver: University of British Columbia Press, 1982), p. 71. P. H. Gordon, "An Arbitrary Boundary," *Beaver*, 302 (Autumn 1971), 50–51.

4. Green, *Boundary Hunters*, pp. 65–74. Bearss, *Klondike Gold Rush*, pp. 149–62.

5. Gordon Bennett, *Yukon Transportation: A History*, Canadian Historic Sites: Occasional Papers in Archaeology and History, No. 19 (Ottawa, 1978), pp. 37–46. Bearss, *Klondike Gold Rush*, pp. 247–68. S. H. Graves, *On the "White Pass" Pay-Roll* (Chicago: Paladin Press, 1908).

6. Berton, *Klondike Fever*, p. 176. Capt. P. H. Ray and Lt. W. P. Richardson, "Suffering and Destitute Miners in Alaska and What Was Done for Their Relief—1898," in *Compilation*, p. 521.

7. Alger to Ray, August 4, 1897, in *Compilation*, p. 9.

8. Ray and Richardson, "Suffering and Destitute Miners," p. 531, describes the panic caused by inadequate stocks of food. Other contemporaries report the hold-up sympathetically to the miners: Adney, *Klondike Stampede*, pp. 191–92; Samuel C. Dunham, "The Alaskan Goldfields and the Opportunities They Offer for Capital and Labor," in *Bulletin of the Department of Labor*, ed. Carroll D. Wright, House Ex. Doc., 55th Cong., 2d sess., no. 206, pt. 3 (1898), p. 366; and Arthur Treadwell Walden, *A Dog-Puncher on the Yukon* (Boston: Houghton Mifflin Company, 1928), pp. 98–99. L. D. Kitchener, *Flag Over the North* (Seattle: Superior Publishing Co., 1954), p. 200, describes the hold-up from the point of view of the companies.

9. Ray and Richardson, "Suffering and Destitute Miners," p. 551. Captain P. H. Ray, "Alaska, 1897—Relief of the Destitute in the Gold Fields," in *Compilation*, p. 501. *Alaska Mining Record*, March 3, 1898, p. 6. *Alaska Weekly*, June 8, 1923, p. 3.

10. Ray and Richardson, "Suffering and Destitute Miners," p. 550.

11. *Alaska Mining Record*, February 16, 1898, p. 4.

12. Ray, "Alaska, 1897—Relief of the Destitute," p. 503.

13. Duane A. Smith, *Rocky Mountain Mining Camps: The Urban Frontier* (Lincoln: University of Nebraska Press, 1967), develops this interpretive theme fully. Rodman Wilson Paul, *Mining Frontiers of the Far West, 1848–1880* (Albuquerque: University of New Mexico Press, 1974), handles mining towns in a generalized fashion. W. Turrentine Jackson, *Treasure Hill: Portrait of a Silver Mining Camp* (Tucson: University of Arizona Press, 1963), examines one hard-rock mining camp from boom to bust. Although less applicable to Alaska, Bradford Luckingham, "The City in the Westward Movement—A Bibliographical Note," *Western Historical Quarterly*, 5 (July 1974), 295–306, continues the theme of the urban frontier.

14. The early history of Eagle City, Alaska, is told in the following works: Dunham, "Alaskan Goldfields," p. 356; Adney, *Klondike Stampede*, p. 457; Harold B. Goodrich, "History and Conditions of Yukon Gold District to 1897," *Eighteenth Annual Report of the United States Geological Survey to the Secretary of the Interior, 1896–97*, pt. 3 (Washington, D. C.: GPO, 1898), p. 119; Josiah Edward Spurr, "Geology of the Yukon Gold District, Alaska," *Eighteenth Annual Report of the United States Geological Survey to the Secretary of the Interior, 1896–97*, pt. 3 (Washington, D. C.: GPO, 1898), p. 156; Lt. Harry Graham, "Military Historical Sketch of Fort Egbert, Alaska," written for Garrison School for Officers, Department of the Columbia, March 31, 1909, p. 2; and Sims letters in *Letters and Papers of the Church Missionary Society*, London, on microfilm at Public Archives of Canada, Ottawa, Reel A-112.

15. Chester Wells Purington, *Methods and Costs of Gravel and Placer Mining in Alaska*, USGS Bulletin 263 (Washington D. C.: GPO, 1905), pp. 41, 43–44.

16. "Short Story of Alaska and the Yukon as told by the Mount Wrangell Company's Explorer" (promotional pamphlet, Boston: Mount Wrangell Company, 1897–98), p. 12. M. D. K. Weimer, *M. D. K. Weimer's True Story of the Alaska Gold Fields* (privately printed, 1900), pp. 138–41. Adney, *Klondike Stampede*, p. 457.

17. Weimer, *True Story of Alaska*, p. 280. Dora Elizabeth McLean, "Early Newspapers on the Upper Yukon Watershed, 1894–1907" (M.A. thesis, University of Alaska, n.d.), p. 38.

18. Samuel C. Dunham, "The Yukon and Nome Gold Regions," *Bulletin of the Department of Labor No. 29* (Washington, D. C.: GPO, 1900), p. 839. City records in EARC, Yellow File #2, 1898, and Yellow File #13, 1900.

19. Alfred Hulse Brooks, "A Reconnaisance from Pyramid Harbor to Eagle City," in *Twenty-first Annual Report of United States Geological Survey, 1899–1900*, pt. 2 (Washington, D. C.: GPO, 1900), p. 337. *Alaska Mining Record*, July 20, 1898, p. 4.

20. Dunham, "Alaskan Goldfields," p. 356.

21. Much confusion exists about which town was named Star City and which was Seventymile City. Alfred Hulse Brooks, "General Information Concerning the Territory by Geographic Provinces: The Yukon District," *Maps and*

Descriptions of Routes of Exploration in Alaska in 1899 (Washington, D. C.: GPO, 1899), p. 80, names Seventymile City and Star City in that order and topographer E. C. Barnard maps them in that order. Louis M. Prindle, *The Gold Placers of Fortymile, Birch Creek, and Fairbanks Regions, Alaska*, USGS Bulletin 251 (Washington, D. C.: GPO, 1905), and Donald J. Orth, *Dictionary of Alaska Place Names*, USGS Professional Paper 567 (Washington, D. C.: GPO, 1967), p. 913, have followed the USGS names, but Adney, *Klondike Stampede*, p. 457, and map opposite p. 460 have the names reversed. Lt. W. P. Richardson to Quartermaster General, February 12–26, 1899, "Records of the Office of the Quartermaster-General," RG 92, NA, places the post office in lower Star City but most of the population in upper Seventymile City. James Wickersham, *Old Yukon: Tales, Trails, and Trials* (St. Paul, Minnesota: West Publishing Co., 1938), p. 62, discusses only Star City. Perhaps the remnants of the town at the mouth and the one two miles upriver eventually became known collectively as "Star City." The ruins of the community were still visible in 1976.

22. *Alaska Mining Record*, August 30, 1898, p. 3. Melvin B. Ricks, *Directory of Alaska Post Offices and Postmasters* (Ketchikan: Tongass Publishing Co., 1965). Richardson to Quartermaster General, February 12–26, 1899. Dunham, "Yukon and Nome Gold Regions," p. 840.

23. "Rules for Organizing a Town-Nation City," June 6, 1898, Yellow File #8, 1899, Claims in EARC. Richardson to Quartermaster General, February 12–26, 1899. Dunham, "Yukon and Nome Gold Regions," p. 840. Only log remnants of Nation City remained in 1976.

24. Richardson to Quartermaster General, February 12–26, 1899.

25. Ibid. Dunham, "Yukon and Nome Gold Regions," p. 840.

26. Dunham, "Alaskan Goldfields," p. 360.

27. The development of the Rampart district is traced in the following works: Erinia Pavaloff Cherosky Callahan, "A Yukon Autobiography," *Alaska Journal*, 5 (Spring 1975), 128; Robert L. Spude, "Navagability Study for Upper Yukon Region, Alaska," draft manuscript (Anchorage: Bureau of Land Management, 1980); L. M. Prindle and F. M. Hess, *Rampart Placer Regions*, USGS Bulletin 259 (Washington, D. C.: GPO, 1905), pp. 104–19; and Hunt, *North of 53°*, pp. 60–62, 88–91, 217–20. Contemporary newspapers, especially, *Alaska Forum* and *Yukon Valley News*, are on microfilm at UAF. See also the contemporary correspondence of Rampart residents and miners in the R. H. Fitzhugh Collection and the Will Ballou Collection, UAF.

28. "The Adventures of the Iowa Goldseekers," ed. and annotated John Clark Hunt, *Alaska Journal*, 3 (Winter 1973), 2–12. Alfred Hulse Brooks, *Blazing Alaska's Trails* (Fairbanks: University of Alaska, 1953), p. 332. Hunt, *North of 53°*, pp. 232–33.

29. Cornelius Osgood, *The Han Indians*, Yale University Publications in Anthropology, No. 74 (New Haven: Yale University Press, 1971), pp. 138–44. Cornelius Osgood, *Contributions to the Ethnography of the Kutchin*, Yale University Publications in Anthropology, No. 14 (New Haven: Yale University Press, 1936), pp. 170–74.

30. Alfred Hulse Brooks, "The Mining Industry in 1909," *Mineral Resources of Alaska: Report on Progress of Investigations in 1909*, USGS Bulletin 442 (Washington, D. C.: GPO, 1910), p. 33.

31. Lt. J. C. Cantwell, *Report of the Operations of the U.S. Revenue Steamer Nunivak on the Yukon River Station, Alaska, 1899–1901*, Senate Ex. Doc., 58th Cong., 2d sess., no. 155 (1904) (Serial 4599), p. 173.

Chapter 7

1. "General Introduction," *Compilation*, p. 6.

2. Robert M. Utley, *Frontiersmen in Blue: The United States Army and the Indian, 1848–1865*. (New York: Macmillan Co., 1967). Robert M. Utley, *Frontier Regulars: The United States Army and the Indian, 1866–1890* (New York: Macmillan Co., 1973).

3. *Annual Report of the Secretary of War, 1987*, House Reps., 55th Cong., 2d sess., no. 2 (1897) (Serial 3630), p. 9. Ibid., 1898, House Reps. 55th Cong. 3d sess., no. 2 (1898) (Serial 3745), p. 180. Edwin C. Bearss, *Proposed Klondike Gold Rush National Historical Park Historic Resource Study* (Washington, D. C.: National Park Service, 1970). pp. 103–04. Pierre Berton, *The Klondike Fever* (Bloomington: Indiana University Press, 1972), pp. 199–200.

4. P. H. Ray and W. P. Richardson, "Suffering and Destitute Miners in Alaska, and What Was Done for Their Relief," in *Compilation*, pp. 519–60.

5. Quoted in Bearss, *Klondike Gold Rush*, p. 156.

6. Bearss, *Klondike Gold Rush*, pp. 155–59, 181–89. "Report of the Major General Commanding the Army" in *Annual Report of the Secretary of War, 1898*, House Reps., 55th Cong., 3d sess., no. 2 (1898) (Serial 3745), p. 180

7. William R. Abercrombie, "A Military Reconnoissance of the Copper River Valley, 1898," in *Compilation*, p. 565.

8. Morgan Sherwood, *Exploration of Alaska* (New Haven: Yale University Press, 1965), p. 159.

9. E. F. Glenn, "A Trip into the Tanana Region, 1898," in *Compilation*, pp. 629–48. H. G. Learnard, "A Trip From Portage Bay to Turnagain Arm and Up the Sushitna," in ibid., pp. 648–77. William Yanert, "A Trip to the Tanana River," ibid., pp. 677–79. Frederick Mathys, "Up the Chickaloon and Down the Talkeetna," ibid., pp. 679–83. Luther S. Kelly, "From Cabin Creek to the Valley of the Yukla, Alaska," ibid., pp. 684–86.

10. J. C. Castner, "A Story of Hardship and Suffering in Alaska," *Compilation*, pp. 686–712.

11. Richardson to Adjutant General, Department of the Columbia, September 19, 1898, in *Annual Report of the Secretary of War, 1899*, House Ex. Doc., 56th Cong., 1st sess., no. 2 (1899) (Serial 3901), pp. 79–81. Walker to Adjutant General, October 10, 1898, ibid., pp. 82–84. W. P. Richardson, "The Mighty Yukon As Seen and Explored," in *Compilation*, pp. 749–51.

12. Richardson to the Adjutant General, Department of the Columbia, February 13, 1899, in *Report of the Secretary of War, 1898* (Serial 3901), pp. 85–89.

13. Walker to Adjutant General, United States Army, July 7, 1899, in *Report of the Secretary of War, 1899* (Serial 3901), pp. 95–103.

14. Sherwood, *Exploration of Alaska*, pp. 166–67. Joseph S. Herron, *Explorations in Alaska, 1899, for an All-American Overland Route from Cook Inlet, Pacific Ocean, to the Yukon*, Senate Ex. Doc., 60th Cong., 2d sess., no. 689 (1901) (Serial 5408).

15. Walter C. Babcock, "The Trans Alaska Military Road," *Compilation*, p. 778.

16. John F. Rice, "From Valdez to Eagle City," *Compilation*, p. 787.

17. Compare Sherwood, *Exploration of Alaska*, pp. 167–68, with William E. Goetzmann, *Exploration and Empire: The Explorer and the Scientist in the Writing of the American West* (New York: Alfred A. Knopf, 1966), pp. 487–88.

18. Medical History of Fort Egbert, Alaska, July 31, 1899, "Medical Histories of Posts, 1868–1913," vol. 812. Records of the Adjutant General's Office, RG 94, NA. Richardson to Quartermaster General, July 15, 1899, Records of the United States Army Continental Commands, Post Records:Fort Egbert, 1899–1904, RG 393, NA.

19. Diary of Charles S. Farnsworth, July 8, 1899, Charles S. Farnsworth Collection, HEH.

20. Farnsworth Diary, September 3–November 27, 1899, HEH. Robert J. Farnsworth, "An Army Brat Goes to Alaska," part 2, *Alaska Journal*, 7 (Autumn 1977), 211–19, was taken from his manuscript, "Alaska, 1899–1901 and 1910–1911," in the Robert J. Farnsworth Collection, UAF.

21. *Annual Report of the Secretary of War, 1900*, part 1, (Washington, D. C.: GPO, 1900), pp. 243–49.

22. Farnsworth Diary, January 22, 1900, HEH. Letters from Ray and Wright, during March 1900, in Records of the U.S. Army Continental Commands, Posts Records: Fort Egbert, 1899–1904, RG 393, NA. Farnsworth to Tillman, April 30, 1900; Farnsworth to Dr. Thrasher, December 3, 1900; Farnsworth to Goodin, January 3, 1901; Farnsworth to Russell, December 1900; C. S. Farnsworth Collection, UAF.

23. Farnsworth Diary, November 27, 1899 to April 12, 1900, HEH.

24. General Orders No. 19, July 30, 1900; Farnsworth to Uncle Sam, August 8, 1900; Farnsworth to Goodin, January 3, 1901, C. S. Farnsworth Collection, UAF. Farnsworth Diary, August 11, 1900. HEH.

25. Quotations come from Farnsworth to Goodin, January 3, 1901; see also Farnsworth to McCoy, August 28, 1900, C. S. Farnsworth Collection, UAF; and Farnsworth to Assistant Adjutant General, St. Michael, August 28, 1900, RG 393, NA.

26. Root to Adjutant General, August 4, 1900, General Orders No. 109, "Selected Documents from the Abandoned Military Reservations File Relating to Fort Egbert," RG 49, NA.

27. Farnsworth to Richardson, October 18, 1900; Farnsworth to Dr.

Thrasher, October 26, 1900; Farnsworth to Will, November 5, 1900, C. S. Farnsworth Collection, UAF.

28. Farnsworth to Adjutant General, September 27, 1900, RG 49, NA. Farnsworth to McCoy, December 2, 1900, C. S. Farnsworth Collection, UAF.

29. Farnsworth describes life at Fort Egbert in his letters to McCoy, December 2, 1900; to Richardson, October 18, 1900; to Mother Galey, January 20, 1901; to Goodin, January 3 and March 3, 1901; to Wright, April 16, 1901; and to his brother, May 15, 1901, C. S. Farnsworth Collection, UAF.

30. Robert J. Farnsworth, "An Army Brat Goes to Alaska," part 1, *Alaska Journal*, 7 (Summer 1977), 160.

31. William Mitchell, "The Opening of Alaska." Microfilm #20 in UAF, from an original manuscript in the Library of Congress, p. 83. See also the published version with the same title, edited by Lyman L. Woodman. (Anchorage: Cook Inlet Historical Society, 1982).

32. J. C. Cantwell, *Report of the Operations of the U.S. Revenue Steamer Nunivak on the Yukon River Station, Alaska, 1899–1901*, Senate Ex. Doc., 58th Cong., 2d sess., no. 155 (1904) (Serial 4599), p. 182. Senator Nelson to Assistant Secretary of War, December 1, 1903, Records of the Judge Advocate General: Reservation File–Fort Egbert, RG 153, NA.

33. "Report of the Chief Signal Officer," in *Annual Report of the Secretary of War, 1901* (Washington, D. C.: GPO, 1901), p. 921 Verden McQueen, "Alaskan Communications, 1867–1914, part 1: A New Territory, 1867–1901," *Airpower Historian*, 8 (October 1961), p. 235.

34. Quoted in McQueen, "Alaskan Communications, Part 1," p. 242. "Report of the Chief Signal Officer," in *Annual Report of the Secretary of War, 1901*, pp. 921–24, 951–59.

35. Farnsworth Diary, March 1901, HEH. Interview with Charlie Steven, Eagle Village, by Mertie Baggen, July 22, 1964, field notes in Anthropology Department, UAF.

36. Mitchell, "The Opening of Alaska," introduction.

37. Quotations come from Mitchell, "The Opening of Alaska," pp. 42, 62, 86, and 184. In his work, Mitchell describes his theories as original to him when in fact many were commonly known truths of the north country already in use with miners and traders.

38. "Report of the Chief Signal Officer," in *Annual Reports of the Secretary of War, 1906*, vol. 2, House Ex. Doc., 59th Cong., 2nd sess., no. 2 (1906), p. 174. *Report of the Secretary of War, 1903*, vol. 1 (Washington, D. C.: GPO, 1903), pp. 30–31.

39. Quoted in *Report of the Secretary of War, 1903*, p. 31.

40. Mitchell, "The Opening of Alaska," pp. 3a–5a.

41. *Report of the Secretary of War, 1904*, vol. 1 (Washington, D. C.:GPO, 1904), pp. 21–25. Ibid., vol. 3, p. 199. "Report of the Quartermaster-General," p. 25, and "Report of the Chief Signal Officer," p. 175, *Annual Report of the Secretary of War, 1906*, vol. 2, House Ex. Doc., 59th Cong., 2d sess., no. 2 (1906) (Serial 5406).

42. "Report of the Chief Signal Officer," in *Annual Report of the Secretary of War, 1916,* vol. 1 (Washington, D. C.: GPO, 1916), pp. 865–69.

43. Quotation from Hanigan to Secretary of War, November 29, 1909; Orange File—1904–10, city records in EARC. Henry David McCary, Historical Tape Recordings H-27, UAF.

44. *Report of the Secretary of War, 1905,* vol. 1 (Washington, D. C.:GPO, 1905), p. 306. "Report of the Chief of Engineers," in *Annual Report of the Secretary of War, 1908,* vol. 5 (Washington, D. C.: GPO, 1908), p. 850.

45. "Report of the Adjutant-General," in *Annual Report of the Secretary of War, 1908,* vol. 1 (Washington, D. C.: GPO 1908), pp. 417–18. *Report of the Secretary of War, 1906,* vol. 1 (Washington, D. C.: GPO, 1906), pp. 58–59.

46. "Report of the Department of the Columbia," *Annual Report of the Secretary of War, 1910,* vol. 3 (Washington, D. C.: GPO, 1910), pp. 157–73. Wilds P. Richardson, "Col. Dick Richardson, Alaska Pioneer, Writes of U. S. Army in the North," *Alaska Weekly,* June 8, 1923, reprinted from *Infantry Journal,* 22 (May 1923), 505–17.

47. *Hearings Before the House Committee on Military Affairs on H. R. 6621 and H. R. 4130,* 74th Cong., 1st sess. (1935), pp. 120–21. Ernest Gruening, *The State of Alaska* (New York: Random House, 1968), pp 307–19.

48. George W. Rogers and Richard A. Cooley, *Alaska's Population and Economy: Regional Growth, Development and Future Outlook,* vol. 2, Division of State Planning (Juneau: Office of the Governor, 1962), p. 8, and Orlando W. Miller, *The Frontier in Alaska and the Matanuska Colony* (New Haven: Yale University Press, 1975), p. 197, declare that the military provided the greatest impetus to Alaskan development.

49. Quoted in Morris Zaslow, *The Opening of the Canadian North, 1870–1914* (Toronto: Hunter Rose Co., 1917), p. 108. Zaslow provides the best synthesis of developments in Yukon Territory during the early twentieth century.

Chapter 8

1. Robert M. Utley, *The Indian Frontier of the American West, 1846–1890,* (Albuquerque: University of New Mexico Press, 1984). Francis Paul Prucha, *American Indian Policy in Crisis: Christian Reformers and the Indian, 1865–1900* (Norman: University of Oklahoma Press, 1976). Francis Paul Prucha, *The Churches and the Indian Schools, 1888–1912* (Lincoln:University of Nebraska Press, 1979).

2. Barbara S. Smith, *Russian Orthodoxy in Alaska* (Anchorage: Alaska Historical Commission, 1980), pp. 55, 123–25, 131. James W. VanStone, *Ingalik Contact Ecology,* Fieldiana Anthropological Series Volume 71 (Chicago: Field Museum, 1979), pp. 94–97, 133–34.

3. Quotations from Hiram Alfred Cody, *An Apostle of the North, Mem-*

oirs of the Right Reverend William Carpenter Bompas (Toronto:Musson Book Co., 1908), pp. 264 and 271.

4. Ibid., pp. 282–83. Williams Douglas Johns, "The Early Yukon, Alaska, and the Klondike Discovery As They Were Before the Great Klondike Stampede Swept Away the Old Conditions Forever By One Who Was There," typescript, UWMC, p. 144.

5. Quoted in Gerard George Steckler, "Charles John Seghers:Missionary Bishop in the American Northwest, 1839–1886" (Ph.D. diss., University of Washington, 1963), p. 388. This biography is thoughtful, insightful, objective, and well written.

6. Quoted in Steckler., p. 457. Steckler, providing a masterful characterization of Seghers with all his contradictions, develops the theme that Segher's personality led to his ultimate tragedy.

7. Quoted in Steckler., p. 476.

8. After the fact, Tosi and Robault claimed they had tried to dissuade the impetuous and stubborn bishop, to no avail. See Steckler, pp. 488–92.

9. A phrase used by one of the Indian reformers to describe Protestant Indian policies. See Francis Paul Prucha's *Americanizing the American Indians: Writings by the "Friends of the Indian" 1880–1900* (Lincoln:University of Nebraska Press, 1978); also Prucha's *The Churches and the Indian Schools*, and *American Indian Policy in Crisis*.

10. *Annual Report of the Commissioner of Indian Affairs to the Secretary of the Interior for the Year 1887* (Washington, D. C.: GPO, 1887), p. xix.

11. "Report of the Commissioner of Education," in *Report of the Secretary of the Interior for the Fiscal Year Ending June 30, 1885*, vol. 4 (Washington, D. C.: GPO, 1886), p. lxiii. Sheldon Jackson, *Alaska and Missions on the North Pacific Coast* (New York: Dodd, Mead, 1880). For biographies of Jackson, see Robert Laird Stewart, *Sheldon Jackson: Pathfinder and Prospector of the Missionary Vanguard in Rocky Mountains and Alaska* (New York: Fleming H. Revell, 1908), which is uncritical and full of praise. For better balance, see a series of articles by Ted C. Hinckley, "The Presbyterian Leadership in Pioneer Alaska," *Journal of American History*, 52 (March 1966), 742–56; "Publicist of the Forgotten Frontier," *Journal of the West*, 4 (January 1965), 27–40; and "Sheldon Jackson as Preserver of Alaska's Native Culture," *Pacific Historical Review*, 33 (November 1964), 411–24.

12. Alice C. Fletcher, *Bureau of Education Special Report, 1888: Indian Education and Civilization*, Senate Ex. Doc., 48th Cong., 2d sess., no. 95 (1888), pp. 163–69.

13. Most of the Alaskan Episcopal Church records are in Austin, Texas. See Patricia L. Davis, *The Alaska Papers, 1884–1939: Guide to Collection of the Domestic and Foreign Missionary Society Papers in the Library and Archives of the Church Historical Society in Austin, Texas* (Austin:Episcopal Church Historical Society, n.d.). See also a number of Chapman's papers in the Episcopal Church in Alaska Collection at UAF. Using the extensive archives of the Episcopal and Catholic churches, VanStone, *Ingalik Contact Ecology*, has writ-

ten one of the better volumes in Alaskan history, all the more remarkable since it is a true ethnohistory—the impact of white culture on Alaskan Natives. See also "Education Report, 1886–1887," in *Report of the Secretary of the Interior for the Fiscal Year Ending June 30, 1887,* vol. 4 (Washington, D. C.: GPO, 1887), pp. 103–4, and John Wight Chapman, *A Camp on the Yukon* (Cornwall-on-Hudson, New York: Idlewild Press, 1948), pp. 19–21.

14. Most of the papers pertaining to the Jesuits in Alaska are deposited in the OPA and have been microfilmed on 42 rolls of film. These contain a wealth of information, such as history, diaries, annual reports, and correspondence. The guide is most useful; see Robert C. Carriker, Jennifer Ann Boharski, Eleanor R. Carriker, and Clifford A. Carroll, S. J., *Guide to the Microfilm Edition of the Oregon Province Archives of the Society of Jesus, Alaska Mission Collection* (Spokane: Gonzaga University, 1980). In particular see Holy Cross Collection Microfilm #8–12 and Nulato Collection, Microfilm #19–22. See also VanStone, *Ingalik Contact Ecology,* pp. 136–41 and William John Loyens, "The Changing Culture of the Nulato Koyukon Indians" (Ph.D. diss., University of Wisconsin, 1966), p. 117.

15. Charles J. Judge, *An American Missionary: A Record of the Work of Rev. William H. Judge, S. J.* (Ossining, New York: Catholic Foreign Mission Society, 1907), p. 49.

16. Sister Mary Joseph Calasanctius, *The Voice of Alaska* (Lachine, Quebec: St. Ann's Press, 1947). pp. 124–25. Louis L. Renner, S.J., "Farming at Holy Cross Mission on the Yukon," *Alaska Journal,* 9 (Winter 1979), 33.

17. Quoted in Richard Mathews, *The Yukon* (New York: Holt, Rinehart and Winston, 1968), p. 236.

18. Father F. Barnum, *Life on the Alaska Mission with an Account of the Foundation of the Mission and the Work Performed* (Woodstock, Maryland: Woodstock College Press, 1893), p. 36.

19. VanStone, *Ingalik Contact Ecology,* pp. 160–62.

20. Quotation from Louis L. Renner, S. J., "Jules Jetté: Distinguished Scholar in Alaska," *Alaska Journal,* 5 (Autumn 1975), 240. See material in the Nulato Collection. Microfilm #19–22 and the Julius Jetté Collection, Microfilm #32, OPA.

21. Prucha, *Churches and the Indian Schools,* pp. 4–9 and 26–40.

22. *Report of the Commissioner of Education for the Year Ending June 30, 1905,* vol. 1 (Washington, D. C.: GPO, 1907), p. xxxiv. "Report on Education in Alaska," in ibid., 1900–1901, vol. 2 (Washington, D. C.: GPO, 1902), p. 1459.

23. VanStone, *Ingalik Contact Ecology,* pp. 224–28. A. Parodi, "Process of the Plague at Holy Cross Mission, Alaska," manuscript written in 1900, on Microfilm #10, OPA.

24. Quoted in VanStone, *Ingalik Contact Ecology,* p. 211. See also correspondence between Rowe and Chapman, Box 1, Episcopal Church Records in Alaska Collection, UAF.

25. Few scholars have traced the missionary effort into the twentieth century and assessed its impact. Here VanStone, *Ingalik Contact Ecology,* excels.

Others include: Renner, "Farming at Holy Cross," and Loyens, "The Changing Culture of the Nulato Koyukon Indians." See also Stuck's diaries in the Hudson Stuck Collection, UAF.

26. Scholars of the American West have not yet synthesized the missionary movement to developing white frontier communities nor assessed their influence on frontier institutions.

27. Judge, *An American Missionary*, pp. 128–267. Pierre Berton, *Klondike: The Last Great Gold Rush, 1896–1899*, rev. ed. (Bloomington:Indiana University Press, 1972), pp. 182–83, 375–80. See also the William Judge Collection, Microfilm #36, OPA.

28. Thomas Jenkins, *The Man of Alaska: Peter Trimble Rowe* (New York: Morehouse-Gorham Co., 1943), pp. 58 and 69.

29. Peter T. Rowe, "First Annual Report of the Bishop of the Missionary District of Alaska, 1896," in Box 7, Episcopal Church Records, UAF.

30. Peter T. Rowe, "Annual Report of the Bishop of the Missionary District of Alaska, 1898," in Box 7, Episcopal Church Records, UAF.

31. James Wickersham, *Old Yukon: Tales, Trails, and Trials* (St. Paul, Minnesota: West Publishing Co., 1938), pp. 144–54. Dora Elizabeth McLean, "Early Newspapers on the Upper Yukon Watershed: 1894–1907" M. A. thesis, University of Alaska, n.d.).

32. Ibid. Jenkins, *Man of Alaska*, p. 92.

33. Clara Heintz Burke (as told to Adele Comandini), *Doctor Hap* (New York: Coward-McCann, Inc., 1961). Paul E. Thompson, "Who Was Hudson Stuck?" *Alaska Journal*, 10 (Winter 1980), 62–65. Arthur Ben Chitty, "The Venerable Dr. Stuck," manuscript in Box 10, Hudson Stuck Collection. See also Microfilm #88, 91, 97 and 98 on Hudson Stuck and UAF, and Hudson Stuck's Diaries, Box 1 and 2 and other material in Boxes 7–10, Hudson Stuck Collection, UAF.

34. Hudson Stuck, *Ten Thousand Miles With a Dog Sled: A Narrative of Winter Travel in Interior Alaska* (New York: Charles Scribner's Sons, 1915); *Voyages on the Yukon and Its Tributaries: A Narrative of Summer Travel in the Interior of Alaska* (New York: Charles Scribners's Sons, 1925); and *The Ascent of Denali: First Complete Ascent of Mt. McKinley, Highest Peak in North America*, 2nd ed. (Snohomish, Washington: Snohomish Publishing Co., 1977).

35. A.H. Savage, "The Alaskan Hercules: Father Monroe," *Dogsled Apostles* (New York: Sheed and Ward, 1942), p. 103. Bishop Joseph R. Crimont, S. J., "A Short Story of a Long-Time Friend: A Retrospect of the 84 Years of Life of Fr. F. P. Monroe," *Jesuit Seminary News*, 7 (1940), 39–40. Father Monroe, manuscript in Monroe Collection, also found on Microfilm #8, 38, and 39, OPA.

36. Quotations from Monroe to Rene, August 28, 1899, Monroe Collection.

37. Ray to Adjutant General, December 14, 1899, RG 49, NA. Letters Received, Adjutant General's Office, January 20, 1900, "Index to General Correspondence of the Adjutant General's Office, 1890–1917," National Archives Microfilm Publications, Microcopy 698, Roll 356, NA.

38. Father F. P. Monroe, "Annual Reports on Eagle, Alaska, St. Xavier's Mission, 1900–1901," Monroe Collection.

39. Rev. Robert M. Dickey. newly ordained, was the first Presbyterian missionary at Skagway and later Dawson. Presbyterian missionaries to the interior were sent to minister to the whites not the Natives. Thora McIlroy Mills, *The Church and the Klondike Gold Rush: The Contribution of the Presbyterian Church to the Yukon During the Gold Rush, 1897–1910* (Toronto: University of Toronto Press for the United Church Archives, 1978). James M. Sinclair, "St. Andrews Church, Lake Bennett," *Alaska Journal*, 4 (Autumn 1974), 242–50. Margaret Carter, *St. Andrew's Presbyterian Church, Lake Bennett, British Columbia*, Canadian Historic Sites: Occasional Papers in Archaeology and History No. 26 (Ottawa: Indian and Northern Affairs, Parks Canada, 1981).

40. James Wollaston Kirk and Anna L. M. Kirk, *Pioneer Life in the Yukon Valley, Alaska* (Buffalo: Ben Franklin Printers, 1936), p. 12.

41. Kirk, *Pioneer Life*, p. 25. J. C. Cantwell, *Report of the Operations of the U. S. Revenue Steamer Nunivak on the Yukon River Station, Alaska, 1899–1901*, Senate Ex. Doc., 58th Cong., 2d sess., no. 155 (1904) (Serial 4599), pp. 170–75. William Mitchell, "The Opening of Alaska," Microfilm #20 in UAF of original manuscript in Library of Congress, n.d., p. 52.

42. Kirk, *Pioneer Life*, pp. 30–31.

43. Charles F. Ensign, "The 'Chechakoo' and the 'Sour Dough'," *Assembly Herald*, 8 (1903), 259. Mary R. Ensign, "An Arctic School," *Assembly Herald*, 8 (1903), 263–64.

44. "Historical Data of Alaskan Missions," *Alaskan Churchmen*, 14 (1920). John G. Brady, *Annual Report of the Governor of Alaska to the Department of the Interior* (Washington, D. C.: GPO, 1905), p. 58.

45. Ernest Gruening, *The State of Alaska* (New York: Random House, 1968), pp. 107–14. Ted C. Hinckley, *Alaskan John G. Brady: Missionary, Businessman, Judge, and Governor, 1878–1918* (Columbus: Ohio State University Press, 1982). pp. 203–6.

46. Wickersham, *Old Yukon*, pp. 1–5, 36–56. Evangeline Atwood, *Frontier Politics: Alaska's James Wickersham* (Portland: Binford & Mort, 1979), pp. 58–78.

47. Wickersham, *Old Yukon*, pp. 40–77.

48. C. S. Farnsworth to McCoy, December 23, 1900, C. S. Farnsworth Collection, UAF.

49. Duane A. Smith, *Rocky Mountain Mining Towns: The Urban Frontier* (Lincoln: University of Nebraska Press, 1967). Richard C. Wade, *The Urban Frontier: Pioneer Life in Early Pittsburgh, Cincinnati, Lexington, Louisville, and St. Louis* (Chicago: University of Chicago Press, 1959).

50. Farnsworth to Boyd, May 9, 1901, C. S. Farnsworth Collection, UAF. Mitchell, "The Opening of Alaska," p. 20. Ferdinand Schmitter, *Upper Yukon Native Customs and Folk-Lore* (Washington, D. C.: Smithsonian Institution, 1910), p. 6. Lt. G. T. Emmons, *Condition and Needs of the Natives of Alaska*, Senate Ex. Doc., 58th Cong., 3d sess., no. 106 (1905) (Serial 4765). Cantwell, *Report of the Nunivak*, p. 183.

51. McLean, "Early Newspapers."

52. John G. Brady, *Report of the Governor of the District of Alaska to the Secretary of the Interior* (Washington, D. C.: GPO, 1902), p. 159. Stuck, *Voyages on the Yukon*, pp. 87–89.

53. Wickersham, *Old Yukon*, p. 48.

54. Terrence Cole in *E. T. Barnette: The Strange Story of the Man Who Founded Fairbanks* (Anchorage: Alaska Northwest Publishing Co., 1981) has ferreted out the basic story primarily from contemporary newspapers.

55. L. M. Prindle, *A Geologic Reconnaissance of the Fairbanks Quadrangle, Alaska*, USGS Bulletin 525 (Washington, D. C.: GPO, 1913), pp. 111–12. Cole, *E. T. Barnette*, p. 66–67.

56. Morris Zaslow, *The Opening of the Canadian North, 1870–1914* (Toronto: McClelland and Stewart, Ltd., 1971), pp. 122–42. See also David Morrison, *The Politics of the Yukon Territory, 1898–1909* (Toronto:University of Toronto Press, 1968).

Chapter 9

1. Oscar Osburn Winther, *The Transportation Frontier: Trans-Mississippi West, 1865–1890* (New York: Holt, Rinehart and Winston, 1964), pp. 10–74. Louis C. Hunter, *Steamboats on the Western Rivers: An Economic and Technological History* (Cambridge: Harvard University Press, 1949) pp. 3–60. Gordon Bennett, *Yukon Transportation: A History*, Canadian Historic Sites: Occasional Papers in Archaeology and History No. 19 (Ottawa: Indian and Northern Affairs, Parks Canada, 1978), p. 69.

2. Robert L. Spude, "Navigability Study for the Upper Yukon Region, Alaska," draft manuscript (Anchorage: Bureau of Land Management, 1980). Allan A. Wright, *Prelude to Bonanza* (Sidney, British Columbia: Gray's Publishing Company, 1976), p. 74.

3. Hunter, *Steamboats on Western Rivers*, p. 74.

4. Compare Hunter, pp. 606–13 with Leroy N. McQuesten, *Recollections of Leroy N. McQuesten of Life in the Yukon, 1871–1885* (Dawson City: Yukon Order of Pioneers, 1952), p. 9.

5. McQuesten, *Recollections of Leroy N. McQuesten*, p. 9.

6. R. N. DeArmond, "The Ill-Favored Steamboat Arctic," *Alaska Journal*, 4 (Autumn 1971), 52–54. Walter R. Curtin, *Yukon Voyage:Unofficial Log of the Steamer Yukoner* (Caldwell, Idaho: Caxton Printers, 1938), p. 278. Alfred Hulse Brooks, *Blazing Alaska's Trails* (Fairbanks:University of Alaska Press, 1973), p. 419. William Ogilvie, *Early Days on the Yukon* (Ottawa: Thorburn and Abbott, 1913), p. 67. William D. MacBride, "Saga of Famed Packets and Other Steamboats of the Mighty Yukon River," *Alaska Weekly*, July 21, 1944, p. 7. William D. Moore, "From Peru to Alaska," typescript, UWMC. Frank But-

eau, "My Experiences in the World," in *Sourdough Sagas*, ed. Herbert L. Heller (New York: Ballantine Books, 1967), p. 97.

7. William Douglas Johns, "The Early Yukon, Alaska and the Klondike Discovery As They Were Before the Great Klondike Stampede Swept Away the Old Conditions Forever By One Who Was There," typescript, UWMC, p. 152. Virginia S. Burlingame, "John J. Healy's Alaskan Adventure," *Alaska Journal*, 8 (Autumn 1978), 310–19.

8. Spude, "Navigability Study." E. S. Harrison, "Steamboating on the Yukon," *Alaska-Yukon Magazine* (May 1907), 9–10; also reprinted in *Alaska Journal*, 9 (Spring 1979), 49–53.

9. Capt. P. H. Ray and W. P. Richardson, "Suffering and Destitute Miners in Alaska and What Was Done for Their Relief—1898," in *Compilation*, p. 539.

10. Lt. John C. Cantwell, *Report of the Operations of the U. S. Revenue Steamer Nunivak on the Yukon River Station, Alaska, 1899–1901*, Senate Ex. Doc., 58th Cong., 2d sess., no. 155 (1904) (Serial 4599), pp. 127–29. *Alaska Mining Record*, June 15, 1898, p. 8. "Short Story of Alaska and the Yukon, As Told by the Mount Wrangell Company's Explorer, 1897–98," pamphlet, James T. Gray Collection, UOE. Spude, "Navigability Study."

11. Quotations from Curtin, *Yukon Voyage*, pp. 7 and 38.

12. Wood to Mrs. Wood, September 16 and November 11, 1900; and pamphlet in Fred J. Wood Collection, UOE.

13. Wood to Mrs. Wood, April 30, 1901, Wood Collection. Bennett, *Yukon Transportation*, p. 62–64. Hunter, *Steamboats on Western Rivers*, p. 624. Cantwell, *Report of the Nunivak*, p. 129. Northern Navigation Company, "To the Alaska Gold Fields," pamphlet (San Francisco: Northern Navigation Company, 1907). William R. Siddall, "The Yukon Waterway in the Development of Interior Alaska," *Pacific Historical Review*, 28 (November 1959), 367. George Leonard Anderson, "The *Koyukuk* of the Northern Navigation Company: A Study in Yukon River Transportation" (M.A. thesis, University of Oregon, 1972), p. 7.

14. MacBride, "Saga of Famed Packets," *Alaska Weekly*, July 21 to September 15, 1944. Cantwell, *Nunivak*, pp. 280–81, lists 47 steamers, 44 barges, 9 tugs, and 4 launches on the Yukon in 1900.

15. Northern Navigation Company, "To the Alaska Gold Fields," p. 5. Ogilvie, *Early Days*, p. 69. William Mitchell, "The Opening of Alaska," Microfilm #20 in UAF of original manuscript in Library of Congress, n.d., pp. 44–46. James Wickersham, *Old Yukon* (St. Paul, Minnesota: West Publishing Co., 1938), p. 47. *Alaska Mining Record*, November 2, 1898, p. 4.

16. Full narrative of the two years is found in Cantwell, *Nunivak*, pp. 1–325. Gary C. Stein, "Ship's Surgeon on the Yukon," *Alaska Journal*, 11 (1981), 228–36.

17. Wood to Mrs. Wood, July 12, 1900, Wood Collection, UOE. Pilcher to University of Alaska, May 2, 1935, George Pilcher Collection, UAF.

18. Cantwell, *Report of the Nunivak*, p. 131. Mitchell, "The Opening of Alaska," p. 44. Harrison, "Steamboating on the Yukon," 223.

19. Bennett, *Yukon Transportation*, p. 73. Siddall, "The Yukon Waterway in the Development of Interior Alaska," 361–76. *Annual Report of the Secretary of War, 1908*, vol. 5 (Serial 5424) (Washington, D. C.: GPO, 1908), pp. 850–51. Spude, "Navigability Study."

20. Cantwell, *Report of the Nunivak*, p. 135. Samuel C. Dunham, "The Alaskan Goldfields and the Opportunities They Offer for Capital and Labor," in *Bulletin of the Department of Labor*, edited by Carroll D. Wright, House Ex. Doc., 55th Cong., 2d sess., no. 206, pt. 3 (1898), p. 399.

21. Anderson, "The *Koyukuk*," p. 14. Norris H. Perkins, "Captain James T. Gray: A Grandfather to Remember," typescript, James T. Gray Collection, UOE. Wood to Mrs. Wood, May 20, 1900, Wood Collection, UOE. James Gray, "Light-Draft Steamer for an Alaskan River," *Marine Engineering* (February 1904), 68–69. Gray to wife Grace, July 31, 1902, Gray Collection, UOE. D. D. Cairnes, *The Yukon-Alaska International Boundary, Between Porcupine and Yukon Rivers*, Canadian Geological Survey Memoir No. 67 (Ottawa: Government Printing Bureau, 1914), pp. 7–8.

22. J. E. Chilberg, "Steamboating on the Yukon River," typescript, UWMC. Cantwell, *Report of the Nunivak*, p. 136. Wood to Mrs. Wood, June 12, 1900, Wood Collection, UOE.

23. Gray to Wickersham, February 20, 1911; and Gray to Secretary of Commerce and Labor, August 21, 1911, Gray Collection, UOE.

24. Curtin, *Yukon Voyage*, p. 293.

25. Hunter, *Steamboats on Western Rivers*, pp. 100–102.

26. Gray to Grace, September 22, 1906, Gray Collection, UOE.

27. MacBride, "Saga of Famed Packets," *Alaska Weekly*, July 28, 1944, p. 7. S. H. Graves, *On the 'White Pass' Pay-Roll* (Chicago: Paladin Press, 1970), pp. 192–216.

28. Cost of wood and methods of cutting and storing from Cantwell, *Report of the Nunivak*, pp. 132–33; Journal of George Pilcher, August 23 and November 1898, Pilcher Collection; Wood Contract of 1902, Gray Collection; Wood to Mrs. Wood, July 2, 1900, Wood Collection; and Samuel C. Dunham, "The Yukon and Nome Gold Regions," in *Bulletin of the Department of Labor*, No. 29 (Washington, D. C.: GPO, 1900), p. 843. See also "List of wood camps of Northern Navigation Company, 1902," Gray Collection.

29. Journal of George Pilcher, July 1898, Pilcher Collection, UAF.

30. Journal of George Pilcher, Thanksgiving 1899, Pilcher Collection.

31. Roger L. Trimble, "Miller's Camp," Bureau of Land Management Antiquities Site Survey, October 5, 1974. *Alaska Weekly*, August 12, 1927, p. 1, and August 1, 1930, p. 4. Interview with Horace Biederman, Jr., September 18, 1976, Eagle, Alaska.

32. Arthur James Collier, *The Coal Resources of the Yukon, Alaska*, USGS Bulletin 218 (Washington, D. C.: GPO, 1903), pp. 30–36. Dunham, "The Yukon and Nome Gold Regions," p. 843. Cantwell, *Report of the Nunivak*, p. 134. L. D. Kitchener, *Flag Over the North: The Story of the Northern Commercial Company* (Seattle: Superior Publishing Co., 1954), p. 201.

33. Interview with George Beck, September 19, 1976, Eagle, Alaska.

34. Collier, *Coal Resources of the Yukon.* Cantwell, *Report of the Nunivak*, pp. 40, 60–61, 119–20.

35. Harrison, "Steamboating on the Yukon," p. 50. Northern Navigation Company, "To the Alaskan Gold Fields," p. 6. A. H. Savage, *Dogsled Apostles* (New York: Sheed and Ward, 1942), p. 14.

36. Anderson, "The *Koyukuk*," p. 55. Spude, "Navigability Study." Harrison, "Steamboating on the Yukon," pp. 49–50. *Alaska Forum*, July 9, 1904, p. 2 and October 15, 1904, p. 2. *Yukon Valley News*, September 14, 1904, p. 3; December 6, 1905, p. 2; and July 17, 1907, p. 4. Bennett, *Yukon Transportation*, pp. 64, 157.

37. Bennett, *Yukon Transportation*, pp. 68–69. Spude, "Navigability Study." "Superintendent's Annual Report of Operation, 1914," American Yukon Navigation Company, White Pass & Yukon Route Records, Yukon Archives, Whitehorse.

38. Bennett, *Yukon Transportation*, p. 69. Anderson, "The *Koyukuk*," pp. 58–59. Spude, "Navigability Study."

39. William H. Wilson, *Railroad in the Clouds: The Alaska Railroad in the Age of Steam, 1914–1945* (Boulder, Colorado: Pruett Publishing Co., 1977), pp. 85, 179. Hunter, *Steamboats on the Western Rivers*, p. 607. *Alaska Weekly*, October 15, 1926, p. 1 and April 29, 1949, p. 1. Bennett, *Yukon Transportation*, p. 106.

40. *Alaska Weekly*, February 14, 1930, p. 1; May 30, 1930, p. 1; and June 27, 1930, p. 1. Wilson, *Alaska Railroad*, p. 237.

41. *Alaska Weekly*, April 1949, p. 1; and January 16, 1953, p. 1.

42. Bennett, *Yukon Transportation*, pp. 69, 104, 111–14, 145–46.

43. Brooks, *Blazing Alaska's Trails*, pp. 414–15. T. A. Rickard, *Through the Yukon and Alaska* (San Francisco: Mining and Scientific Press, 1909), p. 258.

44. Spude, "Navigability Study," breaks new ground in his discussion of these smaller watercraft.

Chapter 10

1. *A Guide for Alaskan Miners, Settlers, and Tourists*, prepared for the Copper River Mining, Trading and Development Co., under the auspices of the Valdez Chamber of Commerce (Seattle: Trade Register Print, 1902), p. 65. James Wollaston and Anna Kirk, *Pioneer Life in the Yukon Valley, Alaska* (Buffalo: Ben Franklin Printers, 1935), p. 74. Samuel C. Dunham, "The Alaska Goldfields and the Opportunities They Offer for Capital and Labor," *Bulletin of the Department of Labor*, ed. Carroll D. Wright, House Ex. Doc., 55th Cong., 2d sess., no. 206, pt. 3 (1898), p. 415.

2. Edwin Tappan Adney, *The Klondike Stampede* (New York: Harper and Brothers Publishers, 1900), pp. 183, 209–13, 221. Edwin Tappan Adney, "The

Sledge Dogs of the North," *Outing*, 39 (May 1901), 131–33. John C. Cantwell, *Report of the Operations of the U. S. Revenue Steamer Nunivak on the Yukon River Station, Alaska, 1899–1901*, Senate Ex. Doc., 58th Cong., 2d sess., no. 155 (1904) (Serial 4599), pp. 155–66. Gordon Bennett, *Yukon Transportation*, Canadian Historic Sites: Occasional Papers in Archaeology and History No. 19 (Ottawa: Indian and Northern Affairs, Parks Canada, 1978), pp. 48–54.

3. James Wickersham, *Old Yukon* (St. Paul, Minnesota: West Publishing Co., 1938), pp. 131–33. Interview with George Beck, September 19, 1976, Eagle, Alaska. Interview with Charlie Biederman (the son of Ed Biederman and the last person to carry mail from Eagle to Circle by dog team), February 12, 1977, Fairbanks, Alaska. Interview with Horace Biederman, Jr. (grandson of Ed Biederman and long-time resident of Eagle, Alaska), September 18, 1976, Eagle. Interview with Wyman Fritsch, September 19, 1976, Eagle, Alaska.

4. Cantwell, *Report of the Nunivak*, pp. 162–64. Wickersham, *Old Yukon*, p. 133. Hudson Stuck, *Ten Thousand Miles with a Dog Sled* (New York: Charles Scribner's Sons, 1915), p. 124. Mike Modrzynski, "Neither Rain nor Sleet nor Snow. . .," *Alaska Journal*, 10 (Spring 1980), 54–55.

5. Interview with Charlie Biederman, June 30, 1976, and February 12–13, 1977. Interview with Horace Biederman, Jr., September 18, 1976. Interview with George Beck, September 19, 1976. Diary Notes on the Yukon and Koyukuk Rivers, Alaska, Summer 1934, Elizabeth Hayes Goddard Collection, UAF.

6. Compare Alfred H. Brooks, *Blazing Alaska's Trails* (Fairbanks: University of Alaska Press, 1973), pp. 403–5, with Arthur Treadwell Walden, *A Dog-Puncher on the Yukon* (Boston: Houghton Mifflin Co., 1928), pp. 35–38, and William Douglas Johns, "The Early Yukon, Alaska and the Klondike Discovery As They Were Before the Great Klondike Stampede Swept Away the Old Conditions Forever By One Who Was There," typescript, UWMC, p. 158. Bennett, *Yukon Transportation*, p. 48.

7. Cantwell, *Report of the Nunivak*, p. 164. Adney, *Klondike Stampede*, p. 183. Josiah Edward Spurr, *Through the Yukon Gold Diggings* (Boston: Eastern Publishing Co., 1900), p. 173. Henry Davis, "Recollections," in *Sourdough Sagas*, ed. Herbert L. Heller (New York: Ballantine Books, 1967), p. 67. Bennett, *Yukon Transportation*, p. 48.

8. Bennett, *Yukon Transportation*, p. 54. Walden, *Dog-Puncher on the Yukon*, p. 169. Letter of William Ogilvie quoted in Joseph Ladue, *Klondyke Nuggets* (Montreal: John Lovell and Son Publishers, 1897), p. 168. Adney, *Klondike Stampede*, p. 430. Kathryn Winslow, *Big Pan-out* (New York:Norton, 1951), p. 153.

9. Michael E. Smith, *Alaska's Historic Roadhouses*, Office of Statewide Cultural Programs, History and Archeology Series No. 6 (Anchorage: Alaska Division of Parks, 1974), pp. 5–7. Walden, *Dog-Puncher on the Yukon*, pp. 32–33, 220. Modrzynski, "Neither Rain nor Sleet," p. 55.

10. Quotations from Wickersham, *Old Yukon*, p. 142–43. For more information on roadhouses see Wickersham, pp. 62–78; Journal of Clarence L. Andrews, August 29, 1904 and August 29, 1905, Andrews Collection, UAF; C.

A. Bryant, "Another Man's Life," typescript, Alaska Historical Library, Juneau, vol. 2, 1937, pp. B–M insert; Spurr, *Through the Yukon*, pp. 169–74, 187; Walden, *Dog-Puncher on the Yukon*, p. 39; Stuck, *Ten Thousand Miles with a Dog Sled*, p. 324; and Cantwell, *Report of the Nunivak*, p. 156.

11. Compare Roald Amundsen, *My Life as an Explorer* (Garden City, New York: Doubleday, Doran, and Co., 1927), pp. 53–59, with John Bockstoce's personality sketch of Mogg in Bernhard Kilian's *The Voyage of the Schooner, 'Polar Bear:' Whaling and Trading in the North Pacific and Arctic, 1913–1914*, ed. John Bockstoce (New Bedford Whaling Museum: Old Dartmouth Historical Society and the Alaska Historical Commission, 1983), pp. vi–vii.

12. Amundsen, *My Life as an Explorer*, pp. 53–59. Iris Warner, "Herschel Island," *Alaska Journal*, 3 (Summer 1973), 130–42. Journal of Clarence L. Andrews, December 12, 1905, Andrews Collection, UAF. *Seattle Post-Intelligencer*, December 6, 1905, p. 1, and December 7, 1905, p. 1.

13. *Alaska Weekly*, March 6 and June 12, 1931, p. 5. Telephone interview with Charlie Biederman, June 30, 1976, Tok, Alaska. Thompson to Johnson, May 17, 1939, and Election Results, Green File #3, 1937–39, EARC.

14. Edwin C. Bearss, *Proposed Klondike Gold Rush National Historical Park: Historic Resource Study* (Washington, D. C.: National Park Service, 1970), pp. 31–33, 199–247. Pierre Berton, *Klondike: The Last Great Gold Rush, 1896–1899* (Bloomington: Indiana University Press, 1972), pp. 356–57.

15. *War Department Annual Reports, 1918*, vol. 3, "Report of the Chief of Engineers" (Washington, D. C.: GPO, 1918), pp. 1988–89. Bennett, *Yukon Transportation*, p. 57.

16. Laura Beatrice Berton, *I Married the Klondike* (Toronto: Little, Brown, Co., 1954), p. 38. Bennett, *Yukon Transportation*, p. 88.

17. Report of William Rucker on Road Work, March 31, 1909, Orange File #14, 1909; Report of August Fritsch on Road Work, March 28, 1908; Report of August Fritsch on Road Work, March 27, 1909; Report of Harry F. Rogers on Road Work, May 12, 1909; Report of B. F. Cordell on Road Work, March 31, 1910; and Eagle Precinct Road, 1908, all in Orange Files, 1904–19, EARC. See also Brooks, *Blazing Alaska's Trails*, p. 423.

18. Valdez Common Council to Mayor and Council of Eagle, July 29, 1904, Orange File, 1904, EARC. *Conditions in Alaska*, Senate Reps., 58th Cong., 2d sess., no. 282, pt. 2 (1904), p. 123. *Seattle Post-Intelligencer*, September 19, 1905, p. 1.

19. Claus-M. Naske, "The Alaska Board of Road Commissioners," *Transportation in Alaska's Past*, ed. Michael S. Kennedy (Anchorage: Alaska Historical Society, 1982), pp. 91–139.

20. Thomas Christmas Riggs, Jr., "Autobiographical Memoir" on Microfilm #66 at UAF, from the original in the Library of Congress.

21. U.S. Alaska Road Commission, *Report of the Board of Road Commissioners for Alaska*, (Washington, D. C.: GPO, 1906–53). *War Department Annual Reports, 1918*, pp. 1986–88. Colonel W. P. Richardson, "The U. S. Army in the North," *Alaska Weekly*, June 8, 1923, p. 7. *Annual Report of the Gover-*

nor of Alaska to the Department of Interior (Washington, D. C.: GPO, 1905).
Brooks, Blazing Alaska's Trails, p. 426. "The Alaska Road Commission," Alaska
Weekly, December 13, 1929, p. 7.

22. War Department Annual Reports, 1918, p. 1919.

23. "Alaska Road Commission," Alaska Weekly, p. 7. Bennett, Yukon
Transportation, pp. 80–82. Evangeline Atwood, Frontier Politics: Alaska's James
Wickersham (Portland: Binford & Mort, 1979), pp. 220, 248, 324.

24. Bennett, Yukon Transportation, p. 82. Grace Edman, Alice Hudson,
and Sam Johnson, Fifty Years of Highways (Alaska Department of Public Works:
Division of Highways, 1960), p. 40. The latter source is largely an unsynthes-
ized compilation of random annual reports from the Alaska Road Commission.

25. "Alaska Road Commission," Alaska Weekly, p. 7. Edman et al, Fifty
Years of Highways, p. 42.

26. War Department Annual Reports, 1919, vol. 2, "Report of the Chief of
Engineers" (Washington, D. C.: GPO, 1919), p. 2101. War Department Annual
Reports, 1920, vol. 2, "Report of the Chief of Engineers" (Washington, D. C.:
GPO, 1920), pp. 61–63. "The Alaska Road Commission," Alaska Weekly, p. 7.

27. Bennett, Yukon Transportation, p. 92–103, 141–45.

28. Edman et al., Fifty Years of Highways, pp. 43, 142–44. Bennett, Yukon
Transportation, p. 143. Reed to Brown, April 26, 1955, Green File #31, 1955;
and Report on the Completion of the Fortymile Road, October 21, 1950, Green
File #22, 1950, EARC. Ernest Gruening, The State of Alaska (New York: Random House, 1968), pp. 443–48.

29. Norman Penlington, The Alaska Boundary Dispute: A Critical Reappraisal (Toronto: McGraw-Hill Ryerson, 1972). Lewis Green, The Boundary
Hunters: Surveying the 141st Meridian and the Alaska Panhandle (Vancouver:
University of British Columbia Press, 1982), pp. 79–94. Alaska Boundary Tribunal, The Argument of the United States Before the Tribunal Convened at London Under the Provisions of the Treaty Between the United States of America
and Great Britain Concluded January 24, 1903 (Washington, D. C.: GPO, 1903).
P. H. Gordon, "An Arbitrary Boundary," Beaver, 302 (Autumn 1971), 51.

30. Green, Boundary Hunters, pp. 143–44.

31. Riggs's description of himself in his unpublished memoirs, Microfilm
#66, UAF.

32. International Boundary Commission, Joint Report upon the Survey and
Demarcation of the International Boundary Between the United States and
Canada Along the 141st Meridian from the Arctic Ocean to Mount St. Elias
(Ottawa and Washington, D. C.: International Boundary Commissioners, 1918),
pp. 118–92. Green, Boundary Hunters, pp. 144–47.

33. For more detail on the transportation methods of the survey teams,
see Richard O. Stern, "Historic Uses of the Kandik and Nation Rivers, East-
Central Alaska," typescript (Anchorage: State of Alaska, Department of Natural Resources, 1978), pp. 36–55.

34. Two men lost their lives in the panhandle during a mudslide. Green,
Boundary Survey, p. 103.

35. Riggs, "Memoir." Thomas Riggs, Jr., "Running the Alaska Boundary," *Beaver*, 276 (September 1945), 43. Christine W. Billman, "Jack Craig and the Alaska Boundary Survey," *Beaver*, 302 (Autumn 1971), 48.

36. Both quotations in Green, *Boundary Hunters*, pp. 164, 175.

37. D. D. Cairnes, *The Yukon-Alaska International Boundary, Between Porcupine and Yukon Rivers*, Canada Geological Survey, Memoir 67 (Ottawa: Government Printing Bureau, 1914). A. G. Maddren, *Geologic Investigations Along Canada-Alaska Boundary*, USGS Bulletin 520K (Washington, D. C.:GPO, 1912).

Chapter 11

1. Gordon Bennett, *Yukon Transportation*, Canadian Historic Sites: Occasional Papers in Archaeology and History No. 19 (Ottawa: Indian and Northern Affairs, Parks Canada, 1978). S. H. Graves, *On the "White Pass" Pay-roll* (Chicago: Paladin Press, reprint of 1908, 1970). Edwin C. Bearss, *Proposed Klondike Gold Rush National Historical Park: Historic Resource Study* (Washington, D. C.: National Park Service, 1970). Lone E. Janson, *The Copper Spike* (Anchorage: Alaska Northwest Publishing Company, 1975). Robert Alden Stearns, "The Morgan-Guggenheim Syndicate and the Development of Alaska, 1906–1915" (Ph.D. diss., University of California, Santa Barbara, 1967).

2. George W. Dickinson, *The Alaska Central Railway* (Seattle:privately printed, 1903). Duane Koenig, "Ghost Railway in Alaska," *Pacific Northwest Quarterly*, 45 (January 1954), 8–12. William R. Siddall, "The Yukon Waterway in the Development of Interior Alaska," *Pacific Historical Review*, 28 (November 1959), 371–73. Franklin Ward Burch, "Alaska's Railroad Frontier: Railroads and Federal Development Policy, 1898–1915" (Ph.D. diss., Catholic University of America, Washington, D. C., 1965).

3. House Committee on the Territories, *Railroads in Alaska*, 60th Cong., 1st sess. (Washington, D. C.: GPO, 1908). Ibid., 61st Cong., 2d sess. (Washington, D. C.: GPO, 1910). Senate Committee on Public Lands, *Government Railroad and Coal Lands in Alaska*, part 1, 62nd Cong., 2d sess. (Washington, D. C.: GPO, 1912). U.S. Alaska Railroad Commission, *Railway Routes in Alaska*, House Ex. Doc., 62nd Cong., 3d sess., no. 1346 (1913). Senate Committee on Territories, *Construction of Railroads in Alaska*, part 1, 63rd Cong., 1st sess. (1913).

4. The archives of the Alaska Railroad, Federal Archives and Records Center, Seattle, are rich and extensive. The best political and economic history is William H. Wilson, *Railroad in the Clouds: The Alaska Railroad in the Age of Steam, 1914–1945* (Boulder: Pruett Publishing Company, 1977). Also see Bernadine LeMay Prince, *The Alaska Railroad in Pictures, 1914–1964*, 2 vols. (Anchorage: Ken Wray, 1964); William H. Wilson, "The Alaska Railroad: Elements of Continuity, 1915–1941," *Transportation in Alaska's Past*, ed. Michael S. Kennedy (Anchorage: Alaska Historical Society, 1982), pp. 317–39; William H. Wilson, "The Alaska Railroad and Coal:Development of a Federal

Policy, 1914–1939," *Pacific Northwest Quarterly*, 73 (April 1982), 66–77; and Edwin M. Fitch, *The Alaska Railroad* (New York:Frederick A. Praeger, 1967). Published government documents also provide data: House Committee on Territories, *The Building of Railroads in Alaska*, 63rd Cong., 2d sess. (1914), and the Alaska Railroad's own newspaper, *Alaska Railroad Record*, Anchorage, November 14, 1916, to June 29, 1920, which provided accurate information on the construction of the railroad and circulated official orders.

5. Wilson, *Railroad in the Clouds*. See also the Alaska Railroad Archives in Seattle, and the Frederick C. Mears Collection, UAF.

6. Wilson, *Railroad in the Clouds*, pp. 75–78.

7. William H. Wilson, "The Mayo Ore Deal: An International 'Gentlemen's Agreement,' " *Alaska Journal*, 9 (Winter 1979), 74–79.

8. The best source on the Alaska Railroad after 1945 is Edwin M. Fitch, *The Alaska Railroad* (New York: Frederick A. Praeger, 1967).

9. Bill Sheffield, "A Guest Editorial by the Governor of Alaska," *Alaskafest* (February 1983), 5. Cleonne R. Compton, *The Alaska Railroad* (Juneau: Committee on Transportation, 1979), pp. 32–43.

10. Sheffield, "Guest Editorial," p. 5. Compton, *The Alaska Railroad*, pp. 43–64.

11. Bennett, *Yukon Transportation*, pp. 145–48.

12. Compare Bennett, p. 146 with "The Little Engines That Can't," *Maclean's*, 93 (October 1, 1979), 25 and "No Railroad, Few Jobs, What Now in Skagway?" *Fairbanks Daily News-Miner*, February 25, 1983, p. 2.

13. U.S. Department of State, *Report of the Commission to Study the Proposed Highway to Alaska, 1933* (Washington, D. C.: GPO, 1933).

14. The two best sources on the Alaska Highway are Bennett, *Yukon Transportation*, and Harold W. Richardson, "Alcan—America's Glory Road:Part I, Strategy," *Engineering News-Record*, 129 (December 17, 1942), 81–98. David A. Remley, *Crooked Road: The Story of the Alaska Highway* (New York: McGraw-Hill Book Company, 1976), fails to live up to its potential and is largely a collection of oral impressions tied loosely together with a historical narrative.

15. Harold W. Richardson, "Alcan—America's Glory Road: Part II, Supply, Equipment, Camps," *Engineering News-Record*, 129 (December 31, 1942), 35–42. Bennett, *Yukon Transportation*, p. 134. Remley, *Crooked Road*, pp. 77–86.

16. The role of the Public Roads Administration is best told in Theodore A. Huntley and R. E. Royall, *Construction of the Alaska Highway* (Washington, D. C.: GPO, 1945).

17. Bennett, *Yukon Transportation*, p. 138, seen from the viewpoint of Yukon Territory, has thoughtfully assessed the impact of the highway.

18. The best synthesis on the Dempster Highway is William G. MacLeod, *The Dempster Highway* (Ottawa: Canadian Arctic Resources Committee, 1979). Others include: Allen A. Wright, "Yukon Hails Opening of the Dempster Highway," *Canadian Geographic*, 98 (June/July 1979), 16–21; Robert Renaud, "The

Dempster: Road to Riches. . . or Ruin?" *Alaska Journal*, 10 (Winter 1980), 14–21;
and "Two Throughways to the Arctic," *Time*, 113 (May 14, 1979), 100–101.

19. The history of the Alaska Pipeline has yet to be written. Best current
synthesis is James P. Roscow, *800 Miles to Valdez: The Building of the Alaska
Pipeline* (Englewood Cliffs, New Jersey: Prentice-Hall, Inc., 1977). Robert
Douglas Mead, *Journeys Down the Line: Building the Trans-Alaska Pipeline*
(New York: Doubleday, 1978), is not very useful. Many other popular articles
and books can be found, but few offer any insight or analysis.

20. Mary Clay Berry, *The Alaska Pipeline: The Politics of Oil and Native
Land Claims* (Bloomington: Indiana University Press, 1975). Robert D. Arnold,
Alaska Native Land Claims (Anchorage: Alaska Native Foundation, 1976).

21. For extensive studies, see U.S. Department of the Interior, *Trans-Alaska
Pipeline Hearings*, 12 vols. (Washington, D. C.: GPO, 1971) and U.S. Department of the Interior, *Final Environmental Impact Statement for the Proposed
Trans-Alaska Pipeline*, 6 vols. (Washington, D. C.: GPO, 1972). For impacts
and postpipeline assessment see U.S. Department of the Interior, *Summary of
Trans-Alaska Oil Pipeline System Critique Session* (Washington, D. C.: GPO,
1977). Several other socioeconomic books have attempted to assess the "new
Alaska," but lack of distance from the event produces distortion and lack of
objectivity.

22. Michael S. Kennedy, "Arctic Flying and Alaskan Bush Pilots: A Synopsis of Early Aviation History," *Transportation in Alaska's Past*, ed. Michael
S. Kennedy (Anchorage: Alaska Historical Society, 1982), pp. 183–238.

23. William Mitchell, "Alaskan Expedition," Microfilm #20 in UAF from
the original in the Library of Congress. Rose Albert, "Ruby Sees Its First Planes,"
Alaska Journal, 11 (1981), 216–17.

24. See Eielson's correspondence with the Second Assistant Postmaster
General of the United States in Eielson's "Summary of Impressions Received
in Two Years Flying in Alaska," on Microfilm #20 in UAF from original in the
William Mitchell Collection at the Library of Congress.

25. Most books on Alaska or Yukon aviation are written for the popular
audience without footnotes or even bibliographies. The Eielson story is told by
Edward A. Herron, *Wings Over Alaska: The Story of Carl Ben Eielson* (New
York: Archway Paperback, 1967); "Adventure Marked Eielson's Life," *Fairbanks
Daily News-Miner*, March 12, 1930, pp. 5–7; and Jean Potter, *The Flying North*
(New York: Macmillian Company, 1945). For Canadian aviation development
and aviators, see Jeanne Harbottle, "Clyde Wann, Father of Yukon Aviation,"
Alaska Journal, 3 (Autumn 1973), 237–45; Jeanne Harbottle, "White Pass Avia-
tion and Its Rivals," *Alaska Journal*, 4 (Autumn 1974), 232–41; and Bennett,
Yukon Transportation, pp. 119–24.

26. Ira Harkey, *Pioneer Bush Pilot: The Story of Noel Wien* (Seattle:
University of Washington Press, 1974), like all books on Alaskan aviation, foc-
uses primarily on the years of bush flying.

27. Statistics quoted in Harkey, p. 265.

28. Bennett, *Yukon Transportation*, p. 120. Archie Satterfield *The Alaska Airlines Story* (Anchorage: Alaska Northwest Publishing Company, 1981), p. 33.

Chapter 12

1. Following statistics and quotations from C. A. "Bert" Bryant, "Another Man's Life," vol. 1 (1937), typescript, Alaska State Historical Library, Juneau.

2. Ibid., pp. 170–72. Norman L. Wimmler, *Placer-Mining Methods and Costs in Alaska*, Bureau of Mines Bulletin 259 (Washington, D. C.: GPO, 1927), pp. 31–36, 89–90. John Power Hutchins, "Prospecting and Mining Gold Placers in Alaska," *Minerals of Alaska in 1907*, USGS Bulletin 345 (Washington, D. C.: GPO, 1908), pp. 54–77. Chester Wells Purington, *Methods and Costs of Gravel and Placer Mining in Alaska*, USGS Bulletin 263 (Washington, D. C.: GPO, 1905), pp. 39–43. Ernest Wolff, *Handbook for the Alaskan Prospector* (Ann Arbor, Michigan: Edward Brothers, 1969), pp. 180–83.

3. Billy Meldrum, Tape Recording Nos. 1 and 2, taped by Terry Haynes, Bureau of Land Management, Fortymile Resource Area, July 11 and 30, 1976.

4. The best description of the geologic process is in J. B. Mertie, Jr., *Geology of the Eagle-Circle District, Alaska*, USGS Bulletin 816 (Washington, D. C.: GPO, 1930), pp. 159–66, but the evolution of geological thought can be traced in Alfred Hulse Brooks, "The Circle Precinct," *Minerals of Alaska in 1906*, USGS Bulletin 314 (Washington, D. C.: GPO, 1907), pp. 187–204; and Brooks, "The Mining Industry in 1906," ibid., pp. 22–34; L. M. Prindle, *The Fortymile Quadrangle: Yukon-Tanana Region, Alaska*, USGS Bulletin 375 (Washington, D. C.: GPO, 1909), p. 32; Prindle, *A Geologic Reconnaissance of the Circle Quadrangle, Alaska*, USGS Bulletin 538 (Washington, D. C.: GPO, 1913), pp. 54–58; Brooks, "The Mineral Deposits of Alaska," *Minerals of Alaska in 1913*, USGS Bulletin 592 (Washington, D. C.: GPO, 1914), pp. 24–26; and Prindle, *The Yukon-Tanana Region, Alaska*, USGS Bulletin 295 (Washington, D. C.: GPO, 1906), pp. 15–25.

5. T. A. Rickard, *Through the Yukon and Alaska* (San Francisco:Mining and Scientific Press, 1909), pp. 207, 222. Wolff, *Handbook for the Prospector*, p. 115. Wimmler, *Placer Mining Methods*, pp. 65–70. Brooks, "The Mineral Deposits of Alaska," p. 31.

6. Rickard, *Through the Yukon and Alaska*, pp. 210–20. Wimmler, *Placer-Mining Methods*, pp. 113–34. Purington, *Methods and Costs of Placer Mining*, pp. 82–99. Norman R. Ball, "The Development of Permafrost Thawing Techniques," paper delivered to the Annual Meeting of the Canadian Society for the Study of the History and Philosophy of Science, Edmonton, Alberta, May 1975. Josiah Edward Spurr, "Geology of the Yukon Gold District, Alaska," *Eighteenth Annual Report of the United States Geological Survey to the Secretary of the Interior, 1896–97*, part 3 (Washington, D. C.: GPO, 1898), p. 390. Chester Wells Purington, "Methods and Costs of Gravel and Placer Mining in

Alaska," *Minerals of Alaska in 1904*, USGS Bulletin 259 (Washington, D. C.: GPO, 1905), p. 32. L. M. Prindle, "Yukon Placer Fields," *Minerals of Alaska in 1905*, USGS Bulletin 284 (Washington, D. C.: GPO, 1906), p. 121.

7. Rickard, *Through the Yukon and Alaska*, p. 215. Ball, "Permafrost Thawing Techniques," p. 3.

8. Wimmler, *Placer-Mining Methods*, pp. 87–112. Purington, *Methods and Costs of Placer Mining*, pp. 55–81. Hutchins, "Prospecting and Mining Gold," pp. 70–71. Prindle, "Yukon Placer Fields," p. 121. Rickard, *Through the Yukon and Alaska*, p. 220.

9. Purington, *Methods and Costs of Placer Mining*, p. 99. Rodman W. Paul, *Mining Frontiers of the Far West, 1848–1880* (New York: Holt, Rinehart and Winston, 1963), pp. 90–91.

10. Wimmler, *Placer-Mining Methods*, pp. 65–71. Hutchins, "Prospecting and Mining Gold Placers in Alaska," pp. 68–70. Alfred Hulse Brooks, "The Mining Industry in 1908," *Minerals of Alaska in 1908*, USGS Bulletin 379 (Washington, D. C.: GPO, 1909), p. 43.

11. Purington, *Methods and Costs of Placer Mining*, pp. 99–156. Hutchins, "Prospecting and Mining Gold," pp. 65–70. Wimmler, *Placer-Mining Methods*, pp. 47–62, 65–71, 132–75. Brooks, "The Mining Industry in 1908," pp. 42–44. Paul, *Mining Frontiers*, pp. 90–91.

12. A synthesis of the history of dredge mining is Clark C. Spence, "The Golden Age of Dredging: The Development of an Industry and Its Environmental Impact," *Western Historical Quarterly*, 11 (October 1980), 401–14. Purington, *Methods and Costs of Placer Mining*, pp. 157–60. Wimmler, *Placer-Mining Methods*, pp. 176–90. Rickard, *Through the Yukon and Alaska*, pp. 220–21. William Rodney, "Pioneer Dredging in the Klondike," *Alaska Journal*, 6 (Winter 1976), 51. Charles Francis Herbert, "Gold Dredging in Alaska" (B.A. thesis, Alaska Agricultural College and School of Mines, 1934). Ernest Patty, *North Country Challenge* (New York:David McKay Co., 1969), pp. 98–99.

13. Ball, "Permafrost Thawing Techniques," p. 6–7. Arthur Gibson, "Thawing Frozen Ground for Placer Mining," *Mining and Scientific Press*, 108 (January 10, 1914), 143. "Cold-Water Thawing in the North," *Mining and Scientific Press*, 124 (February 4, 1922), 147. Hubert I. Ellis, "Thawing Methods at Fairbanks," *Engineering and Mining Journal*, 100 (July 3, 1915), 1. C. H. Birmingham, "Gold Dredging at Sixty Below Zero," *Scientific American*, 116 (June 2, 1917), 555. R. N. Ogburn, "Thawing and Dredging Gold at Fairbanks, Alaska," *Mining and Metals*, 14 (1933), 214–16.

14. Prindle, "The Fortymile Gold-Placer District," *Minerals of Alaska in 1907*, p. 195. Alfred Hulse Brooks, "The Alaskan Mining Industry in 1915," *Minerals of Alaska in 1915*, USGS Bulletin 642 (Washington, D. C.: GPO, 1916), pp. 24–25. Wimmler, *Placer-Mining Methods*, pp. 177–78. Brooks, "The Mining Industry in 1908," pp. 39–42. Hutchins, "Prospecting and Mining Gold," pp. 71–72.

15. Brooks, "Placer Mining in Alaska in 1904," *Minerals of Alaska in 1904*, pp. 25–28. Prindle, "Yukon Placer Fields," pp. 110–23. Alfred Hulse Brooks,

"The Mining Industry in 1906," *Minerals of Alaska in 1906*, pp. 35–37. Brooks, "The Mining Industry in 1907," *Minerals of Alaska in 1907*, pp. 38–43. C. E. Ellsworth, "Placer Mining in the Yukon-Tanana Region," *Minerals of Alaska in 1909*, USGS Bulletin 442 (Washington, D. C.: GPO, 1910), pp. 230–34.

16. Brooks, "The Circle Precinct," pp. 187–204. Alfred Hulse Brooks, "Placer Gold Mining in Alaska in 1902," *Contributions to Economic Geology, 1902*, USGS Bulletin 213 (Washington, D. C.: GPO, 1903), pp. 47–48. Brooks, "Placer Gold Mining in Alaska," ibid., 1903, USGS Bulletin 225 (Washington, D. C.: GPO, 1904), pp. 43–57. Friese to Johanson, February 4, 1903, and List of Claims, Orange Files, EARC. Brooks, "Placer Mining in Alaska in 1904," p. 29. Prindle, *The Yukon-Tanana Region, Alaska*, pp. 14–27. Brooks, "Railway Routes," *Minerals of Alaska in 1905*, USGS Bulletin 284 (Washington, D. C.: GPO, 1906), pp. 13–15. Purington, *Methods and Costs of Placer Mining*, pp. 1–204. Purington, "Methods and Costs of Placer Mining," pp. 36–41. Prindle, "Yukon Placer Fields," pp. 109–10.

17. *Conditions in Alaska*, Hearings before Subcommittee of Committee on Territories, Senate Reps., 58th Cong., 2d sess., no. 282, part 2 (1904). T. A. Rickard, "Mining Law in Alaska," *Mining and Scientific Press*, 97 (December 26, 1908), 855.

18. Alfred Hulse Brooks, "The Mining Industry in 1907," *Minerals of Alaska in 1907*, USGS Bulletin 345 (Washington, D. C.: GPO, 1908), pp. 30–50. Prindle, "The Fortymile Gold-Placer District," pp. 189–96. Prindle, *The Fortymile Quadrangle*, pp. 45–46. Brooks, "The Mining Industry in 1908," pp. 21–53. Brooks, "The Mining Industry in 1909," pp. 20–26. Ellsworth, "Placer Mining in the Yukon-Tanana Region," pp. 234–44. Brooks, "The Mining Industry in 1910," *Minerals of Alaska in 1910*, USGS Bulletin 480 (Washington, D. C.: GPO, 1911), pp. 21–39. C. E. Ellsworth and G. L. Parker, "Placer Mining in the Yukon-Tanana Region," ibid., pp. 153–72. Brooks, "The Mining Industry in 1911," *Minerals of Alaska in 1911*, USGS Bulletin 520 (Washington, D. C.: GPO, 1912), pp. 19–41. E. A. Potter, "Placer Mining in the Fortymile, Eagle, and Seventymile River Districts," ibid., 211–18. Brooks, "The Mining Industry in 1912," *Minerals of Alaska in 1912*, USGS Bulletin 542 (Washington, D. C.: GPO, 1913), pp. 18–45. C. E. Ellsworth and R. W. Davenport, "Placer-Mining in the Yukon District," ibid., pp. 210–20. Brooks, "The Alaska Mining Industry in 1913," *Minerals of Alaska in 1913*, pp. 45–69. Theodore Chapin, "Placer Mining in the Yukon-Tanana Region," ibid., pp. 361–62. Brooks, "The Alaskan Mining Industry in 1914," *Minerals of Alaska in 1914*, USGS Bulletin 622 (Washington, D. C.: GPO, 1915), pp. 15–66.

19. Brooks, "The Mining Industry in 1908," p. 21.

20. Ibid., p. 33. Brooks, "The Alaskan Mining Industry in 1913," p. 45.

21. Alfred Hulse Brooks, "The Alaskan Mining Industry in 1915," *Minerals of Alaska in 1915*, USGS Bulletin 642 (Washington, D. C.: GPO, 1916), pp. 16–67. Brooks, "The Alaska Mining Industry in 1916," *Minerals of Alaska in 1916*, USGS Bulletin 662 (Washington, D. C.: GPO, 1918), pp. 11–60. See

also Red Files, 1914–25, EARC. Sumner S. Smith, *The Mining Industry in the Territory of Alaska During the Calendar Year 1916*, Bureau of Mines Bulletin 153 (Washington, D. C.: GPO, 1919), p. 53.

22. G. C. Martin, "The Alaska Mining Industry in 1917," *Minerals of Alaska in 1917*, USGS Bulletin 692 (Washington, D. C.: GPO, 1919), pp. 17, 37. G. C. Martin, "The Alaskan Mining Industry in 1918," *Minerals of Alaska in 1918*, USGS Bulletin 712 (Washington, D. C.: GPO, 1920), pp. 11, 33. Alfred Hulse Brooks and G. C. Martin, "The Alaskan Mining Industry in 1919," *Minerals of Alaska in 1919*, USGS Bulletin 714 (Washington, D. C.:GPO, 1921), p. 60. Brooks, *The Alaska Mining Industry in 1920*, USGS Bulletin 722-A (Washington, D. C.: GPO, 1921), p. 10. Brooks, "The Alaskan Mining Industry in 1921," *Minerals of Alaska in 1921*, USGS Bulletin 739 (Washington, D. C.: GPO, 1923), p. 43. Brooks and S. R. Capps, "The Alaskan Mining Industry in 1922," *Minerals of Alaska in 1922*, USGS Bulletin 755 (Washington, D. C.: GPO, 1924), pp. 12–13, 33. *Report of the Governor of Alaska to the Secretary of the Interior, 1919* (Washington, D. C.: GPO, 1919).

23. Brooks, *The Alaskan Mining Industry in 1920*, pp. 14–17. Brooks, "The Alaskan Mining Industry in 1921," p. 5. Brooks and Capps, "The Alaskan Mining Industry in 1922," pp. 11–13. *Alaska Weekly*, June 13, 1930, p. 6.

24. Fred H. Moffit, "Mineral Industry in Alaska in 1925," *Minerals of Alaska in 1925*, USGS Bulletin 792 (Washington, D. C.: GPO, 1929), p. 4. *Alaska Weekly*, April 12, 1929, p. 1; February 7, 1930, p. 1. Philip S. Smith, "Mineral Industry of Alaska in 1926," *Minerals of Alaska in 1926*, USGS Bulletin 797 (Washington, D. C.: GPO, 1929), pp. 14–24. Smith, "Mineral Industry in Alaska in 1927," *Minerals of Alaska in 1927*, USGS Bulletin 810 (Washington, D. C.: GPO, 1930), pp. 18–31. Smith, "Mineral Industry of Alaska in 1928," *Minerals of Alaska in 1928*, USGS Bulletin 813 (Washington, D. C.: GPO, 1930), pp. 19–49.

25. Philip S. Smith, "Mineral Industry in Alaska in 1927," p. 18. Smith, "Mineral Industry of Alaska in 1928," p. 5. *Alaska Weekly*, editorial, July 19, 1929, p. 4.

26. Philip S. Smith, "Mineral Industry of Alaska in 1931," *Minerals of Alaska in 1931*, USGS Bulletin 844 (Washington, D. C.: GPO, 1934), p. 24. Smith, "Mineral Industry of Alaska in 1932," *Minerals of Alaska in 1932*, USGS Bulletin 857 (Washington, D. C.: GPO, 1934), pp. 9, 31.

27. Smith, *Mineral Industry of Alaska in 1929*, USGS Bulletin 824-A (Washington, D. C.: GPO, 1930), pp. 24–41. Smith, "Mineral Industry of Alaska in 1930," *Minerals of Alaska in 1930*, USGS Bulletin 836 (Washington, D. C.: GPO, 1933), pp. 23–42. Smith, "Mineral Industry of Alaska in 1931," pp. 24–42. Smith, "Mineral Industry of Alaska in 1932," pp. 22–53. Smith, *Mineral Industry of Alaska in 1934*, USGS Bulletin 868-A (Washington, D. C.: GPO, 1936), pp. 26–45.

28. Patty, *North Country Challenge*, pp. 93–94.

29. Philip S. Smith, *Mineral Industry of Alaska in 1940*, USGS Bulletin

933-A (Washington, D. C.: GPO, 1942), pp. 27–51. Smith, *Mineral Industry of Alaska in 1941 and 1942*, USGS Bulletin 943-A (Washington, D. C.: GPO, 1944), pp. 9–11.

30. Patty, *North Country Challenge*, pp. 96–120.

31. Philip S. Smith, *Mineral Industry of Alaska in 1935*, USGS Bulletin 880-A (Washington, D. C.: GPO, 1937), pp. 4, 33, 43. Smith, *Mineral Industry of Alaska in 1937*, USGS Bulletin 910-A (Washington, D. C.: GPO, 1939), pp. 5–7, 44–57. J. B. Mertie, Jr., *Gold Placers of the Fortymile, Eagle, and Circle Districts, Alaska*, USGS Bulletin 897-C (Washington, D. C.: GPO, 1938), pp. 251–57.

32. Patty, *North Country Challenge*, pp. 119–20. Interview with Ernest Wolff, August 3, 1976, Fairbanks. Interview with Joe Vogler, August 6, 1976, Woodchopper Creek. Interview with Jim Layman, August 8–9, 1976, Ben Creek. *Alaska Weekly*, January 1942 through December 1950.

33. "Alaska's Oil/Gas & Minerals Industry," *Alaska Geographic*, 9 (1982), 34.

34. Cited in Gordon Bennett, *Yukon Transportation: A History*, Canadian Historic Sites: Occasional Papers in Archaeology and History No. 19 (Ottawa: Indian and Northern Affairs, Parks Canada, 1978), pp. 59–95.

35. The best synthesis of the Treadgold story is Lewis Green's *The Gold Hustlers* (Anchorage: Alaska Northwest Publishing Co., 1977).

36. Bennett, *Yukon Transportation*, pp. 95, 141. Canada, Department of Mines, *The Yukon Territory: A Brief Description of its Administration, Resources and Development* (Ottawa: Bureau of Northwest Territories and Yukon Affairs, 1944).

37. Janet E. Macpherson, "The Cyprus Anvil Mine," *Northern Transitions*, ed. Everett B. Peterson and Janet B. Wright, vol. 1, (Ottawa:Canadian Arctic Resources Committee, 1978), pp. 113–44. D. B. Craig, "Yukon Mining and Exploration, 1975," *Western Miner*, 48 (October 1975), 16–18. "Mining Industry Left $70-Million (Plus) in Canadian North in 1974," *Western Miner*, 48 (April 1974), 19–24. Frank Duerden, *The Development and Structure of the Settlement System in the Yukon* (Whitehorse:Department of Library and Information Resources, 1981).

38. "United Keno Layoff," *Canadian Mining Journal*, 103 (August 1982), 11. "From Ketchikan to Barrow," *Alaska*, 48 (November 1982), 27.

Chapter 13

1. The best book on the agricultural development of Alaska and the subsequent myths of homesteading and rugged individualism is Orlando W. Miller, *The Frontier in Alaska and the Matanuska Colony*, (New Haven:Yale University Press, 1975). The statistics quoted come from pages 17, 22–23, and 208 respectively.

2. Evelyn Berglund Shore, *Born on Snowshoes* (Boston: Houghton Mifflin Co., 1954). Quotation comes from page 130.

3. Ibid., p. 209. Other Alaskan trappers have expressed similar contentment: James A. Carroll, *The First Ten Years in Alaska: Memoirs of a Fort Yukon Trapper, 1911–1922* (New York: Exposition Press, 1957); Erik Munsterhjelm, *The Wind and the Caribou: Hunting and Trapping in Northern Canada* (London: George Allen and Unwin, 1953); Erik Munsterhjelm, *Fool's Gold: A Narrative of Prospecting and Trapping in Northern Canada* (London: George Allen and Unwin, 1957); Jeanne Connolly Harbottle and Fern Grice Credeur, *Woman in the Bush* (Pelican Publishing Company, 1966); and Chick Ferguson, *Mink, Mary and Me: The Story of a Wilderness Trapline* (New York: M. S. Mill Co., 1946).

4. The best work on trapping in Alaska is Richard K. Nelson's *Hunters of the Northern Forest: Designs for Survival Among the Alaskan Kutchin* (Chicago: University of Chicago Press, 1973). Also informative is *The Manitoba Trappers' Guide* (Manitoba: Department of Renewable Resources and Transportation Services, 1976) and Bob Hoffman's *Master Trapping Methods* (Tacoma: Mercury Press, 1976). More oriented to lower forty-eight trapping is S. Stanley Hawbaker's *Trapping the North American Furbearers* (Clearfield, Pennsylvania: Kurtz Bros., 1974). A historic source is Ned Dearborn's *Trapping on the Farm*, an extract from the U.S. Department of Agriculture Yearbook of 1919, facsimile reproduction (Seattle: Shorey Book Store, 1973).

5. Jim Rearden, "The New Boom in Furs: An Old Trade Comes to Life," *Alaska*, 47 (January 1981), 33.

6. No historian in Alaska or the American West has attempted to write a history of twentieth-century trapping. The following chronology and generalizations are synthesized from Alaska Game Commission Reports, fur auction prices, and contemporary newspaper articles.

7. Nelson, *Hunters of the Northern Forest*, p. 166. Nelson H. H. Graburn and Stephen B. Strong, *Circumpolar Peoples: An Anthropological Perspective* (Pacific Palisades, California: Goodyear Publishing, 1973), p. 102. Carroll, *The First Ten Years in Alaska*, p. 70.

8. J. B. Marshall, "Evolution of Fur Trade," *Alaska Weekly*, December 7, 1928, p. 6. Nelson, *Hunters of the Northern Forest*, p. 166. Redington to Gunnell, October 24, 1928, Folder on Fur Resources: Marten, Box 159, Fish and Wildlife Service Records, RG 22, NA. "Annual Report of Alaska Game Commission to the Secretary of the Interior, 1941," Box 6, RG 22, NA. *Alaska Weekly*, May 11, 1928, p. 5. Ferguson, *Mink, Mary and Me*, p. 9. Carroll, *The First Ten Years in Alaska*, p. 70. "The Twelfth Annual Report of the Executive Officer to the Alaska Game Commission for the period November 1, 1936, to December 31, 1937," Folder 9, Alaska Game Commission Reports, UAF. See also *Alaska Weekly*, April 23, 1926, to September 27, 1929, which contain each month's fur auction prices at the Seattle Fur Exchange.

9. Nelson, *Hunters of the Northern Forest*, p. 167. *Alaska Weekly*, January 25, 1929, p. 2; February 9, 1929, p. 2; August 9, 1929, p. 2; and February 7, 1930, p. 7; March 22, 1929, p. 2; October 3, 1930, p. 7; July 24, 1931, p. 6; December 25, 1931, p. 8; October 19, 1934, p. 3; and May 3, 1935, p. 3.

10. *Alaska Weekly,* December 1936, p. 1; February 26, 1937, p. 1; and January 14, 1938, p. 1. See also *Alaska Weekly,* November 22, 1929, to June 13, 1941, which quotes each month's fur prices for the Seattle Fur Exchange and the West Coast Fur Sales, Inc., and "Annual Report of the Alaska Game Commission to the Secretary of the Interior," 1939 and 1941, RG 22, NA.

11. See game warden reports for Fort Yukon (District 10) in "Annual Report of the Alaska Game Commission to the Secretary of Agriculture," for the years 1928–33, Folders 3–7, UAF.

12. See mileage reports of distance traveled in the thirteen annual reports of the Alaska Game Commission to the Secretary of Agriculture for the years 1925–39, Folders 1–12, UAF

13. *Alaska Weekly,* February 7, 1941, p. 8; April 11, 1941, p. 4; and May 12, 1944, p. 2. L. D. Kitchener, *Flag Over the North* (Seattle: Superior Publishing Co., 1954), pp. 269–70.

14. Nelson, *Hunters of the Northern Forest,* p. 167. Graburn and Strong, *Circumpolar Peoples,* p. 102. *Alaska Weekly,* April 24, 1942, to February 23, 1945, which sporadically quote the fur auction prices of the Seattle Fur Exchange and the West Coast Fur Sales, Inc. See also specific articles in *Alaska Weekly,* December 13, 1940, p. 4; January 31, 1941, p. 8; and February 14, 1941; May 2, 1941, p. 8; March 20, 1942; November 13, 1942, p. 5; May 21, 1943, p. 3; and January 7, 1944, p. 1. "Annual Report of the Alaska Game Commission to the Secretary of the Interior," 1941, 1942, and 1943, Box 6, RG 22, NA.

15. "Annual Report of the Alaska Game Commission to the Secretary of the Interior, 1946," Box 6, RG 22, NA. Nelson, *Hunters of the Northern Forest,* p. 167. Graburn and Strong, *Circumpolar Peoples,* p. 103. *Alaska Weekly,* editorial and article, November 12, 1948, p. 4. Interview with Elmer Nelson, September 19–20, 1976.

16. Trapping in Yukon Territory, unlike in Alaska, has benefited from an excellent synthesis, Adrian Tanner, *Trappers, Hunters, and Fishermen:Wildlife Utilization in the Yukon Territory,* Yukon Research Project Series No. 5 (Ottawa: Department of Northern Affairs and Natural Resources, 1966).

17. Compare statistics in Tanner, p. 11, with "The Twelfth Annual Report of the Executive Officer to the Alaska Game Commission for the period November 1, 1936, to December 31, 1937," p. 56, Folder 10, UAF, and "Annual Reports of the Alaska Game Commission to the Secretary of the Interior, " for years 1940–50, RG 22, NA.

18. Tanner, *Trappers, Hunters, and Fishermen,* p. 23.

19. Rearden, "New Boom in Furs," pp. 32–33.

20. John Haines, "Of Traps and Snares," *Alaska,* 47 (March 1981), 68.

21. Through conversations with the "river people" and especially David Evans, identified in the introduction, the author observed an intense interest in early frontier history. Some trappers actually tried to live, as closely as possible, the life of early mountain men. Others spent considerable time talking to Natives and trappers from the 1930s to learn additional knowledge of the land and trapping skills.

22. Frederick Jackson Turner, *The Frontier in American History* (New York: Holt, Rinehart, and Winston, 1963), p. 37.

23. Miller, *The Frontier in Alaska and the Matanuska Colony*, p. 223.

24. Ernest Gruening, *The State of Alaska: A Definitive History of America's Northernmost Frontier* (New York: Random House, 1968). Robert Marshall, *Arctic Village* (New York: Literary Guild, 1933). John McPhee, *Coming into the Country* (New York: Farrar, Straus and Giroux, 1977). Joe McGinniss, *Going to Extremes* (New York: Alfred A. Knopf, 1980). Arguments on the Alaska National Interest Lands issue—the amount of public land to be preserved and protected in parks and wildlife refuges—can be found in Alaskan newspapers and magazines of environmental organizations throughout the 1970s.

25. U.S. Department of the Interior, "Rampart Project, Alaska: Market for Power and Effect of Project on Natural Resources" (Juneau, 1965).

Selected Bibliography

I. Archival Collections

GOVERNMENT DEPOSITORIES

Washington, D.C., National Archives and Records Service.
Records of the Fish and Wildlife Service. Record Group 22.
Records of the General Land Office. Record Group 49. Selected Documents
    from Abandoned Military Reservation Files.
Records of the Office of the Quartermaster General. Record Group 92.
Records of the Adjutant General's Office. Record Group 94. Medical Histories
    of Posts, 1868–1913.
Records of the Office of Territories. Record Group 126. Selected Documents
    Relating to Eagle Townsite and Fur and Game Resources.
Records of the Judge Advocate General. Record Group 153. Reservation File,
    Fort Egbert.
Records of the U.S. Army Continental Commands Post Records. Record
    Group 393.
National Archives Microfilm Publications. Microcopy 617: Returns from U.S.
    Military Posts, 1800–1916. Roll 342: Fort Egbert, Alaska, June
    1899–August 1911.
———. Microcopy 698: Index to General Correspondence of the Adjutant
    General's Office, 1890–1917. Roll 228: Circle City, Alaska. Roll 356:
    Fort Egbert, Alaska.

Seattle. Federal Archives and Records Center.
Alaska Railroad Archives.
Papers of the Governors of Alaska. (Now housed in State Archives Building,
    Juneau, Alaska.)

Ottawa. Public Archives of Canada

Letters and Papers of the Church Missionary Society, London. Microfilm
A-112: Vincent C. Sims Papers.
———. Microfilm A-103 and A-110: Robert McDonald Letters and Journals.

OTHER DEPOSITORIES

Eagle, Alaska. Records of Eagle City with copies in Anchorage at the State
Division of Parks Office and microfilm at the University of Alaska
Archives at Fairbanks.
Eugene, Oregon. University of Oregon Library. C. L. Andrews Collection.
———. University of Oregon. James T. Gray Collection.
———. University of Oregon. Fred J. Wood Collection.
Fairbanks, Alaska. University of Alaska Archives. Alaska Game Commission
Records.
———. University of Alaska Archives. Clarence Leroy Andrews Collection.
———. University of Alaska Archives. Arctic Village Journals.
———. University of Alaska Archives. William B. Ballou Collection.
———. University of Alaska Archives. Frank Buteau Collection.
———. University of Alaska Archives. Episcopal Church in Alaska
Collection.
———. University of Alaska Archives. Charles S. Farnsworth Collection.
———. University of Alaska Archives. Robert J. Farnsworth Collection.
———. University of Alaska Archives. Robert Hunter Fitzhugh Collection.
———. University of Alaska Archives. James Geoghegan Collection.
———. University of Alaska Archives. Elizabeth Hayes Goddard Collection.
———. University of Alaska Archives. Martin Harrais Collection.
———. University of Alaska Archives. N. V. Hendricks Collection.
———. University of Alaska Archives. Frederick C. Mears Collection.
———. University of Alaska Archives. George Pilcher Collection.
———. University of Alaska Archives. Shad Reid Collection.
———. University of Alaska Archives. Hudson Stuck Collection.
———. University of Alaska Archives. Joe Ward Collection.
———. University of Alaska Archives. Sam O. White Collection.
Spokane, Washington. Gonzaga University. Oregon Province Archives of
Society of Jesus. Alaska Mission Collection. Microfilmed on 42 reels.
———. Gonzaga University. Oregon Province Archives of Society of Jesus.
Father Francis P. Monroe Collection.
San Marino, California. Henry E. Huntington Library. Charles S. Farnsworth
Collection.
———. Henry E. Huntington Library. Frederick Jackson Turner Collection.
Seattle, Washington. University of Washington Archives. Charles S. Bulkley
Collection.
Whitehorse, Yukon Territory. Yukon Archives. American Yukon Navigation
Company Records.

II. Unpublished Materials

MANUSCRIPTS

Alaska Commercial Company. "Minutes of Meetings, October 19, 1868, to October 9, 1918." Microfilm #13. From the original in California Historical Society, San Francisco.

Andrews, Elizabeth. "Niibeeo Zhoo: An Early Historic Han Athapaskan Village Site, Interim Report." Typescript. Fairbanks: University of Alaska Cooperative Park Studies Unit, 1976.

Ball, Norman R. "The Development of Permafrost Thawing Techniques." Paper presented at Annual Meeting of the Canadian Society for the Study of the History and Philosophy of Science, May 1975, at Edmonton, Alberta.

Bowers, Peter M. Hoch, David M. "An Archeological Reconnaisance of the Copper Creek Drainage, Upper Charley River Area, East-Central Alaska." Typescript. Fairbanks: University of Alaska Cooperative Park Studies Unit, 1976.

Bryant, C. A. "Another Man's Life." 2 vols. Typescript. Juneau: Alaska Historical Library, n.d.

Bulkley, C. S. "Journal of the U.S. Russo-American Telegraph Expedition, 1865–1867." Microfilm #3. Fairbanks: University of Alaska Archives.

Carriker, Robert C.; Boharski, Jennifer Ann; Carriker, Eleanor R.; and Carroll, Clifford A. *Guide to the Microfilm Edition of the Oregon Province Archives of the Society of Jesus, Alaska Mission Collection.* Spokane: Gonzaga University, 1980.

Chilberg, J. E. "Steamboating on the Yukon River." Typescript. Seattle: University of Washington Manuscript Collection, n.d.

Chitty, Arthur Ben. "The Venerable Dr. Stuck." Typescript. Fairbanks: Hudson Studk Collection, University of Alaska Archives.

Davis, Patrica L. "The Alaska Papers, 1884–1939: Guide to the Collection of the Domestic and Foreign Missionary Society Papers in the Library and Archives of the Church Historical Society in Austin, Texas." Austin: Espiscopal Church Historical Society, n.d.

Deranja, John E. "A Short Autobiography of John Deranja, as Told to His Daughter, Mary, During Spring of 1933 When He Was Seventy Years Old." Typescript. Seattle: University of Washington Manuscript Collection, 1933.

Eielson, Carl Ben. "Summary Impressions Received in Two Years Flying in Alaska." Microfilm #20. From the original in William Mitchell Collection in Library of Congress. Fairbanks: University of Alaska Archives.

Graham, Harry, Lt. "Military Historical Sketch of Fort Egbert." Paper written for Garrison School for Officers, Department of Columbia, 1908–09.

Grauman, Melody Webb. "Eagle: Focus on the Yukon." Typescript. Fairbanks: National Park Service, 1975.

Hall, Edwin S., Jr. "Aboriginal Occupations of the Charley River and Adjacent Yukon River Drainage, East-Central Alaska." Typescript. Fairbanks: National Park Service, 1974.

Heimer, Virginia Doyle. "Alaska Mining History: An Annotated Review of Selected Literature, an Alphabetical Index of Mining Towns with Notes on Their Location and Associated References, and Miscellaneous Other Information." Typescript. Fairbanks: University of Alaska Museum, 1975.

Hildebrandt, James. "History of Placer Mining in Alaska." Typescript. Fairbanks: University of Alaska Library, 1942.

Jetté, Jules. "Jottings of an Alaskan Missionary." Microfilm #96, Reel 33. From the original in Jules Jetté Collection in Jesuit Alaska Mission Records at Oregon Province Archives of the Society of Jesus at Gonzaga University in Spokane. Fairbanks: University of Alaska Archives.

Johns, William Douglas. "The Early Yukon, Alaska, and the Klondike Discovery as They Were Before the Great Klondike Stampede Swept Away the Old Conditions Forever By One Who Was There." Typescript. Seattle: University of Washington Manuscript Collection, n.d.

Mercier, François. Untitled manuscript, translated by Linda Finn Yarborough, handwritten. In Francis Monroe Papers. Spokane, Washington: Oregon Province Archives of the Society of Jesus Gonzaga University, n.d.

Miners' Association of Circle, Alaska. Vol. 1: Constitution, By-Laws, and Membership of the Miners' Association. Vol. 2: Minutes. Juneau: Alaska Historical Library, 1895.

Mitchell, William. "Alaskan Expedition." Microfilm #20. From the original manuscript in William Mitchell Collection in Library of Congress. Fairbanks: University of Alaska Archives.

Mitchell, William. "Opening of Alaska." Microfilm #20. From the original manuscript in William Mitchell Collection in Library of Congress. Fairbanks: University of Alaska Archives.

Monroe, Francis P. Untitled manuscript on Eagle. Spokane: Oregon Province Archives of the Society of Jesus, Gonzaga, University, n.d.

Moore, William D. "From Peru to Alaska." Typescript. Seattle: University of Washington Manuscript Collection, n.d.

Naske, Claus-M. "The Historical Fortymile District." Anchorage: Bureau of Land Management, 1974.

Parodi, A. "Process of the Plague at Holy Cross Mission, Alaska." Microfilm #96, Reel 10. From the original in Oregon Province Archives Records at Gonzaga University in Spokane. Fairbanks: University of Alaska Archives, 1900.

Perkins, Norris H. "Captain James T. Gray: A Grandfather to Remember." Typescript. Eugene: University of Oregon, 1969.

Riggs, Thomas Christmas, Jr. "Autobiographical Memoir." Microfilm #66. From the original in Library of Congress. Fairbanks: University of Alaska Archives.

Sackinger, Patricia M. "An Historical Survey of Eagle City, Alaska."
Typescript. Fairbanks: University of Alaska History Department, 1975.

Schieffelin, Edward. "Edward Schieffelin's Trip to Alaska." Typescript.
Berkeley: Bancroft Library, University of California.

Stern, Richard O. "Historic Uses of the Kandik and Nation Rivers, East-
Central Alaska." Typescript. Anchorage: Alaska Department of Natural
Resources, 1978.

Tritt, Albert. "The Story of the Early Natives and Their Church." Typescript.
Fairbanks: University of Alaska Archives.

Utley, Robert M. "A Personal View of the Western Experience." Paper
presented at The West: Its Literature and History, Western Writers'
Conference, Logan, Utah, June 1973.

Vlmer, Joseph. "History of the Circle Mining District, Alaska." Handwritten.
Fairbanks: University of Alaska Archives, n.d.

Westdahn, Ferdinand. "Interview at Anderson Insland, Puget Sound, June
7, 1878, Concerning Experiences on the Pacific Coast Since 1865,
Especially with the Western Union Telegraph Expedition." Typescript.
Berkeley: Bancroft Library, University of California.

THESES AND DISSERTATIONS

Anderson, George Leonard. "The *Koyukuk* of the Northern Navigation
Company: A Study in Yukon River Transportation." Master's thesis,
University of Oregon, 1972.

Herbert, Charles Francis. "Gold Dredging in Alaska." Bachelor's thesis,
Alaska Agricultural College and School of Mines, 1934.

Laatsch, William Ganfield. "Yukon Mining Settlement: An Examination of
Three Communities." Ph.D dissertation, University of Alberta, 1972.

Loyens, William John. "The Changing Culture of the Nulato Koyukon
Indians." Ph.D dissertation, University of Wisconsin, 1966.

McLean, Dora Elizabeth. "Early Newspapers on the Upper Yukon Watershed,
1894–1907." Master's thesis, University of Alaska, n.d.

Marshall, John W. "A History of Protestant Missions in Alaska." Master's
thesis, Pasadena College, 1954.

Matthews, Raymond T. "Placer Mining Methods and Costs in Circle
District." Bachelor's thesis, University of Alaska, 1940.

Murray, David F. "Some Factors Affecting the Production and Harvest of
Beaver in the Upper Tanana River Valley, Alaska." Master's thesis,
University of Alaska, 1961.

Stearns, Robert Alden. "The Morgan-Guggenheim Syndicate and the
Development of Alaska, 1906–1915." Ph.D. dissertation, University of
California at Santa Barbara, 1967.

Steckler, Gerard George. "Charles John Seghers: Missionary Bishop in the
American Northwest, 1836–1886." Ph.D. dissertation, University of
Washington, 1963.

INTERVIEWS

George Beck, resident of Yukon-Kandik area during 1930s and 1940s who hunted, fished, mined, and trapped area. Interviewed by author on September 19–20, 1976, in Eagle, Alaska.

Charlie Biederman, son of Ed Biederman, grew up in middle Yukon, and was the last person to carry mail from Eagle to Circle by dog team. Interviewed by author on June 30 and November 11, 1976, in Tok, Alaska, and February 12–13, 1977, in Fairbanks, Alaska.

Horace Biederman, Jr., grandson of Ed Biederman and long-time resident of Eagle, Alaska. Interviewed by author on September 18, 1976, in Eagle, Alaska.

Dan Colben, co-owner of Coal Creek mining claim on the Yukon River. Interviewed by author on August 6, 1976, at Coal Creek, Alaska.

Wyman Fritsch, long-time resident of Eagle, Alaska. Interviewed by author on September 19, 1976, in Eagle, Alaska.

Barney Hansen, miner of the Seventymile and Fourth of July Creek and resident of Eagle, Alaska. Interviewed by author on December 13, 1976, in Fairbanks, Alaska.

Jess and Cathryne Knight, long-time residents of Eagle and Circle, Alaska. Interviewed by author on September 20, 1976, in Eagle, Alaska.

Jim Layman, owner of Ben Creek mining claim on the Yukon River. Interviewed by author on August 8–9, 1976, at his cabin on Ben Creek, Alaska.

Henry David McCary, soldier at Fort Egbert, Alaska. Interviewed on Historical Tape Recordings H-27, University of Alaska Archives, Fairbanks.

Elmer Nelson, former trapper in upper Charley River area. Interviewed by author on September 19–20, 1976, in Eagle, Alaska.

Charlie Stevens, native of Eagle Village. Interviewed by Mertie Baggen on July 22 and September 16, 1964, in Eagle Village, Alaska.

Joe Vogler, owner of Woodchopper Creek patented mine on the Yukon River. Interviewed by author on August 6–7, 1976, at his camp at the mouth of Mineral Creek, Alaska.

Ernest Wolff, University of Alaska mining professor and co-owner of Coal Creek mining claim on the Yukon River. Interviewed by author on August 3, 1976, in Fairbanks, Alaska.

III. Public Documents

UNITED STATES DOCUMENTS—BY AUTHOR

Abercrombie, William R. "Copper River Exploring Expedition, 1899." *Compilation of Narratives of Exploration in Alaska.* Senate Reps., 56th Cong., 1st sess., No. 1023 (1900) (Serial 3896), pp. 755–68.

———. "A Military Reconnoissance of the Copper River Valley." *Compilation of Narratives of Exploration in Alaska.* Senate Reps., 56th Cong., 1st sess., No. 1023 (1900) (Serial 3896), pp. 563–90.

Allen, Henry T. "A Military Reconnaissance of the Copper River Valley, 1885." *Compilation of Narratives of Exploration in Alaska.* Senate Reps., 56th Cong., 1st sess., No. 1023 (1900) (Serial 3896), pp. 411–88.

Babcock, Walter. "The Trans Alaska Military Road." *Compilation of Narratives of Exploration in Alaska.* Senate Reps., 56th Cong., 1st sess., No. 1023 (1900) (Serial 3896), pp. 70–80.

Barnard, E. C. "Report of the Forty Mile Expedition." *Maps and Descriptions of Routes of Exploration in Alaska in 1899.* Washington, D. C.: GPO, 1899.

Beardslee, L. A. *Reports of Captain L. A. Beardslee, U.S. Navy, Relative to Affairs in Alaska,* Senate Ex. Doc., 47th Cong., 1st sess. (1982).

Bearss, Edwin C. *Proposed Klondike Gold Rush National Historical Park Historic Resource Study.* Washington, D. C.: National Park Service, 1970.

Bell, Edwin. "What I Saw, Heard, and Did in and about Rampart City, Alaska." *Compilation of Narratives of Exploration in Alaska.* Senate Reps., 56th Cong., 1st sess., No. 1023 (1900) (Serial 3896), pp. 752–53.

Brooks, Alfred Hulse. "General Information Concerning the Territory by Geographic Provinces: The Yukon District." *Maps and Descriptions of Routes of Exploration in Alaska in 1899,* pp. 85–131. Washington, D. C.: GPO, 1899.

———. "A Reconnaissance from Pyramid Harbor to Eagle City." *Twenty-first Annual Report of the United States Geological Survey, 1899–1900,* pt. 2, pp. 331–91. Washington, D. C.: GPO, 1900.

———. "Placer Gold Mining in Alaska in 1902." *Contributions to Economic Geology, 1902.* USGS Bulletin No. 213, pp. 41–49. Washington, D. C.: GPO, 1903.

———. "Placer Gold Mining in Alaska in 1903." *Contributions to Economic Geology, 1903.* USGS Bulletin No. 225, pp. 43–59. Washington, D. C.: GPO, 1904.

———. "Placer Mining in 1904." *Mineral Resources of Alaska: Report on Progress of Investigation in 1904.* USGS Bulletin No. 259, pp. 18–31. Washington, D. C.: GPO, 1905.

———. "Railway Routes." *Mineral Resources of Alaska: Report on Progress* of Investigation in 1905. USGS Bulletin No. 284, pp. 10–18. Washington, D. C.: GPO, 1906.

———. "The Circle Precinct." *Mineral Resources of Alaska: Report on Progress of Investigation in 1906*. USGS Bulletin No. 314, pp. 187–204. Washington, D. C.: GPO, 1907.

———. "The Mining Industry in 1906." *Mineral Resources of Alaska: Report on Progress of Investigation in 1906*. USGS Bulletin No. 314, pp. 22–34. Washington, D. C.: GPO, 1907.

———. "The Mining Industry in 1907." *Mineral Resources of Alaska: Report on Progress of Investigation in 1907*. USGS Bulletin No. 345, pp. 30–53. Washington, D. C.: GPO, 1908.

———. "The Mining Industry in 1908." *Mineral Resources of Alaska: Report on Progress of Investigation in 1908*. USGS Bulletin No. 379, pp. 21–62. Washington, D. C.: GPO, 1909.

———. "The Mining Industry in 1909." *Mineral Resources of Alaska: Report on Progress of Investigation in 1909*. USGS Bulletin No. 442, pp. 20–46. Washington, D. C.: GPO, 1910.

———. "The Mining Industry in 1910." *Mineral Resources of Alaska: Report on Progress of Investigation in 1910*. USGS Bulletin No. 480, pp. 21–42. Washington, D. C.: GPO, 1911.

———. "The Mining Industry in 1911." *Mineral Resources of Alaska: Report on Progress of Investigation in 1911*. USGS Bulletin No. 520, pp. 17–44. Washington, D. C.: GPO, 1912.

———. "The Mining Industry in 1912." *Mineral Resources of Alaska: Report on Progress of Investigation in 1912*. USGS Bulletin No. 542, pp. 18–51. Washington, D. C.: GPO, 1913.

———. "The Mineral Deposits of Alaska." *Mineral Resources of Alaska: Report on Progress of Investigation in 1913*. USGS Bulletin No. 592, pp. 24–26. Washington, D. C.: GPO, 1914.

———. "The Alaskan Mining Industry in 1914." *Mineral Resources of Alaska: Report on Progress of Investigation in 1914*. USGS Bulletin No. 622, pp. 15–66. Washington, D. C.: GPO, 1915.

———. "The Alaskan Mining Industry in 1915." *Mineral Resources of Alaska: Report on Progress of Investigation in 1915*. USGS Bulletin No. 642, pp. 16–72. Washington, D. C.: GPO, 1916.

———. "The Alaska Mining Industry in 1916." *Mineral Resources of Alaska: Report on Progress of Investigation in 1916*. USGS Bulletin No. 662, pp. 11–62. Washington, D. C.: GPO, 1918.

———. *The Alaska Mining Industry in 1920*. USGS Bulletin No. 722-A. Washington, D. C.: GPO, 1921.

———. "The Alaskan Mining Industry in 1921." *Mineral Resources of Alaska: Report on Progress of Investigation in 1921*. USGS Bulletin No. 739, pp. 1–44. Washington, D. C.: GPO, 1923.

Brooks, Alfred Hulse, and Capps, S. R. "The Alaskan Mining Industry in 1922." *Mineral Resources of Alaska: Report on Progress of Investigation* in 1922. USGS Bulletin No. 755, pp. 3–50. Washington, D. C.: GPO, 1924.

Brooks, Alfred Hulse, and Martin, G.C. "The Alaskan Mining Industry in 1919." *Mineral Resources of Alaska: Report on Progress of Investigation in 1919.* USGS Bulletin No. 714, pp. 59–96. Washington, D. C.: GPO, 1921.

Cantwell, J. C. *Report of the Operations of the U. S. Revenue Steamer 'Nunivak' on the Yukon River Station, Alaska, 1899–1901.* Senate Ex. Doc., 58th Cong., 2d sess., No. 155 (1904) (Serial 4599).

Castner, J. C. "A Story of Hardship and Suffering in Alaska." *Compilation of Narratives of Exploration in Alaska.* Senate Reps., 56th Cong., 1st sess., No. 1023 (1900) (Serial 3896), pp. 686–712.

Chapin, Theodore. "Placer Mining in the Yukon-Tanana Region." *Mineral Resources of Alaska: Report on Progress of Investigation in 1913.* USGS Bulletin No. 592, pp. 357–62. Washington, D. C.: GPO, 1914.

Collier, Arthur James. *The Coal Resources of the Yukon, Alaska.* USGS Bulletin No. 218. Washington, D. C.: GPO, 1903.

Compton, Cleonne R. *The Alaska Railroad.* Juneau: State Committee on Transportation, 1979.

Dunham, Samuel C. "The Alaskan Goldfields and the Opportunities They Offer for Capital and Labor." *Bulletin of the Department of Labor*, pp. 297–425. Edited by Carroll D. Wright. House Ex. Doc., 55th Cong., 2d sess., No. 206, pt. 3 (1898).

———. "The Yukon and Nome Gold Regions." *Bulletin of the Department of Labor No. 29*, pp. 832–72. Washington, D. C.: GPO, 1900.

Edman, Grace; Hudson, Alice; and Johnson, Sam. *Fifty Years of Highways.* Juneau: Alaska Department of Public Works, Division of Highways, 1960.

Ellsworth, C. E. "Placer Mining in the Yukon-Tanana Region." *Mineral Resources of Alaska: Report on Progress of Investigation in 1909.* USGS Bulletin No. 442, pp. 230–45. Washington, D. C.: GPO, 1910.

Ellsworth, C. E., and Parker, G. L. "Placer Mining in the Yukon-Tanana Region." *Mineral Resources of Alaska: Report on Progress of Investigation in 1910.* USGS Bulletin No. 480, pp. 153–72. Washington, D. C.: GPO, 1911.

Ellsworth, C. E., and Davenport, R. W. "Placer Mining in the Yukon District." *Mineral Resources of Alaska: Report on Progress of Investigation in 1912.* USGS Bulletin No. 542, pp. 210–20. Washington, D. C.: GPO, 1913.

Emmons, G. T. *Condition and Needs of the Natives of Alaska.* Senate Ex. Doc., 58th Cong., 3d sess., No. 106 (1905) (Serial 4765).

Fletcher, Alice C. *Bureau of Education Special Report, 1888: Indian Education and Civilization.* Senate Ex. Doc., 48th Cong., 2d sess., No. 95 (1888).

"General Introduction." *Compilation of Narratives of Exploration in Alaska.*

Senate Reps., 56th Cong., 1st sess., No. 1023 (1900) (Serial 3896), pp. 5–18.

Glenn, E. F. "A Trip into the Tanana Region, 1898." *Compilation of Narratives of Exploration in Alaska.* Senate Reps., 56th Cong., 1st sess., No. 1023 (1900) (Serial 3896), pp. 629–47.

———. "Explorations in and about Cook Inlet, 1899." *Compilation of Narratives of Exploration in Alaska.* Senate Reps., 56th Cong., 1st sess., No. 1023 (1900) (Serial 3896), pp. 713–24.

Goodrich, Harold B. "History and Conditions of Yukon Gold District to 1897." *Eighteenth Annual Report of the United States Geological Survey to the Secretary of the Interior, 1896–97,* pt. 3, pp. 103–33. Washington, D. C.: GPO, 1898.

Griffiths, C. E. "From Knik Station to Eagle City." *Compilation of Narratives of Exploration in Alaska.* Senate Reps., 56th Cong., 1st sess., No. 1023 (1900) (Serial 3896), pp. 724–33.

Herron, Joseph S. *Explorations in Alaska, 1899, for an All-American Overland Route from Cook Inlet, Pacific Ocean, to the Yukon.* Senate Ex. Doc., 60th Cong., 2d sess., No. 689 (1901) (Serial 5408).

Huntley, Theodore A., and Royall, R. E. *Construction of the Alaska Highway.* Washington, D. C.: GPO, 1945.

Hutchins, John Power. "Prospecting and Mining Gold Placers in Alaska." *Mineral Resources of Alaska: Report on Progress of Investigation in 1907.* USGS Bulletin No. 345, pp. 54–77. Washington, D. C.: GPO, 1908.

Janin, Charles. *Recent Progress in Thawing Frozen Gravel in Placer Mining.* Bureau of Mines Technical Paper No. 309. Washington, D. C.: GPO, 1922.

Jones, Strachan. "The Kutchin Tribes." *Annual Report of the Smithsonian Institution for 1866,* pp. 320–21. Washington, D. C.: GPO, 1872.

Kelly, Luther S. "From Cabin Creek to the Valley of the Yukla, Alaska." *Compilation of Narratives of Exploration in Alaska.* Senate Reps., 56th Cong., 1st sess., No. 1023 (1900) (Serial 3896), pp. 684–86.

Kirkby, W. W. "A Journey to the Youcan, Russian America." *Annual Report, Smithsonian Institution, 1864,* pp. 416–20. Washington, D. C.: GPO, 1872.

Learnard, H. G. "A Trip From Portage Bay to Turnagain Arm and up the Sushitna." *Compilation of Narratives of Exploration in Alaska.* Senate Reps., 56th Cong., 1st sess., No. 1023 (1900) (Serial 3896), pp. 648–77.

Lowe, P. G. "From Valdez Inlet to Belle Isle, on the Yukon." *Compilation of Narratives of Exploration in Alaska.* Senate Reps., 56th Cong., 1st sess., No. 1023 (1900) (Serial 3896), pp. 591–93.

McManus, George. "A Reconnaissance Between Circle City and the Tanana." *Compilation of Narratives of Exploration in Alaska.* Senate Reps., 56th Cong., 1st sess., No. 1023 (1900) (Serial 3896), pp. 751–52.

Maddren, A. G. *Geologic Investigations Along Canada-Alaska Boundary.* USGS Bulletin No. 520-K. Washington, D. C.: GPO, 1912.

Martin, G. C. "The Alaska Mining Industry in 1918." *Mineral Resources of Alaska: Report on Progress of Investigation in 1918.* USGS Bulletin No. 712, pp. 11–42. Washington, D. C.: GPO, 1920.

Mathys, Fredrick. "Up the Chickaloon and Down the Talkeetna." *Compilation of Narratives of Exploration in Alaska.* Senate Reps., 56th Cong., 1st sess., No. 1023 (1900) (Serial 3896), pp. 679–83.

Mertie, J. B., Jr. *Geology of the Eagle-Circle District, Alaska.* USGS Bulletin No. 816. Washington, D. C.: GPO, 1930.

———. *Gold Placers of the Fortymile, Eagle, and Circle Districts, Alaska.* USGS Bulletin No. 897-C. Washington, D. C.: GPO, 1938.

Moffit, Fred H. "Mineral Industry in Alaska in 1925." *Mineral Resources of Alaska: Report on Progress of Investigation in 1925.* USGS Bulletin No. 792, pp. 1–40. Washington, D. C.: GPO, 1929.

Nelson, Edward W. *Report Upon the Natural History Collections Made in Alaska, 1877–1881.* Senate Misc. Doc., 49th Cong., 1st sess., No. 156 (1887) (Serial 2349).

———. *The Eskimo About Bering Strait.* Eighteenth Annual Report of Bureau of American Ethnology, pt. 1. Washington, D. C.: GPO, 1899.

Orth, Donald J. *Dictionary of Alaska Place Names.* USGS Professional Paper No. 567. Washington, D. C.: GPO, 1967.

Petrov, Ivan. *Population and Resources of Alaska.* House Ex. Doc., 46th Cong., 3d sess., No. 40 (1881).

———. "Population and Resources of Alaska." *Compilation of Narratives of Exploration in Alaska.* Senate Reps., 56th Cong., 1st sess., No. 1023 (1900) (Serial 3896), pp. 55–284.

Porter, E. A. "Placer Mining in the Fortymile, Eagle, and Seventymile River Districts." *Mineral Resources of Alaska: Report on Progress of Investigation in 1911.* USGS Bulletin No. 520, pp. 211–18. Washington, D. C.: GPO, 1912.

Prindle, L. M. *The Gold Placers of Fortymile, Birch Creek, and Fairbanks Regions, Alaska.* USGS Bulletin No. 251. Washington, D. C.: GPO, 1905.

———. "Yukon Placer Fields." *Mineral Resources of Alaska: Report on Progress of Investigation in 1905.* USGS Bulletin No. 284, pp. 109–27. Washington, D. C.: GPO, 1906.

———. *The Yukon-Tanana Region, Alaska.* USGS Bulletin No. 295. Washington, D. C.: GPO, 1906.

———. "The Fortymile Gold-Placer District." *Mineral Resources of Alaska: Report on Progress of Investigation in 1907.* USGS Bulletin No. 345, pp. 187–97. Washington, D. C.: GPO, 1908.

———. *The Fortymile Quadrangle: Yukon-Tanana Region, Alaska.* USGS Bulletin No. 375. Washington, D. C.: GPO, 1909.

———. *A Geologic Reconnaissance of the Fairbanks Quadrangle, Alaska.* USGS Bulletin No. 525. Washington, D. C.: GPO, 1913.

Prindle, L. M., and Hess, F. M. *Rampart Placer Regions.* USGS Bulletin No. 259. Washington, D. C.: GPO, 1905.

Purington, Chester Wells. "Methods and Costs of Gravel and Placer Mining in Alaska." *Mineral Resources of Alaska: Report on Progress of Investigation in 1904.* USGS Bulletin No. 259, pp. 32–46. Washington, D. C.: GPO, 1905.

―――. *Methods and Costs of Gravel and Placer Mining in Alaska.* USGS Bulletin No. 263. Washington, D. C.: GPO, 1905.

Ray, P. H. "Alaska, 1897—Relief of the Destitute in the Goldfields." *Compilation of Narratives of Exploration in Alaska.* Senate Reps., 56th Cong., 1st sess., No. 1023 (1900) (Serial 3896), pp. 497–503.

Ray, P. H., and Richardson, W. P. "Suffering and Destitute Miners in Alaska and What was Done for Their Relief—1898." *Compilation of Narratives of Exploration in Alaska.* Senate Reps., 56th Cong., 1st sess., No. 1023 (1900) (Serial 3896), pp. 519–63.

Raymond, Charles W. *Report of a Reconnaissance of the Yukon River, Alaska Territory, July to September, 1869.* Senate Ex. Doc., 42nd Cong., 1st sess., No. 12 (1871).

Rice, John F. "From Valdez to Eagle City." *Compilation of Narratives of Exploration in Alaska.* Senate Reps., 56th Cong., 1st sess., No. 1023 (1900) (Serial 3896), pp. 784–90.

Richardson, Wilds P. "The Mighty Yukon as Seen and Explored." *Compilation of Narratives of Exploration in Alaska.* Senate Reps., 56th Cong., 1st sess., No. 1023 (1900) (Serial 3896), pp. 745–51.

―――. "Relief of the Destitute in the Gold Fields, 1897." *Compilation of Narratives of Exploration in Alaska.* Senate Reps., 56th Cong., 1st sess., No. 1023 (1900) (Serial 3896), pp. 504–11.

Rogers, George W., and Cooley, Richard A. *Alaska's Population and Economy: Regional Growth, Development and Future Outlook.* Vol. 2. Juneau: Division of State Planning, 1962.

Schmitter, Ferdinand. *Upper Yukon Native Customs and Folk-lore.* Washington, D. C.: Smithsonian Institution, 1910.

Schwatka, Frederick. *Report of a Military Reconnaissance in Alaska, Made in 1883.* Senate Ex. Doc., 48th Cong., 2d sess., No. 2 (1885) (Serial 2261).

―――. "A Reconnaissance of the Yukon Valley, 1883." *Compilation of Narratives of Exploration in Alaska.* Senate Reps., 56th Cong., 1st sess., No. 1023 (1900) (Serial 3896), pp. 285–364.

Shimkin, Demitri B. *Fort Yukon, Alaska: An Essay in Human Ecology.* Juneau: Alaska Development Board, 1951.

Smith, Michael E. *Alaska's Historic Roadhouses.* History and Archeology Series No. 6. Anchorage: Alaska Division of Parks, 1974.

Smith, Philip S. "Mineral Industry of Alaska in 1924." *Mineral Resources of Alaska: Report on Progress of Investigation in 1924.* USGS Bulletin No. 783, pp. 1–30. Washington, D. C.: GPO, 1926.

―――. "Mineral Industry of Alaska in 1926." *Mineral Resources of Alaska: Report on Progress of Investigation in 1926.* USGS Bulletin No. 797, pp.

1–50. Washington, D. C.: GPO, 1929.

———. "Mineral Industry of Alaska in 1927." *Mineral Resources of Alaska: Report on Progress of Investigation in 1927.* USGS Bulletin No. 810, pp. 1–64. Washington, D. C.: GPO, 1930.

———. "Mineral Industry of Alaska in 1928." *Mineral Resources of Alaska: Report on Progress of Investigation in 1928.* USGS Bulletin No. 813, pp. 1–72. Washington, D. C.: GPO, 1930.

———. *Mineral Industry of Alaska in 1929.* USGS Bulletin No. 824-A. Washington, D. C.: GPO, 1930.

———. "Mineral Industry of Alaska in 1930." *Mineral Resources of Alaska: Report on Progress of Investigation in 1930.* USGS Bulletin No. 836, pp. 1–84. Washington, D. C.: GPO, 1933.

———. "Mineral Industry of Alaska in 1931." *Mineral Resources of Alaska: Report on Progress of Investigation in 1931.* USGS Bulletin No. 844, pp. 1–82. Washington, D. C.: GPO, 1934.

———. "Mineral Industry of Alaska in 1932." *Mineral Resources of Alaska: Report on Progress of Investigation in 1932.* USGS Bulletin No. 857, pp. 1–78. Washington, D. C.: GPO, 1934.

———. "Mineral Industry of Alaska in 1933." *Mineral Resources of Alaska: Report on Progress of Investigation in 1933.* USGS Bulletin No. 864, pp. 1–82. Washington, D. C.: GPO, 1936.

———. *Mineral Industry of Alaska in 1934.* USGS Bulletin No. 868-A. Washington, D. C.: GPO, 1936.

———. *Mineral Industry of Alaska in 1935.* USGS Bulletin No. 880-A. Washington, D. C.: GPO, 1937.

———. *Mineral Industry of Alaska in 1937.* USGS Bulletin No. 910-A. Washington, D. C.: GPO, 1939.

———. *Mineral Industry of Alaska in 1940.* USGS Bulletin No. 933-A. Washington, D. C.: GPO, 1942.

———. *Mineral Industry of Alaska in 1941 and 1942.* USGS Bulletin No. 943-A. Washington, D. C.: GPO, 1944.

Smith, Sumner S. *The Mining Industry in the Territory of Alaska During the Calendar Year 1916.* Bureau of Mines Bulletin No. 153. Washington, D. C.: GPO, 1919.

Spurr, Josiah Edward. "Geology of the Yukon Gold District, Alaska." *Eighteenth Annual Report of the United States Geological Survey to the Secretary of the Interior, 1896–97.* Pt. 3. Washington, D. C.: GPO, 1898.

Wahrhaftig, Clyde. *Physiographic Divisions of Alaska.* USGS Professional Paper No. 482. Washington, D. C.: GPO, 1965.

Wells, E. Hazard. "Up and Down the Yukon, 1897." *Compilation of Narratives of Exploration in Alaska.* Senate Reps., 56th Cong., 1st sess., No. 1023 (1900) (Serial 3896), pp. 511–19.

Wimmler, Norman. *Placer-Mining Methods and Costs in Alaska.* Bureau of Mines Bulletin No. 259. Washington, D. C.: GPO, 1927.

Yanert, William. "A Trip to the Tanana River." *Compilation of Narratives of Exploration in Alaska.* Senate Reps., 56th Cong., 1st sess., No. 1023 (1900) (Serial 3896) , pp. 677–79.

UNITED STATES DOCUMENTS—GENERAL

Alaska Game Commission. *Annual Report of the Alaska Game Commission to the Secretary of Agriculture,* 1925–1939.

———. *Annual Report of the Alaska Game Commission to the Secretary of the Interior,* 1939–1950.

———. *Annual Report of the Executive Officer to the Alaska Game Commission,* 1925–1940.

U.S. Alaska Boundary Tribunal. *The Case of the United States Before the Tribunal Convened at London Under the Provisions of the Treaty Between the United States of America and Great Britain Concluded January 24, 1903.* Washington, D. C.: GPO, 1903.

———. *The Counter Case of the United States Before the Tribunal Convened at London Under the Provisions of the Treaty Between the United States of America and Great Britain Concluded January 24, 1903.* Washington, D. C.: GPO, 1903.

———. *The Argument of the United States Before the Tribunal Convened at London Under the Provisions of the Treaty Between the United States of America and Great Britain Concluded January 24, 1903.* Washington, D. C.: GPO, 1903.

U.S. Alaska Railroad Commission. *Railway Routes in Alaska.* House Ex. Doc., 62nd Cong., 3d sess., No. 1346 (1913).

U.S. Bureau of Education. *Report of the Commissioner of Education,* 1902–1910.

U.S. Bureau of Indian Affairs. *Annual Report of the Commissioner of Indian Affairs,* 1887–1890.

U.S. Congress. House. Committee on Military Affairs. *Hearings on H.R. 6621 and H.R. 4130.* 74th Cong., 1st sess. (1935).

———. Committee on Territories. *The Building of Railroads in Alaska.* 63rd Cong., 2d sess. (1914).

U.S. Congress. Senate. Committee on Public Lands. *Government Railroad and Coal Lands in Alaska.* 62nd Cong., 2d sess. (1912).

———. Committee on Territories. *Conditions in Alaska.* Senate Reps., 58th Cong., 2d sess., No. 282, Pt. 2 (1904).

———. Committee on Territories. *Construction of Railroads in Alaska.* 63rd Cong., 1st sess. (1913).

U.S. Department of the Interior. *Annual Report of the Governor of Alaska to the Department of the Interior,* 1890–1935.

———. *Annual Report of the Secretary of the Interior,* 1885–1920.

———. Census Office. *Report on Population and Resources of Alaska at the Eleventh Census: 1890.* Washington, D. C.: GPO, 1893.

———. Census Office. *Twelfth Census of the United States Taken in the Year 1900.* 2 vols. Washington, D. C.: GPO, 1901.

———. *Final Environmental Impact Statement for the Proposed Trans-Alaska Pipeline.* 6 vols. Washington, D. C.: GPO, 1972.

———. *Rampart Project, Alaska: Market for Power and Effect of Project on Natural Resources.* Juneau, 1965.

———. *Summary of Trans-Alaska Oil Pipeline System Critique Session.* Washington, D. C.: GPO, 1977.

———. *Trans-Alaska Pipeline Hearings.* 12 vols. Washington, D. C.: GPO, 1971.

U.S. Department of State. *Report of the Commission to Study the Proposed Highway to Alaska, 1933.* Washington, D. C.: GPO, 1933.

U.S. International Boundary Commission. *Joint Report Upon the Survey and Demarcation of the International Boundary Between the United States and Canada Along the 141st Meridian from the Arctic Ocean to Mount St. Elias.* Ottawa and Washington, D. C.: International Boundary Commissioners, 1918.

U.S. War Department. *Annual Report of the Secretary of War, 1897–1925.*

CANADIAN DOCUMENTS

Bennett, Gordon. *Yukon Transportation: A History.* Canadian Historic Sites Occasional Papers in Archaeology and History No. 19. Ottawa: Indian and Northern Affairs, Parks Canada, 1978.

Bostock, H. S. *Yukon Territory: Selected Field Reports of the Geological Survey of Canada, 1898 to 1933.* Geological Survey of Canada Memoir 284. Ottawa: Queen's Printer, 1957.

Bush, Edward F. *The 'Dawson Daily News': Journalism in the Klondike.* Canadian Historic Sites Occasional Papers in Archaeology and History No. 21. Ottawa: Indian and Northern Affairs, Parks Canada, 1979.

Cairnes, D. D. *The Yukon-Alaska International Boundary, Between Porcupine and Yukon Rivers.* Canadian Geological Survey Memoir No. 67. Ottawa: Government Printing Bureau, 1914.

Canada. Department of Mines and Resources. *The Yukon Territory: A Brief Description of its Administration, Resources and Development.* Ottawa: Bureau of Northwest Territories and Yukon Affairs, Lands, Parks, and Forest Branch, 1944.

Carter, Margaret. *St. Andrew's Presbyterian Church, Lake Bennett, British Columbia.* Canadian Historic Sites Occasional Papers in Archaeology and History No. 26. Ottawa: Indian and Northern Affairs, Parks Canada, 1981.

Constantine, Charles. "Report of Inspector Constantine, October 10, 1894." *Report of the Commissioner of the North-West Mounted Police Force, 1894.* Ottawa: Queen's Printer, 1895.

Dawson, George M. *Report on an Exploration in the Yukon District, N.W.T.*

and Adjacent Northern Portion of British Columbia. Ottawa: Queen's
Printer, 1887.

Duerden, Frank. *The Development and Structure of the Settlement System in
the Yukon*. Whitehorse: Department of Library and Information
Resources, 1981.

MacLeod, William G. *The Dempster Highway*. Ottawa: Canadian Arctic
Resources Committee, 1979.

MacPherson, Janet E. "The Cyprus Anvil Mine." *Northern Transitions*.
Edited by Everett B. Peterson and Janet B. Wright. 2 vols. Vol. 1, pp.
113–44. Ottawa: Canadian Arctic Resources Committee, 1978.

Manitoba. Department of Renewable Resources and Transportation Services.
The Manitoba Trappers' Guide, 1976.

Murray, Alexander Hunter. *Journal of the Yukon, 1847–48*. Edited by L. J.
Burpee. Publications of the Canadian Archives No. 4. Ottawa:
Government Printing Bureau, 1910.

Ogilvie, William. "Exploratory Survey from the Pelly-Yukon to Mackinzie
River by Way of Tat-on-duc, Porcupine, Bell, Trout and Peel Rivers."
Department of the Interior Annual Report, 1889. Part 8, section 3.
Ottawa: Brown Chamberlin, 1897.

———. *Exploratory Survey of Part of the Lewes, Tat-on-Duc, Porcupine, Bell,
Trout, Peel, and Mackenzie Rivers, 1887–88*. Ottawa: Government
Printing Bureau, 1889.

———. *Information Respecting the Yukon District*. Ottawa: Government
Printing Bureau, 1897.

Tanner, Adrian. *Trappers, Hunters and Fishermen: Wildlife Utilization in
the Yukon Territory*. Yukon Research Project Series No. 5. Ottawa:
Department of Northern Affairs and Natural Resources, 1966.

IV. Newspapers

Alaska Forum. Rampart, Alaska. 1900–1906.

Alaska Mining Record. Juneau, Alaska. 1898.

Alaska Railroad Record. Anchorage, Alaska. 1916–1920.

Alaska Weekly. Seattle, Washington. 1923–1950.

Alaskan. Sitka, Alaska. 1885–1907.

Fairbanks Daily News-Miner. 1909–1916, 1974–1983.

Fairbanks Daily Times. 1907–1908.

Fairbanks Sunday Times. 1906–1908.

Fairbanks Times. 1906–1907.

Fairbanks Weekly News. 1903–1904.

Northern Light. Fairbanks, Alaska. 1906–1907.

Polar Record. 1968–1972.

Seattle Post-Intelligencer. 1905–1906.

Tanana Miner. Fairbanks, Alaska. 1906–1907.

Tanana Tribune. Fairbanks, Alaska. 1907–1908.

Washington Daily News. 1937.
Yukon Press. Circle and Fort Adams, Alaska. 1894–1899.
Yukon Valley News. Rampart, Alaska. 1904–1907.

V. Maps

Map of Alaska, 1894. Rare map in University of Alaska Documents.

Map of Alaska and Northwest Goldfields. By Charles O. Richardson, Board of Trade, Pueblo, Colorado, 1897. University of Alaska Documents.

Map of Alaska and Surroundings Showing the Klondike Gold Fields and Routes to Mining Camps. By Charles L. Moll, Reading, Pennsylvania, 1898. University of Alaska Documents.

Map of Alaska. By Harry King, General Land Office, Department of the Interior, 1898. University of Alaska Documents.

Map of Alaska. By Rand-McNally, 1898. University of Alaska Documents.

Map of Alaska. Alaskan Military Reconnaissance of 1898. By Emil Mahlo. From *Compilation of Narratives of Explorations of Alaska*, Senate Reps., 58th Cong., 1st sess., No. 1023 (1900) (Serial 3896).

Maps of Alaska and the Koyukuk, Tanana, Copper, Chittyn, and Unalaklik rivers. Henry T. Allen's Expedition of 1885. By H. T. Allen, J. H. Colwell, and Paul Eaton. From *Compilation of Narratives of Explorations in Alaska*, Senate Reps., 58th Cong., 1st sess., No. 1023 (1900) (Serial 3896).

Maps of Alaska. By Department of War cartographers and topographers, 1898 to 1920. *Annual Reports of the Secretary of War*, Washington, D. C.: GPO.

Maps of Alaska and Vicinity. By USGS crews, 1898 to 1940. See bulletins listed under Government Documents.

Map of Northwest Part of Dominion of Canada. By J. Johnston and Jacob Smith of the Department of the Interior, 1898. James T. Gray Collection, University of Oregon.

Map of Alaska and Yukon Territory. By C. O. Richardson, Pueblo, Colorado, for the North American Transportation and Trading Company, 1899. James T. Gray Collection, University of Oregon.

Map of a Portion of Birch Creek, Alaska. By the United States Survey Party of J. E. Spurr, 1897. From *Eighteenth Annual Report of United States Geological Survey*, pt. 1, House Ex. Doc., 55th Cong., 2d sess., No. 5 (1897).

Map of Vicinity of Eagle, Alaska. By E. J. Chamberlain, U. S. Deputy Surveyor and Notary Public, Eagle, Alaska, approximately 1900. University of Alaska Archives.

Map of Eagle City, Alaska. By J. E. Snevely, U.S. Mineral Surveyor, 1899. University of Alaska Archives.

Map of Eagle District. By the Alaska Road Commission, 1925. Files of Bureau of Land Management, Anchorage, Alaska.

Map of Fort Egbert, Alaska. Survey under the direction of Major Edwin H. Plummer, 3rd Infantry, 1906. University of Alaska Archives.

Map of Fort Egbert, Alaska. Among records of Alaska Road Commission, 1935.

Map of Fortymile. By E. C. Barnard, USGS topographer, 1898. Files of Bureau of Land Management, Anchorage, Alaska.

Map of Forty Mile, Eagle City, and Seventy Mile Mining Districts. By B. W. Lenont, Map and Blue Print Company, Seattle, Washington, 1900.

Map of Yukon. Frederick Schwatka's Expedition of 1883. By Charles A. Homan. From *Compilation of Narratives of Explorations of Alaska*, Senate Reps., 58th Cong., 1st sess., No. 1023 (1900) (Serial 3896).

Track Chart of the Yukon. By Charles Y. Malmquist, 1900–1911. James T. Gray Collection. University of Oregon.

Track Chart of the Yukon. By James T. Gray, drawn in 1902 from information of 1898–99 with corrections made 1912. James T. Gray Collection. University of Oregon.

Track Chart of Yukon. Microfilm #2073 in University of Alaska Archives.

VI. Books

Adams, George R. *Life on the Yukon, 1865–1867*. Studies in Alaska History, No. 22. Edited by Richard A. Pierce. Kingston, Ontario: Limestone Press, 1982.

Adney, Edwin Tappan. *The Klondike Stampede*. New York: Harper and Brothers Publishers, 1900.

The Alaska Almanac: Facts About Alaska. Anchorage: Alaska Northwest Publishing Co., 1981.

Amundsen, Roald. *My Life as an Explorer*. Garden City, New York: Doubleday, Doran, and Co., 1927.

Anthony, Leo Mark, and Tunley, Arthur. *Introductory Geography and Geology of Alaska*. Anchorage: Polar Publishing, 1976.

Arnold, Robert D. *Alaska Native Land Claims*. Anchorage: Alaska Native Foundation, 1976.

Atwood, Evageline. *Frontier Politics: Alaska's James Wickersham*. Portland: Binford & Mort, 1979.

Atwood, Evageline, and DeArmond, Robert N. *Who's Who in Alaskan Politics: A Biographical Dictionary of Alaskan Political Personalities, 1884–1974*. Portland: Binford & Mort for the Alaska Historical Commission, 1977.

Bancroft, Hubert Howe. *History of Alaska, 1730–1885*. 1886; reprint ed., introduction by Ernest Gruening. Darien, Conn.: Hafner Publishing Co., 1970.

Barhouse, J. C. *George Dawson: The Little Giant*. Toronto: Clark, Irwin and Co., 1974.

Barnum, F. *Life on the Alaska Mission with an Account of the Foundation of* the Mission and the Work Performed. Woodstock, Maryland: Woodstock College Press, 1893.

Berry, Mary Clay. *The Alaska Pipeline: The Politics of Oil and Native Land Claims*. Bloomington: Indiana University Press, 1975.

Berton, Laura Beatrice. *I Married the Klondike*. Toronto: Little, Brown Co., 1954.

Berton, Pierre. *The Klondike Fever: The Life and Death of the Last Great Gold Rush*. 2d ed., rev. Bloomington: Indiana University Press, 1972.

Billington, Ray Allen, ed. *The Frontier Thesis: Valid Interpretation of American History*. New York: Holt, Rinehart and Winston, 1966.

———. *The Genesis of the Frontier Thesis: A Study in Historical Creativity*. San Marino, California: Huntington Library, 1971.

———. *Frederick Jackson Turner: Historian, Scholar, Teacher*. New York: Oxford University Press, 1973.

———. *America's Frontier Heritage*. Histories of the American Frontier Series. Albuquerque: University of New Mexico Press, 1974.

Billington, Ray Allen, and Ridge, Martin. *Westward Expansion: A History of the American Frontier*. 5th ed., rev. New York: Macmillan Publishing Co., 1982.

Boorstin, Daniel J. *The Americans: The National Experience*. Vol. 2. New York: Random House, Vintage Books, 1965.

———. *The Americans: The Democratic Experience*. Vol. 3. New York: Random House, Vintage Books, 1973.

Brooks, Alfred Hulse. *Blazing Alaska's Trails*. Fairbanks: University of Alaska Press, 1973.

Bryan, Alan Lyle, ed. *Early Man in America: From a Circum-Pacific Perspective*. University of Alberta Department of Anthropology Occasional Paper No. 1. Edmonton: Archaeological Researches International, 1978.

Burke, Clara Heintz (as told to Adele Comandini). *Doctor Hap*. New York: Coward-McCann, Inc., 1961.

Calasanctius, Mary Joseph. *The Voice of Alaska*. Lachine, Quebec: St. Ann's Press, 1947.

Campbell, Robert. *Two Journals of Robert Campbell, 1808 to 1853*. Seattle: John W. Todd, Jr., 1958.

Carroll, James A. *The First Ten Years in Alaska: Memoirs of a Fort Yukon Trapper, 1911–1922*. New York: Exposition Press, 1957.

Caulfield, Richard A. *Subsistence Use In and Around the Proposed Yukon-Charley National Rivers*. Anthropology and Historic Preservation Occasional Paper, No. 20. Fairbanks: University of Alaska Cooperative Park Studies Unit, 1979.

Chapman, John Wight. *A Camp on the Yukon*. Cornwall-on-Hudson, New York: Idlewild Press, 1948.

Chase, Will H. *Reminiscences of Captain Billie Moore*. Kansas City: Burton Publishing Co., 1947.

Chevigny, Hector. *Russian America: The Great Alaskan Venture, 1741–1867*. Portland: Binford & Mort, 1965.

Chittenden, Hiram Martin. *A History of the American Fur Trade of the Far West*. 2 vols. Stanford, California: Academic Reprints, 1954.

Clark, Annette McFadyen. *Koyukuk River Culture*. Canadian Ethnology Service, Paper No. 18. Ottawa: National Museums of Canada, 1974.

Cody, Hiram Alfred. *An Apostle of the North: Memoirs of the Right Reverend William Carpenter Bompas*. Toronto: Musson Book Co., 1908.

Cole, Terrence. *E. T. Barnette: The Strange Story of the Man Who Founded Fairbanks*. Anchorage: Alaska Northwest Publishing Co., 1981.

Colliery Engineer Company. *Placer Mining: A Handbook for Klondike and Other Miners and Prospectors*. Scranton, Pennsylvania: Colliery Engineer Co., 1897. Facsimile reproduction, Seattle: Shorey Book Store, 1965.

Cook, Alan, and Holland, Clive. *The Exploration of Northern Canada: 500 to 1920, A Chronology*. Toronto: Arctic History Press, 1978.

Coolidge., L. A. *Klondike and the Yukon Country*. Philadelphia: Henry Altemus, 1897.

Copper River Mining, Trading and Development Co. *A Guide for Alaskan Miners, Settlers, and Tourists*. Seattle: Trade Register Print for the Valdez Chamber of Commerce, 1902.

Curtin, Walter R. *Yukon Voyage: Unofficial Log of the Steamer 'Yukoner'*. Caldwell, Idaho: Caxton Printers, 1938.

Dall, William H. *Alaska and its Resources*. 1870; reprint. New York: Arno Press, 1970.

Davidson, George. *The Alaska Boundary*. San Francisco: Alaska Packers Association, 1903.

Davydov, G. I. *Two Voyages to Russian America, 1802–1807*. Translated by Colin Bearne. Edited by Richard A. Pierce. Materials for the Study of Alaska History, No. 10. Kingston, Ontario: Limestone Press, 1977.

Dearborn, Ned. *Trapping on the Farm*. Facsimile reproduction of U.S. Department of Agriculture Yearbook of 1919. Seattle: Shorey Book Store, 1973.

DeVoto, Bernard. *Across the Wide Missouri*. Boston: Houghton Mifflin, 1947.

De Windt, Henry. *Through the Gold-Field of Alaska to Bering Straits*. New York: Harper and Brothers Publishers, 1898.

Dumond, Don E. *The Eskimos and Aleuts*. London: Thames and Hudson Ltd., 1977.

Fedorova, Svetlana G. *The Russian Population in Alaska and California, Late 18th Century–1867*. Translated by Richard A. Pierce and Alton S. Donnelly. Materials for the Study of Alaska History, No. 4. Kingston, Ontario: Limestone Press, 1973.

Ferguson, Chick. *Mink, Mary and Me: The Story of a Wilderness Trapline*. New York: M. S. Mill Co., 1946.

Fisher, Raymond H. *Bering's Voyages: Whither and Why.* Seattle: University of Washington Press, 1977.

Fitch, Edwin M. *The Alaska Railroad.* New York: Frederick A. Praeger Publishers, 1967.

Florinsky, Michael T. *Russia: A Short History.* New York: Macmillan Co., 1964.

Galbraith, John S. *The Hudson's Bay Company as an Imperial Factor, 1821–1869.* Octagon Books. New York: Farrar, Straus and Giroux, 1977.

Gibson, James R. *Imperial Russia in Frontier America: The Changing Geography of Supply of Russian America, 1784–1867.* New York: Oxford University Press, 1976.

Giddings, J. Louis. *Ancient Men of the Arctic.* New York: Alfred A. Knopf, 1971.

Gilder, William H. *Ice-Pack and Tundra: An Account of the Search for the 'Jeannette' and a Sledge Journey through Siberia.* London: Sampson Low, Marston, Searle & Rivington, 1883. Excerpt reprinted as "St Michael, 1881." *Alaska Journal,* 3 (Spring 1973), 122–24.

Goetzmann, William H. *Exploration and Empire: The Explorer and the Scientist in the Writing of the American West.* New York: Alfred A. Knopf, 1966.

Graburn, Nelson H. H., and Strong, Stephen B. *Circumpolar Peoples: An Anthropological Perspective.* Pacific Palisades, California: Goodyear Publishing, 1973.

Graves, S. H. *On the 'White Pass' Pay-Roll.* 1908; reprint. Chicago: Paladin Press, 1970.

Green, Lewis. *The Boundary Hunters: Surveying the 141st Meridian and the Alaskan Panhandle.* Vancouver: University of British Columbia Press, 1982.

———. *The Gold Hustlers.* Anchorage: Alaska Northwest Publishing Co., 1977.

Gressley, Gene M., ed. *American West: A Reorientation.* Laramie: University of Wyoming Press, 1966.

Gruening, Ernest. *The State of Alaska.* New York: Random House, 1968.

Hamiliton, Walter R. *The Yukon Story: A Sourdough's Record of the Goldrush Days and Yukon Progress from the Earliest Times to the Present Day.* Vancouver, Canada: Mitchell Press, 1964.

Hamlin, C. S. *Old Times on the Yukon: Decline of Circle City; Romances of the Klondyke.* Los Angeles: Wetzel Publishing Co., 1928.

Harbottle, Jeanne Connolly, and Credeur, Fern Grice. *Woman in the Bush.* Pelican Publishing Co., 1966.

Harkey, Ira. *Pioneer Bush Pilot: The Story of Noel Wien.* Seattle: University of Washington Press, 1974.

Hartman, Charles W., and Johnson, Philip R. *Environmental Atlas of Alaska.* Fairbanks: University of Alaska, 1978.

Hawbaker, Stanley S. *Trapping North American Furbearers: A Complete Guide on Trapping All North American Furbearers for Both Amateur and Professional.* Clearfield, Pennsylvania: Kurtz Bros., 1974.

Haycox, Stephen W. and Betty J., eds. *Melvin Ricks' Alaska Bibliography: An Introductory Guide to Alaskan Historical Literature.* Portland: Binford & Mort for the Alaska Historical Commission, 1977.

Heller, Herbert L., ed. *Sourdough Sagas.* New York: Ballantine Books, 1967.

Helm, June, ed. *Handbook of North American Indians: Subarctic.* Vol. 6. Washington, D. C.: Smithsonian Institution, 1981.

Herron, Edward A. *Wings Over Alaska: The Story of Carl Ben Eielson.* New York: Archway Paperback, 1967.

Hill, Douglas. *The Opening of the Canadian West.* New York: John Day Co., 1967.

Hinckley, Ted C. *The Americanization of Alaska, 1867–1897.* Palo Alto, California: Pacific Books, 1972.

———. *Alaskan John G. Brady: Missionary, Businessman, Judge, and Governor, 1878–1918.* Columbus: Ohio State University Press, 1982.

Hoffman, Bob. *Master Trapping Methods.* Tacoma: Mercury Press, 1976.

Hofstadter, Richard. *The Progressive Historians: Turner, Beard, Parrington.* New York: Alfred A. Knopf, 1968.

Hopkins, David, ed. *The Bering Land Bridge.* Palo Alto: Stanford University Press, 1968.

Hulley, Clarence C. *Alaska: Past and Present.* 3rd ed. Portland: Metropolitan Press, 1970.

Hunt, William R. *North of 53°: The Wild Days of the Alaska-Yukon Mining Frontier, 1870–1914.* New York: Macmillan Publishing Co., 1974.

Hunter, Louis C. *Steamboats on the Western Rivers: An Economic and Technological History.* Cambridge, Massachusetts: Harvard University Press, 1949.

Jackson, Sheldon. *Alaska and Missions on the North Pacific Coast.* New York: Dodd, Mead, 1880.

Jackson, W. Turrentine. *Treasure Hill: Portrait of a Silver Mining Camp.* Tucson: University of Arizona Press, 1963.

Jacobsen, Johan Adrian. *Alaskan Voyage, 1881–1883: An Expedition to the Northwest Coast of America.* Translated by Erna Gunther. Chicago: University of Chicago Press, 1977.

James, James Alton. *The First Scientific Exploration of Russian America and the Purchase of Alaska.* Northwestern University Studies in Social Science, No. 4. Chicago: Northwestern University, 1942.

Jansen, Lone E. *The Copper Spike.* Anchorage: Alaska Northwest Publishing Co., 1975.

Jenkins, Thomas. *The Man of Alaska: Peter Trimble Rowe.* New York: Morehouse-Gorham Co., 1943.

Jensen, Ronald J. *The Alaska Purchase and Russian-American Relations.* Seattle: University of Washington, 1975.

Johnson, Samuel, ed. *Alaska Commercial Company, 1868–1940.* San Francisco: E. E. Wachter, 1940.

Judge, Charles J. *An American Missionary: A Record of the Work of Rev. William H. Judge, S. J..* Ossining, New York: Catholic Foreign Mission Society, 1907.

Kennedy, Michael S., ed. *Transportation in Alaska's Past.* Anchorage: Alaska Historical Society, 1982.

Kilian, Bernhard. *The Voyage of the Schooner, 'Polar Bear': Whaling and Trading in the North Pacific and Arctic, 1913–1914.* Edited by John Bockstoce. New Bedford Whaling Museum: Old Dartmouth Historical Society and Alaska Historical Commission, 1983.

Kirk, James Wollaston and Anna L. M. *Pioneer Life in the Yukon Valley, Alaska.* Buffalo: Ben Franklin Printers, 1936.

Kitchener, Lois D. *Flag Over the North: The Story of the Northern Commerical Company.* Seattle: Superior Publishing Co., 1954.

Knutson, Artur E. *Sternwheelers on the Yukon.* Kirland, Washington: Knutson Enterprises, Inc., 1979.

Koutsky, Kathryn. *Early Days on Norton Sound and Bering Strait: The St. Michael and Stebbins Area.* Vol. 8. Anthropology and Historic Preservation Occasional Paper, No. 29. Fairbanks: University of Alaska Cooperative Park Studies Unit, 1982.

Krause, Aurel. *The Tlingit Indians.* Translated by Erna Gunther. Seattle: American Ethnological Society, 1976.

Ladue, Joseph. *Klondyke Nuggets.* Montreal: Jonh Lovell and Son Publishers, 1897.

McClellan, Catherine. *My Old People Say: An Ethnographic Survey of Southern Yukon Territory.* 2 vols. Publications in Ethnology, No. 6. Ottawa: National Museum of Canada, 1975.

McConnell, R. G. *Report on an Exploration in the Yukon and Mackenzie Basins, N. W. T.* Montreal: William Foster Brown & Co., 1891.

McGinniss, Joe. *Going to Extremes.* New York: Alfred A. Knopf, 1980.

McKennan, Robert. *The Upper Tanana Indians.* Yale University Publications in Anthropology, No. 55. New Haven: Yale University Press, 1959.

———. *The Chandalar Kutchin.* Arctic Institute of North America Technical Paper, No. 17. Montreal: Arctic Institute of North America, 1965.

McPhee, John. *Coming into the Country.* New York: Farrar, Straus and Giroux, 1976.

McQuesten, Leroy N. *Recollections of Leroy N. McQuesten of Life in the Yukon, 1871–1885.* Dawson City: Yukon Order of Pioneers, 1952.

Mackenzie, Alexander. *Voyages from Montreal Through the Continent of North America to the Frozen and Pacific Oceans in the Years 1789 and 1793, with an Account of the Rise and State of the Fur Trade.* New York: G. F. Hopkins, 1802.

Marshall, Robert. *Arctic Village.* New York: Literary Guild, 1933.

Mathews, Richard. *The Yukon.* New York: Holt, Rinehart and Winston, 1968.

Mead, Robert Douglas. *Journeys Down the Line: Building the Trans-Alaska Pipeline*. New York: Doubleday, 1978.

Michael, Henry N., ed. *Lieutenant Zagoskin's Travels in Russian America, 1842–1844: Yukon and Kuskokwim Valleys of Alaska*. Arctic Institute of North America. Anthropology of the North: Translations from Russian Sources, No. 7. Toronto: University of Toronto Press, 1967.

Miller, David Hunter. *The Alaska Treaty*. Studies in Alaska History, No. 8. Kingston, Ontario: Limestone Press, 1981.

Miller, Orlando W. *The Frontier in Alaska and the Matanuska Colony*. Yale Western Americana, No. 26. New Haven: Yale University Press, 1975.

Mills, Thora McIlroy. *The Church and the Klondike Gold Rush: The Contribution of the Presbyterian Church to the Yukon During the Gold Rush, 1897–1910*. Toronto: University of Toronto Press for the United Church Archives, 1978.

Mitchell, William. *The Opening of Alaska*. Edited by Lyman L. Woodman. Anchorage: Cook Inlet Historical Society, 1982.

Morlan, Richard E. *Taphonomy and Archaeology in the Upper Pleistocene of the Northern Yukon Territory: A Glimpse of the Peopling of the New World*. Archaeological Survey of Canada Paper No. 94. Ottawa: National Museum of Man, 1980.

Morrison, David R. *The Politics of the Yukon Territory, 1898–1909*. Toronto: University of Toronto Press, 1968.

Mountfield, David. *A History of Polar Exploration*. New York: Dial Press, 1974.

Munsterhjelm, Erik. *The Wind and the Caribou: Hunting and Trapping in Northern Canada*. London: George Allen and Unwin, 1953.

———. *Fool's Gold: A Narrative of Prospecting and Trapping in Northern Canada*. London: George Allen and Unwin, 1957.

Nash, Gerald D. *The American West in the Twentieth Century: A Short History of an Urban Oasis*. Albuquerque: University of New Mexico Press, 1977.

Naske, Claus-M. *An Interpretative History of Alaskan Statehood*. Anchorage: Alaska Northwest Publishing Co., 1973.

Naske, Claus-M., and Slotnick, Herman E. *Alaska: A History of the 49th State*. Grand Rapids, Michigan: William B. Eerdmans Publishing Co., 1979.

Nelson, Richard K. *Hunters of the Northern Forest: Designs for Survival Among the Alaskan Kutchin*. Chicago: University of Chicago Press, 1973.

Ogilvie, William. *The Klondike Official Guide*. Toronto: Hunter, Rose Co., 1898.

———. *Early Days on the Yukon*. Ottawa: Thorburn and Abbott, 1913.

Osgood, Cornelius. *Contributions to the Ethnography of the Kutchin*. Yale University Publications in Anthropology, No. 14. New Haven: Yale University Press, 1936.

————. *The Distribution of the Northern Athapaskan Indians.* Yale University Publications in Anthropology, No. 7. New Haven: Yale University Press, 1936.

————. *Ingalik Material Culture.* Yale University Publications in Anthropology, No. 22. New Haven: Yale University Press, 1940.

————. *Ingalik Social Culture.* Yale University Publications in Anthropology, No. 53. New Haven: Yale University Press, 1958.

————. *Ingalik Mental Culture.* Yale University Publications in Anthropology, No. 56. New Haven: Yale University Press, 1959.

————. *The Han Indians: A Compilation of Ethnographic and Historical Data on the Alaska-Yukon Boundary Area.* Yale University Publications in Anthropology, No. 74. New Haven: Yale University Press, 1971.

Oswalt, Wendell H. *Alaskan Eskimos.* San Francisco: Chandler Publishing Co., 1967.

————. *Kolmakovskiy Redoubt: The Ethnoarchaeology of a Russian Fort in Alaska.* Monumenta Archaeologica, vol. 8. Institute of Archaeology. Los Angeles: University of California, 1980.

Patty, Ernest. *North Country Challenge.* New York: David McKay Co., 1969.

Paul, Rodman W. *California Gold: The Beginning of Mining in the Far West.* Lincoln: University of Nebraska Press, 1947.

————. *Mining Frontiers of the Far West, 1848–1880.* Histories of the American Frontier. Albuquerque: University of New Mexico Press, 1974.

Penlington, Norman. *The Alaska Boundary Dispute: A Critical Reappraisal.* Toronto: McGraw-Hill Ryerson, 1972.

Phillips, Paul C. *The Fur Trade.* 2 vols. Norman: University of Oklahoma Press, 1961.

Pierce, W. H. *Thirteen Years of Travel and Exploration in Alaska, 1877–1889.* Edited by R. N. DeArmond. Anchorage: Alaska Northwest Publishing Co., 1977.

Pike, Warburton. *Through the Sub-Arctic Forest.* 1896; reprint. New York: Arno Press, 1967.

Potter, Jean. *The Flying North.* New York: Macmillan Co., 1945.

Prince, Bernadine LeMay. *The Alaska Railroad in Pictures, 1914–1964.* 2 vols. Anchorage: Ken Wray, 1964.

Prucha, Francis Paul. *American Indian Policy in Crisis: Christian Reformers and the Indian, 1865–1900.* Norman: University of Oklahoma Press, 1976.

————. *Americanizing the American Indians: Writings by the "Friends of the Indian," 1880–1900.* Lincoln: University of Nebraska Press, 1978.

————. *The Churches and the Indian Schools, 1888–1912.* Lincoln: University of Nebraska Press, 1979.

Ray, Dorothy Jean. *The Eskimos of Bering Strait, 1650–1898.* Seattle: University of Washington Press, 1975.

Remley, David A. *Crooked Road: The Story of the Alaska Highway.* New York: McGraw-Hill Book Co., 1976.

Rich, E. E. *The Fur Trade and the Northwest to 1857*. Canadian Centenary Series. Toronto: McClelland and Steward Ltd., 1967.

Rickard, T. A. *Through the Yukon and Alaska*. San Francisco: Mining and Scientific Press, 1909.

Ricks, Melvin B. *Directory of Alaska Post Offices and Postmasters*. Ketchikan: Tongass Publishing Co., 1965.

Roscow, James P. *800 Miles to Valdez: The Building of the Alaskan Pipeline*. Englewood Cliffs, New Jersey: Prentice-Hall Inc., 1977.

Sackett, Russell. *The Chilkat Tlingit: A General Overview*. Anthropology and Historic Preservation Occasional Paper, No. 23. Fairbanks: University of Alaska Cooperative Park Studies Unit, 1979.

Satterfield, Archie. *The Alaska Airlines Story*. Anchorage: Alaska Northwest Publishing Company, 1981.

Savage, A. H. *Dogsled Apostles*. New York: Sheed and Ward, 1942.

Schwatka, Frederick. *Along Alaska's Great River*. New York: Cassell and Co., 1885.

Sherwood, Morgan B. *Exploration of Alaska, 1865–1900*. Yale Western Americana, No. 7. New Haven: Yale University Press, 1965.

————, ed. *Alaska and Its History*. Seattle: University of Washington Press, 1967.

————. *Big Game in Alaska: A History of Wildlife and People*. Yale Western Americana, No. 33. New Haven: Yale University Press, 1981.

Shore, Evelyn Berglund. *Born on Snowshoes*. Boston: Houghton Mifflin Co., 1954.

Simeone, William E. *A History of Alaskan Athapaskans*. Anchorage: Alaska Historical Commission, n.d.

Smith, Barbara. *Russian Orthodoxy in Alaska: A History, Inventory, and Analysis of the Church Archives in Alaska with an Annotated Bibliography*. Anchorage: Alaska Historical Commission, 1980.

Smith, Duane A. *Rocky Mountain Mining Camps: The Urban Frontier*. Lincoln: University of Nebraska Press, 1967.

Spence, Clark C. *Mining Engineers and the American West: The Lace-Boot Brigade, 1849–1933*. Yale Western Americana, No. 22. New Haven: Yale University Press, 1970.

Spude, Robert L. *Chilkoot Trail: From Dyea to Summit with the '98 Stampeders*. Anthropology and Historic Preservation Occasional Paper, No. 26. Fairbanks: University of Alaska Cooperative Park Studies Unit, 1980.

Spurr, Josiah Edward. *Through the Yukon Gold Diggings: A Narrative of Personal Travel*. Boston: Eastern Publishing Co., 1900.

Stewart, Robert Laird. *Sheldon Jackson: Pathfinder and Prospector of the Missionary Vanguard in the Rocky Mountains and Alaska*. New York: Fleming H. Revell, 1908.

Stuck, Hudson. *Ten Thousand Miles with a Dog Sled: A Narrative of Winter Travel in Interior Alaska*. New York: Charles Scribner's Sons, 1915.

———. *Voyages on the Yukon and Its Tributaries: A Narrative of Summer Travel in the Interior of Alaska.* New York: Charles Scribner's Sons, 1925.

———. *The Ascent of Denali: First Complete Ascent of Mt. McKinley, Highest Peak in North America.* 2nd ed. Snohomish, Washington: Snohomish Publishing Co., 1977.

Tikhmenev, P. A. *A History of the Russian-American Company.* Translated and edited by Richard A. Pierce and Alton S. Donnelly. Seattle: University of Washington Press, 1978.

Trimmer, F. Mortimer, ed. *The Yukon Territory.* London: Downey & Co., 1898.

Turner, Frederick Jackson. *Rise of the New West, 1819–1829.* American Nation Series, No. 14. New York: Harper and Brothers Publishers, 1906.

———. *The United States, 1830–1850: The Nation and Its Sections.* New York: Henry Holt & Co., 1935.

———. *The Frontier in American History.* New York: Holt, Rinehart and Winston, 1963.

Twichell, Heath, Jr. *Allen: The Biography of an Army Officer, 1859–1930.* New Brunswick: Rutgers University Press, 1974.

Utley, Robert M. *Frontiersman in Blue: The United States Army and the Indian, 1848–1865.* New York: Macmillan Publishers, 1967.

———. *Frontiers Regulars: The United States Army and the Indian, 1866–1891.* New York: Macmillan Publishers, 1974.

———. *The Indian Frontier of the American West, 1846–1890.* Histories of the American Frontier. Albuquerque: University of New Mexico Press, 1984.

VanStone, James W. *Athapaskan Adaptations: Hunters and Fishermen of the Subarctic Forests.* Chicago: Aldine Publishing Co., 1974.

———. *Ingalik Contact Ecology: An Ethnohistory of the Lower-Middle Yukon, 1790–1935.* Fieldiana Anthropology, No. 71. Chicago: Field Museum, 1979.

Wade, Richard C. *The Urban Frontier: Pioneer Life in Early Pittsburgh, Cincinnati, Lexington, Louisville, and St. Louis.* Chicago: University of Chicago Press, 1959.

Walden, Arthur Treadwell. *A Dog-Puncher on the Yukon.* New York: Houghton Mifflin Co., 1928.

Weimer, M. D. K. *M. D. K. Weimer's True Story of the Alaska Gold Fields.* Privately printed, 1900.

Wharton, David. *The Alaska Gold Rush.* Bloomington: Indiana University Press, 1972.

Who Was Who in America. Vol. 1. Chicago: A. N. Marquis Co., 1942.

Who Was Who in America: Historical Volume, 1607–1896. Chicago: A. N. Marquis Co., 1963.

Whymper, Frederick. *Travel and Adventure in the Territory of Alaska.* London: John Murray, Albemarle Street, 1868.

Wickersham, James. *Old Yukon: Old Tales, Trails, and Trials*. St. Paul, Minnesota: West Publishing Co., 1938.

Wilson, Clifford. *Campbell of the Yukon*. Toronto: Macmillan of Canada, 1970.

Wilson, William H. *Railroad in the Clouds: The Alaska Railroad in the Age of Steam, 1914–1945*. Boulder, Colorado: Pruett Publishing Co., 1977.

Wilson, V. *Guide to the Yukon Gold Fields: Where They Are and How to Reach Them*. Seattle: Colvert Co., 1895.

Winther, Oscar Osburn. *The Transportation Frontier: Trans-Mississippi West, 1865–1890*. Histories of the American Frontier. New York: Holt, Rinehart and Winston, 1964.

Wolff, Ernest. *Handbook for the Alaskan Prospector*. Ann Arbor, Michigan: Edward Brothers, 1969.

Wrangell, Ferdinand Petrovich. *Russian America: Statistical and Ethnographic Information*. Translated by Mary Sadouski. Edited by Richard A. Pierce. Materials for the Study of Alaska History, No. 15. Kingston, Ontario: Limestone Press, 1980.

Wright, Allen A. *Prelude to Bonanza: The Discovery and Exploration of the Yukon*. Sidney, British Columbia: Gray's Publishing, 1976.

Young, Otis E. *Western Mining: An Informal Account of Precious-Metals Prospecting, Placering, Lode Mining, and Milling on the American Frontier From Spanish Times to 1893*. Norman: University of Oklahoma Press, 1970.

Zaslow, Morris. *The Opening of the Canadian North, 1870–1914*. Canadian Centenary Series. Toronto: McClelland and Stewart, 1971.

VII. Articles

Adney, Edwin Tappan. "Moose Hunting with the Tro-chu-tin." *Harper's New Monthly Magazine*, 100 (February 1900), 494–507.

———. "The Sledge Dogs of the North." *Outing*, 39 (May 1901), 131–33.

Agnew, William McGarry. "Alaska's Grand Old Man." *Jesuit Missions: A Magazine of Apostolic Endeavor*, 14 (1940), 108–09.

"Alaska's Oil/Gas & Minerals Industry." *Alaska Geographic*, 9 (1982).

Albert, Rose. "Ruby Sees Its First Planes." *Alaska Journal*, 11 (1981), 216–17.

Andrews, C. L. "The U. S.-Siberian Telegraph." *Alaska Life*, 8 (September 1945), 36–39.

Anon. "A Sequel to Mrs. Bean's Murder." In *Sourdough Sagas*, edited by Herbert L. Heller, pp. 113–14. New York: Ballantine Books, 1967.

Bender, Jim. "Early Days in Alaska." In *Sourdough Sagas*, edited by Herbert L. Heller, pp. 78–85. New York: Ballantine Books, 1967.

Berkhofer, Robert F., Jr. "Space, Time, Culture and the New Frontier." *Agricultural History*, 38 (October 1964), 21–30.

———. "The North American Frontier as Process and Context." In *The Frontier in History: North America and Southern Africa Compared*, edited by Howard Lamar and Leonard Thompson, pp. 43–75. New Haven: Yale University Press, 1981.

Bettles, Gordon C. "Some Early Yukon River History." In *Sourdough Sagas*, edited by Herbert l. Heller, pp. 109–12. New York: Ballantine Books, 1967.

Billman, Christine W. "Jack Craig and the Alaska Boundary Survey." *Beaver*, 302 (Autumn 1971), 48–50.

Birmingham, C. H. "Gold Dredging at Sixty Below Zero." *Scientific American*, 116 (June 2, 1917), 555.

Bloom, Jo Tice. "Cumberland Gap Versus South Pass." *Western Historical Quarterly*, 3 (April 1972), 153–68.

Boon, Thomas, C. B. "William West Kirkby: First Anglican Missionary to the Loucheux." *Beaver*, 295 (Spring 1965), 36–43.

Brigham, H. A. "Examine and Fitting a Hydraulic Mine." *Engineering and Mining Journal*, 86 (December 26, 1908), 1257–60; and 87 (January 2, 1909), 23–29.

Burlingame, Virginia S. "John J. Healy's Alaskan Adventure." *Alaska Journal*, 8 (Autumn 1978), 310–14.

Burpee, Lawrence J. "Campbell of the Yukon." *Canadian Geographical Journal*, 30 (April 1945), 200–201. Also reprinted in *Alaska and Its History*, edited by Morgan Sherwood, pp. 115–20. Seattle: University of Washington Press, 1967.

Buteau, Frank. "My Experiences in the World." In *Sourdough Sagas*, edited by Herbert L. Heller, pp. 86–112. New York: Ballantine Books, 1967.

Callahan, Erinia Pavaloff Cherosky. "A Yukon Autobiography." *Alaska Journal*, 5 (Spring 1975), 127–28.

Canby, Thomas Y. "The First Americans." *National Geographic*, 156 (September 1979), 330–63.

Caughey, John W. "The Insignificance of the Frontier in American History or 'Once Upon a Time There Was an American West.' " *Western Historical Quarterly*, 5 (January 1974), 5–16.

Chapman, J. E. "Interview." *The Alaskan* (Sitka) (October 30, 1886).

Clark, John A. "From Valdez to Fairbanks in 1906 by Bicycle, Blizzard and Strategy." In *Sourdough Sagas*, edited by Herbert L. Heller, pp. 163–94. New York: Ballantine Books, 1967.

"Cold-Water Thawing in the North." *Mining and Scientific Press*, 124 (February 4, 1922), 147–48.

Coleman, William. "Science and Symbol in the Turner Frontier Hypothesis." *American Historical Review*, 72 (October 1966), 22–49.

Cooney, M. J. "Airmail Not Yet Adequate for Interior." *Alaska Weekly* (June 12, 1931), 5.

Couch, Jim. "The Wizard of Eagle." *Alaska Sportsman*, 23 (1957), 16–17.

Craig, D. B. "Yukon Mining and Exploration, 1975." *Western Mining*, 48 (October 1975), 16–18.

Crimont, Joseph R. "A Short Story of a Long-Time Friend: A Retrospect of the 84 Years of the Life of Fr. F. P. Monroe." *Jesuit Seminary News*, 7 (1940), 39–40.

Crow, John R., and Obley, Philip R. "Han." In *Handbook of North American Indians: Subarctic*, edited by June Helm, pp. 506–13. Washington, D. C.: Smithsonian Institution, 1981.

Dall, William H. "A Yukon Pioneer, Mike Lebarge." *National Geographic Magazine*, 9 (April 1898), 137–139.

———. "The Future of Yukon Goldfields." *National Geographic Magazine*, 9 (April 1898), 117–20.

Davis, Henry. "Recollections." In *Sourdough Sagas*, edited by Herbert L. Heller, pp. 24–78. New York: Ballantine Books, 1967.

Dawson, George M. "Extracts From the Report on an Exploration Made in 1887 in the Yukon District N.W.T. and Adjacent Northern Portion of British Columbia." In *The Yukon Territory*, edited by F. Mortimer Trimmer. London: Downey & Co., 1898.

DeArmond, R. N. "The Ill-Favored Steamboat, *Arctic*." *Alaska Journal*, 4 (Autumn 1971), 52–54.

———. "A Letter to Jack McQuesten: 'Gold on the Fortymile.' " *Alaska Journal*, 3 (Spring 1973), 114–21.

Dennis, F. J. "Modern Methods of Gravel Excavation—Steam Shovel and Dragline." *Mining and Scientific Press*, 125 (August 3, 1922), 136–40.

"Eagle Notes." *Assembly Herald*, 6 (1902), 238–39.

Eddy, L. H. "Bagley Scraper for Gravel Mining." *Engineering and Mining Journal*, 100 (August 14, 1915), 257.

Elkins, Stanley, and McKitrick, Eric. "A Meaning for Turner's Frontier, Part I: Democracy in the Old Northwest." *Political Science Quarterly*, 69 (September 1954), 321–53.

Ellis, Hubert I. "Hydraulic Mining at Circle." *Engineering and Mining Journal*, 98 (December 19, 1914), 1104; and 100 (December 11, 1915), 962.

———. "Thawing Methods at Fairbanks." *Engineering and Mining Journal*, 100 (July 3, 1915).

Emmons, Samuel Franklin. "Alaska and Its Mineral Resources." *National Geographic Magazine*, 9 (April 1898), 139–72.

Ensign, Charles F. "The 'Chechakoo' and the 'Sour Dough.' " *Assembly Herald*, 8 (1903), 259.

Ensign, Mary R. "An Arctic School." *Assembly Herald*, 8 (1903), 263–64.

Farnsworth, Robert J. "An Army Brat Goes to Alaska." Part 1. *Alaska Journal*, 7 (Summer 1977), 160–65.

———. "An Army Brat Goes to Alaska." Part 2. *Alaska Journal*, 7 (Autumn 1977), 211–19.

Forbes, Jack. "Frontiers in American History and the Role of the Frontier Historian." *Ethnohistory*, 15 (Spring 1968), 203–35.

"From Ketchikan to Barrow." *Alaska*, 48 (November 1982), 27.

Fulcomer, Anna. "The Three R's at Circle City." *Century Magazine*, 56 (June 1898), 223–29.

Funston, Frederick. "Frederick Funston's Alaska Trip." *Harper's Weekly*, 39 (May 25, 1895), 491–93.

———. "Over the Chilkoot Pass in 1893." *Scribner's Magazine*, (November 1896). Also reprinted in *Alaska Journal*, 2 (Summer 1972), 16–24.

———. "Along Alaska's Eastern Boundary." *Harper's Weekly*, 40 (February 1, 1898), 103.

Gibson, Arthur. "Thawing Frozen Ground for Placer Mining." *Mining and Scientific Press*, 108 (January 17, 1914), 143.

Glave, E. J. "The Leslie Expedition." *Frank Leslie's Illustrated Newspaper*, November 15, 22, 29 and December 6, 13, 20, 27, 1890 and January 3, 10, 1891.

———. "Pioneer Packhorses in Alaska." *Century*, 44 (September 1892), 671–82.

Gordon, P. H. "An Arbitrary Boundary." *Beaver*, 302 (Autumn 1971), 50–51.

Goring, W. B. "Is the Old Prospector Necessary?" *Alaska Weekly* (April 26, 1929), 6.

Gray, James. "Light-Draft Steamer for an Alaskan River." *Marine Engineering* (February 1904), 68–69.

Gressley, Gene M. "The Turner Thesis: A Problem in Historiography." *Agricultural History*, 32 (October 1958), 227–49.

Guthrie, R. D. "Paleoecology of the Large Mammal Community in Interior Alaska During the Late Pleistocene." *American Midland Naturalist*, 79 (April 1968), 346–63.

Haines, John. "Of Traps and Snares." *Alaska*, 47 (March 1981), 34–37.

Harbottle, Jeanne. "Clyde Wann, Father of Yukon Aviation." *Alaska Journal*, 3 (Autumn 1973), 237–45.

———. "White Pass Aviation and Its Rivals." *Alaska Journal*, 4 (Autumn 1974), 232–41.

Harrison, E. S. "Steamboating on the Yukon." *Alaska-Yukon Magazine* (May 1907), 9–10. Also reprinted in *Alaska Journal*, 9 (Spring 1979), 49–53.

Hayes, Charles W. "An Expedition Through the Yukon District." *National Geographic Magazine*, 4 (May 1892), 117–62.

Hinckley, Ted C. "Sheldon Jackson as Preserver of Alaska's Native Culture." *Pacific Historical Quarterly*, 33 (November 1964), 411–24.

———. "Publicist of the Forgotten Frontier." *Journal of the West*, 4 (January 1965), 27–40.

———. "The Presbyterian Leadership in Pioneer Alaska." *Journal of American History*, 52 (March 1966), 742–56.

Hirshberg, M. R. "My Bicycle Trip Down the Yukon [in 1900]." *Alaska*, 44 (February 1978), 26–28.

"Historical Data of Alaskan Missions." *Alaskan Churchman*, 14 (1920).

Hunt, John Clark, ed. "The Adventures of the Iowa Goldseekers." *Alaska*

Journal, 3 (Winter 1973), 2–12.

Irving, William N. "Recent Early Man Research in the North." *Arctic Anthropology*, 8 (1971), 68–82.

Jensen, Richard. "On Modernizing Frederick Jackson Turner: The Historiography of Regionalism." *Western Historical Quarterly*, 11 (July 1980), 307–22.

Kennedy, Michael S. "Arctic Flying and Alaskan Bush Pilots: A Synopsis of Early Aviation History." In *Transportation in Alaska's Past*, edited by Michael S. Kennedy, pp. 183–238. Anchorage: Alaska Historical Society, 1982.

Kennicott, Robert. "The Journal of Robert Kennicott, May 19, 1959–February 11, 1862." In *The First Scientific Exploration of Russian America and the Purchase of Alaska*, edited by James Alton James, pp. 46–135. Evanston, Illinois: Northwestern University, 1942.

Lain, B. D. "The Fort Yukon Affair, 1869." *Alaska Journal*, 7 (Winter 1977), 12–17.

Lamar, Howard, and Thompson, Leonard. "Comparative Frontier History." In *The Frontier in History: North America and Southern Africa Compared*, edited by Howard Lamar and Leonard Thompson, pp. 3–13. New Haven: Yale University Press, 1981.

Lantis, Margaret. "Edward William Nelson." *Anthropological Papers of the University of Alaska*, 3 (December 1954), 5–16.

"The Little Engines That Can't." *Maclean's*, 93 (October 1, 1979), 25.

Luckingham, Bradford. "The City in the Westward Movement—A Bibliographical Note." *Western Historical Quarterly*, 5 (July 1974), 295–306.

Lyon, William H. "The Third Generation and the Frontier Thesis." *Arizona and the West*, 4 (Spring 1962), 45–50.

MacBride, William D. "Saga of Famed Packets and Other Steamboats of the Mighty Yukon River." *Alaska Weekly* (July 21, 1944), 7; (July 28, 1944), 7; (August 4, 1944), 7; (August 11, 1944), 7; (August 18, 1944), 7; (August 25, 1944), 7; (September 1, 1944), 7; (September 8, 1944), 7; and (September 15, 1944), 7.

McDermott, John Francis. "The Frontier Re-examined." In *The Frontier Re-examined*. Urbana: University of Illinois Press, 1967.

McGrath, J. E. "The Alaska Boundary Survey: II. The Boundary South of Fort Yukon." *National Geographic Magazine*, 4 (February 1893), 181–88.

McQueen, Verden. "Alaskan Communications, 1867–1914, Part I: A New Territory, 1867–1901." *Airpower Historian*, 8 (1961), 232–43.

———. "Alaskan Communications, 1867–1914, Part II: Technical Pioneering, 1901–1903." *Airpower Historian*, 11 (1964), 16–22.

Marshall, J. B. "Evolution of Fur Trade." *Alaska Weekly* (December 7, 1928), 6.

Mendenhall, T. C. "The Alaska Boundary Survey: I. Introduction." *National Geographic Magazine*, 4 (February 1893), 177–80.

"Mining Industry Left $70 Million (Plus) in Canadian North in 1974." *Western Mining*, 48 (April 1974), 19–24.

Mitchell, William. "Building the Alaska Telegraph System." *National Geographic Magazine*, 9 (April 1898), 172–78.

———. " Billy Mitchell in Alaska." *American Heritage*, 12 (February 1961), 65–79.

Modrzynski, Mike. "Neither Rain nor Sleet nor Snow . . ." *Alaska Journal*, 10 (Spring 1980), 54–55.

Nash, Gerald D. "The Census of 1890 and the Closing of the Frontier." *Pacific Northwest Quarterly*, 71 (July 1980), 98–100.

Naske, Claus-M. "The Alaska Board of Road Commissioners." In *Transportation in Alaska's Past*, edited by Michael S. Kennedy, pp. 91–139. Anchorage: Alaska Historical Society, 1982.

Nichols, David. "Civilization Over Savage: Frederick Jackson Turner and the Indian." *South Dakota History*, 2 (Fall 1972), 384–405.

Northern Navigation Company. "To the Alaska Gold Fields." Pamphlet. San Francisco: Northern Navigation Company, 1907.

Ogburn, R. H. "Thawing and Dredging Gold at Fairbanks, Alaska." *Mining and Metallurgy*, 14 (May 1933), 214–16.

Ogilvie, William. "Extracts from the Report of an Exploration Made in 1896–1897." In *The Yukon Territory*, edited by F. Mortimer Trimmer. London: Downey & Co., 1898.

Peake, F. A. "Robert McDonald (1829–1913): The Great Unknown Missionary of the Northwest." *Canadian Church Historical Society Journal*, 17 (September 1975), 54–72.

Pomeroy, Earl. "Towards a Reorientation of Western History: Continuity and Environment." *Mississippi Valley Historical Review*, 41 (March 1955), 579–600.

Putnam, Jackson K. "The Turner Thesis and the Westward Movement: A Reappraisal." *Western Historical Quarterly*, 7 (October 1976), 377–404.

Pyle, Ernie. "A Footless Dog-Team Postman Who's Sixty-eight and Tough as Nails." *Washington Daily News* (July 15, 1937), 23.

Ransom, Jay Ellis. "Alaxsxaq—Where the Sea Breaks Its Back." *Alaska Journal*, 8 (Summer 1978), 199.

Rearden, Jim. "The New Boom in Furs: An Old Trade Comes to Life." *Alaska*, 47 (January 1981), 32–33.

Renaud, Robert. "The Dempster: Road to Riches . . . or Ruin?" *Alaska Journal*, 10 (Winter 1980), 14–21.

Renner, Louis L. "Jules Jetté: Distinguished Scholar in Alaska." *Alaska Journal*, 5 (Autumn 1975), 239–47.

———. "Farming at Holy Cross Mission on the Yukon." *Alaska Journal*, 9 (Winter 1979), 32–37.

Richardson, David. "The Geoghegan Brothers of Alaska." *Alaska Journal*, 6 (Winter 1976), 17–24.

Richardson, Harold W. "Alcan—America's Glory Road: Part 1, Strategy."

Engineering News-Record, 129 (December 17, 1942), 81–98.

———. "Alcan—America's Glory Road: Part II, Supply, Equipment, Camps." *Engineering News-Record*, 129 (December 31, 1942), 35–42.

Richardson, Wilds P. "Col. Dick Richardson, Alaska Pioneer, Writes of U. S. Army in North." *Infantry Journal*, 22 (May 1923). Reprinted in *Alaska Weekly* (June 8, 1923), 3.

Rickard, T. A. "Dredging in the Yukon." *Mining and Scientific Press*, 97 (August 29, 1908), 290–93.

———. "Mining Law in Alaska." *Mining and Scientific Press*, 97 (December 26, 1908), 855–56.

———. "Mining Methods in the North, Part II." *Mining and Scientific Press*, 98 (January 9, 1909), 86–89.

Riggs, Thomas C. Jr. "Running the Alaska Boundary." *Beaver*, 276 (September 1945), 43–45.

Rodney, William. "Pioneer Dredging in the Klondike." *Alaska Journal*, 6 (Winter 1976), 50–54.

Rowe, Peter T. "Historical Data of Alaskan Missions." *Alaskan Churchman*, 14 (1920).

Rundell, Walter, Jr. "Concepts of the 'Frontier 'and the 'West.' " *Arizona and the West*, 1 (Spring 1959), 13–41.

Russell, Israel C. "A Journey up the Yukon River." *Journal of the American Geographical Society*, 27 (1895), 143–60.

Schanz, Alfred Brunot. "The Alaskan Boundary Survey." *Harper's Weekly*, 35 (September 12, 1891), 699–700.

———. "The Leslie Expedition." *Frank Leslie's Illustrated Newspaper*, September 26, October 3, 10, 17, 24, 31, and November 7, 28, 1891.

Scheiber, Harry. "Turner's Legacy and the Search for a Reorientation of Western History: A Review Essay." *New Mexico Historical Review*, 45 (July 1969), 231–48.

Schwatka, Frederick. "Yukon River." *Century*, 8 (September 1885), 739; and (October 1885), 820.

Sheffield, Bill. "A Guest Editorial by the Governor of Alaska." *Alaskafest* (February 1983), 5.

Sherman, Ro. "Down the Yukon and Up the Fortymile." *Alaska Journal*, 4 (Autumn 1974), 205–13.

———. "Exploring the Tanana River Region." *Alaska Journal*, 5 (Winter 1975), 41–48.

Sherwood, Morgan. "The Mysterious Death of Frederick Schwatka." *Alaska Journal*, 9 (Summer 1979), 74–75.

Shimkin, Demitri B. "The Economy of a Trapping Center: The Case of Fort Yukon, Alaska." *Economic Development and Culture Changes*, 3 (1955), 219–40.

Shipley, Nan. "Anne and Alexander Murray." *Beaver*, 298 (Winter 1967), 33–37.

"Short Story of Alaska and the Yukon as Told by the Mount Wrangell

Company's Explorer." Promotional pamphlet. Boston: Mount Wrangell
Company, 1897–98.

Siddall, William R. "The Yukon Waterway in the Development of Interior
Alaska." *Pacific Historical Review*, 28 (November 1959), 361–76.

Sinclair, James M. "St. Andrews Church, Lake Bennett." *Alaska Journal*, 4
(Autumn 1974), 242–50.

Slobodin, Richard. "Kutchin." In *Handbook of North American Indians:
Subarctic*, edited by June Helm, pp. 514–32. Washington, D. C.:
Smithsonian Institution, 1981.

Sloss, Frank H. "Who Owned the Alaska Commercial Company?" *Pacific
Northwest Quarterly*, 68 (July 1977), 120–30.

Sloss, Frank H., and Pierce, Richard A. "The Hutchinson, Kohl Story: A Fresh
Look." *Pacific Northwest Quarterly*, 62 (January 1971), 1–6.

Snow, Jeanne H. "Ingalik." In *Handbook of North American Indians:
Subarctic*, edited by June Helm, pp. 602–17. Washington, D. C.:
Smithsonian Institution, 1981.

Spence, Clark C. "The Golden Age of Dredging: The Development of an
Industry and Its Environmental Impact." *Western Historical Quarterly*,
11 (October 1980), 401–14.

Stein, Gary C. "Ship's Surgeon on the Yukon." *Alaska Journal*, 11 (1981),
228–36.

Taggart, H. F., ed. "Journal of William H. Ennis, Member, Russian-American
Telegraph Exploring Expedition." *California Historical Society
Quarterly*, 33 (March 1954), 1–12; and (June 1954), 147–68.

Tero, Richard D. "E. J. Glave and the Alsek River." *Alaska Journal*, 3
(Summer 1973), 180–88.

Thompson, Paul E. "Who Was Hudson Stuck?" *Alaska Journal*, 10 (Winter
1980), 62–65.

Turner, Frederick Jackson. "The West—1876 and 1926: Its Progress in a
Half-Century." *World's Work*, 52 (July 1926), 319–27.

———. "The Significance of the Frontier in American History." In *The
Frontier in American History*, pp. 1–38. New York: Holt, Rinehart and
Winston, 1963.

———. "Contributions of the West to American Democracy." In *The Frontier
in American History*, pp. 243–68. New York: Holt, Rinehart and
Winston, 1963.

Turner, J. Henry. "The Alaska Boundary Survey: III. The Boundary North of
Fort Yukon." *National Geographic Magazine*, 4 (February 1893), 189–97.

"Two Throughways to the Arctic." *Time*, 113 (May 14, 1979), 100–101.

"United Keno Layoff." *Canadian Mining Journal*, 103 (August 1982), 11.

VanStone, James. "Russian Exploration in Interior Alaska: An Extract from
the Journal of Andrei Glazunov." *Pacific Northwest Quarterly*, 50 (April
1959), 37–47.

Vevier, Charles. "The Collins Overland Line and American Continentalism."
Pacific Historical Review, 27 (August 1959), 237–53. Reprinted in

Alaska and Its History, edited by Morgan Sherwood, pp. 208–30. Seattle: University of Washington Press, 1967.

Warner, Iris. "Herschel Island." *Alaska Journal*, 3 (Summer 1973), 130–42.

Well, E. H. "The Leslie Expedition." *Frank Leslie's Illustrated Newspaper*, July 4, 11, 18, 25; August 1, 8, 29; and September 5, 19, 1891.

Wilson, Clifford. "The Surrender of Fort Yukon One Hundred Years Ago." *Beaver*, 300 (Autumn 1969), 47–51.

Wilson, William H. "The Mayo Ore Deal: An International 'Gentlemen's Agreement.' " *Alaska Journal*, 9 (Winter 1979), 74–79.

———. "The Alaska Railroad: Elements of Continuity, 1915–1941." In *Transportation in Alaska's Past*, edited by Michael S. Kennedy, pp. 317–39. Anchorage: Alaska Historical Society, 1982.

———. "The Alaska Railroad and Coal: Development of a Federal Policy, 1914–1939." *Pacific Northwest Quarterly*, 73 (April 1982), 66–77.

Wimmler, W. L. "Placer Mining in Interior Alaska." *Alaska Weekly* (October 12, 1923), 5.

Woods, Benton S. "Yukon Pioneer Longs to Hear from Oldtimers." *Alaska Weekly* (March 14, 1924), 7.

Wright, Allen A. "Yukon Hails Opening of the Dempster Highway." *Canadian Geographic*, 98 (June/July 1979), 16–21.

Young, Hall S. "The Situation in Alaska." *Assembly Herald* (June 1902), 231–36.

———. "Yukon Presbytery Redevivus." *Assembly Herald* (June 1911), 277–82.

INDEX

References to illustrations are printed in bold face.

Abercrombie, William R., 107,
146–48, 150–51, 165
Adams, George R., 321
Africa, 116, 118
Agassiz, Louis, 54
agriculture, 100, 113, 148, 178, 179,
229, 240, 247, 248, 250, 254, 255,
291, 294, 356
Air Commerce Act of 1926, 266
Air Mail Act of 1925, 266
airplanes. *See* aviation
Alaska, xi, 2; Aleut name for, 46,
319; and Athapaskan Indians, 12,
14, 171–201 *passim*, 315; climate
of, 6, 8, 207–8; and education, 84,
95, 172, 178–87, 201; explorers and
scientists, 99–121 *passim*, **200;**
and Frederick Jackson Turner, 2,
307–8; and fur trade, 48, 51, 56;
and Klondike gold rush, 141;
mining in, 77–97 *passim*, 136–40,
191, 208–22, 223–24, 245, 269–89;
and missionaries, 72–75, 171–97,
177, 181, 185, 188, 200; and
Mitchell, 159–64, 167; and
Natives, 1, 4, 10–19, **15, 17,** 21–50
passim, 72–74, 143, 148–67
passim, 171–97, **188,** 198–201,
200; and *posse comitatus*, 152;
purchase of, 46, 48, 55, 64, 72, 172,
319, 321; and transportation,

205–68 *passim*; trapping in,
291–308; and Turner thesis, 2; and
U.S. Army, 104–10, 130, 143–70
passim, **166.** *See also* Russian
America
Alaska (steamboat), 221
Alaska Airways, Inc., 264
Alaska Boundary Tribunal, 242
Alaska Central Railroad. *See* Alaska
Northern Railway
Alaska Coal and Coke Company, 220
Alaska Commercial Company, 48,
50, 56–75 *passim*, **57, 87,** 132, 137,
176, 191, 200, 219–20, 321; and
competition, 64–66, 67, 71, 86–88,
92, 209, 211; and explorers and
scientists, 109, 116; and
McQuesten, Harper, and Mayo, 61,
64; and mining, 75, 77, 84, 208;
and missionaries, 176, 179, 191;
and the NAT & T Company, 86,
88, 92, 208–9. *See also*
Hutchinson, Kohl & Company
Alaska Communications System,
167
Alaska earthquake, 253
Alaska Engineering Commission,
248, **249,** 250, 256
Alaska Exploration Company, 137,
209, 211
Alaska Forum (newspaper), 140, 332

Alaska Game Commission, 300, 301, 302–4, 357

Alaska Highway (Ak.-Canada), 117, 168, 255–58, 259, 267, 308, 350. *See also* Alcan Military Highway

Alaska Home Rule Act of 1912, 248

Alaska Mining Record (newspaper), 133

Alaska National Interest Lands Conservation Act, 307–8, 359

Alaska Native Claims Settlement Act, 259, 308

Alaska Northern Railway, 247, 248

Alaska Peninsula, 319

Alaska Pipeline, 253, **258,** 259–60, 308, 350–51

Alaska purchase, 46, 48, 55, 64, 72, 172, 319, 321

Alaska Railroad, 147, 167, 221–22, 240, 248–55, **249, 251, 252,** 267, 283, 349

Alaska Railroad's River Boat Service, 221–22

Alaska Range, 2, 6, 107, 109, 149

Alaska Road Commission, 166, 236–42, **237,** 239, 250, 256, 257, 347

Alaska Statehood Act, 308

Alaska Yukon Navigation Company, 222

Alberta (Canadian province), 110

Alcan Military Highway, 168, 254, 255–58. *See also* Alaska Highway

Alder Creek (Ak.), 270, 271, 283

Aleutian Islands (Ak.), 22, 198

Alger, Russell A., 145

Alice (steamboat), 221

Allen, Henry Tureman, xii, 80, 106–10, **108,** 117, 118, 146, 151

Alsek River (Ak.-British Columbia), 117

American Boundary Survey Expedition, 118

American Creek (Ak.), 133, 134, 140, 270, 280, 282, 292

American Ethnological Society, 181

American Expeditionary Force, 157

American Fur Company, 37

American Geographical Society, 104

American West: and fur trade, 62, 306; and mining camps, 134, 187; and missionaries, 171, 176–78, 183, 187; and transportation, 205, 206, 211, 225, 235, 260, 267; and Turner thesis, xi, 1–2; and U.S. Army, 104, 143, 151, 170

American Yukon Navigation Company, 221, 222

AMTRAK, 253

Amundsen, Roald, xxi, 230–34, **233**

Anchorage (Ak.), 167, 221, 248, 249, 250, 253, 254, 262, 264

Anderson, Thomas M., 145, 146

Anglican church, 72, 73, 74, 84, 171–74, **173,** 196

Antarctic, 263

Antrim, Ireland, 59

Anvik (Ak.), 106, 176; and missionaries, 176, 179–83, **181, 185,** 186, 189, 197

Anvik River (Ak.), 27

Aphoon (Ak.). *See* Apoon

Apoon (Ak.), 26, 207

Arctic (steamboat), 84, 85, 87, 115, 208

Arctic Express Company, 138

Arctic Ocean, 39, 115, 243, 245, **258,** 259, **261,** 263, 302

Argo (steamboat), 151

Arizona, 70

Arkansas, 8

Arrowsmith, 59

asbestos, 288

Ash, Harry, 93

Asia, 21, 46

Athabasca River (Alberta), 111

Athapaskan Indians, 10–19, **15, 17,** 314; and cultural change, 47–48, 184–87, 198–201, **200;** description of, 13, 14–18, **15, 17;** and explorers and scientists, 30, 36, 104, 107, 109, 115, 117, 118, **200;** and Hudson's Bay Company, 30–31; and mining, 184, **188;** and missionaries, 58–59, 72–74, 84, 95,

102, 171–97, **181, 185,** 186, **188, 200;** population of, 102, 315. *See also* Natives; and individual Athapaskan groups
Atkins, J. D. C., 178
Atlantic Ocean, 8, 52, 54
Audubon Club, Chicago, Ill., 51
aviation, 222, 229, 234, 241, 255, 257, 260–68, **263, 265,** 286, 295, 302, 304, 351

Baird, Spencer, 99
Baltic Sea, 22, 31
Bancroft, Hubert Howe, 100
Baranov, Aleksandr Andreevich, 28
Barnard, John J., 40–43, 66, 318
Barnette, Elbridge Truman "E. T.," 201
Barney Creek (Ak.), 271
Barr, John C., 208
Barrow (Ak.), 263
Bates Rapids (Ak.), 201
Beach, Rex, 203
Bean, Edmund, 69, 71
Bean, James M., 55, 65–66, 69, 81
bear, x, 164, 194, 230, 294, 297
Beardslee, L. A., 69
beaver, 62, 294, 296, 297, 298, 299, 300, 301, 302, 303–4
Belkhov, Zachary, 172, 179
Bell, John, 31, 37, 114
Bell River (Yukon Territory), 37, 60, 114
Bella (steamboat), 132
Belle Isle (Ak.), 70, 71, 72, 75, 79, 89, 136, 146, 323
Bellevue Hospital Medical College, 104
Ben Creek (Ak.), 287
Bennett (Yukon Territory), **131** 147. *See also* Lake Bennett
Bering, Vitus, 21, 48, 316
Bering land bridge, 3
Bering Sea, 4, 6, 8, 179, 207
Berlin, Germany, 104
Berlin Museum, 103
Berry, C. J., 273

Bettles (Ak.), 215
Bettles, Gordon, 79, 140
Billings, Joseph, 24
Biederman, Bella, **228**
Biederman Camp (Ak.), 229
Biederman, Charlie, 229, 345
Biederman, Horace, 229
Biederman, Max Adolphas "Ed," 226–29, **228**
Birch Creek (Ak.), 89–96, 131, 133, 140, 326
Black River (Ak.), 292
Black Sea, 22, 45
Black Wolf Squadron, 260, 261
Bohemia, 226
Bompas, Charlotte Selina Cox, 172
Bompas, William Carpenter, 43, 171–74, **173,** 188, 189, 194
Bonanza (whaling ship), 232
Bonanza Creek (Yukon Territory), 124, 209
Bonfield, Frank, 61
Boundary (Ak.), 243
Boundary, International, xi, x, 1, 4, 14, 50, 58, 72, 111, 113, 114, 116, 117, **120,** 146, 302, 309; boundary survey, 111, 113, 115–16, 119, **120,** 242–46, **243,** 320; dispute over, 129, 144–45, 158; mining near, 88, 119, 134, 269; and U.S. Army, 132, 144, 148, **150,** 155, 158, 170. *See also* International Boundary Commission
Bowen, R. J., 174, 189
Brackett, George, 235
Brady, John G., 130, 145, 194
Bremen, Germany, 103
Bremner, John, 80, 81, 107, 109, 140
British American Steamship Company, 209
British Columbia (Canadian province), xi, 2, 4, 52, **55,** 59, 69, 77, 78, **111,** 112, 155, 245
British North America Boundary Commission, 110
British Yukon Navigation Company, 211, 221, 222

Brooks, Alfred Hulse, 151, **281,** 332

Brooks Range (Ak.), 2, 4, 6, 232, **233**

Bryan, William Jennings, 96

Bryant, C. A. "Bert," 269–71, 274, 289

Bulkley, Charles, 52

Bureau of Catholic Indian Missions, 183

Burke, Grafton "Hap," 190

Burnside (ship), 165

Buteau, Frank, 79, 82, 84, **94**

Butte Creek (Ak.), 283

Byres, Michael, 323

Cairnes, DeLorme Donaldson, 245

California, 2, 22, 32, 77, 82, 93, 94, 97, 123, 141, 220, 274, 275, 276, 278, 280

California gold rush, 59, 77, 94, 125, 324

California-Oregon Trail, 205

Callahan, Erinia Pavaloff Cherosky, 64, 75, 90, 322

Camp Colonna (Ak.), 115

Camp Davidson (Ak.), 115

Campbell, Robert, 30, 31, 37, 39, **41,** 54, 61, 84, 106, 112, 116, **120**

Canada: and American fur trade, 56–75; and Athapaskan Indians, 12, 14, 169; climate of, 6, 8; Dominion of, 46; and explorers and scientists, 103–5, 110–21, 232; and Hudson's Bay Company, 46; and mining, 59, 71, 75, 77–80, 84–89, 202–3, 287–89; and missionaries, 43, 72–74, 171, 172–74; and telegraphs, **153,** 155, 158, 159, 170; and transportation, 205–68 *passim;* trapping in, 301, 302, 304, 305–8; and United States, 129, 144–45, 155, 158, 159, 170 242–46, 255

Canadian (steamboat), 222

Canadian Department of Public Works, 214

Canadian Game Department, 304

Canadian Geological Survey, 245, 271

Canadian Pacific Navigation Company, 209

Cantwell, John C., 213

Canyon City (Ak.), 126

Cape Nome (Ak.), 149

caribou, 16, 156, 162, 164, 194, 230, 259–60, 271, 292, 294

Carcross (Yukon Territory), 174

Carmack, George Washington, 112, 123, **124,** 209

Caspian Sea, 31, 32

Castner, J. C., 147

Chapman, Henry, 186

Chapman, John Wight, 179–86, **181,** 189

Chapman, Mary Seely, 179, 182, 189

Chaffee, Adnar, 152

Chandalar River (Ak.), 215

Charley River (Ak.), 81, 134, 138, 220, 270

Charley's Village (Ak.), 67, 102, 113

Chena (Ak.), 201

Chena River (Ak.), 201

Cherokee Strip (Oklahoma), 117

Cherosky, Erinia Pavaloff. *See* Callahan, Erinia Pavaloff Cherosky

Cherosky, Sergi Gologoff, 64, 70, 75, 89, 140

Chicago, 52, 86, 96

Chicago Academy of Sciences, 99

Chicago fire, 99, 320

Chickaloon River (Ak.), 147

Chilberg, J. E., 216

Chilkat Indians, 18, 69, 102, 112, 125, 145; description of, 18, 316; and trade, 39, 40

Chilkat Pass (Ak., British Columbia), 18

Chilkoot (Ak.), 102

Chilkoot Pass (Ak.–British Columbia), 18, 69, 71, 78, 79, 86, 103, 105, 112, 113, 114, 116, 118, 119, 125, **127, 128,** 168, 175, 187, 214, 242

Chilkoot Trail (Ak.-Canada), **127,** 144, 168, 175, 187, 214
Chisana (Ak.), 245
Chitina River (Ak.), 107
Chukotsk Peninsula (Siberia), 102
Chulitna River (Ak.), 147
Church of England. *See* Anglican church
Churchill, W. L., 278
Circle (Ak.). *See* Circle City
Circle City (Ak.), 90–97, **92,** 129, 138, 202, 216, 241, 325, 326; description of, 91, **92,** 197–201, **202,** 325; and Klondike gold rush, 123, 144, 174; mail delivery to, 226–27, **229,** 345; and McQuesten, 90–92; **92,** 93; as mining town, 90–97, 188, 216, 269, 280, 283, 286; and missionaries, 174, 187, 188, 191, 193, 200; and Natives, 91, 93, 141, 188–89; population of, 134, 140; and starvation scare, 131, 138, 148–49, 209; and U.S. Army, 143, 144, 146, 149, 151, 154, 162, 168, 209
Civil Aeronautics Act of 1938, 266
Civil Aeronautics Board, 266
Civil Codes of 1900, 154, 197, 198, **199,** 200
Cleary Creek (Ak.), 201, 280
Close Brothers, 129
Clut, Father Isidore, 58–59, 61, 171
coal, 203, 219–20, 248
Coal Creek (Ak.), 133, 138, 285, 286
Coast Range (Ak.-Canada), 2, 6, 262
Colben, Dan, 286
Coleen River (Ak.), 232
Collins, Perry McDonough, 52
Colorado, 77, 78
Columbia River, 208, 211, 214
Columbian (steamboat), 217
Colville River (Ak.), 39
Colville (Washington), 174
Commodore (ship), 48
Congo, 116

Constantine, Charles, 88, **89,** 119, 168–69
consumption. *See* tuberculosis
Cook Inlet (Ak.), 24, 26, 28, 31, 39, 144, 146, 147, 149
Coolidge, Calvin, 262
copper, 203, 270, 287, 288, 289
Copper Center (Ak.), 150, 186
Copper Creek (Ak.), 270
Copper River (Ak.), 80, 107, 110, 118, 128, 146, 147, 150
Copper River & Northwestern Railway, 247
Copper River Delta (Ak.), 107, 146
Cordova (Ak.), 234, 247
Craig, J. D., **243**
Creoles, 26, 27, 28, 29, 32, 37, 47, 54, 62, 64, 65, 66, 70, 80, 89, 102, 172, 316
Crimean War, 36, 45
Criminal Codes of 1899, 152, 154, 197, 198
Crooked Creek (Ak.), 283
Cuba, 110, 152, 164
Cudahy (Yukon Territory), 87
Cudahy, Jack, 87
Cudahy, Michael, 87
Cumberland Gap, 1, 6
Customs Acts, 295
Cyprus Anvil Mining Corporation, 289

Dakota Territory, 152
Dall River (Ak.), 213
Dall, William H., **53,** 54, 62, 99, 100, 106
Dalton, Jack, 117, 128, 145, 235
Dalton Highway (Ak.), **261,** 308
Dalton Trail, 117, 128, 145, 146, 225, 235
dancehalls, 92–93, 213
David's Village (Ak.), 68, 70, 74, 102
Davis, Henry, 79
Dawson (Yukon Territory), 120, **120, 125,** 130, **131,** 146, 151, 155, 162, 168, 202, 260, 261, 273, 287, 305;

beginning of, 97, 208; decline of, 203, 211, 220–21, 234, 287, **288, 288**–89, 308; life in, 123–24; and missionaries, **173,** 174, 187, 190, 340; name of, 123; and Natives, 141, **173,** 174; and North-West Mounted Police, 168–70; roads to, 223, 235–36, 241, 257, 258–59; and starvation scare, **127,** 130–33, 138, 144, 189, 209, 330; steamboats into, 210, 213, 214, 216, 220–21, 222, 223, 224, 225

Dawson, George Mercer, 110–14, **111, 120,** 123, 323

De Windt, Henry, 91

Deadwood Creek (Ak.), 90, 286

Deane, Elizabeth, 189

Dease Lake (British Columbia), 112, 114

Delta (steamboat), 215

Delta River (Ak.), 147

Dempster Highway (Canada), 258–59, 308, 350

Denmark, 167

Department of Alaska (U.S. Army), 152, 164

Depression, 252, **252,** 284, 285, 286, 288, 301, 302

Deriabin, Vasili, 29, 33, 42, 43, 66

District of Alaska (U.S. Army), 149

District of North Alaska (U.S. Army), 152

Dixon, E. D., 208

Dunham, Samuel, 140

Dyea (Ak.), 86, 112, 125, 129, 144–45, 146

Eagle (Ak.). *See* Eagle City

Eagle City (Ak.), 133, 162, 225, **233,** 262; beginning of, 136, 323, 331; government of, 137, 156, 197–200; life in, 193–96; **195,** 196, 270–71; mail delivery to, 266–27, **227, 228,** 229, 234–35, 345; mining near, 136–37, 286, 292; and missionaries, 189, 191–97, **192, 195;** population

of, 134, 191, 196, 198, 235; roads to, 235, 236, 241

Eagle City Tribune (newspaper), 137

Eagle Creek (Ak.), 283

Eagle Reporter (newspaper), 137

Eagle Village (Ak.), 141, 197, 198–201

economics. *See* trade; mining; trapping; and names of specific companies

Edes, William C., 248, **249,** 250

Edinburgh, Scotland, 110

Edmonton (Alberta), 255

education, 178–87; in Anvik, 179–86, **181;** in Circle City, 95; in Eagle City, 196; in Fortymile, 84, 172; in Holy Cross, 180–86, **185;** in Nulato, 183

Eielson, Carl Ben, 262–64, **263,** 264

Eldorado Creek (Yukon Territory), 124

Ellingen, Casper, 96

Empire Transportation Company, 209, 211

England. *See* Great Britain

English, Robert, 90

Ennis, William H., 54

Ensign, Charles F. and Mary, 196

Enterprise (ship), 40

Episcopal church, 95, 136, 179–91, **188,** 196–97, 200

Eskimos, 10, **10, 13,** 18, 19, 28, 36, 73, 102, 103, 104, 179, 206, 232, 314. *See also* Natives

Ester Creek (Ak.), 201

ethnography. *See* Natives

Etholen, Adolf Karlovich, 26

Europe, 21

Evans, David, ix, x, 359

Everett, Pinyit, **63**

Excelsior (ocean steamer), 123

Explorer (riverboat), 80

explorers, 21–48, 99–121 *passim*, 143–68, 213, 223–24

Fairbanks (Ak.), x, **161,** 162, 165, 167, 190, **192,** 193, **199,** 291; and aviation, 260, 262, **263,** 263, 264; founding of, 201; government of, 201–2,; mining near, 201, 220, 247, 254, 269, 280, 282, 283, 284, 286; population of, 201–2; and transportation, 215, 220, 221, 224, 241, 247, 248, 249, 254, 255, 258, 259, 267

Fairbanks, Charles W., 201

Fairbanks Creek (Ak.), 201

Fairbanks Exploration Company, 284, 286

Farnsworth, Charles Stewart, 151–57, **153,** 158, 159, 194, 335

Farnsworth, Helen, 152, **153,** 156

Farnsworth, Robert, 152

Farcoit, Charles, 70, 71

Faro (Yukon Territory), **288,** 289

Farthest North Airplane Company, 262

Federal Aid Highway Act, 241

Fickett, Fred, **108**

Finlay River (British Columbia), 59

Firth River (Ak.–Yukon Territory), 232

Fish Camp (Ak.), 90

Five Finger Rapids (Yukon Territory), 127, 214

Flume Creek (Ak.), 270

Fort Benton (Montana), 191

Fort Constantine (Yukon Territory), 88

Fort Cudahy (Yukon Territory), 119, 168

Fort Davis (Ak.), 158, 167

Fort Egbert (Ak.), 149, **150,** 151, **153,** 153–57, 158, 159–67, **161, 166,** 198, 232, 234, 269; abandonment of, 167; life at, 153–57, 162, 165–66, **166,** 335

Fort Gibbon (Ak.), 149, 151, **153,** 153, 154, 156, 158, 162, 165, 167, 189, 221

Fort Keogh (Montana), 107

Fort Liscum (Ak.), 150, 152, 153, 159, 162, 164, 165, 167

Fort McPherson (Northwest Territories), 31, 114

Fort Nelson (British Columbia), 78, 79

Fort Providence (Northwest Territories), 114

Fort Reliance (Yukon Territory), 61, **63;** abandonment of, 78–79; and American fur trade, 64, 68; as landmark, 62, **63,** 88; and missionaries, 75; population of, 102; and prospecting, 71–72, 79

Fort Ross (Calif.), 32

Fort St. John (British Columbia), 169

Fort St. Michael (Ak.), 148, 152, 158, 164, 165, 167

Fort Selkirk (Yukon Territory), 39, 40, 54, **55,** 61, 84, 89, 105, 112, 113, 116, 117, 118, 128, 146–47, 175, 235

Fort Simpson (Northwest Territories), 40, 43, 59

Fort Youcon (Ak.), 38. *See also* Fort Yukon

Fort Yukon (Ak.), 37–38, 44, **44,** 48–50, 60, 214, 220, 232, 264; and American fur trade, **44,** 48, 50, 57, 61, 64, 72; and explorers and scientists, 51, 54, 115; and missionaries, 43, 58, 73, 171, **173,** 190; and Murray, 37–38, **44;** population of, 102, 134; and starvation scare, 130, 132, 144, 148; and trade, 38, 40, 45, 50, 220; and trapping, 292, 294, 302; and the Western Union Telegraph Expedition, 54

Fortymile (Yukon Territory), 77–91 *passim,* 120, 129, 220; and explorers and scientists, 113–20, 143, 146, 244; and Klondike, 123, 220; life in, 84, **85,** 87, **87, 89,** 91, 325; and mining, 79, 84–88, 172, 173, 187, 208, 209, 234, 241, 278, 280, 282; and missionaries, 171, **173,** 187, 191, **192,** 193; and Natives, 91, 171, 172, **173;** and North-West Mounted Police, 124; population of, 134

Fortymile River (Ak.–Yukon Territory), **63,** 81, 117, 128, 133, 146; and prospecting, 68, 78

Fourth of July Creek (Ak.), 134, 138, 280, 282, 283

France, 21, 183

Frances Lake (Yukon Territory), 30, 39, 40, 112

Frances River (Yukon Territory), 30

Frank Leslie's Illustrated Newspaper, 116

Franklin, Howard, 71, 79

Franklin, John, 40, 104

Franklin Expedition. *See* Franklin, Sir John

Franklin Gulch (Yukon Territory), 82

Fraser River (British Columbia), 25, 59

French Canadians, 55, 56, 71

Frenchy, 81

Fulcomer, Anna, 95

Fuller, Frank, 175–76

Funston, Frederick, 119

Galena (Ill.), 104

Galvin, Pat, 209–10

Gen. Jeff C. Davis (steamboat), 221, 250

Gen. J. W. Jacobs (steamboat), 221, 250

Geographical Society of Bremen, 102

Geological Survey of Canada, 110, 114

geology, xii, 3, 77, 113, 116, 118, 121, 245, 271, 272, **281,** 288, 352

Germany, 110

Gillam, C. Harold, 234

Giordano, Carmelo, 180

Gjoa (gasoline sloop), 232, 234

glaciation, 3, 107, 118, 146, 147

Glave, Edward James, 116, 117

Glazunov, Andrei, 26, 29, 317

Glenallen (Ak.), 186

Glenn, Edward F., 147–48, 149–51

Glenton, Mary V., 182

gold. *See* mining

Goodpaster River (Ak.), 147, **161,** 162. *See also* Volkmar River

Grand Forks (Yukon Territory), 235

Grant, Ulysses S., 171

Gray, James T., 211, 214–16, **215**

Great Britain, 22–50, 300; and exploration, 22, 24–25, 30–31, 37–43, 44–45; and Hudson's Bay Company, 25, 30–31, 37–43, **44,** 320; and Natives, 22, 24–25, 30–31, 37–43, 44–45; and Russia, 25, 31, 37, 44, 45, 205, 318; and United States, 46, 48, 158, 242; and the Western Union Telegraph Expedition, 52

Great Northern Railroad, 248

Great Slave Lake (Northwest Territories), 58, 60

Greely, Adolphus Washington, 158–60, 164

Green Mountains (Vermont), 179

Greene, Frank, 158

Greenland, 103, 232

Gruening, Ernest, 307

Gulf of Alaska (Ak.), 258

Haines (Ak.), 138, 146, 147, 167, 247, 257

Haines Cutoff (Ak.–Canada), 117

Haines Mission. *See* Haines

Halleck, Henry W., 48

Hamburg, Germany, 26, 31

Hammontree, C. O., 262

Han Indians, 14, 38, 39, 113, 136, 162, **200;** and Fort Reliance, 61, 66; and hostility to whites, 81; and Klondike gold rush, 141; and missionaries, 74, 194, **200.** *See also* Athapaskan Indians; Natives

Hannah (steamboat), 211, **212**

Harding, Warren G., 250

Harper, Arthur, **60,** 66, 75, 88–89, 116, 175; and prospecting/mining, 59, 68, 79, 89

Hayes, Charles Willard, 118

Healy, John J., 86, 87, **87,** 92, 125, 172–74, 208
Helena (Montana), 209
Henderson, Robert, 89, 123
Hendrick, N. V., 140
Heney, Michael J., 129, **131**
Herron, Joseph S., 149, 152
Herschel Island (Yukon Territory), 232
Hill, Barney, 88, 90
Hill, Manny, 90
Hitler, Adolf, 167
Hoare, A. R., 196
Holikachuk Indians, 14. *See also* Athapaskan Indians; Natives
Holt, George, 69
Holy Cross (Ak), 116, 180–86, **185,** 187, 191, 197. *See also* Koserefsky
homesteads, 291, 308, 356
hooch, 69, 189
Howard, Oliver O., 214
Hudson's Bay Company, 25–26, 30–31, 37–43, 45, 48–50, 74, 84, 112, 113, 114, 115; and Alaska Commercial Company, 48–50; and Canada, 46; and exploration, 25–26, 30–31, 37–43, 52, 323; and Fort Yukon, 37–40, 44–45, 48–50; and fur trade, 25–26, 30–31, 37–43, 48–50, 55, **57,** 58, 59, 84, 112–15, 205–6, 320
Hurricane Gulch (Ak.), 250
Hutchinson, Fred, 82
Hutchinson, Kohl & Company, 48, 55. *See also* Alaska Commercial Company

Idaho, 77, 78, 86, 244
Iditarod River (Ak.), 184, 185, 215, 269, 280, 282, 286
Ikogmĭut (Ak.), 28
Iliamna Lake (Ak.), 24
Illinois, 51
Independence (Ak.), 134, 138
Indian Rights Association, 176, **183**

Indians. *See* Athapaskan Indians; Natives
Industrial Workers of the World (IWW), 250
Ingalik Indians, 14, **181,** 181–86, 187. *See also* Athapaskan Indians; Natives
Innoko River (Ak.), 27, 36, 100, 184
International Boundary Survey, 224, 242–46, **243,** 248, 320, 348. *See also* Boundary, International
International Polar Expedition, 131
Inuvik (Northwest Territories), 258
Isbister, Alexander Kennedy, 31
Ivanov, Aleksey, 24, 25, 26
Ivy City (Ak.), 134, 138

Jack Wade Creek (Ak.), 270, 286
Jackson, Sheldon, 178–179, 180, 184
Jacobsen, Johan Adrian, 103
Jamestown (ship), 69
Japan, 255, 257
Jetté, Julius, 183, 186, 318
John Cudahy (steamboat), 213
John River (Ak.), 80
Johns, William Douglas, 96
Jones, Strachan, 43, 45, 319
Joseph, Chief, 162, **200**
Judge, William H., 187, 189, 190
Juneau (Ak.), 70, 71, 78, 93, 118, 133, 145, 158, 175, 197, 198, 262
Kandik River (Ak.–Yukon Territory), ix, 67, 227, 244
Kansas, 156
Kechumstuck Summit (Ak.), 162
Kenai Peninsula (Ak.), 247
Kenai Redoubt (Ak.), 24, 26, 28
Kennecott (Ak.), 247
Kennicott, Robert, 51, 52, **53,** 99, 320, 321
Keno (steamboat), 222
Keno Hill, (Yukon Territory), 287, 289
Kentucky, 60
Ketchikan (Ak.), 190
Ketchum, Frank, 54, 55

Keystone Canyon (Ak.), 147
King, Tom, 96
King, W. F., 242
King William Island (Northwest
   Territories), 104
Kirk, James W. and Anna, 191,
   193–96, **195**
Kirkby, William West, 43, 44, 171
Klondike, 143, 202, 225; and
   backwash, 140, 144, 197, 202–03,
   269; and Canadian law, 129,
   168–69; comparison of, 140;
   discovery of, 123, **124,** 187, 330;
   and mining methods, 136, 276,
   278, **288;** rush to, 97, 174, 184,
   187, 189, 202, 208, 211, 216, 244,
   269, 330; significance of, 137, 203,
   209, 287, 288, 308; trails to,
   125–29, 241. *See also* Dawson;
   Klondike gold rush
Klondike gold rush, **60,** 79, 95, 99,
   114, 121, 123–41 *passim,* **124,** 143,
   174, 184, 189, 211, **212,** 225, 235,
   244; and Canadian government,
   124, 168–70; first report of, 119,
   208, 269, 330; and Natives, 141,
   184; riches of, 123, 287;
   significance of, 123, 141, 197, 209,
   288, 308. *See also* Dawson;
   Klondike
Klondike River (Yukon Territory),
   61, 89, 119; and discovery of gold,
   123, **124, 125**
Kluane Lake (Yukon Territory), 117
Kolmakov Redoubt (Ak.), 27, 28, 44
Korgenikoff, Ivan, 64, 66, 81, 322
Koserefsky (Ak.), 27, 180, 186. *See
   also* Holy Cross
Kotzebue, Otto von, 24, 32
Kotzebue Sound (Ak.), 32, 33, 149
Koyukon Indians, 14, 62, 80, 109,
   184; and missionaries, 37, 73, 183,
   184, 185; and Nulato Massacre,
   40–43, 318. *See also* Athapaskan
   Indians; Natives
Koyukuk (steamboat), 215
Koyukuk River (Ak.), 2, 28, 33, 40,

73, 80, 102, 109, 140, 149, 176, **215,**
   215, 264, 318
Krause, Arthur, 102, 105, 117
Krause, Aurel, 102
Kronshtadt Naval Cadet Corps, 31
Kronshtadt Navigation College, 28
Krusenstern, Ivan Fedorovich, 32
Kusawa Lake (Yukon Territory), 117
Kuskokwim River (Ak.), 6, 26, 37, 44,
   70, 262, 302; and American fur
   trade, 56, 62; and exploration, 24,
   25, 26, 28, 32, 36, 149
Kutchin Indians, 14, **15, 17,** 31, 37,
   39, 44, 45, 58, 315, 318; and
   Klondike gold rush, 141; and
   missionaries, 43, 72–74, 172, **173,**
   186–87, 188–89. *See also*
   Athapaskan Indians; Natives
Kvikhpak River, 318; Eskimo and
   Russian name for Yukon, 26; and
   Yukon, 26, 39, 44. *See also* Yukon
   River.

La Brie (New Brunswick), 220
Ladd Field (Ak.), 167
La Pierre House (Yukon Territory),
   37, 38, 43, 52, 74, 114
Ladue, Joseph, 71, 79, 89, 97, 123
Lake Bennett (British Columbia),
   106, 126, **128,** 235
Lake Clark (Ak.), 117
Lake Laberge, 214, 223
Lake Lindeman (British Columbia),
   103, 105, 175
Lake Marsh (British Columbia). *See*
   Marsh Lake
Lake Mohonk (New York), 176
Lake Nebagamon (Wisconsin), 263
land otter, 62
Lapland, 103, 138
lead-zinc, **288,** 289
Lebarge, Michael, 54, 55, 64
Lebedev-Lastochkin Company, 24
Lecorre, Father August, 58, 72
Leo (ocean schooner), 106
Leo XIII, Pope, 174–75
Lewes River (Yukon Territory), 30,

31, 39, 106, 112, 113. *See also* Kvikhpak River; Pelly River; Yukon River

Lewis and Clark Expedition, 110

Liard River (British Columbia–Yukon Territory), 30, 40, 59, 111, 114

liquor traffic, 88, 148, 172

Little Minook Creek (Ak.), 140

Livengood (Ak.), 266

Lizzie Horner (steamboat), 320

London, England, 43, 44, 72, 110, 129, 209, 210

London, Jack, 203

Long Island Sound (New York), 158

Lorenz, Moise, 68

Lowe, P. G., 146, 151

Lukin, Ivan, 44, 54, 318

Lukin, Semen, 27, 44, 318

Lynn Canal (Ak.), 102, 126, 235

lynx, 230, 293, 294, 296, 297, 298–99, 300, **301**, 302, **303**, 304, 306

McConnell, Richard George, 111, 113–14

McDonald, Robert, 43, 72, 74, 171, 174, 194

McDougall, James, 114

McDougall Pass (Yukon Territory), 114

McGill University, 110, 111, 114

McGrath, J. E., 114, 115, 117, 243

McGrath (Ak.), 262, **263**

Mackenzie, Alexander, 22, 24, 39

Mackenzie Bay (Canada), 232

Mackenzie Mountains (Northwest Territories), 2

Mackenzie River (Northwest Territories), 22, 24, 30, 35, 40, 48, 52, 58, 61, 114, 119, 205, 258

McKinley, William, 155

McQuesten, Harper & Mayo, 71, 72, 77, 79, 97

McQuesten, Leroy Napoleon "Jack," **92, 94**, 100, 116, 322, 323, 325; and Circle City, 90, **92**; and fur trade,

60, 61–62, 70, **87,** 206; and mining, 59, 68, 71, 77

McRae, A. D., 286

Maddren, A. G., 245

Madison, Harry, 71, 79

mail delivery, 169, 226–29, **227, 228,** 241, 262, **263,** 264, 265, 266

Malakhov, Petr, 28, 29, 33

Malakhov, Vasilii, 28

Mammoth Creek (Ak.), 90, 140, 280, 282, 286

Mandart, Father Joseph, 72

Manila, Philippines, 210

Manitoba (Canadian province), 43

Manook, John. *See* Minook, John

Margaret (steamboat), 208

Marsh Lake (British Columbia), 69, 106, 223

marten, 62, 218, 293, 294, 296, 297, 298, 300, 301, **301,** 302

Martin, James, 260

Mary Ellen Galvin (steamboat), 210

Mason, Skookum Jim, 112, 119, 123, **124**

Massachusetts Institute of Technology, 248

Mastodon Creek (Ak.), 90, 140, 282, 283

Matanuska River (Ak.), 147, 248

Matlock, George, 79, 82, 84, 85, **94,** 96, 172, 270

Matteson, Edward E., 274

Maud (barge), 210

Mayo, Alfred, 59, 68, 75, 90, **94**

Mayo (Yukon Territory), 222, 223, 241, 250, 257, 287–89, **288**

Meade River (Ak.), 131

Mears, Frederick, 248–50, **249**

Mendenhall, W. C., 147

Mentasta Pass (Ak.), 80, 128, 146

Merchants' Yukon Line, 220

Mercier, François, 56, **57,** 58, 61, 65, 67, 69, 71, 73, 75, 89, 136, 323

Mercier, Moise, 56, 58, 61, 64

Merriam, Henry C., 146, 148

Mesozoic era, 272

Mexican Cession, 46

Mexican Punitive Expedition, 110, 157

Mexico, 3, 59

Michigan, 156, 187

Mikhailovskii. *See* St. Michael Redoubt

Miles, John H, 278

Miles, Nelson A., 104, **105**, 106, **108**, 110

Miles Canyon (Yukon Territory), 106, **128**, 168, 201

Miles Pass (Ak.), 107

Miles Rapids (Yukon Territory), 106

Miller, Frank Charles "Heine," 219

Miller's Camp (Ak.), 227

Miners Association, 93, 326

miners' associations, 93

miners' meetings, 94, 131, 148, 198, **199**

mining, x, xii, **60,** 77–97 *passim,* 100, 113, **281,** 291, 295, 306, 307, 308; in Alaska, 136, 137, 140, 191, 248; in American West, 77, 323–24; Canadian laws of, 113, 133, 174; dredge mining, 272, 274, 276, **277,** 278, 280, 282, 283, 284, 286, 353; drift mining, 82, 270, 272, 273, 274, 278, 280, 284; history of Yukon, 279–89; hydraulic mining, 82, 140, 271, 272, 274, **275,** 276, 278, 280, 282, 283, 284, 286; and Klondike gold rush, 136, 141, 144–45, 148, 269, 289, 295, 308; and law and order, **89,** 94, 144–45, 148, 152, 174, 187–97, **192,** 213, 279, 280; laws of, 80, 279, 280; life of, 269–72; methods of, 82, 84, 90, 136, 270, 271, 272–78, **273, 275, 277,** 279, 280, **285,** 286, 289; and missionaries, 74, 187–97, **188,** 340; and Natives, 141, 184; open-cut mining, 90, 136, 270, 272, **273,** 274, 278, 280, 282, 284; sluice mining, 270, **273,** 274, 275, **275,** 278, 286; strikes, 77, 79, 89, 120, 137, 149, 193, 197, 269, 278, 281, 286, 289; thawing ground for, 273,

276, 278, **279,** 280, 282, **285,** 286; and transportation, 166, 205–24 *passim,* 235, 236, 240–41, 250, 254, 255, 257, 268, 286, 288; in Yukon Basin, 77–97 *passim,* 133, 136, 137, 140, 254, 260–89

Mining and Scientific Press (magazine), 282

mining camps: and Klondike gold rush, 141, 144, 148, 150, 187, 279; life in, 193–96, **196,** 201, 203, 234, 236, 279, 286; of Rocky Mountains, 134, 331; of Yukon Basin, 134–40, 144, 148, 150, 187, **188, 192,** 201, 286, **288,** 289, 291

Minnesota, 270

Minook, John, 64, 80, 140

Minook Creek (Ak.), 140

Mission Creek (Ak.), 132, 134, 144

missionaries, 100, 171–97, 203, 337, 339; Anglican, 43, 72, 73, 74, 84, 171–74, **173;** Episcopal, 95, 136, 179–91, **181, 188,** 196–97, 200; and fur traders, **57,** 74; and Natives, 36–37, 43–44, 47, 58, 72–74, 84, 95, 102, 171–97 *passim;* Presbyterian, 156, 191, 193–97, **195,** 340; and prospectors/miners, 74, 187–97, **188;** Roman Catholic, 43, 58, 72, 74, 171–72, 174–87, **177, 185,** 189, 191–93, **192,** 197; Russian Orthodox, 36, 43, 47, 72, 102, 172, 179, 182

Mississippi River, 56, 206, 208, 211, **212**

Missouri River, 206, 208, 217

Mitchell, William, xii, 159–64, **161, 163,** 167, 260, 335

Mogg, William, 232, 346

Monarch (steamboat), 216

Monroe, Francis P., 191–93, **192**

Montana, 77, 86, 152, 156, 191, 244

Montreal (Quebec), 58, 75

Moore, Capt. Billie, 88

Moore, William, 112

Mosquito Creek (Ak.), 286

mosquitoes, x, 6, 7, 35, 38, 43, 73, 91,

103, 158, 162, **163,** 164, 244–45, 292

Mount Katmai, 186

Mount Saint Elias (Ak.), 106, 117, 118, 245

mounties. *See* North-West Mounted Police

Murray, Alexander Hunter, 37, 39, 40, **44,** 114, 318

Murray, Anne Campbell, 37

muskeg, 7, 159, 256

muskrat, 296, 297, **298,** 306

Napoleonic wars, 25

Nasutlin (steamboat), 222

Nation City (Ak.), 134, 138, 227, 292

Nation River (Ak.), 219

National Park Service, x

NAT & T Company. *See* North American Transportation and Trading Company

Natives, 1, 4, 10–19, **15, 17,** 21–50 *passim,* 148–67 *passim,* 171–97, 314; and American fur trade, 55–79 *passim,* **60,** 106, 110; and British exploration, 22, 24, 30–31, 37–43, 44–45; and communities, 91, 140; and cultural change, 47–48, 166, 170, 184–87, 190, **200,** 198–201, 260, 295–96, 308, 309, 338; and disease, 28, 33, 102, 170, 186, 189–90, 200, **200,** 244, 315; and education, 84, 95, 172, 178–87, 197, 201; and explorers and scientists, 52, 99–121 *passim,* 147–48, 149, **200;** and hostilities to whites, 65, 66, 80, 81, 318, 322; and Klondike, 123, 141; land claims of, 259, 308; and mining, 77, 79, 141, 184; and missionaries, 36–37, 43–44, 47, 58, 72–74, 84, 95, 102, 171–97, **173, 177, 181, 185, 188, 200,** 338–39, 340; and Nulato Massacre, 40–43, 318; population of, 102, 178, 315; and Russian exploration, 22, 24, 26–29, 44–45, 316, 318; and steamboats,

50, 184, 206, 207, 208, 213, 214, 219; and trade, 36, 39, 180, **200;** and trade with Siberia, 21–22, 32, 33; and trapping, 295, 300, 302, 305, 359; and United States, 25, 166, 213; and U.S. Army, 104, 107, 109–10, 143, 147–48, 149, 152, 166–67, 256; of Yukon Basin, 10–50 *passim,* 72–74, 84, 95, 102, 166–67, 171–97, **173, 177, 181, 185, 188, 200, 228;** and Zagoskin, 32–36. *See also* Athapaskan Indians; Eskimos; and individual Native groups

Nebraska Bar Association, 104

Nelson, Edward William, 78, 99, 100

Nelson River (Manitoba), 59

Nenana (steamboat), 222

Nenana (Ak.), 221, 249, 250, 262

Netsvetov, Iakov, 37

Nevada, 77

New Archangel (Ak.). *See* Sitka

New Brunswick (Canadian province), 46

New Orleans (Louisiana), 51

New Racket (steamboat), 70, 71, 72, 74, 103, 117, 206

New Rampart House (Yukon Territory), **301,** 320

New York, 269, 270

New York City, 59, 104, 260, 261

New Zealand, 276

newspapers, 116

Nicolai, 118

Ninth Infantry, 152

Nome (Ak.), 158, 194, 197, 213, 226, 234, 247, 260, 264

Nome gold rush, 137, 140, 149, 152, 184, 191, 194, 200, 226, 244, 247

Norge (airship), 234

North American Transportation and Trading Company, 87, **87,** 132, 213, 220–21; and competition with Alaska Commercial Company, 87–92, 208–9, 211

North British American Trading and Transportation Company, 209–10

North Dakota, 96, 262
North Pole, 232, 234, 263
North Slope (Ak.), 258
North West Company, 22, 25
North-West Mounted Police, **87,** 88,
    89, 119, 124, 127, **128,** 129, 130,
    132, 168–70, **169,** 174, 229, 255,
    305; compared to U.S. Army, 143,
    168; in conflict with U.S. Army,
    144–45; life in, 168–70, 234; and
    miners, 88, 174
Northern Navigation Company, 211,
    215, **215,** 217, 220–21, 224
Northern Commercial Company,
    211, 226, 229, 302
Northern Pacific Railroad, 107
Northwest Passage, 230, 232, **233,**
    234
Northwest Territories, 245
Northwestern University Museum of
    Natural History, 51
Norton Bay (Ak.), 26
Norway, 167, 234
Nova Scotia (Canadian province), 46
Nowitna River (Ak.), 35, 45, 100
Nuklako (Yukon Territory), 61
Nuklukayet (Ak.), 43, 44, 45, **63,** 64,
    319; and American fur trade, 56,
    61, 65; and missionaries, 58, 73,
    176, 180
Nulato (Ak.), **29,** 44; and American
    fur trade, 65, 66, 70; and explorers
    and scientists, 33, 36, 54, 100; and
    missionaries, 73, 175, **177,** 180,
    182, 183, 186, 187, 197; and
    Nulato Massacre, 40–43, 318;
    population of, 102; settling of, 28,
    29, **29,** 197; and steamboats, 87,
    220; and trade, 42, 62
Nulato River (Ak.), 28
Nunivak (steamboat), 213

O'Brien, Michael, 79
O'Brien, Red Tom, 81
Ogilvie (Yukon Territory), 89
Ogilvie, William, 88, 111, 113, 116,
    119, **120,** 124, 243, 328

Ohlson, Otto F., 251–52, **252**
oil, 258–60, 287, 308
Oklahoma, 117
Old Crow (Yukon Territory), 305
Old Portage (Ak.), 90
opium, 118
Oregon, 179, 214, 215
Oregon Code, 94
Organic Act of 1884, 144, 178
Ottawa (Ontario), 110, 112, 113, 114,
    120, 169
Overland Trail (Yukon Territory),
    235–36, 238, 241
Oxford, England, 287

Pacific Ocean, 30, 117
Panama, 240
Panama Railroad, 248, 250
Parker, Octavius, 179–82
Pastol Bay (Ak.), 26
Patty, Ernest, 285, 286
Pavaloff, Erinia. *See* Callahan, Erinia
    Pavaloff Cherosky, 64
Pavaloff, Ivan, 62, 66, 70, 80
Pavaloff, Ivan (son of Ivan Sr.). *See*
    Minook, John
Pavaloff, Malanka or Marina, 64, 80
Pavaloff, Pitka, 64, 80, 89, 140
Payne, Henry M., 278
Peace River (Alberta–British
    Columbia), 110
Pearl Harbor (Hawaii), 164, 255
Pedro, Felix, 201
Peekskill Military Academy, 107
Peel River (Yukon Territory), 31, 52,
    113
Pelican (gasoline launch), 190
Pelly River (Yukon Territory), 2, 4,
    30, 31, 39, 40, 54, 84, 106, 112,
    113, 119, 175. *See also* Kvikhpak
    River; Lewes River; Yukon River
Pennsylvania, 151–52, 251
permafrost, 4, 7, 82, 159, **163,** 238,
    239, 244, 249, **251,** 256, 257, 264,
    270, 272, 274, 277, 279, **279,** 280,
    286, 287, 291
Pershing, John J., 110, 157

Peter the Great, 21
Petrov, Ivan, 100, 106, 327
Philadelphia, 193, 196, 226
Philippines, 110, 154, 156, 159, 248
Pierce, Walter H., 78, 324
Pike, Warburton, 119
Pilcher, George, 218–19
Pioneer Company, 56, 65
Pitka Bar (Ak.), 89
pneumonia, 152, 180, 187
Point Barrow (Ak.), 106, 131, 149
polio, 267
population: of Yukon Basin, 100
Porcupine River (Ak.–Yukon
   Territory), 2, 4, 31, 37, 43, 52, 58,
   60, 74, 114, 215, 232, 292, **301**;
   exploration of, 31, 37, 244, 245;
   and trade, 40, 205–6, 320
Port Safety (Ak.), 158, 165. *See also*
   Safety Harbor
Portland (Oregon), 105, 118, 176, 215
Portus B. Weare (steamboat), 87, 132,
   208
Powell, John Wesley, 151
Presbyterian Board of Home
   Missions, 193, 196
Presbyterian church, 156, 191,
   193–97, **195,** 340
Prest, Clarence, 260
Prevost, Jules L., 95, 189, 190, 200
Prince George (British Columbia),
   254
Prince William Sound (Ak.), 144,
   147, 149, 150, 280
Princeton, 244
promyshlenniks, 22, 24
prospecting, 86, 103, 133, 140,
   269–89, 271, **284,** 295; in
   American West, 77; and Yukon
   Basin, 59, 72, 75, 269–89. *See also*
   mining
Prospector's Aid Act, 284
Protestant Episcopal Mission Board,
   179
Prudhoe Bay (Ak.), 258, 259
Puget Sound, 208
Pyramid Harbor (Ak.), 128

Queen Charlotte Islands (British
   Columbia), 110
Queen's University, 114
Quikpok River. *See* Kvikhpak River;
   Yukon River
Ragaru, Aloysius, 180
railroads, 129–30, **131,** 147, 148, 193,
   202, 221–22, 236, 240, 247–55,
   249, 251, 252, 282, 283, 284
Rampart (Ak.), 97, 102, 134, 140, 141,
   148, 151, 190, 213, 126, 220, 222,
   332
Rampart Dam (Ak.), 309
Rampart House (Yukon Territory),
   58, 74, 115, 171, 172, 232, 320
ramparts of Yukon (Ak.), 4, 70, 207
Randall, George M., 144, 148, 152,
   164
Rat River (Yukon Territory), 31, 37,
   40, 114
Ray, Patrick Henry, 130–34, 144,
   149, 150, 153–54, 191, 213
Raymond, Charles W., 48–50, 100,
   106, 172
Red River (Manitoba), 51
reindeer, 138, 146, 147, 184
Resurrection Bay (Ak.), 147
Rice, John, 151
Richardson Highway (Ak.), 238, 241,
   251
Richardson, John, 38
Richardson Mountains (Northwest
   Territories–Yukon Territory), 31
Richardson, Wilds P.: with Alaska
   Road Commission, 236–40, **237,**
   239; during Klondike, 130, 138,
   144, 148, 149, **150,** 151, 166, 332
Rickard, Tex, 96
Riggs, Thomas C., 236, **243,** 243–45,
   248, **249,** 250
Rink Rapids, 214
road building, 144, 150, 152, 166,
   169, 170, 205, 223, 235–42, **237,**
   247, **251,** 254, 255–60, 272, 279,
   280, 284, 288, 302, 305, 308
roadhouses, 90, 226, 227, 228, 230,
   234–35, 267, 346

Robaut, Aloysius, 174–76, 179–80,
   186, 337
Robertson, Cady, **108**
Rock Island (steamboat), 213
Rocky Mountain Presbyterian
   (journal), 179
Rocky Mountain Trench (Canada),255
Rocky Mountains, 59, 134
Roman Catholic church, 43, **57,** 58,
   72, 74, 171–72, 174–87, **177, 185,**
   189, 191–93, **192,** 197
Rome, Italy, 174
Root, Elihu, 158
Rowe, Peter Trimble, 187–91, **188,**
   194, 196
Royal Canadian Mounted Police. *See*
   North-West Mounted Police
Royal Geographical Society, 114
Royal North-West Mounted Police.
   See North-West Mounted Police
Royal Society of England, 114
Ruby (Ak.), 260
Rupert's Land, 46
Russell, Israel C., 116, 118
Russia, 21, 25–29, 31–37, 40–43,
   300; and exploration, 21, 25–29,
   31–37, 40–43, 318; and Great
   Britain, 25, 31–32, 37, 39, 44, 45,
   48, **173,** 205, 318; impact on
   Natives of, 47, 319; and Peter the
   Great, 21; and United States, 25,
   45–46, 48, 240, 255, 265; and the
   Western Union Telegraph
   Expedition, 52
Russian America, 22, 24–29, 31–37,
   40–43, 44–48, 316; and Kennicott,
   52, **53;** and the Western Union
   Telegraph Expedition, 52–55, **55.**
   See also Alaska
Russian-American Company, 25, 37,
   45, **57,** 242, 316; and explorers and
   scientists, 25–29, 31–37, 40–43,
   100; formation of, 24; and Natives,
   25–29, 42–46, 62, 319; and Siberia,
   21, 36
Russian-American Telegraph
Exploring Expedition. *See* Western

Union Telegraph Company
Russian Mission (Ak.), 28, 36, 37, 73,
   102, 172, 210, 218
Russian Orthodox church, 36, 47,
   68, 72, 73, 102, 172, 179, 182, 318

Safety Harbor (Ak.), 165. *See also*
   Port Safety
St. James Mission, 189
St. Michael (Ak.), 78, 81, 191, 202;
   and American fur trade, 57, 61, 66,
   67, 71; description of, 67; and
   explorers and scientists, 100, 103,
   106, 109, 114, 115, 117; and
   miners, 84, 149; and missionaries,
   59, 72, 172, 176, 179, 180, 191;
   population of, 100, 134; and
   prospecting, 70, 78; and steamboats,
   87, 125, 146, 208, 209, 210, 213,
   214, 216, 220, 222; and trade, 48,
   191; and U.S. Army, 130, 132, 144,
   148; and the Western Union
   Telegraph Expedition, 54, 55
St. Michael (steamboat), 67, 71, 182,
   206
St. Michael Canal (Ak.), 166, 214
St. Michael Redoubt (Ak.), **27,** 40,
   316; and exploration, 28, 32; and
   Russian exploration, **27,** 27, 28;
   and trade, 36, 42
St. Petersburg, Russia, 24, 28, 45
Salcha River (Ak.), 164
Salem (Oregon), 104
salmon, 64, 162, 225, 229, 292
Salmon River (Ak.), 292
Sam Creek (Ak.), 138
San Francisco, 45, 48, 54, 58, 59, 64,
   68, 70, 75, 79, 81, 103, 106, 109,
   115, 116, 117, 123, 125, 155, 172,
   176, 208, 209, 213, 226, 234, 321
Santa Fe Trail, 205
Sarah (steamboat), 211, **212,** 213, 220
Scammon, Capt. Charles M., 52
Schanz, A. B., 116, 117
Schieffelin, Edward, 70, 103, 140
Schieffelin, Eff, 70, 140
Schrader, F. C., 147

Schwatka, Frederick, 104–6, **105,** 110, 112, 117, 118

Scientific Corps, Western Union Telegraph Company, 52

scientists, 99–121 *passim*

scurvy, 22, 78, 109, 113, 149, 150, 174, 189

Seattle Fur Exchange, 300, 358

Seattle Post-Intelligencer (newspaper), 234

Seattle, 125, 146, 158, 165, 210, 221

Seattle-Yukon Transportation Company, 209–11, 214, 215

Seghers, Archbishop Charles John, 59, 72–74, 171, 174–77, **177,** 179, 337

Sequin, Father Jean, 43

Service, Robert, 203

Seventh Infantry, 149, 151, 153

Seventymile City (Ak.), 137, 138, 332. *See also* Star City

Seventymile River (Ak.), **67,** 88, 90, 133, 137, 270, 271, 280, 282

Seward (Ak.), 147, 167, 221, 247, 248, 253

Seward Peninsula (Ak.), 148–49, 152, 167

Seward, William H., 52

Shakespeare, William, 85

Sharpsburg, Kentucky, 106

Sheenjek River (Ak.), 292

Sheep Camp (Ak.), 126

Shore, Evelyn Berglund, 291–95, **293**

Siberia, 52, 263; and Yukon Basin, 21–22, 32, 33, 36, 42, 47

Sierra Club, x

silver-lead, 203, 221, 222–23, 241, 250, 254, 287, **288,** 288

Simpson, George, 25, 30, 31, 37, 39

Sims, Rev. Vincent C., 74–75, 107, 136, 171

Sitka (Ak.), 32, 36, 69, 81, 103, 316

Sixtymile (Yukon Territory), 97

Sixtymile River, 69, 89, 119

Skagway (Ak.), 126, 129, **131,** 144–45, 146, 147, 151, 158, 168,

197, 198, 211, 235, 254–55, 289, 340

Slana River (Ak.), 150

smallpox, 28, 29, 33, 245

Smith, Jefferson "Soapy," 145

Smith, Noel, 252

Smithsonian Institution, 51, 52, **53**

Snake River (Idaho), 221

Snow, George, 93

South Pass (Wyoming), 1, 6

South Pole, 234

southeast panhandle (Ak.-Canada), 145, 174, 178, 242, 348

Southern Pacific Railroad, 248

Soviet Union. *See* Union of Soviet Socialist Republics

Spain, 21, 22

Spanish-American War, 152

Spaulding, O. L., 149

Spencer Fullerton Baird, 51

Spitsbergen, Greenland, 234, 263

Spurr, Josiah Edward, 85, 91, 93, 136

Stanley, Henry M., 116

Star City (Ak.), 134, 138, 332. *See also* Seventymile City

steamboats, 48–49, 61, 67, 103, 109, 115, 117, 130–32, 169, 198, 203, 205–23, 245, 302, 308; and American fur trade, 51, **57,** 72, 201, 206–9; captains of, 214–16, **215;** competition among, 209, 211, 213, 220–23; costs of, 216–17; decline of, 220–23, 268; disasters of, 217; fuels of, 210, 211, **212,** 217–20, **218,** 308, 344; and Klondike gold rush, 125, 130–32, 209–17; and mining, 70–71, 80, 84, 85, 87, 184, 201, 280, 295; and missionaries, 182, 184; and U.S. Army, 146, 148, 158, 166

Steele, Samuel Benfield, 88, 129, 168

Steese Highway (Ak.), 241, 284

Steese, James Gordon, 240, 250

Stewart River (Yukon Territory), 39, 69, 75, 77, 78, 93, 136, 175, 222, 223

Stikine River (Ak.-British Columbia), 25, 26, 32, 111
Stoeckl, Edouard de, 45
Stony River (Ak.), 27
Stuart Island (Ak.), 26
Stuck, Hudson, 190–91
Susie (steamboat), 211, **212**
Susitna River (Ak.), 147, 148, 149, 150, 250
Swiftwater Bill, 96
Switch Creek (Ak.), 283

T. C. Powers (steamboat), 213
Tacoma (Washington), 198, 244
Taft, William Howard, 248
Tagish Charley, 112, 119, 123, **124**
Tagish Indians, 14. *See also* Athapaskan Indians; Natives
Taku River (Ak.), 118
Talkeenta River (Ak.), 147
Tanacross Junction (Ak.), 162
Tanana Highlands (Ak.), 147
Tanana (steamboat), 215, 245
Tanana Indians, 14, 74–75, 324. *See also* Athapaskan Indians; Natives
Tanana River (Ak.), 2, 4, 80, 110, 128, 201, 291, 295; and American fur trade, 56, 62, 65; and explorers and scientists, 104, 106, 107, 117, 144, 146, 205; mining on, 89, 193, 201, 269; and missionaries, 74, 189, 190; and Native hostility to whites, 65, 80; population along, 102; and prospecting, 68, 70; and trade, 44, 45, 205; transportation on, 215, **215,** 221, 250, 259; and U.S. Army, 132, 144, 146, 148, 149, 151, **153,** 162, 164
Tanana Station (Ak.), 61, **63,** 72, 89, 96, 109, 144, 200, 226; and missionaries, 74, 189, 200; and Native hostility to whites, 65–66; population of, 134. *See also* Nuklukayet
Tanana Valley Railroad, 247, 248, 251

Taral (Ak.), 107, 118
Tatonduk River (Ak.-Yukon Territory), 113, 219
Taylor Highway (Ak.), 241
Teben'kov, Mikhail Dmit'rievich, 26
telegraph, 153, **153,** 155, 156, 157–67, **161, 163, 166,** 170, 184, 193, 232, **233,** 234, 235, 243, 249, 260
tenth census, 102
Tertiary period, 272
Teslin River (Yukon Territory), 118
Third Cavalry, 104
Third Judicial District, 198, **199,** 200, 201
Thompson Pass, (Ak.), 147
Tillman, Benjamin, 156–57, 159
Tittman, O. H., 242
Tlingit Indians. *See* Chilkat Indians
Todd Creek (Ak.), 138
Tok River (Ak.–Yukon Territory), 117
Tombstone (Arizona), 70
Tosi, Pascal, 174–76, 180, 183, 186, 187, 337
trade, 10–50 *passim,* 51, 100, 106, 113, 207, 211; in American West, 51, 320; and Americans, 52, 55–57; with China, 21–22, 45, 46; and exploration, 25–29, 31–37, 43, 44–45; and Great Britain, 22, 24–25, 30–31, 37–43, 44–45, 205; and Hudson's Bay Company, 25–26, 30–31, 37–43, 45, 48; and mining, 84, 143, 208–24; and Natives, 10–50 *passim,* 51, 79, 110, 116, 180, 198–201, **200,** 205; and Russia, 25–29, 31–37, 40–43, 205; and Siberia, 21–22, 32, 33; and United States, 25, 37
trading posts. *See* names of specific trading posts
trails, ix, 6, 29, 52, 90, 113, 114, 117, 125–29, 141, 143, 145, 146, 148, 149, 159, 160, 162, 166, 168, 169–70, 175, 187, 198, 205,

225–35, **227, 233, 237,** 238, 240,
241, 244, 247, 280, 292, 293, 294,
298, 302, 306
Trans-Alaskan Military Road,
165
transportation, 100, **161,** 170,
205–68, 269, 274, 282, 291, 296; by
airplane, 222, 229, 234, 241, 255,
257, 260–69, **263,** 265, 286, 288,
295, 302, 304, 351; by boat (other
than steamboat), x, 6, 16, 26, 30,
32, 35–36, 37, 38, 39–40, 42, 44,
48, 54, 60, 66, 73, 75, 78, 80, 89,
100, 104, 105–6, 107, 112, 115,
119, 127, 164, 175, 187, 189, 190
205–06, 207, **207,** 222, **223,** 225,
248, 267, 292, 294, 295, 302; by
dog team, 32–33, 70, 113, 144, 147,
159, 162, **163,** 169–70, 176, 190,
198, 211, 220, 225–34, **227, 233,**
263, 267, 268, 269, 270, 293, **293,**
294, 295, 302; by horse or mule,
159, 160–62, **163,** 169, 220, 225,
227, 229–30, **239,** 244–45, 248,
267, 269; by railroad, 129–30, **131,**
147, 148, 193, 202, 221–22, 236,
240, 247–55, **249, 251, 252,** 282,
283, 284; by revenue cutter, 109,
116, 144, 176, 213; and roads, 144,
150, 152, 166, 169, 170, 205,
235–42, **237,** 247, **251,** 254,
255–60, 272, 279, 280, 284, 288,
302, 305, 308; by steamboat, 48–49,
51, 57, **57,** 61, 67, 70, 71–72, 80, 84,
85, 87, 103, 109, 115, 117, 130–32,
146, 158, **158,** 166, 169, 182, 184,
198, 201, 203, 205–23, **212, 215,**
218, 225, 227, 245, 280, 295, 302,
320; by trail, ix, 6, 29, 52, 90, 113,
114, 117, 125–29, 141, 143, 145, 146
148, 149, 159, 160, 162, 166, 168,
169–70, 175, 187, 198, 205,
225–35, **227, 233, 237,** 238, 240,
241, 244, 247, 267, 269, 280, 292,
293, 294, 298, 302, 306. *See also*
Alaska Railroad; specific

steamboats; Yukon and White Pass
Railway
trapping, ix, x, 40, 51, 269, 271, 283,
291–309; animals of, 62, 218, 293,
294, 296, 297–99, **298, 299;**
economics of, 294, 300–306, **301,**
357; life-style of, 291–300, **293,**
306–8, 357, 359; methods of,
295–300, **298, 299,** 357; and
Natives, 51, 295; and transportation,
224, 230, 235, 236, 256, 268,
293–94, 295, 296, 302, 304, 306
Treadgold, Arthur Newton Christian,
287–88, 356
Treaty of 1825, 25, 242
Treaty of Paris, 45
Treaty of Peking, 46
tuberculosis, 72, 78, 97, 152, 200
tungsten, 288
Turkey, 45
Turner, Frederick Jackson, xi, 1, 2, 6,
10, 97, 307–8. *See also* Turner
thesis
Turner, J. H., 114, 320
Turner thesis, xi, 1, 315; and Alaska,
2, 307–8; and Indians, 10, 19; and
United States, 1, 19, 313. *See also*
Turner, Frederick Jackson
Tutchone Indians, 14, 30. *See also*
Athapaskan Indians; Natives
typhoid fever, 180

Uffington, England, 43
Unalakleet portage, 117
Unalakleet River (Ak.), 29, 33, 73
Union of Soviet Socialist Republics,
168
United States: and Alaska, 236, 255,
260; and Canada, 129, 144–45,
155, 158, 159, 242–46; and Great
Britain, 48–50, 158, 172, 242; and
posse comitatus, 152; and Russia,
25, 46–48; and trade, 25, 37, 300;
and Turner thesis, 1, 19, 313
U.S. Army, 80, 100, 143–68, 170,
171, 172, 193, 198, 270, 308; and

conflict with Canada, 144–45; and
exploration, 104–10, 143, 144–51,
159, 162, 164; and Klondike,
130–33, 134, 144–46, 209, 269; life
in, 152–58, 160–68, **166,** 191; and
transportation, 211, 238, 250,
252–53, 254, 256–57, 260
U.S. Army Air Service, 260, 263
U.S. Army Corps of Engineers, 166,
214, 236, 255–56
U.S. Army Signal Corps, 78, 99,
158–67, **161,** 164, 165, 167, 184,
197
U.S. Biological Survey, 100
U.S. Bureau of Education, 95, 178,
179, 184
U.S. Bureau of Indian Affairs, 178
U.S. Bureau of Public Roads, 242
U.S. Coast and Geodetic Survey, 114,
116, 214, 242
U.S. Congress, 235, 236, 237, 248,
252, 252, 253, 255, 259
U.S. Department of Commerce, 242,
266
U.S. Department of the Interior, 178,
235, 241, 253
U.S. Department of Justice, 156, 201
U.S. Department of Labor, 140
U.S. Department of Transportation,
253
U.S. Department of the Treasury, 50,
160, 176
U.S. Geological Survey, 85, 116, 118,
136, 147, 148, 151, 224, 245, 271,
272, 280, **281,** 282, 283, 284, 291
U.S. Military Academy, 104, 131
U.S. Navy, 69
U.S. Office of Indian Affairs. *See* U.S.
Bureau of Indian Affairs
U.S. Post Office, 226, 234, 262–63
U.S. Public Roads Administration,
256–57, 350
U.S. Revenue Cutter Service, 213
U.S. War Department, 144–47, 149,
150, 152, 154, 158, 164, 166, 235,
241, 255–56, 257

Union Gulch (Ak.), 134
University of Alaska, x, 267, 286
University of North Dakota, 152
Utah, 244

Valdez (Ak.), 80, 146, 150, 159, 165,
190, 193, 202; and transportation,
225, 235, 238, 241, 259
Valdez Glacier (Ak.), 128, 146, 147
Vancouver Barracks (Washington),
146, 147, 164
Vancouver Island (British Columbia),
72, 243
Vermont, 179
Victoria (British Columbia), 174
Vogler, Joe, 286
Volkmar River (Ak.), 147. *See also*
Goodpaster River

Wade, Jack, 79
Walden, Arthur, 91, 95
Walker, E. S., 149
Walker Fork (Ak.), 286
WAMCATS. *See* Washington-Alaska
Military Cable and Telegraph
System
Washburn, 86, 172
Washington-Alaska Military Cable
and Telegraph System
(WAMCATS), 158–67, **161, 163,
166,** 235
Washington Creek (Ak.), 220
Washington, D. C., 45, 100, 159
Watson Lake (Yukon Territory), 305
Watt, James L., 189–90
Weare, Portus B., 87, 208
Weimer, W. D. K., 137
Wells, E. Hazard, 116–17
West Coast Fur Sales, 300, 358
West Point (New York), 104, 107,
110, 131, 152, 240
Westdahl, Ferdinand, 55
Western Fur and Trading Company,
64, 66, 67, 70, 71
Western Union Telegraph Company,
52, **55**

Western Union Telegraph Expedition, 52–55, **53, 55, 56,** 62, 99, 320, 323; significance of, 54
westward movement, xi, xii
whalers, 73, 232, 234
White Pass (Ak.–British Columbia), 69, 112, 125, **128,** 147, 168, 225, 235, 242
White Pass and Yukon Railway, 147, 211, 222, 289; construction of, 129–30, **131,** 235; value of, 247, 250, 254–55, 256, 257
White River (Yukon Territory), 2, 4, 39, 61, 69, 106, 118
Whitehorse (Yukon Territory), 168, 202–3, 223, 224, 260, 305; beginnings of, 127, **128,** 202; mining near, 287–89; roads to, 235, 241, 254–55, 255–56, 258; and White Pass and Yukon Railway, 130, 202–3, 211
Whitehorse Canyon (Yukon Territory). *See* Whitehorse Rapids
Whitehorse Rapids (Yukon Territory), 127, 175, 201
Whymper, Frederick, 54, **55, 56,** 62, 99
Wickersham, James, 197–201, **199,** 230, 236, 240, 332
Wien, Noel, 263–65, **265,** 267
Wilder (steamboat), 320
Wilkins, George Hubert, 263
Willamette River (Oregon), 221
Wilson, Woodrow, 248, **249**
Winn, James "Slim Jim," 69, 71
Winnipeg (Manitoba), 174
wolf, 293, 294, 296, 297, **301, 303**
Wolff, Ernest, 286
Wood, W. D., 210–11
Woodchopper Creek (Ak.), 227, 280, 283, 286
woodchopping, 61, 213, 217–19, **218,** 226, 230, 269, 270, 271, 283, 344
Woods, Benton S., 96
World War I, 110, 157, 164, 240, 241, 249, 260, 262, 278, 283, 287, 300, 304

World War II, 164, 167, 222, 223, 229, **252,** 252, 253, 254, 255–57, 266, **281,** 285, 286, 288, 291, 304
Wrangell (Ak.), 112
Wrangell, Baron Ferdinand Petrovich von, 25, 28, 31, 45
Wrangell Mountains (Ak.), 148, 150, 245, 247
Wright, W. K., 151, 153–54

Y.O.O.P. *See* Yukon Order of Pioneers
Yakutat (Ak.), 119
Yenta River (Ak.), 149
Youcon River, 31, 40. *See also* Yukon River
Yukon (steamboat), 48, 57, 61, 71, 106, 109, 114, 115, 206, 221; replaces first *Yukon* (steamboat), 67
Yukon Basin, xi, **5, 41;** and American fur trade, 62; and Athapaskan Indians, 14–50 *passim,* 58, 72–74, 141, 171–97; climate of, 6, 207–8, 267, 269, 274, 278, 289, 291, 306; description of, 2, 4, 206–8, 214, 279, 289, 308–9, 313; explorers and scientists in, 99–121, 143–68; and Klondike gold rush, 123–41 *passim,* 269–89; life on, 152–58, 160–68, **166,** 191, 193–96, **195, 196,** 210, **218,** 269–72; and mining camps and communities, 134–40, 144, 148, 150, 187, **188, 192,** 201, 247, 249, 268, 280–89; mining in, 69–70, 77–97, 99, 119–21, 269–89, **273, 275, 277, 279, 281, 285, 288;** and missionaries, 36, 43, 47, 58, 72–75, 84, 95, 102, 171–97, **173, 177;** Natives of, 10–19, 21–50 *passim,* 104, 107, 109–10, 143, 147–49, 152, 166, 170, 171–97, **228,** 315; population of, 100, 133, 138; prospecting in, 69–71, 75, 77, 269–89; starvation scare of, 130–33, 138, 144, 189, 209; and

trade with Siberia, 21–22, 32, 33, 36, 42, 47; transportation in, 205–68, **207, 212, 215, 223, 227, 233, 237, 239, 243**; trapping in, 291–309, **293**; and U.S. Army, 132, 143–69, **150**, 170. *See also* Klondike gold rush; Yukon River
Yukon-Charley National Rivers, x
Yukon Consolidated Gold Corporation, 288
Yukon Delta, 4, 6, 12, 100, 314; and steamboats, 70, 166, 214, 217, 320
Yukon Expedition, 110–14, **111**, 116
Yukon Field Force, 168
Yukon Flats (Ak.), 4, 37, 91, 130, 162, 207, 214, 269
Yukon Game Department, 305
Yukon Gold Company, 278
Yukon Order of Pioneers, 93, **94**
Yukon Press (newspaper), 96, 189, 200
Yukon River, ix, 1, 2, **3**, 30–39, 40, 267; and American fur trade, 56–75; bridge over, 259, **261**; and British exploration, 22, 24–25, 30–31, 37–43, 44–45; description of, 2, 4, 308–9, 313; and explorers and scientists, 21–50 *passim*, 52–55, **53**, 99–121, **105**, 143–51, 159, 162; and Kvikhpak, 26, 39, 44; and McQuesten, Harper, and Mayo, 60, **60**, 70, 75, 87, **87**, 88–90,

92, 94, 100; mail trail, 226, **227, 228**, 230, 232, 234, 235; and missionaries, 36–37, 43, 47, 58, 72–75, 84, 95, 102, 171–97, **173, 177**; and name, 26, 31; and prospecting, 59, 68, 69–71, 75, 77, 86, 103, 133, 140, 269–89; and Russian exploration, 21, 25–29, 31–37, 40–43; steamboats on, 48–49, 51, 57, **57**, 61, 67, 70, 71–72, 80, 84, 85, 87, 103, 109, 115, 117, 130–32, 146, 158, 166, 169, 182, 184, 198, 201, 203, 205–23, 320; towns along, 28–29, 33, 36, 40–43, 49, 90–97, 102, 129, 134, 138, 140, 193–201; transportation on, 205–24, **207, 212, 215, 223**, 267–69; tributaries of, 106, 113; and U.S. Army, 132, 143–70, **150**; Western Union Telegraph Expedition, 52–55. *See also* Kvikhpak River; Lewes River; Pelly River; Yukon Basin
Yukon Territory (Canadian territory), xi, 2, 120, 202, 222, 241, 245, 254, **288**, 304–5, 336, 350, 358
Yukon Valley News (newspaper), 140, 332
Yukoner (steamboat), 210

Zagoskin, Lavrentiy Alekseyevich, 31–36, 42, 318